Grade 6

Glencoe
Georgia Math

Volume ②

Mc
Graw
Hill
Education

Bothell, WA • Chicago, IL • Columbus, OH • New York, NY

Cover: (tl) Georgia state butterfly the Eastern Tiger Swallowtails of yellow and dark varieties feeding on flowers, (tr) Close up of the Georgia state amphibian the Green Treefrog (Hyla cinerea), (b) A Brown Thasher (Toxostoma rufum), the Georgia state bird, on it's perch.

connectED.mcgraw-hill.com

STEM McGraw-Hill is committed to providing instructional materials in Science, Technology, Engineering, and Mathematics (STEM) that give all students a solid foundation, one that prepares them for college and careers in the 21st century.

Send all inquiries to:
McGraw-Hill Education
STEM Learning Solutions Center
8787 Orion Place
Columbus, OH 43240

ISBN: 978-0-07-665484-0 (*Volume 2*)
MHID: 0-07-665484-2

Printed in the United States of America.

11 12 13 14 15 QVS 22 21 20 19 18

Our mission is to provide educational resources that enable students to become the problem solvers of the 21st century and inspire them to explore careers within Science, Technology, Engineering, and Mathematics (STEM) related fields.

CONTENTS IN BRIEF

 Units organized by the Georgia Grade 6 Curriculum Map

attribute categorical (handwritten)

$$\frac{\begin{array}{r}196\\176\end{array}}{16}$$ (handwritten)

GO digital

it's all at **connectED.mcgraw-hill.com**

Go to the Student Center for your eBook, Resources, Homework, and Messages.

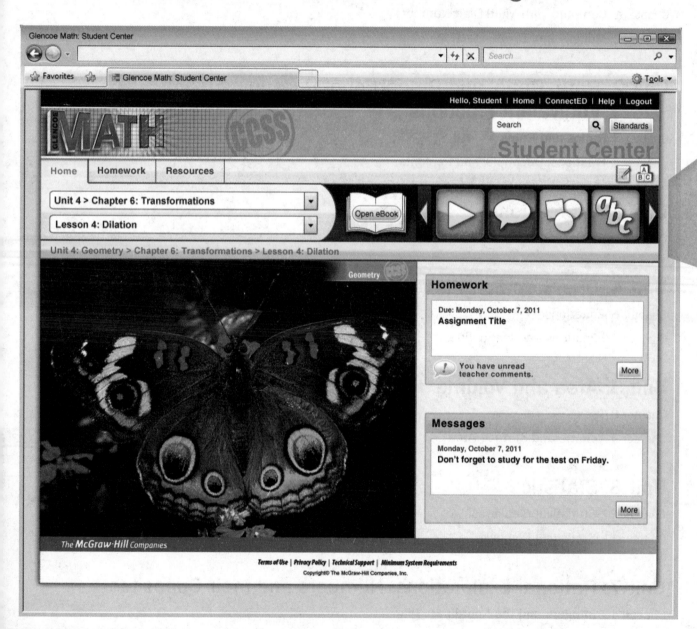

Write your Username ___abatchu (IXL)___ Password ___93arrive (IXL)___

Get your resources online to help you in class and at home.

Vocab

Find activities for building vocabulary.

Watch

Watch animations and videos.

Tutor

See a teacher illustrate examples and problems.

Tools

Explore concepts with virtual manipulatives.

Check

Self-assess your progress.

eHelp

Get targeted homework help.

Masters

Provides practice worksheets.

GO mobile

Scan this QR code with your smart phone* or visit mheonline.com/apps.

*May require quick response code reader app.

v

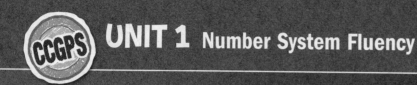

UNIT 1 Number System Fluency

Chapter 1
Compute with Multi-Digit Numbers

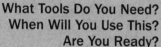

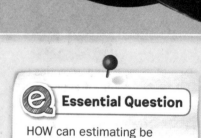

Essential Question

HOW can estimating be helpful?

Chapter 2
Multiply and Divide Fractions

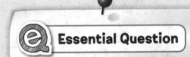

Essential Question

WHAT does it mean to multiply and divide fractions?

* These lessons are prerequisites for MCC6.NS.1 and also address the Georgia Transition Standards.

Chapter 3
Ratios and Rates

Essential Question

HOW do you use equivalent rates in the real world?

DLILLC/Corbis (t); Punchstock/Brand X Pictures (b)

Copyright © The McGraw-Hill Companies, Inc.

Chapter 4
Fractions, Decimals, and Percents

e Essential Question

WHEN is it better to use a fraction, a decimal or a percent?

Chapter 5
Expressions

ⓔ Essential Question

HOW is it helpful to write numbers in different ways?

Steve Mason/Getty Images (t); Jupiterimages/Getty Images (b)   Copyright © The McGraw-Hill Companies, Inc.

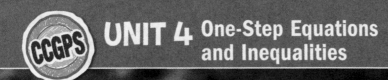

UNIT 4 One-Step Equations and Inequalities

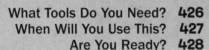

Chapter 6
Equations

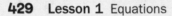

ⓔ **Essential Question**

HOW do you determine if two numbers or expressions are equal?

Chapter 7
Functions and Inequalities

Essential Question

HOW are symbols, such as <, >, and =, useful?

CCGPS UNIT 5 Area and Volume

Chapter 8
Area

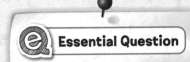

Essential Question

HOW does measurement help you solve problems in everyday life?

xiii

Chapter 9
Volume and Surface Area

e **Essential Question**

HOW is shape important when measuring a figure?

Philipp Nemenz/The Image Bank/Getty Images (t); Joshua Ets-Hokin/Getty Images (c); Mitch Reardon/Stone/Getty Images (b)   Copyright © The McGraw-Hill

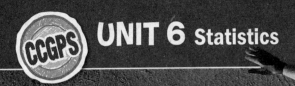

Chapter 10
Statistical Measures

Essential Question

HOW are the mean, median, and mode helpful in describing data?

Chapter 11
Statistical Displays

 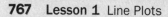
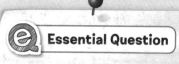

Essential Question

WHY is it important to carefully evaluate graphs?

Doug Armand/Stone/Getty Images (t); Clarissa Leahy/Getty Images (c); Laurence Mouton/Photo Alto/Age Fotostock (b)

Copyright © The McGraw-Hill Companies, Inc.

Chapter 12
Integers and the Coordinate Plane

Essential Question

HOW are integers and absolute value used in real-world situations?

Georgia Grade 6 Curriculum Map

Georgia Math, Grade 6, focuses on teaching the CCGPS standards in the order of the Georgia Grade 6 Curriculum map.

Unit 1: Number System Fluency

MCCS addressed in Unit 1:

MCC6.NS.1 Interpret and compute quotients of fractions, and solve word problems involving division of fractions by fractions, e.g., by using visual fraction models and equations to represent the problem.

MCC6.NS.2 Fluently divide multi-digit numbers using the standard algorithm.

MCC6.NS.3 Fluently add, subtract, multiply, and divide multi-digit decimals using the standard algorithm for each operation.

MCC6.NS.4 Find the greatest common factor of two whole numbers less than or equal to 100 and the least common multiple of two whole numbers less than or equal to 12. Use the distributive property to express a sum of two whole numbers 1–100 with a common factor as a multiple of a sum of two whole numbers with no common factor.

Transition Standard to be addressed:

MCC5.NF.6 Solve real world problems involving multiplication of fractions and mixed numbers, e.g., by using visual fraction models or equations to represent the problem.

Unit 2: Rate, Ratio, and Proportional Reasoning Using Equivalent Fractions

MCCS addressed in Unit 2:

MCC6.RP.1 Understand the concept of a ratio and use ratio language to describe a ratio relationship between two quantities.

MCC6.RP.2 Understand the concept of a unit rate a/b associated with a ratio $a: b$ with $b \neq 0$ (b not equal to zero), and use rate language in the context of a ratio relationship.

MCC6.RP.3 Use ratio and rate reasoning to solve real-world and mathematical problems, e.g., by reasoning about tables of equivalent ratios, tape diagrams, double number line diagrams, or equations.

> **MCC6.RP.3a** Make tables of equivalent ratios relating quantities with whole-number measurements, find missing values in the tables, and plot the pairs of values on the coordinate plane. Use tables to compare ratios.
>
> **MCC6.RP.3b** Solve unit rate problems including those involving unit pricing and constant speed.
>
> **MCC6.RP.3c** Find a percent of a quantity as a rate per 100 (e.g., 30% of a quantity means 30/100 times the quantity); solve problems involving finding the whole given a part and the percent.
>
> **MCC6.RP.3d** Use ratio reasoning to convert measurement units; manipulate and transform units appropriately when multiplying or dividing quantities.

Additional MCCS incorporated in Unit 2 (from Unit 1):

MCC6.NS.1 Interpret and compute quotients of fractions, and solve word problems involving division of fractions by fractions, e.g., by using visual fraction models and equations to represent the problem.

MCC6.NS.2 Fluently divide multi-digit numbers using the standard algorithm.

MCC6.NS.3 Fluently add, subtract, multiply, and divide multi-digit decimals using the standard algorithm for each operation.

MCC6.NS.4 Find the greatest common factor of two whole numbers less than or equal to 100 and the least common multiple of two whole numbers less than or equal to 12. Use the distributive property to express a sum of two whole numbers 1–100 with a common factor as a multiple of a sum of two whole numbers with no common factor.

Unit 3: Expressions

MCCS addressed in Unit 3:

MCC6.EE.1 Write and evaluate numerical expressions involving whole-number exponents.

MCC6.EE.2 Write, read, and evaluate expressions in which letters stand for numbers.

MCC6.EE.2a Write expressions that record operations with numbers and with letters standing for numbers.

MCC6.EE.2b Identify parts of an expression using mathematical terms (sum, term, product, factor, quotient, coefficient); view one or more parts of an expression as a single entity.

MCC6.EE.2c Evaluate expressions at specific values for their variables. Include expressions that arise from formulas in real-world problems. Perform arithmetic operations, including those involving whole-number exponents, in the conventional order when there are no parentheses to specify a particular order (Order of Operations).

MCC6.EE.3 Apply the properties of operations to generate equivalent expressions.

MCC6.EE.4 Identify when two expressions are equivalent (i.e., when the two expressions name the same number regardless of which value is substituted into them).

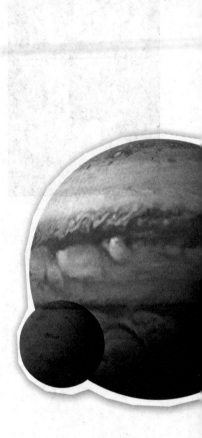

Additional MCCS incorporated in Unit 3 (from Unit 1):

MCC6.NS.1 Interpret and compute quotients of fractions, and solve word problems involving division of fractions by fractions, e.g., by using visual fraction models and equations to represent the problem.

MCC6.NS.2 Fluently divide multi-digit numbers using the standard algorithm.

MCC6.NS.3 Fluently add, subtract, multiply, and divide multi-digit decimals using the standard algorithm for each operation.

MCC6.NS.4 Find the greatest common factor of two whole numbers less than or equal to 100 and the least common multiple of two whole numbers less than or equal to 12. Use the distributive property to express a sum of two whole numbers 1–100 with a common factor as a multiple of a sum of two whole numbers with no common factor.

Also incorporates parts of MCC6.EE.1 Use variables to represent numbers and write expressions when solving a real-world or mathematical problem; understand that a variable can represent an unknown number, or, depending on the purpose at hand, any number in a specified set.

Unit 4: One-Step Equations and Inequalities

MCCS addressed in Unit 4:

MCC6.EE.5 Understand solving an equation or inequality as a process of answering a question: which values from a specified set, if any, make the equation or inequality true? Use substitution to determine whether a given number in a specified set makes an equation or inequality true.

MCC6.EE.6 Use variables to represent numbers and write expressions when solving a real-world or mathematical problem; understand that a variable can represent an unknown number, or, depending on the purpose at hand, any number in a specified set.

MCC6.EE.7 Solve real-world and mathematical problems by writing and solving equations of the form $x + p = q$ and $px = q$ for cases in which p, q and x are all nonnegative rational numbers.

MCC6.EE.8 Write an inequality of the form $x > c$ or $x < c$ to represent a constraint or condition in a real-world or mathematical problem. Recognize that inequalities of the form $x > c$ or $x < c$ have infinitely many solutions; represent solutions of such inequalities on number line diagrams.

MCC6.EE.9 Use variables to represent two quantities in a real-world problem that change in relationship to one another; write an equation to express one quantity, thought of as the dependent variable, in terms of the other quantity, thought of as the independent variable. Analyze the relationship between the dependent and independent variables using graphs and tables, and relate these to the equation.

MCC6.RP.3 Use ratio and rate reasoning to solve real-world and mathematical problems, e.g., by reasoning about tables of equivalent ratios, tape diagrams, double number line diagrams, or equations.

> **MCC6.RP.3a** Make tables of equivalent ratios relating quantities with whole-number measurements, find missing values in the tables, and plot the pairs of values on the coordinate plane. Use tables to compare ratios.

> **MCC6.RP.3b** Solve unit rate problems including those involving unit pricing and constant speed.

> **MCC6.RP.3c** Find a percent of a quantity as a rate per 100 (e.g., 30% of a quantity means 30/100 times the quantity); solve problems involving finding the whole given a part and the percent.

> **MCC6.RP.3d** Use ratio reasoning to convert measurement units; manipulate and transform units appropriately when multiplying or dividing quantities.

Additional MCCS incorporated in Unit 4 (from Unit 1):

MCC6.NS.1 Interpret and compute quotients of fractions, and solve word problems involving division of fractions by fractions, e.g., by using visual fraction models and equations to represent the problem.

MCC6.NS.2 Fluently divide multi-digit numbers using the standard algorithm.

MCC6.NS.3 Fluently add, subtract, multiply, and divide multi-digit decimals using the standard algorithm for each operation.

MCC6.NS.4 Find the greatest common factor of two whole numbers less than or equal to 100 and the least common multiple of two whole numbers less than or equal to 12. Use the distributive property to express a sum of two whole numbers 1–100 with a common factor as a multiple of a sum of two whole numbers with no common factor.

Unit 5: Area and Volume

MCCS addressed in Unit 5:

MCC6.G.1 Find area of right triangles, other triangles, special quadrilaterals, and polygons by composing into rectangles or decomposing into triangles and other shapes; apply these techniques in the context of solving real-world and mathematical problems.

MCC6.G.2 Find the volume of a right rectangular prism with fractional edge lengths by packing it with unit cubes of the appropriate unit fraction edge lengths, and show that the volume is the same as would be found by multiplying the edge lengths of the prism. Apply the formulas $V = lwh$ and $V = bh$ to find volumes of right rectangular prisms with fractional edge lengths in the context of solving real-world and mathematical problems.

MCC6.G.4 Represent three-dimensional figures using nets made up of rectangles and triangles, and use the nets to find the surface area of these figures. Apply these techniques in the context of solving real-world and mathematical problems.

Additional MCCS incorporated in Unit 5:

MCC6.EE.2c Evaluate expressions at specific values for their variables. Include expressions that arise from formulas in real-world problems. Perform arithmetic operations, including those involving whole-number exponents, in the conventional order when there are no parentheses to specify a particular order (Order of Operations).

MCC6.NS.1 Interpret and compute quotients of fractions, and solve word problems involving division of fractions by fractions, e.g., by using visual fraction models and equations to represent the problem.

MCC6.NS.2 Fluently divide multi-digit numbers using the standard algorithm.

MCC6.NS.3 Fluently add, subtract, multiply, and divide multi-digit decimals using the standard algorithm for each operation.

MCC6.NS.4 Find the greatest common factor of two whole numbers less than or equal to 100 and the least common multiple of two whole numbers less than or equal to 12. Use the distributive property to express a sum of two whole numbers 1–100 with a common factor as a multiple of a sum of two whole numbers with no common factor.

Unit 6: Statistics

MCCS addressed in Unit 6:

MCC6.SP.1 Recognize a statistical question as one that anticipates variability in the data related to the question and accounts for it in the answers.

MCC6.SP.2 Understand that a set of data collected to answer a statistical question has a distribution which can be described by its center, spread, and overall shape.

MCC6.SP.3 Recognize that a measure of center for a numerical data set summarizes all of its values with a single number, while a measure of variation describes how its values vary with a single number.

MCC6.SP.4 Display numerical data in plots on a number line, including dot plots, histograms, and box plots.

MCC6.SP.5 Summarize numerical data sets in relation to their context, such as by:

a. Reporting the number of observations.

b. Describing the nature of the attribute under investigation, including how it was measured and its units of measurement.

c. Giving quantitative measures of center (median and/or mean) and variability (interquartile range and/or mean absolute deviation), as well as describing any overall pattern and any striking deviations from the overall pattern with reference to the context in which the data was gathered.

d. Relating the choice of measures of center and variability to the shape of the data distribution and the context in which the data was gathered.

Additional MCCS incorporated in Unit 6 (from Unit 1):

MCC6.NS.1 Interpret and compute quotients of fractions, and solve word problems involving division of fractions by fractions, e.g., by using visual fraction models and equations to represent the problem.

MCC6.NS.2 Fluently divide multi-digit numbers using the standard algorithm.

MCC6.NS.3 Fluently add, subtract, multiply, and divide multi-digit decimals using the standard algorithm for each operation.

MCC6.NS.4 Find the greatest common factor of two whole numbers less than or equal to 100 and the least common multiple of two whole numbers less than or equal to 12. Use the distributive property to express a sum of two whole numbers 1–100 with a common factor as a multiple of a sum of two whole numbers with no common factor.

Unit 7: Rational Explorations: Numbers and their Opposites

MCCS addressed in Unit 7:

MCC6.NS.5 Understand that positive and negative numbers are used together to describe quantities having opposite directions or values (e.g., temperature above/below zero, elevation above/below sea level, debits/credits, positive/negative electric charge); use positive and negative numbers to represent quantities in real-world contexts, explaining the meaning of 0 in each situation.

MCC6.NS.6 Understand a rational number as a point on the number line. Extend number line diagrams and coordinate axes familiar from previous grades to represent points on the line and in the plane with negative number coordinates.

MCC6.NS.6a Recognize opposite signs of numbers as indicating locations on opposite sides of 0 on the number line; recognize that the opposite of the opposite of a number is the number itself, e.g., $-(-3) = 3$, and that 0 is its own opposite.

MCC6.NS.6b Understand signs of numbers in ordered pairs as indicating locations in quadrants of the coordinate plane; recognize that when two ordered pairs differ only by signs, the locations of the points are related by reflections across one or both axes.

MCC6.NS.6c Find and position integers and other rational numbers on a horizontal or vertical number line diagram; find and position pairs of integers and other rational numbers on a coordinate plane.

MCC6.NS.7 Understand ordering and absolute value of rational numbers.

MCC6.NS.7a Interpret statements of inequality as statements about the relative position of two numbers on a number line diagram.

MCC6.NS.7b Write, interpret, and explain statements of order for rational numbers in real-world contexts.

MCC6.NS.7c Understand the absolute value of a rational number as its distance from 0 on the number line; interpret absolute value as magnitude for a positive or negative quantity in a real-world situation.

MCC6.NS.7d Distinguish comparisons of absolute value from statements about order.

MCC6.NS.8 Solve real-world and mathematical problems by graphing points in all four quadrants of the coordinate plane. Include use of coordinates and absolute value to find distances between points with the same first coordinate or the same second coordinate.

MCC6.G.3 Draw polygons in the coordinate plane given coordinates for the vertices; use coordinates to find the length of a side joining points with the same first coordinate or the same second coordinate. Apply these techniques in the context of solving real-world and mathematical problems.

Unit 8: Show What We Know

MCCS addressed in Unit 8:
ALL

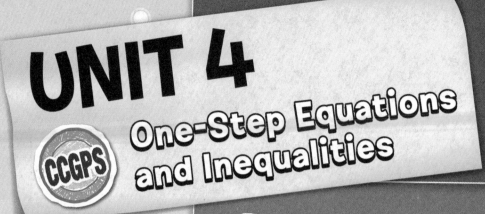

UNIT 4

CCGPS One-Step Equations and Inequalities

 Essential Question

HOW can you communicate mathematical ideas effectively?

Chapter 6
Equations

Variables are used to represent an unknown number in an expression or equation. In this chapter, you will write and solve one-variable addition, subtraction, multiplication, and division equations.

Chapter 7
Functions and Inequalities

Functions can be represented using words, equations, tables, and graphs. In this chapter, you will represent and analyze the relationship between two variables using functions. You will also write, graph, and solve one-variable inequalities.

Chapter 6
Equations

Essential Question

HOW do you determine if two numbers or expressions are equal?

Common Core GPS

Content Standards
MCC6.EE.5, MCC6.EE.7, MCC6.RP.3

Mathematical Practices
1, 2, 3, 4, 5, 7

Math in the Real World

Zip lines can be used for entertainment or to access remote areas such as a rainforest canopy.

The speed differs based on the angle of the cable. On one zip line, the average speed is 44 ft/s. It takes 8 seconds to travel the length of the zip line. Fill in the table to find the distance.

Rate (ft/s)	×	Time (s)	=	Distance (ft)
44	×	1	=	
44	×	2	=	
44	×	3	=	
44	×	4	=	
44	×	5	=	
44	×	6	=	
44	×	7	=	
44	×	8	=	

FOLDABLES®
Study Organizer

 1 Cut out the correct Foldable from the FL pages in the back of this book.

 2 Place your Foldable on the Key Concept page toward the end of this chapter.

 3 Use the Foldable throughout this chapter to help you learn about equations.

What Tools Do You Need?

 Vocabulary

Addition Property of Equality	inverse operations
Division Property of Equality	Multiplication Property of Equality
equals sign	solution
equation	solve
expressions	Subtraction Property of Equality

Study Skill: Studying Math

Simplify the Problem Read the problem carefully to determine what information is needed to solve the problem.

Step 1 | **Read the problem.**

Kylie wants to order several pairs of running shorts from an online store. They cost $14 each, and there is a one-time shipping fee of $7. What is the total cost of buying any number of pairs of shorts?

Step 2 | **Rewrite the problem to make it simpler. Keep all of the important information but use fewer words.**

Kylie wants to buy some _____ that cost _____ each plus a shipping

fee of _____. What is the total cost for any number of pairs of shorts.

Step 3 | **Rewrite the problem using even fewer words. Write a variable for the unknown.**

The total cost of x shorts is _____ + _____.

Step 4 | **Translate the words into an expression.**

_____

Use the method above to write an expression for each problem.

1. Akira is saving money to buy a bicycle. He has already saved $80 and plans to save an additional $5 each week. Find the total amount he has saved after any number of weeks.

2. A taxi company charges $1.50 per mile plus a $10 fee. What is the total cost of a taxi ride for any number of miles?

Watch Play it online!

Your Turn! You will solve this problem in the chapter.

Try the Quick Check below.
Or, take the Online Readiness Quiz.

 Check ✓

Example 1

Find 1.37 − 0.75.

$$\begin{array}{r} \overset{1}{\cancel{1}}.37 \\ -\ 0.75 \\ \hline 0.62 \end{array}$$

Line up the decimal points.
Subtract.

Example 2

Find $\frac{3}{4} - \frac{5}{9}$.

The LCD of $\frac{3}{4}$ and $\frac{5}{9}$ is 36.

Write the problem.   Rename using the LCD, 36.   Subtract the numerators.

$$\begin{array}{l} \frac{3}{4} \rightarrow \frac{3 \times 9}{4 \times 9} = \frac{27}{36} \rightarrow \frac{27}{36} \\ -\frac{5}{9} \rightarrow \frac{5 \times 4}{9 \times 4} = -\frac{20}{36} \rightarrow -\frac{20}{36} \\ \hline \frac{7}{36} \end{array}$$

Quick Check

Subtract Decimals Find each difference.

1. 2.34 − 1.23 = _____

2. 1.26 − 0.78 = _____

3. 3.65 − 0.96 = _____

 Show your work.

Subtract Fractions Find each difference. Write in simplest form.

4. $\frac{7}{8} - \frac{1}{4} =$ _____

5. $\frac{5}{6} - \frac{1}{2} =$ _____

6. $\frac{3}{5} - \frac{2}{7} =$ _____

7. Pamela ran $\frac{7}{10}$ mile on Tuesday and $\frac{3}{8}$ mile on Thursday. How much farther did she run on Tuesday?

_____

 **How Did You Do?**

Which problems did you answer correctly in the Quick Check?
Shade those exercise numbers below.

① ② ③ ④ ⑤ ⑥ ⑦

Equations

What You'll Learn

Scan the lesson. Predict two things you will learn about equations.

• _____

_____

• _____

_____

 Essential Question

HOW do you determine if two numbers or expressions are equal?

 Vocabulary

equation
equals sign
solve
solution

CCGPS Common Core GPS

Content Standards
MCC6.EE.5

Mathematical Practices
1, 2, 3, 4, 7

Vocabulary Start-Up

An **equation** is a mathematical sentence showing two expressions are equal. An equation contains an **equals sign**, =.

Equation	Expression
Definition	Definition
_____	_____
_____	_____
Example	Example
_____	_____

How are an equation and an expression similar?

_____

How are an equation and an expression different?

_____

Real-World Link

Shopping Anna bought a package of 6 pair of socks. She writes the equation below to find how much she paid per pair. Circle the *solution* of the equation.

$$6x = \$9$$

$\$0.50$ $\$1.50$ $\$2.00$

Solve Addition and Subtraction Equations Mentally

When you replace a variable with a value that results in a true sentence, you **solve** the equation. That value for the variable is the **solution** of the equation.

$$2 + x = 9$$
$$2 + 7 = 9$$
$$9 = 9$$

The value for the variable that results in a true sentence is 7. So, 7 is the solution.

This sentence is true.

Examples

Tutor

1. Is 3, 4, or 5 the solution of the equation $a + 7 = 11$?

Value of a	$a + 7 \stackrel{?}{=} 11$	Are Both Sides Equal?
3	$3 + 7 \stackrel{?}{=} 11$ $10 \neq 11$	no
4	$4 + 7 \stackrel{?}{=} 11$ $11 = 11$	yes ✓
5	$5 + 7 \stackrel{?}{=} 11$ $12 \neq 11$	no

The solution is 4.

2. Solve $g - 7 = 3$ mentally.

$$g - 7 = 3 \qquad \text{Think} \quad \text{What number minus 7 equals 3?}$$
$$10 - 7 = 3 \qquad \text{You know that } 10 - 7 = 3.$$
$$3 = 3$$

The solution is 10.

3. The total cost of a pair of skates and kneepads is $63. The skates cost $45. Use the *guess, check, and revise* strategy to solve the equation $45 + k = 63$ to find k, the cost of the kneepads.

Use the *guess, check, and revise* strategy.

Try 14.
$$45 + k = 63$$
$$45 + 14 \stackrel{?}{=} 63$$
$$59 \neq 63$$

Try 16.
$$45 + k = 63$$
$$45 + 16 \stackrel{?}{=} 63$$
$$61 \neq 63$$

Try 18.
$$45 + k = 63$$
$$45 + 18 \stackrel{?}{=} 63$$
$$63 = 63 ✓$$

So, the kneepads cost $18.

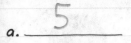

Got It? Do these problems to find out.

a. Is 4, 5, or 6 the solution of the equation $c + 8 = 13$?

b. Solve $9 - x = 2$ mentally.

c. The difference between an ostrich's speed and a chicken's speed is 31 miles per hour. An ostrich can run at a speed of 40 miles per hour. Use mental math or the *guess, check, and revise* strategy to solve the equation $40 - c = 31$ to find c, the speed a chicken can run.

a. _____ 5

b. _____ 7

c. _____ 9

Solve Multiplication and Division Equations Mentally

Multiplication and division equations are solved in a similar way to addition and subtraction equations.

Examples

 Tutor

4. Is 3, 4, or 5 the solution of the equation $18 = 6z$?

Value of z	$18 \stackrel{?}{=} 6z$	Are Both Sides Equal?
3	$18 \stackrel{?}{=} 6 \cdot 3$ $18 = 18$	yes ✓
4	$18 \stackrel{?}{=} 6 \cdot 4$ $18 \neq 24$	no
5	$18 \stackrel{?}{=} 6 \cdot 5$ $18 \neq 30$	no

The solution is 3.

5. Solve $16 \div s = 8$ mentally.

$16 \div s = 8$ Think 16 divided by what number equals 8?

$16 \div 2 = 8$ You know that $16 \div 2 = 8$.

$\quad\quad 8 = 8$

The solution is 2.

Show your work.

Got It? Do these problems to find out.

d. Is 2, 3, or 4 the solution of the equation $4n = 16$?

e. Solve $24 \div w = 8$ mentally.

d. _____ 4

e. _____ 3

Example

6. Mason bought 72 sticks of gum. There are 8 sticks of gum in each package. Use the *guess, check, and revise* strategy to solve the equation $8 \cdot p = 72$ to find p, the number of packages Mason bought.

Use the *guess, check, and revise* strategy.

Try 7.	Try 8.	Try 9.
$8 \cdot p = 72$	$8 \cdot p = 72$	$8 \cdot p = 72$
$8 \cdot 7 \stackrel{?}{=} 72$	$8 \cdot 8 \stackrel{?}{=} 72$	$8 \cdot 9 \stackrel{?}{=} 72$
$56 \neq 72$	$64 \neq 72$	$72 = 72$ ✓

So, Mason bought 9 packages of gum.

Guided Practice

Identify the solution of each equation from the list given. (Examples 1 and 4)

1. $9 + w = 17$; 7, 8, 9   *8*

2. $8 \div c = 8$; 0, 1, 2   *1*

Solve each equation mentally. (Examples 2 and 5)

3. $x - 11 = 23$

34

4. $4x = 32$

8

5. Mississippi and Georgia have a total of 21 electoral votes. Mississippi has 6 electoral votes. Use mental math or the *guess, check, and revise* strategy to solve the equation $6 + g = 21$ to find g, the number of electoral votes Georgia has. (Example 3)

15 votes

6. Riley and her sister collect stickers. Riley has 220 stickers in her sticker collection. Her sister has 55 stickers in her collection. Riley has how many times as many stickers as her sister? Use mental math or the *guess, check, and revise* strategy to solve the equation $55x = 220$. (Example 6)

4 times

7. **Building on the Essential Question** How do you solve an equation? *You have to use inverse operations.*

Work with a partner. Solve each equation using cups and counters.
Draw cups and counters to show your work.

3. $1 + x = 8$

x = _____7_____

 Show your work.

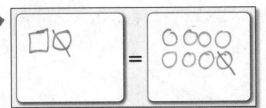

4. $x + 2 = 7$

x = _____5_____

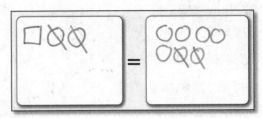

5. $3 + x = 6$

x = _____3_____

6. $x + 5 = 7$

x = _____2_____

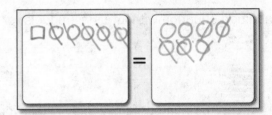

Work with a partner. Solve each addition equation using the model of your choice.

7. $9 = x + 3$

x = _____6_____

8. $4 + x = 6$

x = _____2_____

9. Terrell bought an MP3 player. He spent the rest of his money on an Internet music subscription for $25.95. If he started with $135, how much was the MP3 player? Write and solve an equation using a bar diagram.

$$x + \$25.95 = 135 \ / \ x = \$109.05$$

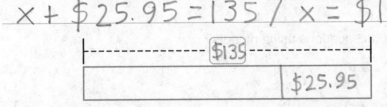

```
  135
- 25.95
-------
109.05
```

Work with a partner to complete the table. The first one is done for you.

	Addition Equation	Subtraction Sentence	Solution
	$x + 1 = 3$	$3 - 1 = x$	$x = 2$
10.	$y + 9 = 12$	$12 - 9 = y$	$y = 3$
11.	$14 = 7 + m$	$14 - 7 = m$	$m = 7$
12.	$8 + f = 20$	$20 - 8 = f$	$f = 12$
13.	$47 = 17 + v$	$47 - 17 = v$	$v = 30$
14.	$100 + c = 129$	$129 - 100 = c$	$c = 29$
15.	$h + 89.4 = 97.4$	$97.4 - 89.4 = h$	$h = 9$

16. **CCGPS** **Reason Inductively** Write a rule that you can use to solve an addition equation without using models. You can use inverse operations.

17. How can the number family 3, 4, 7 help you to solve the equation $3 + x = 7$? I can subtract 3 from 7 to get "x" as 4.

18. **CCGPS** **Model with Mathematics** Write a real-world problem for the equation modeled below. Then write the equation and solve.

|---------- 6 weeks ----------|
length of vacation, v	2 weeks

Jane and her family are away for 6 weeks. They spent 2 weeks.

19. **Inquiry** HOW do you solve addition equations using models? I can use inverse operations.

Solve and Write Addition Equations

What You'll Learn

Scan the lesson. List two real-world scenarios in which you would use addition equations.

• _____
_____

• _____
_____

 Essential Question

HOW do you determine if two numbers or expressions are equal?

 Vocabulary

inverse operations
Subtraction Property
    of Equality

 Common Core GPS

Content Standards
MCC6.EE.5, MCC6.EE.7

Mathematical Practices
1, 2, 3, 4, 5

 ## Real-World Link

 Tools

Miniature Golf On the second hole of miniature golf, it took Anne 3 putts to sink the golf ball. Her score is now 5. She represents this situation with cups and counters.

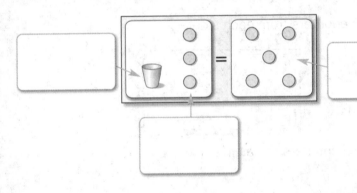

1. Fill in the boxes above using the phrases below:
   • Her score on the first hole is unknown.
   • Her score in now 5.
   • She scored a 3 on the second hole.

2. Write the addition equation shown in the figure.

   _____

3. Explain how to solve the equation.

   _____

4. What was Anne's score on the first hole? ☐

Lesson 2 Solve and Write Addition Equations   **441**

Solve an Equation By Subtracting

In Lesson 1, you mentally solved equations. Another way is to use **inverse operations**, which *undo* each other. For example, to solve an addition equation, use subtraction.

Example

Tutor

1. **Solve 8 = x + 3. Check your solution.**

> **Method 1** Use models.

Model the equation using counters for the numbers and a cup for the variable.

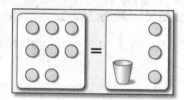

Remove 3 counters from each side.

There are 5 counters remaining.

> **Method 2** Use symbols.

$$8 = x + 3$$ Write the equation.

$$\underline{-3 = \quad -3}$$ Subtract 3 from each side to "undo" the addition of 3 on the right.

$$5 = x$$

Check

$$8 = x + 3$$ Write the equation.

$$8 \overset{?}{=} 5 + 3$$ Replace x with 5.

$$8 = 8 \checkmark$$ This sentence is true.

Using either method, the solution is 5.

> **Got It?** Do these problems to find out.

Solve each equation. Check your solution.

   a. $c + 2 = 5$ **b.** $6 = x + 5$ **c.** $3.5 + y = 12.75$

a. _____3_____ ← Show your work.

b. _____1_____

c. _____9.25_____

Subtraction Property of Equality

Words   If you subtract the same number from each side of an equation, the two sides remain equal.

Examples

Numbers	Algebra
$5 = 5$	$x + 2 = 3$
$-3 = -3$	$-2 = -2$
$2 = 2$	$x = 1$

When you solve an equation by subtracting the same number from each side of the equation, you are using the **Subtraction Property of Equality**.

 Example   Tutor

2. Ruben and Tariq have **245.5 downloaded minutes of music. If Ruben has 132 minutes, how many belong to Tariq? Write and solve an addition equation to find how many minutes belong to Tariq.**

Words   Ruben and Tariq have 245.5 minutes of music.

Variable   Let t represent the number of minutes that belong to Tariq.

Bar Diagram

Tariq's minutes, t

|--------- 245.5 minutes ---------|

132	Tariq's minutes, t

Equation $132 + t = 245.5$

$$132 + t = 245.5 \quad \text{Write the equation.}$$
$$-132 = -132 \quad \text{Subtract 132 from each side.}$$
$$t = 113.5 \quad \text{Simplify.}$$

So, 113.5 minutes belong to Tariq.

Check $132 + 113.5 = 245.5$ ✓

Got It?   Do this problem to find out.

d. Suppose Ruben had 147.5 minutes of the 245.5 that were downloaded. Write and solve an addition equation to find how many minutes belong to Tariq.

> **Checking Solutions**
> You should always check your solution. You will know immediately whether your solution is correct or not.

$$\begin{array}{r} 245 \\ -147 \\ \hline 98 \end{array}$$

 Show your work.

d. ___98___

Example

3. A male gorilla weighs 379 pounds on average. This is 181 pounds more than the weight of the average female gorilla. Write and solve an addition equation to find the weight of an average female gorilla.

Words	181 pounds plus the weight of an average female gorilla is 379 pounds.
Variable	Let w represent the weight of an average female gorilla.
Bar Diagram	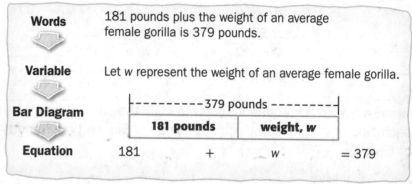
Equation	$181 + w = 379$

$$181 + w = 379 \qquad \text{Write the equation.}$$
$$\underline{-181 \qquad = -181} \qquad \text{Subtract 181 from each side.}$$
$$w = 198 \qquad 379 - 181 = 198$$

So, an average female gorilla weighs 198 pounds.

Check $181 + 198 = 379$ ✓

Guided Practice

Solve each equation. Check your solution. (Example 1)

1. $y + 7 = 10$

3

2. $10 = 6 + e$

4

3. A board that measures 19.5 meters in length is cut into two pieces. One piece measures 7.2 meters. Write and solve an equation to find the length of the other piece. (Example 2)

12.3 m

4. It takes 43 facial muscles to frown. This is 26 more muscles than it takes to smile. Write and solve an equation to find the number of muscles it takes to smile. (Example 3) $43 = x + 26$

5. **Building on the Essential Question** How can the Subtraction Property of Equality be used to solve addition equations?

The property uses an inverse operation.

Rate Yourself!

How confident are you about writing and solving addition equations? Check the box that applies.

I'm on target.

I need help.

For more help, go online to access a Personal Tutor.

FOLDABLES Time to update your Foldable!

Photo 24/Getty Images

Copyright © The McGraw-Hill Companies, Inc.

Name _____ My Homework _____

Go online for Step-by-Step Solutions

Independent Practice

Solve each equation. Check your solution. (Example 1)

1. $c + 3 = 6$

 Show your work.

3

2. $9 = 2 + x$

7

3. $7 + a = 9$

2

4. Zacarias and Paz together have $756.80. If Zacarias has $489.50, how much does Paz have? Write and solve an addition equation to find how much money belongs to Paz. (Example 2) $x + \$489.50 =$ $\$756.80.$ $x = \$267.30$

5. The average length of a King Cobra is 118 inches, which is 22 inches longer than a Black Mamba. Write and solve an addition equation to find the average length of a Black Mamba. (Example 3) $y + 22 = 118.$ $y = 96$ inches

6. CCGPS **Model with Mathematics** Refer to the graphic novel frame below for Exercises a–b.

Watch ▶ Replay it online!

READING REWARD
50 Points = Pizza Party

ITEM READ	POINTS
Book	5
Magazine	1
Newspaper	1

Remember, I need 50 points for the pizza party.

a. If Mei has already earned 30 points, write and solve an addition equation to find the number of points she still needs.

$30 + x = 50$ $x = 20$

b. Suppose Julie has already earned 36 points. Write and solve an addition equation to find the number of points she still needs to earn the pizza party. $36 + y = 50$

Solve each equation. Check your solution.

7. $a + \frac{1}{10} = \frac{5}{10}$

$a = 4/10$

8. $m + \frac{1}{3} = \frac{2}{3}$

$m = 1/3$

9. $\frac{3}{4} = x + \frac{1}{2}$

$x = 1/4$

H.O.T. Problems Higher Order Thinking

10. CCGPS **Reason Abstractly** Write two different addition equations that have 12 as the solution. $3 + x = 15, \quad y + 15 = 27$

11. CCGPS **Persevere with Problems** In the equation $x + y = 5$, the value for x is a whole number greater than 2 but less than 6. Determine the possible solutions for y.

$x > 2, < 6 \quad x = 3, \quad y = 2$

12. CCGPS **Which One Doesn't Belong?** Identify the equation that does not belong with the other three. Explain your reasoning.

| $6 + x = 9$ | $15 = x + 12$ | $x + 9 = 11$ | $7 + x = 10$ |

Equation C, because its solution is 2.

Georgia Test Practice

13. The model represents the equation $x + 4 = 7$.

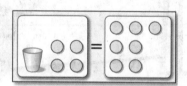

What is the first step in finding the value of x?

Ⓐ Add 4 counters to each side.

Ⓑ Subtract 7 counters from each side.

Ⓒ Add 7 counters to each side.

Ⓓ Subtract 4 counters from each side.

Extra Practice

Solve each equation. Check your solution.

14. $x + 5 = 11$

Homework Help →

$$\begin{array}{r} x + 5 = 11 \\ -5 = -5 \\ \hline x \quad\ = \ 6 \end{array}$$

15. $7 = 4 + y$

$y = 3$

16. $5 + g = 6$

$g = 1$

17. $d + 3 = 8$

$d = 5$

18. $x + 4 = 6$

$x = 2$

19. $3 + f = 8$

$f = 5$

20. Enrique and Levi together have 386 trading cards. If Enrique has 221 trading cards, how many does Levi have? Write and solve an addition equation to find how many trading cards are Levi's.

$221 + y = 386; \ y = 165 \ cards$

21. Eliott is 63 inches tall, which is 9 inches taller than his cousin, Jackson. Write and solve an addition equation to find Jackson's height.

$63 = x + 9; \ x = 54 \ inches$

22. (CCGPS) **Use Math Tools** The table shows the heights of three monster trucks. Bigfoot 5 is 4.9 feet taller than Bigfoot 2. Write and solve an addition equation to find the height of Bigfoot 2. $15.4 =$

$x + 4.9; \ x = 10.5 \ ft. \ tall$

Truck	Height (ft)
Bigfoot 5	15.4
Swamp Thing	12.2
Bigfoot 2	■

Solve each equation. Check your solution.

23. $t + \dfrac{8}{10} = \dfrac{9}{10}$

$t = 1/10$

24. $\dfrac{5}{8} + n = \dfrac{7}{8}$

$n = 1/4$

25. $t + \dfrac{1}{4} = \dfrac{3}{4}$

$t = 1/2$

Georgia Test Practice

26. Niko wants to buy a skateboard that costs $85. He has already saved $15. Which equation represents the amount of money Niko still needs to buy the skateboard?

Ⓐ $t - 15 = 85$ Ⓒ $15 - t = 85$

Ⓑ $t + 15 = 85$ Ⓓ $t = 15 + 85$

27. Refer to Exercise 26. How much money does Niko still need to save?

Ⓕ $100   Ⓗ $65

Ⓖ $70   Ⓘ $60

28. Short Response The table shows the point values from a bag toss game.

Scoring Toss	Points
went through hole	3
landed on board	1

Before Wes's last toss, he had a score of 15 points. After tossing the bag five more times, he had a score of 24 points. Write and solve an equation to show how many points Wes scored on the five tosses.

$15 + x = 24$

 Common Core Review

Subtract. MCC4.NBT.4

29. $22 - 8 =$ ___ 14

30. $72 - 34 =$ ___ 38

31. $34 - 19 =$ ___ 15

32. $51 - 32 =$ ___ 19

33. $66 - 14 =$ ___ 52

34. $49 - 32 =$ ___ 17

35. Tyrone ate $\frac{1}{2}$ of a pizza. Jackie ate $\frac{1}{6}$ of a pizza. How much more pizza did Tyrone eat than Jackie? MCC5.NF.1 ___ Tyrone ate $\frac{1}{3}$ of a pizza more.

36. The table shows the distances three friends hiked. How much farther did Isabella hike than Devon? MCC5.NBT.7 ___ 0.4 mi more

Name	Distance Hiked (mi)
Devon	1.85
Franco	2.55
Isabella	2.25

Download more Extra Practice at **connectED.mcgraw-hill.com.**

Inquiry HOW do you solve subtraction equations using models?

CCGPS Content Standards
MCC6.EE.5,
MCC6.EE.7

Mathematical Practices
1, 3, 4

Trading Cards Zack gave 5 trading cards to his sister. Now he has 41 cards. How many cards did he have originally?

What do you know? _Zack gave away 5 cards and he has 41._

What do you need to find? _How many he has originally_

Investigation

Watch ▶

Step 1 Define a variable. Use the variable c to represent the number of cards Zack had originally.

Step 2 Use a bar diagram to help write the equation.

original number of cards, c
-------- 41 cards ------- ┤5 cards├

The total length of the diagram shows ___C cards___.

The number 41 represents _____.

The number 5 represents _given away_.

☐ – ☐ = ☐

Step 3 Work backward. Rewrite the equation as an addition sentence and solve.

☐ + ☐ = ☐

So, Zack originally had ☐ trading cards.

Collaborate

Work with a partner. Write and solve a subtraction equation using a bar diagram.

1. Mariska gave her friend Elise 8 beads and was left with 37 beads. How many did she have originally?

2. Clinton has $12 after buying a snack at the mall. The snack cost $5. How much money did Clinton have originally?

3. The Martin County Cat Shelter placed 8 cats with new owners on Monday. On Tuesday, 31 cats remained at the shelter. How many cats were at the shelter originally?

Reflect

4. **CCGPS Reason Inductively** Write a rule for solving equations like $x - 4 = 7$.

5. **CCGPS Model with Mathematics** Write a real-world subtraction problem for the equation modeled below. Then write the equation and solve.

miles driven, m
----- 128 miles -----+--67 miles--

6. **Inquiry** HOW do you solve subtraction equations using models?

Solve and Write Subtraction Equations

What You'll Learn

Scan the lesson. Predict two things you will learn about solving and writing subtraction equations.

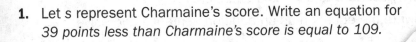

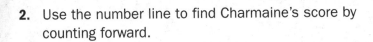

 Essential Question

HOW do you determine if two numbers or expressions are equal?

 Vocabulary

Addition Property of Equality

 Common Core GPS

Content Standards
MCC6.EE.5, MCC6.EE.7
Mathematical Practices
1, 3, 4, 5

 ## Real-World Link 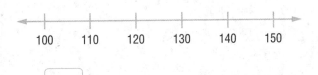 Watch ▶

Bowling Meghan's bowling score was 39 points less than Charmaine's. Meghan's score was 109.

1. Let *s* represent Charmaine's score. Write an equation for *39 points less than Charmaine's score is equal to 109.*

_____

_____

2. Use the number line to find Charmaine's score by counting forward.

<----+-------+-------+-------+-------+-------+---->
     100   110   120   130   140   150

s = ☐

3. What operation does counting forward suggest?

_____

_____

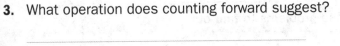

Solve an Equation by Adding

Because addition and subtraction are inverse operations, you can solve a subtraction equation by adding.

Example

1. **Solve $x - 2 = 3$. Check your solution.**

Method 1 Use models.

Model the equation.

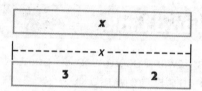

Work backward to solve the equation.

Rewrite the equation as an addition sentence and solve.

$3 + 2 = 5$

Method 2 Use symbols.

$x - 2 =$	3	Write the equation.
$+ 2 = + 2$		Add 2 to each side.
$x \quad =$	5	Simplify.

Check

$x - 2 = 3$	Write the equation.
$5 - 2 \overset{?}{=} 3$	Replace x with 5.
$3 = 3$ ✓	This sentence is true.

Using either method, the solution is 5.

Got It? Do these problems to find out.

Solve each equation. Check your solution.

    a. $x - 7 = 4$ **b.** $y - 6 = 8$ **c.** $9 = a - 5$

Show your work.

a. _____ 11

b. _____ 14

c. _____ 14

Addition Property of Equality

Words	If you add the same number to each side of an equation, the two sides remain equal.

Examples

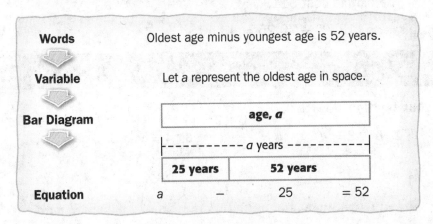

Numbers

$5 = 5$
$+3 = +3$
$8 = 8$

Algebra

$x - 2 = 3$
$+2 = +2$
$x = 5$

When you solve an equation by adding the same number to each side of the equation, you are using the **Addition Property of Equality**.

Example

Tutor

2. **STEM** At age 25, Gherman Titov of Russia was the youngest person to travel into space. This is 52 years less than the oldest person to travel in space, John Glenn. How old was John Glenn? Write and solve a subtraction equation.

Words	Oldest age minus youngest age is 52 years.
Variable	Let a represent the oldest age in space.

Bar Diagram

age, a

$\leftarrow$ -------- a years --------- $\rightarrow$

25 years	52 years

| Equation | a | $-$ | 25 | $= 52$ |

$a - 25 = 52$ Write the equation.
$+25 = +25$ Add 25 to each side.
$a = 77$ Simplify.

John Glenn was 77 years old.

Check $77 - 25 = 52$ ✓

Got It? Do this problem to find out.

d. Georgia's height is 4 inches less than Sienna's height. Georgia is 58 inches tall. Write and solve a subtraction equation to find Sienna's height.

$x - 4 = 58$

Show your work.

d. ___62___

Tutor

Example

3. Raheem's rollerblades cost $70.25 less than his bicycle. His rollerblades cost $43.50. How much did his bicycle cost? Write and solve a subtraction equation.

$$14.95$$
$$+ \; 7.55$$
$$22.50$$

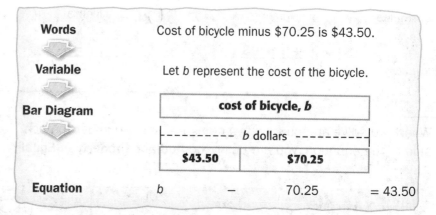

		Words	Cost of bicycle minus $70.25 is $43.50.

Variable — Let *b* represent the cost of the bicycle.

Bar Diagram

cost of bicycle, *b*	
$43.50	$70.25

b dollars

Equation — *b*   −   70.25   = 43.50

$$b - 70.25 = 43.50 \quad \text{Write the equation.}$$
$$\underline{+\,70.25 = +\,70.25} \quad \text{Add 70.25 to each side.}$$
$$b \quad = 113.75 \quad \text{Simplify.}$$

The bicycle cost $113.75.

Check $113.75 - 70.25 = 43.50$ ✓

Guided Practice

Check

Solve each equation. Check your solution. (Example 1)

1. $a - 5 = 9$

Show your work.

14

2. $b - 3 = 7$

10

3. $4 = y - 8$

12

4. Catherine studied 1.25 hours for her science test. This was 0.5 hour less than she studied for her algebra test. Write and solve a subtraction equation to find how long she studied for her algebra test. (Examples 2 and 3)

1.75 hours

5. **ⓔ Building on the Essential Question** How can the Addition Property of Equality be used to solve subtraction equations?

It is just the inverse.

Independent Practice

Go online for Step-by-Step Solutions eHelp

Solve each equation. Check your solution. (Examples 1 and 3)

1. $c - 1 = 8$

9

2. $t - 7 = 2$

9

3. $1 = g - 3$

4

4. $a - 2.1 = 5.8$

3.7

5. $a - 1.1 = 2.3$

1.2

6. $4.6 = e - 3.2$

7.8

7. Pete is 15 years old. This is 6 years younger than his sister Victoria. Write and solve a subtraction equation to find Victoria's age. (Example 2)

$X - 6 = 15$ $X = 21$ years

8. A CD costs \$14.95. This is \$7.55 less than the cost of a DVD. Write and solve a subtraction equation to find the cost of the DVD. (Example 3)

$X - 7.55 = 14.95$ $X = \$22.50$

21

9. If $b - 10 = 5$, what is the value of $b + 6$? _____ 21

Solve each equation. Check your solution.

10. $m - \frac{1}{3} = \frac{2}{3}$

1

11. $n - \frac{1}{4} = \frac{3}{4}$

1

12. $s - \frac{1}{3} = \frac{7}{9}$

$1\frac{1}{9}$

13. Alejandra spent her birthday money on a video game that cost \$24, a controller for \$13, and a memory card for \$16. The total tax was \$3. Write and solve a subtraction equation to find how much money Alejandra gave the cashier if she received \$4 in change.

$X - 56 = 4$ $X = \$60$

14. **CCGPS** **Multiple Representations** The bar diagram represents a subtraction equation.

x°F	
74°F	13°F

a. **Words** Write a real-world problem that can be represented by the bar diagram. Today's temperature is 13°F than x degrees total yesterday (74°F). What is the total temp?

b. **Algebra** Write a subtraction equation that can be represented by the bar diagram. $x - 74 = 13$

c. **Numbers** Solve the equation you wrote in part b. 87°F

H.O.T. Problems Higher Order Thinking

15. **CCGPS** **Find the Error** Elisa is explaining how to solve the equation $d - 6 = 4$. Find her mistake and correct it. You have to ADD 6 to each side.

Subtract 6 from each side.

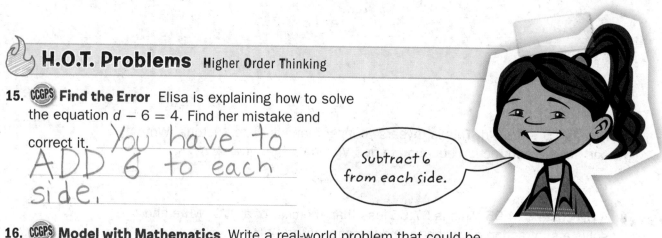

16. **CCGPS** **Model with Mathematics** Write a real-world problem that could be represented by $d - 32 = 64$. Today, I have $64, which is $32 less yesterday.

17. **CCGPS** **Persevere with Problems** Another type of subtraction equation is $16 - b = 7$. Explain how you would solve this equation then solve it. I would just subtract 7 from each side.

Georgia Test Practice

18. Which of the following is true concerning $x - 5 = 13$?

(A) To find the value of x, add 5 to each side.

(B) To find the value of x, subtract 5 from each side.

(C) To find the value of x, add 13 to each side.

(D) To find the value of x, subtract 13 from each side.

Extra Practice

Solve each equation. Check your solution.

19. $f - 1 = 5$

$$f - 1 = 5$$
$$\underline{+ 1 = + 1}$$
$$f = 6$$

20. $2 = e - 1$

3

21. $r - 3 = 1$

4

22. $z - 6.3 = 2.1$

8.4

23. $t - 9.25 = 5.45$

14.7

24. $k - 32.9 = 16.5$

$$\begin{array}{r} 32.9 \\ \underline{+} \\ 49.4 \end{array}$$

49.4

25. **CCGPS** **Use Math Tools** North Carolina has 12 less electoral votes than Florida. Write and solve a subtraction equation to find the number of electoral votes for Florida. $x - 12 = 15;$
$x = 27$

Electoral Votes	
State	**Number of Votes**
Florida	■
North Carolina	15

26. Marty's cat weighs 10.4 pounds. This is 24.4 pounds less than the weight of his dog. Write and solve a subtraction equation to find the weight of Marty's dog. Marty's dog weighs 34.8 lbs.

27. Find the value of t if $t - 7 = 12$. t is 19; since 12 + 7 = 19.

Solve each equation. Check your solution.

28. $s - \frac{1}{2} = \frac{1}{2}$

1

29. $h - \frac{1}{4} = \frac{1}{4}$

1/2

30. $c - 1 = \frac{3}{4}$

$1^3/4$

31. At a movie, Angelo bought a medium popcorn for $4, a small drink for $3, and a box of fruit snacks for $5. Write and solve a subtraction equation to find how much money Angelo gave the cashier if he received $3 in change.
$x - 12 = \$3$

Georgia Test Practice

32. Arizona became a state 96 years later than Indiana. Which equation can be used to find the year y Arizona became a state?

State	Year it Became a State
Arizona	■
Indiana	1816

Ⓐ $y = 1816 - 96$ Ⓒ $y - 1816 = 96$
Ⓑ $y + 96 = 1816$ Ⓓ $1816 - y = 96$

33. Xavier's age is 3 less than Paula's age. Xavier is 11 years old. Which subtraction equation represents this situation?

Ⓕ $a + 11 = 3$
Ⓖ $11 - 3 = a$
Ⓗ $a - 3 = 11$
Ⓘ $3 - a = 11$

34. Short Response Owen bought a pair of shoes and the shirt shown. The cost of the shirt was $42 less than the price of the shoes. How much did Owen spend on shoes?

$62

$22

Common Core Review

Multiply. MCC4.NBT.5

35. $63 \times 8 =$ _504_

36. $19 \times 6 =$ _114_

37. $27 \times 5 =$ _135_

38. $13 \times 8 =$ _104_

39. $36 \times 4 =$ _144_

40. $21 \times 3 =$ _63_

41. The table shows how much four people earned washing cars. If Gabrielle earns $5 for each car she washes, how many cars did she wash? MCC4.NBT.6 _16 cars_

42. The Cozy Cat Shop has 3 calico cats for every gray cat. If they have 9 calico cats available, how many gray cats do they have?

MCC4.NBT.6 _3 gray cats_

Name	Amount Earned ($)
Eli	70
Gabrielle	80
Marcus	60
Sasha	64

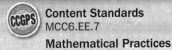

CCGPS **Content Standards**
MCC6.EE.7
Mathematical Practices
1, 3, 4

Case #1 Smart Money

Damian received $100 for his birthday to pay for guitar lessons. The gift money was in $20 bills and $10 bills. When he paid for his lesson, he gave his teacher 8 bills.

How many $20 bills and how many $10 bills did Damian receive?

Understand *What are the facts?*

· Damian received 8 bills that add to $100.
· The money was in $20 bills and $10 bills.

Plan *What is your strategy to solve this problem?*

Make a guess until you find an answer that makes sense for the problem.

Solve *How can you apply the strategy?*

Use addends that have a sum of 8 to find the number of $20 and $10 bills.

Number of $20 bills	Number of $10 bills	Total Amount	Compare to $100
1	7	1($20) + 7($10) = $	
2	6	2($20) + 6($10) = $	
3	5	3($20) + 5($10) = $	
4	4	4($20) + 4($10) = $	

Check *Does the answer make sense?*

The other combinations are either less than or greater than $100.

Analyze the Strategy

CCGPS **Reason Inductively** Damian's sister received $100 in $10 and $5 bills, including eight $10 bills. Use the equation $x + 80 = 100$ to find how much money x was given to her in $5 bills. How many $5 bills did she receive?

Case #2 Anime Adventure

A book store sells used graphic novels in packages of 5 and new graphic novels in packages of 3.

If Amy buys a total of 16 graphic novels, how many packages of new and used graphic novels did she buy?

 Understand

Read the problem. What are you being asked to find?

I need to find _____

_____ .

**Underline key words and values in the problem.
What information do you know?**

The _____ novels come in packages of ☐ and the _____ novels

come in packages of ☐. Amy buys ☐ graphic novels.

Is there any information that you do *not* need to know?

I do not need to know _____ .

Plan

Choose a problem-solving strategy.

I will use the _____ strategy.

Solve

Use your problem-solving strategy to solve the problem. Make a guess.

2 used packages and 1 new package   ☐(5) + ☐(3); ☐ < 16

3 used packages and 2 new packages   ☐(5) + ☐(3); ☐ > 16

2 used packages and 2 new packages   ☐(5) + ☐(3); ☐ = 16

So, _____ .

 Check

Use information from the problem to check your answer.

Make a list of multiples of 3 and a list of multiples of 5. Look for a combination of these multiples that add to 16.

_____

_____

Collaborate Work with a small group to solve the following cases. Show your work on a separate piece of paper.

Case #3 Quizzes

On a science quiz, Ivan earned 18 points. There are six problems worth 2 points each and two problems worth 4 points each.

Find the number of problems of each type Ivan answered correctly.

_____

_____

Case #4 Numbers

Kathryn is thinking of four numbers from 1 through 9 with a sum of 18. Each number is used only once.

Find the numbers.

_____

Case #5 Equations

Use the symbols +, −, ×, or ÷ to make the following equation true. Use each symbol only once.

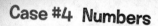

_____

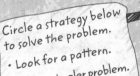

Circle a strategy below to solve the problem.
- *Look for a pattern.*
- *Solve a simpler problem.*
- *Act it out.*
- *Work backward.*

Case #6 Money

Nathaniel is saving money to buy a new graphics card for his computer that costs $250.

If he is saving $20 a month and already has $160, in how many more months will he have enough money for the graphics card?

_____

Mid-Chapter Check

Vocabulary Check

1. Define *equation*. Give an example of a number sentence that is an equation and a number sentence that is not an equation. (Lesson 1)

   An equation is a complete math statement. An example of an equation is $ax^2 + bx + c = 0$. A number sentence is $(p+8)q$.

2. Fill in the blank in the sentence below with the correct term. (Lesson 2)

   You can solve equations using _inverse operations_, which undo each other.

Skills Check and Problem Solving

Circle the solution of the equation from the list given. (Lesson 1)

3. $x + 22 = 27$; ⑤, 6, 7

4. $17 + n = 24$; 6, ⑦, 8

Solve each equation. Check your solution. (Lessons 2 and 3)

5. $63 + d = 105$

   $\begin{array}{r} -63 \\ \hline 42 \end{array}$

   $d = 42$

6. $h + 7.9 = 13$

   $h = 5.1$

7. $a + 1.6 = 2.1$

   $a = .5$

8. $p - 13 = 29$

   $p = 42$

9. $y - 9 = 26$

   $y = 35$

10. $r - 5\frac{1}{6} = 10$

    $r = 15\frac{1}{6}$

11. **CCGPS** **Use Math Tools** The difference between the water levels for high and low tide was 3.6 feet. Write and solve an equation to find the water level at high tide. (Lesson 3)

    _$x - 3.6 = 0.2$; $x = 3.8$_

Tide Level at the Lake Worth Pier

High	■
Low	0.2 foot

12. **Georgia Test Practice** Fonzi spent a total of 90 minutes completing his chores this week. Which of the following equations represents the number of minutes Fonzi spent washing the dishes? (Lesson 2)

    Ⓐ $m = 42 + 90$

    Ⓑ $42 - m = 90$

    Ⓒ $m + 42 = 90$

    Ⓓ $90 = m - 42$

Chore	Time (min)
Vacuuming	42
Dishes	■

Inquiry HOW do you solve multiplication equations using models?

CCGPS Content Standards
MCC6.EE.5,
MCC6.EE.7

Mathematical Practices
1, 3, 4

Running In 5 days, Nicole ran a total of 10 miles. She ran the same amount each day. How much did she run each day?

What do you know? _____

_____

What do you need to find? _____

_____

Investigation 1

Step 1 Define a variable. Use the variable d to represent the distance run in one day.

Step 2 Use a bar diagram to help write the equation.

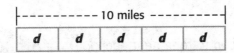

The total length of the diagram shows _____.

The variable d appears in the diagram ☐ times.

☐ $d =$ ☐

Step 3 Work backward. Rewrite the equation as a division sentence and solve.

☐ $\div$ ☐ $= d$

So, Nicole ran ☐ miles each day.

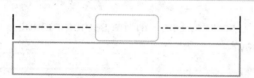

Collaborate

Work with a partner. Define the variable. Then write and solve a multiplication equation using a bar diagram.

1. Suppose Nicole ran 12 miles in four days. If she ran the same distance *d* each day, how many miles did she run in one day?

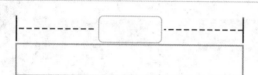

2. Krista has owned her cell phone for 8 months, which is twice as long as her sister Allie has owned her cell phone. How many months *m* has Allie had her cell phone?

Investigation 2

Tools

Solve $3x = 12$. Check your solution.

Step 1   Model the equation. Use one cup to represent each *x*.

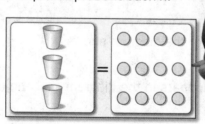

Step 2   Use the model above. Divide the 12 counters equally by circling 3 groups. There are ☐ counters in each group.

So, the solution is ☐.

Check $3\boxed{} = 12$ Write the original equation.

     $3\left(\boxed{}\right) \stackrel{?}{=} 12$ Replace *x* with your solution.

     $\boxed{} = 12$ Is the sentence true? _____

Work with a partner. Solve each equation using cups and counters.

3. $4n = 8$

$n =$ _____

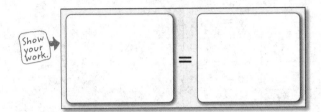

4. $3x = 9$

$x =$ _____

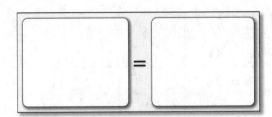

5. $10 = 5x$

$x =$ _____

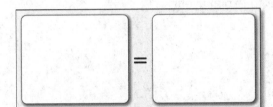

6. $6x = 12$

$x =$ _____

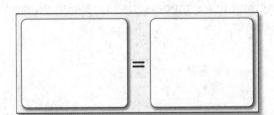

Define a variable. Then write and solve a multiplication equation using a bar diagram.

7. The average lifespan of a horse is 40 years, which is five times longer than the average lifespan of a guinea pig. Use the bar diagram below to find the average lifespan of a guinea pig. Label each section

of the diagram. _____

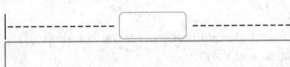

8. Kosumi is saving an equal amount each week for 4 weeks to buy a $40 video game. Use the bar diagram below to find how much he is saving each week. Label each section of the diagram.

_____

Work with a partner to complete the table. The first one is done for you.

	Multiplication Equation	Coefficient	Variable	Product	Division Sentence	Solution
	$7g = 14$	7	g	14	$14 \div 7 = g$	$g = 2$
9.	$21 = 3y$					$y =$
10.	$5m = 45$					$m =$
11.	$48 = 8d$					$d =$
12.	$16f = 32$					$f =$
13.	$39 = 13b$					$b =$

14. **CCGPS Reason Inductively** Write a rule for solving equations like $2x = 24$ without using models. Use a related division sentence to explain your answer.

_____

_____

15. Write and solve an equation to represent the situation modeled below.

16. **CCGPS Model with Mathematics** Write a real-world problem for the equation modeled below. Then write the equation and solve.

$-------------- \$12 --------------$			
c	c	c	c

_____

_____

17. **inquiry** HOW do you solve multiplication equations using models?

_____

_____

_____

Solve and Write Multiplication Equations

What You'll Learn

Scan the lesson. Predict two things you will learn about solving and writing multiplication equations.

- _____
  _____

- _____
  _____

  Essential Question

HOW do you determine if two numbers or expressions are equal?

Vocab abc **Vocabulary**

Division Property of Equality

CCGPS **Common Core GPS**

Content Standards
MCC6.EE.5, MCC6.EE.7, MCC6.RP.3

Mathematical Practices
1, 2, 3, 4, 5

Vocabulary Start-Up

The equation $3x = 9$ is a multiplication equation. In $3x$, 3 is the coefficient of x because it is the number by which x is multiplied.

Fill in the table. The first one is done for you.

Prefix	Root Word	New Word	Meaning
co-	pilot	copilot	the second pilot that flies with the primary pilot of the plane
co-	author		
co-	operate		
co-	efficient		

Real-World Link

Ringtones Matthew is downloading ringtones. The cost to download each ringtone is $2. When Matthew is finished he has spent a total of $10. Let x represent the number of ringtones. What does the expression $2x$ represent?

_____

Solve a Multiplication Equation

A multiplication equation is an equation like $2x = 10$ because the variable x is multiplied by 2. Multiplication and division are inverse operations. So, to solve a multiplication equation, use division.

Examples

 Watch   Tutor

1. **Solve $2x = 10$. Check your solution.**

$$2x = 10 \qquad \text{Write the equation.}$$
$$\frac{2x}{2} = \frac{10}{2} \qquad \text{Divide each side by the coefficient 2.}$$
$$x = 5$$

Check $\quad 2x = 10 \qquad$ Write the original equation.

$\qquad 2(5) \overset{?}{=} 10 \qquad$ Replace x with 5.

$\qquad 10 = 10 \qquad$ This sentence is true. ✔

2. **Solve $3x = 6$. Check your solution.**

Fill in the boxes below.

$$3x = 6 \qquad \text{Write the equation.}$$
$$\frac{3x}{\boxed{}} = \frac{6}{\boxed{}} \qquad \text{Divide each side by the coefficient } \boxed{}.$$
$$x = \boxed{}$$

Check $\quad 3\boxed{} = 6 \qquad$ Write the original equation.

$\qquad 3\left(\boxed{}\right) \overset{?}{=} 6 \qquad$ Replace x with $\boxed{}$.

$\qquad \boxed{} = 6 \qquad$ This sentence is $\boxed{}$. ✔

 Show your work.

Got It? Do these problems to find out.

Solve each equation. Check your solution.

a. $3x = 15$ **b.** $8 = 4x$ **c.** $2x = 14$

a. _____5_____

b. _____2_____

c. _____7_____

Division Property of Equality

Words	If you divide each side of an equation by the same nonzero number, the two sides remain equal.

Examples

Numbers

$$18 = 18$$
$$\frac{18}{6} = \frac{18}{6}$$
$$3 = 3$$

Algebra

$$3x = 12$$
$$\frac{3x}{3} = \frac{12}{3}$$
$$x = 4$$

When you solve an equation by dividing both sides of the equation by the same number, you are using the **Division Property of Equality**.

Example

3. Vicente and some friends shared the cost of a package of blank CDs. The package cost $24 and each person contributed $6. How many people shared the cost of the CDs?

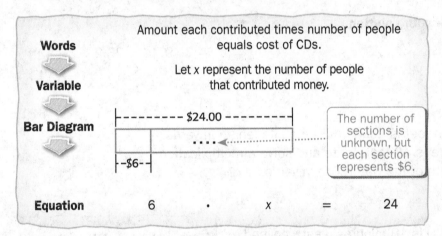

Words	Amount each contributed times number of people equals cost of CDs.
Variable	Let x represent the number of people that contributed money.
Bar Diagram	┄┄┄ $24.00 ┄┄┄ ┄$6┄ The number of sections is unknown, but each section represents $6.
Equation	6 · x = 24

$6x = 24$ Write the equation.

$\dfrac{6x}{6} = \dfrac{24}{6}$ Divide each side by 6.

$x = 4$ Simplify.

Check $6 \times 4 = 24$ ✓

There were 4 people who split the cost of the CDs.

Got It? Do this problem to find out.

d. In 2004, Pen Hadow and Simon Murray walked 680 miles to the South Pole. The trip took 58 days. Suppose they traveled the same distance each day. Write and solve a multiplication equation to find about how many miles they traveled each day.

STOP and Reflect

What is the coeffienct in the equation in Example 3?

$$\begin{array}{r} 580 \\ 58 \\ + \\ \hline 638 \end{array}$$

$$58x = 680$$

Show your work.

d. _____

Example

4. **Solve 3.28x = 19.68. Check your solution.**

$3.28x = 19.68$ Write the equation.

$\dfrac{3.28x}{3.28} = \dfrac{19.68}{3.28}$ Divide each side by 3.28.

$x = 6$

Check $3.28x = 19.68$ Write the original equation.

$3.28(6) \overset{?}{=} 19.68$ Replace x with 6.

$19.68 = 19.68$ This sentence is true. ✓

 Show your work.

e. _____

f. _____

g. _____

Got It? Do these problems to find out.

Solve each equation. Check your solution.

e. $2.25n = 6.75$ **f.** $1.7b = 8.5$ **g.** $6.15y = 55.35$

Guided Practice

 Check ✓

Solve each equation. Check your solution. (Examples 1, 2, and 4)

1. $2a = 6$

$a = 3$

2. $20 = 4c$

$c = 5$

3. $9.4g = 28.2$

$g = 3$

Show your work.

4. The length of an object in feet is equal to 3 times its length in yards. The length of a waterslide is 48 feet. Write and solve a multiplication equation to find the length of the waterslide in yards. (Example 3)

$3x = 48; \; x = 16$

5. The total time to burn a CD is 18 minutes. Last weekend, Demitri spent 90 minutes burning CDs. Write and solve a multiplication equation to find the number of CDs Demitri burned last weekend. Explain how you can check your solution. (Example 3) $18x = 90, \; x = 5$

You can divide.

6.  **Building on the Essential Question** How can the Division Property of Equality be used to solve multiplication equations? It is the total inverse.

Rate Yourself!

How well do you understand solving and writing multiplication equations? Circle the image that applies.

Clear   Somewhat Clear   Not So Clear

For more help, go online to access a Personal Tutor. Tutor

 FOLDABLES Time to update your Foldable!

Independent Practice

Go online for Step-by-Step Solutions

Solve each equation. Check your solution. (Examples 1, 2, and 4)

1. $4g = 24$

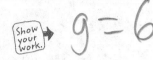 $g = 6$

2. $5d = 30$

$d = 6$

3. $36 = 6e$

$e = 6$

4. $1.5x = 3$

$x = 2$

5. $2.5y = 5$

$y = 2$

6. $8.1 = 0.9a$

$a = 9$

7. A jewelry store is selling a set of 4 pairs of gemstone earrings for $58, including tax. Neva and three of her friends want to buy the set so each could have one pair of earrings. Write and solve a multiplication equation to find how much each person should pay. (Example 3)

$4x = 58 \quad x = \$14.50$

Solve each equation. Check your solution.

8. $39 = 1\frac{3}{10}b$

$*\ b = 30$

9. $\frac{1}{2}e = \frac{1}{4}$

$e = \frac{1}{2}$

10. $\frac{2}{5}g = \frac{3}{5}$

$1\,^3/_{10}$

11. CCGPS **Use Math Tools** Use the table that shows football data.

a. George Blanda played in the NFL for 26 years. Write and solve an equation to find how many points he averaged each year.

$26x = 2002$

b. Norm Johnson played in the NFL for 16 years. Write and solve an equation to find how many points he averaged each year.

$16y = 1736$

Top NFL Kickers	
Player	**Career Points**
Gary Anderson	2,434
Morten Andersen	2,437
George Blanda	2,002
John Carney	1,749
Norm Johnson	1,736

12. STEM An average person's heart beats about 103,680 times a day. Write and solve an equation to find about how many times the average person's heart beats in one minute.

$1440x = 103680$

13. **Model with Mathematics** Problems involving constant speed can be solved by the formula distance = rate × time. Fernando's family traveled 272 miles on a road trip last weekend. They drove for 4 hours. What was the rate at which Fernando's family traveled? Write and solve a multiplication equation.

distance	=	rate	×	time
272		68		4

Fernando's family traveled an average rate of __68__ miles per hour.

H.O.T. Problems Higher Order Thinking

14. 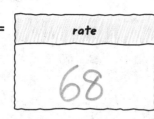 **Find the Error** Noah is solving $5x = 75$. Find his mistake and correct it.

Noah h

$5x = 75$
$5x = \dfrac{75}{5}$
$5x = 15$
$x = 3$

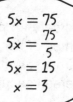

15. 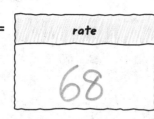 **Which One Doesn't Belong?** Identify the equation that does not belong with the other three. Explain your reasoning.

| $5x = 20$ | $4b = 7$ | $8w = 32$ | $12y = 48$ |

16. 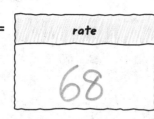 **Persevere with Problems** Explain how you know that the equations $\frac{1}{4} = 2x$ and $\frac{1}{4} \div x = 2$ have the same solution. Then, find the solution.

Georgia Test Practice

17. The Walkers traveled 182 miles in $3\frac{1}{2}$ hours. The equation $3.5m = 182$ can be used to find their mean rate of travel. What is the value of m?

   Ⓐ 60   Ⓑ 52   Ⓒ 50   Ⓓ 48

Extra Practice

Solve each equation. Check your solution.

18. $4c = 16$

$4c = 16$
$\dfrac{4c}{4} = \dfrac{16}{4}$
$c = 4$

19. $5t = 25$

20. $5a = 15$

21. $3f = 12$

22. $21 = 3g$

23. $6x = 12$

24. $5.9q = 23.6$

25. $2.55d = 17.85$

26. $6.5a = 32.5$

27. The Raimonde family drove 1,764 miles across the United States on their vacation. If it took a total of 28 hours, write and solve a multiplication equation to find their average speed in miles per hour.

28. **CCGPS** **Reason Abstractly** Four friends went bowling one afternoon. Use the table that shows the bowling data.

Player	Score
Bryan	320
Carson	366
Jana	522
Pilar	488

a. Carson bowled 3 games. Write and solve an equation to find how many points he averaged each game. _____

b. Jana bowled 5 games. Write and solve an equation to find how many points she averaged each game. _____

Copy and Solve **Solve each equation. Show your work on a separate piece of paper.**

29. $1\frac{2}{5}x = 7$

30. $3\frac{1}{2}r = 28$

31. $2\frac{1}{4}w = 6\frac{3}{4}$

32. $2\frac{3}{4}a = 19\frac{1}{4}$

33. $1\frac{1}{2}c = 6$

34. $3\frac{3}{4}m = 33\frac{3}{4}$

35. If a horse could maintain its average speed for 4 hours, it could travel 120 miles. What is the average speed of the horse?

Ⓐ 30 miles per hour

Ⓑ 33 miles per hour

Ⓒ 120 miles per hour

Ⓓ 480 miles per hour

36. If Mr. Solomon bikes at a constant speed of 12 miles per hour, which method can be used to find the number of hours it will take him to bike 54 miles?

Ⓕ Add 12 to 54.

Ⓖ Subtract 12 from 54.

Ⓗ Multiply 54 by 12.

Ⓘ Divide 54 by 12.

37. **Short Response** Marguerite's bottle of iced tea has this label. The equation $2c = 64$, where c represents the amount of sugar in each serving, can be used to find the amount of sugar in one serving. How many grams of sugar are in each serving?

_____

Nutrition Facts
Servings per container about 2
Calories 80
Total Fat 0g
Sodium 50mg
Total Carbohydrate 64g
Sugars 64g

Divide. MCC5.NTB.6

38. 138 ÷ 6 = _____

39. 80 ÷ 5 = _____

40. 208 ÷ 4 = _____

41. 217 ÷ 7 = _____

42. 216 ÷ 24 = _____

43. 378 ÷ 6 = _____

44. The table shows the cost of concessions at a concert. Evan spent $31.50 buying popcorn for his class. How many bags of popcorn did Evan buy?
MCC5.NTB.7

_____

Item	Cost ($)
Nachos	$3.00
Popcorn	$1.50
Water	$2.00

45. After dinner, $\frac{3}{4}$ of a pie remains. If Tasha eats $\frac{1}{6}$ of the remaining pie, how much of the total pie does Tasha eat? MCC6.NS.1

_____

Inquiry HOW do you solve division equations using models?

CCGPS Content Standards
MCC6.EE.5,
MCC6.EE.7

Mathematical Practices
1, 3, 4

Concerts Four friends decided to split the cost of season concert tickets equally. Each person paid $35. Find the total cost of the season concert tickets.

What do you know? _____

_____

What do you need to find? _____

_____

Investigation

Step 1 Define a variable. Use the variable c to represent the total cost of the tickets.

Step 2 Use a bar diagram to help write the equation.

←————————————— total cost, c —————————————→

amount each person pays	amount each person pays	amount each person pays	amount each person pays

←——— $35 ———→

The total length of the diagram shows _____.

The number 35 represents _____.

There are four equal sections because _____.

$$\boxed{} \div \boxed{} = \boxed{}$$

Step 3 Work backward. Rewrite the equation as a multiplication sentence and solve.

$$\boxed{} \times \boxed{} = c$$

So, the total cost of the season tickets was $ \boxed{} .

Collaborate

CCGPS **Model with Mathematics** Work with a partner. Write and solve a division equation using a bar diagram.

1. Three teachers went to a conference. They shared the cost of gasoline g equally. Each teacher paid $38.50. Draw a bar diagram to find the total cost of gasoline.

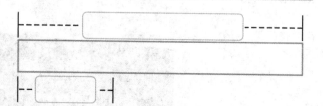

2. Silvia has completed 8 math exercises e. This is one fourth of the assignment. How many exercises were assigned?

_____

3. Antonio bought a shirt for $\frac{1}{2}$ off. He paid $21.75 for the shirt s. Draw a bar diagram to find the original cost of the shirt.

_____

4. Six friends are sharing the cost for a pizza party p equally. Each person paid $15.25. Find the total cost of the pizza party.

_____

Reflect

5. **CCGPS** **Model with Mathematics** Write a real-world division problem for the equation modeled below. Then write the equation and solve.

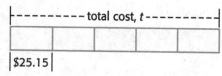

_____

_____

_____

6. **Inquiry** HOW do you solve division equations using models?

_____

_____

_____

Solve and Write Division Equations

What You'll Learn

Scan the lesson. List two real-world scenarios in which you would use division equations.

- _____
- _____

Essential Question

HOW do you determine if two numbers or expressions are equal?

Vocabulary

Multiplication Property of Equality

Common Core GPS

Content Standards
MCC6.EE.5, MCC6.EE.7
Mathematical Practices
1, 2, 3, 4, 7

Real-World Link

Allowances Leslie spends $5 a month on snacks at school, which is one fourth of her monthly allowance. Complete the questions below to find Leslie's monthly allowance.

1. Draw a bar diagram to represent $5 as one fourth of Leslie's monthly allowance.

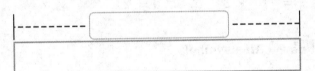

2. What is Leslie's monthly allowance? ☐

3. What operation did you use to find Leslie's allowance?
   _____

4. How can you check your answer to determine if it
   is accurate? _____
   _____
   _____

Solve Division Equations

In the situation on the previous page, equation $\frac{a}{4} = 5$, where a represents the monthly allowance, means the monthly allowance *divided by* 4 equals \$5. Since multiplication and division are inverse operations, use multiplication to solve division equations.

Example

1. Solve $\frac{a}{3} = 7$. **Check your solution.**

Method 1 Use models.

Model the equation.

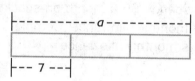

Solve the equation. Work backward.

Since $\frac{a}{3} = 7$, $7 \times 3 = a$. So, $a = 21$.

Method 2 Use symbols.

$\frac{a}{3} = 7$ Write the equation.

$\frac{a}{3}(3) = 7(3)$ Multiply each side by 3.

$a = 21$ Simplify.

Check $\frac{a}{3} = 7$ Write the original equation.

$\frac{21}{3} \overset{?}{=} 7$ Replace a with 21.

$7 = 7$ This is a true sentence. ✔

Using either method, the solution is 21.

Got It? Do these problems to find out.

Solve each equation. Check your solution.

a. $\frac{x}{8} = 9$ **b.** $\frac{y}{4} = 8$

c. $\frac{m}{5} = 9$ **d.** $30 = \frac{b}{2}$

a. _____

b. _____

c. _____

d. _____

Multiplication Property of Equality

Words	If you multiply each side of an equation by the same nonzero number, the two sides remain equal.

Examples

Numbers

$3 = 3$

$3(6) = 3(6)$

$18 = 18$

Algebra

$\frac{x}{4} = 7$

$\frac{x}{4}(4) = 7(4)$

$x = 28$

STOP and Reflect

How is solving a multiplication equation similar to solving a division equation? How is it different? Explain below.

When you solve an equation by multiplying each side of the equation by the same number, you are using the **Multiplication Property of Equality**.

 Example

Tutor

2. **The weight of an object on the Moon is one sixth that of its weight on Earth. If an object weighs 35 pounds on the Moon, write and solve a division equation to find its weight on Earth.**

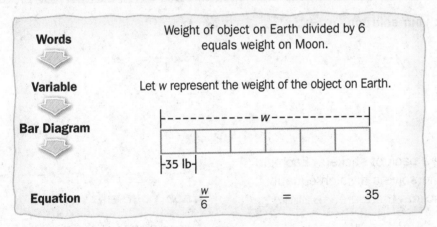

Words — Weight of object on Earth divided by 6 equals weight on Moon.

Variable — Let w represent the weight of the object on Earth.

Bar Diagram

Equation — $\frac{w}{6} = 35$

$\frac{w}{6} = 35$ Write the equation.

$\frac{w}{6}(6) = 35(6)$ Multiply each side by 6.

$w = 210$ $6 \times 35 = 210$

The object weighs 210 pounds on Earth.

Got It? Do this problem to find out.

e. Nathan picked a total of 60 apples in $\frac{1}{3}$ hour. Write and solve a division equation to find how many apples Nathan could pick in 1 hour.

Show your work.

e. _____

Example

3. Carla is buying ribbon for costumes. She wants to divide the ribbon into 8.5 inch pieces for 16 costumes. Write and solve a division equation to find the length of ribbon Carla should buy.

Let r represent the length of ribbon Carla should buy.

$$\frac{r}{8.5} = 16$$ Write the equation.

$$\frac{r}{8.5}(8.5) = 16(8.5)$$ Multiply each side by 8.5.

$$r = 136$$ $8.5 \times 16 = 136$

Carla should buy 136 inches of ribbon.

Got It? Do this problem to find out.

f. Allison is baking a pie. She wants 4.5 strawberries in each serving for 8 people. Write and solve a division equation to find how many strawberries Alison will need.

f. _____

Guided Practice

Solve each equation. Check your solution. (Example 1)

1. $\frac{m}{6} = 10$

2. $\frac{k}{5} = 11$

3. $\frac{v}{13} = 14$

4. Kerry and Tya are sharing a pack of stickers. Each girl gets 11 stickers. Write and solve a division equation to find how many total stickers there are. (Example 2)

_____

5. Chen is buying a ham. He wants to divide it into 6.5-ounce servings for 12 people. Write and solve a division equation to find what size ham Chen should buy. (Example 3) _____

6. **ⓔ** **Building on the Essential Question** When solving an equation, why is it necessary to perform the same operation on each side of the equals sign?

_____

Rate Yourself!

Are you ready to move on?
Shade the section that applies.

I have a few questions.

I'm ready to move on.

I have a lot of questions.

For more help, go online to access a Personal Tutor.

FOLDABLES Time to update your Foldable!

Independent Practice

Go online for Step-by-Step Solutions

Solve each equation. Check your solution. (Examples 1 and 3)

1. $5 = \dfrac{p}{4}$

Show your work.

2. $17 = \dfrac{w}{6}$

3. $4.7 = \dfrac{g}{3.2}$

Write and solve a division equation to solve each problem. (Examples 2 and 3)

4. Sophia is buying party favors. She has a budget of $2.75 a person for 6 people. How much can Sophia spend on party favors?

_____

5. Caroline baked 3 dozen oatmeal raisin cookies for the bake sale at school. This is one fourth the number of dozens of cookies she baked in all. How many dozens of cookies did she bake in all?

_____

6. **CCGPS** **Model with Mathematics** Refer to the graphic novel frame below for Exercises a–b.

a. If Mei has earned 30 points, write and solve a multiplication equation to find how many books she needs to read. _____

b. Suppose Mei has read 7 books. Write and solve a division equation to find the number of points she has earned. $\quad x/5 = 7$

7. **CCGPS** **Identify Structure** Write the property used to solve each type of equation.

+	−

×	÷

8. **CCGPS** **Reason Abstractly** Write a division equation that has a solution of 42.

_____

_____

9. **CCGPS** **Reason Inductively** *True* or *false*: $\frac{x}{3}$ is equivalent to $\frac{1}{3}x$. Explain your reasoning.

_____

_____

10. **CCGPS** **Persevere with Problems** Explain how you would solve $\frac{16}{c} = 8$. Then solve the equation.

_____

_____

11. Which value of x makes this equation true?

$$\frac{x}{7} = 14$$

Ⓐ 98　　　　Ⓒ 2

Ⓑ 21　　　　Ⓓ 0.5

Extra Practice

Solve each equation. Check your solution.

12. $4 = \frac{r}{8}$

$4 = \frac{r}{8}$

$4(8) = \frac{r}{8}(8)$

$32 = r$

(Homework Help)

13. $12 = \frac{q}{7}$

14. $18 = \frac{r}{2}$

15. $\frac{h}{13} = 13$

16. $\frac{j}{12} = 11$

17. $\frac{z}{7} = 8$

18. $\frac{c}{0.2} = 7$

19. $\frac{d}{12} = 0.25$

20. $\frac{m}{16} = 0.5$

CCGPS Identify Structure Write and solve a division equation to solve each problem.

21. One third of a bird's eggs hatched. If 2 eggs hatched, how many eggs did the bird lay? _____

_____

22. Marcel is purchasing a board to build a bookcase. He wants to divide the board into 1.75-foot sections. He needs 6 sections. What size board does Marcel need? _____

_____

23. Blake is cutting a piece of rope into fourths. If each piece is 16 inches long, what is the length of the entire rope? _____

_____

24. CCGPS Justify Conclusions A model plane is $\frac{1}{48}$ the size of the actual plane. If the model plane is 28 inches long, how long is the actual plane? Explain your reasoning to a classmate. _____

_____

25. Alfred does chores to earn money in the summer. The table shows the amount he earns per chore.

Chore	Amount Earned ($)
mow lawn	$10
wash car	$5
weed garden	$8

Suppose Alfred weeded the garden 6 times in the summer. How much did he earn weeding?

Ⓐ $30   ⓒ $60

Ⓑ $48   ⓓ $75

26. Devon is saving his allowance to purchase the telescope shown.

If he saves $7 a week for 14 weeks, which of the following equations can be used to find the total cost of the telescope?

Ⓕ $7 + x = 14$ Ⓗ $\frac{x}{14} = 7$

Ⓖ $x - 7 = 14$ ① $7x = 14$

27. Short Response Shana ran 6 miles in one week. This was one third of what she ran in the month. Write and solve a division equation to find how far she ran in the month. _____

Fill in each ◯ with <, >, or = to make a true sentence. MCC4.NF.7

28. 6.5 ◯ 5.2

29. 1.9 ◯ 1.7

30. 2.2 ◯ 2.2

31. 5.6 ◯ 6.5

32. 4.2 ◯ 3.9

33. 5.5 ◯ 5.7

34. The table shows the number of inches in different number of feet. How many inches are in 5 feet? MCC4.OA.5

_____

_____

35. What is the next number in the pattern below? MCC4.OA.5

4, 8, 12, 16, 20, 24. . .

_____

Feet	Inches
1	12
2	24
3	36
4	48

21ST CENTURY CAREER
in Music

Sound Engineer

Do you enjoy using electronics to make music sound better? If so, you might want to explore a career in sound engineering. Sound engineers, or audio technicians, prepare the sound equipment for recording sessions and live concert performances. They are responsible for operating consoles and other equipment to control, replay, and mix sound from various sources. Sound engineers adjust the microphones, amplifiers, and levels of various instrument and voice tones so that everything sounds great together.

College & Career
READINESS

Explore college and careers at ccr.mcgraw-hill.com

Is This the Career for You?

Are you interested in a career as a sound engineer? Take some of the following courses in high school.

◆ Algebra
◆ Electronic Technology
◆ Music and Computers
◆ Physics
◆ Sound Engineering

Find out how math relates to a career in Music.

Amping the Band!

Use the information in the table and the diagram to solve each problem.

1. In the diagram, the distance between the microphones is 6 feet. This is 3 times the distance *d* from each microphone to the sound source. Write an equation that represents this situation. _____

2. Solve the equation that you wrote in Exercise 1. Explain the solution. _____

_____

3. The distance from the microphone to the acoustic guitar sound hole is about 11 inches less than what it should be. Write an equation that models this situation. _____

4. Solve the equation that you wrote in Exercise 3. Explain the solution. _____

_____

5. The microphone is about 9 times farther from the electric guitar amplifier than it should be to produce a natural, well-balanced sound. Write and solve an equation to find how far from the amplifier the microphone should be placed.

_____

Microphone Mistakes		
Sound Source	**Location of Microphone**	**Resulting Sound**
Acoustic guitar	3 inches from sound hole	very bassy
Electric guitar amplifier	36 inches from amp	thin, reduced bass

6 ft

Career Project

It's time to update your career portfolio! Go to the *Occupational Outlook Handbook* online and research careers in sound engineering. Make a list of the advantages and disadvantages of working in that field.

_____

_____

_____

_____

List several challenges associated with this career.

- _____
- _____
- _____
- _____
- _____

Vocabulary Check

Write the correct term for each clue in the crossword puzzle.

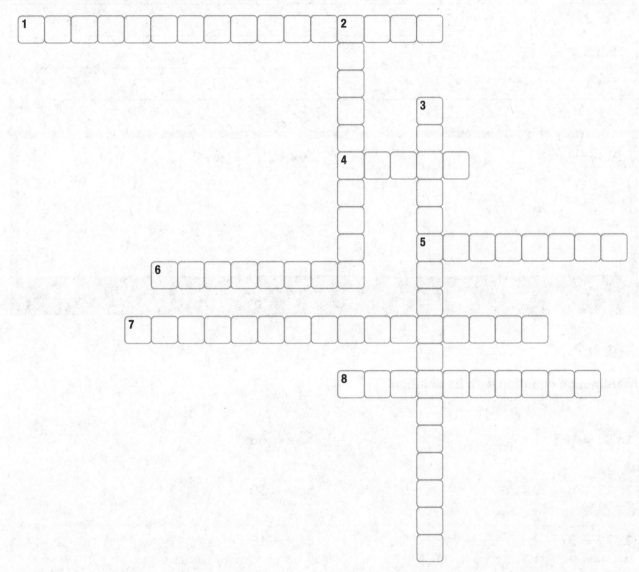

Across

1. property of equality used to solve multiplication equations

4. replace a variable with a value that results in a true sentence

5. the value of a variable that makes an equation true

6. mathematical sentence showing two expressions are equal

7. property of equality used to solve subtraction equations

8. a combination of numbers, variables, and at least one operation

Down

2. a symbol of equality

3. operations which undo each other

Key Concept Check

Use Your FOLDABLES

Use your Foldable to help review the chapter.

Tape here

Tab 4

Tab 3

Tab 2

Tab 1

Models   Symbols

Got it?

Match each equation with its solution.

1. $8x = 128$ **a.** $x = 68$

2. $13 + x = 29$ **b.** $x = 39$

3. $72 = 3x$ **c.** $x = 18$

4. $x - 22 = 17$ **d.** $x = 16$

5. $\frac{x}{4} = 17$ **e.** $x = 24$

6. $x - 18 = 33$ **f.** $x = 51$

Problem Solving

1. The equation $7h = 63$ can be used to find how many hours h a person needs to work to earn $63 at $7 per hour. How many hours does a person need to work to earn $63? (Lesson 1) _____

   _____

2. The equation $18 + p = 34$ represents the sum of Reese's and Ana's ages, where p represents Reese's age. How old is Reese? (Lesson 1)

   _____

   _____

3. When Sean stands on a box, he is 10 feet tall. If the box is 4 feet tall, write and solve an addition equation to find Sean's height. (Lesson 2)

   _____

   _____

4. **CCGPS Use Math Tools** The amount of money Felise has in her account is shown. She has $8 less than her brother. Write and solve a subtraction equation to find how much money her brother has. (Lesson 3)

   _____

   _____

BANK STATEMENT	
Felise Smith 1234 Street Town, US 00200	
CHECKING ACCOUNT	
Previous Balance:	$0.00
Checks:	$0.00
Withdrawals:	$0.00
Deposits:	$39.00
Current Balance:	$39.00

5. A store is selling blank CDs in packages of 25 for $5. Write and solve a multiplication equation to find the cost of one blank CD. (Lesson 4)

   _____

   _____

6. The speed limit in front of Meadowbrook Middle School is shown. It is one third the speed limit of a major street two blocks away. Write and solve a division equation to find the speed limit of the major street.

   (Lesson 5) _____

   _____

7. Milo is baking chicken and the preparation time is 10 minutes, which is one fourth of the baking time. Write and solve a division equation to find the baking time. (Lesson 5)

   _____

   _____

Answering the Essential Question

Use what you learned about expressions and equations to complete the graphic organizer.

 Essential Question

HOW do you determine if two numbers or expressions are equal?

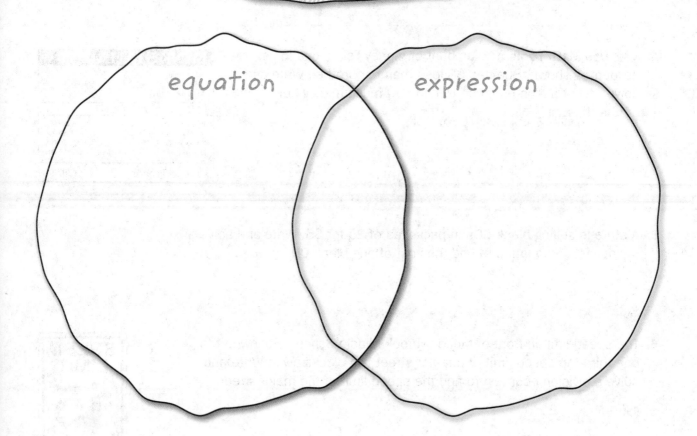

equation

expression

 Answer the Essential Question. HOW do you determine if two numbers or expressions are equal?

_____

_____

_____

Chapter 7
Functions and Inequalities

Essential Question

HOW are symbols, such as <, >, and =, useful?

Common Core GPS

Content Standards
MCC6.EE.2, MCC6.EE.2c, MCC6.EE.5, MCC6.EE.6, MCC6.EE.8, MCC6.EE.9

Mathematical Practices
1, 2, 3, 4, 5, 6, 7, 8

Math in the Real World

Ocean Life In the ocean, clownfish and sea anemones benefit one another. Clownfish chase away different species of fish that eat the sea anemone. Sea anemones have tentacles that are coated in poison. These tentacles protect the clownfish from predators.

A clownfish can be up to 3.5 inches in length. Some species of sea anemones can be up to 39 inches wide. Compare 3.5 inches and 39 inches.

[ ] < [ ]

FOLDABLES
Study Organizer

1 Cut out the correct Foldable from the FL pages in the back of this book.

2 Place your Foldable on the Key Concept page toward the end of this chapter.

3 Use the Foldable throughout this chapter to help you learn about functions and inequalities.

What Tools Do You Need?

 Vocabulary

arithmetic sequence	independent variable
dependent variable	inequality
function	linear function
function rule	sequence
function table	term
geometric sequence	

Study Skill: Writing Math

Describe Data

When you *describe* something, you represent it in words.

Mark surveyed his class to find their favorite flavor of sugarless gum. Describe the data.

- Eight more people favor peppermint gum over cinnamon gum.
- The total number of people surveyed is 40.

These statements describe the data. What other ways can you

describe the data? _____

Favorite Flavor of Sugarless Gum	
Flavor	**Number**
Cinnamon	10
Peppermint	18
Watermelon	12

Describe the data below.

1.

Least Favorite "Bug"	
Kind	**Number**
Centipede	2
Cockroach	18
Spider	30

2.

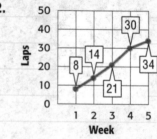

 **Are You Ready?**

Try the Quick Check below.
Or, take the Online Readiness Quiz.

 Check ✓

CCGPS **Quick Review**

Common Core Review MCC4.NBT.2, MCC6.EE.7

Example 1

Fill in the ◯ with <, >, or = to make a true statement.

71,238 ◯ 71,832

71,238   Use place value. Line up the digits.
71,832   Compare the hundreds place. 2 < 8

So, 71,238 < 71,832.

Example 2

Solve $54 + x = 180$.

$$54 + x = 180$$
$$\underline{-54 \qquad = -54}$$ Write the equation.
$$x = 126$$ Subtract.

Check $54 + 126 \overset{?}{=} 180$
$180 = 180$ ✓

Quick Check

Compare Numbers Fill in each ◯ with <, >, or =, to make the inequality true.

1. 302,788 ◯ 203,788   **2.** 54,300 ◯ 543,000   **3.** 892,341 ◯ 892,431

 Show your work.

4. The table shows the number of bones in humans. Compare 300 and 206. _____

Bones in Humans	
Baby	300
Adult	206

Solve Equations Solve each equation.

5. $x + 44 = 90$ _____   **6.** $x - 7 = 18$ _____   **7.** $16m = 48$ _____

8. In the first two basketball games, Lee scored a total of 40 points. If he scored 21 points in the second game, how many points did he score in the first game?

_____

 **How Did You Do?**

Which problems did you answer correctly in the Quick Check? Shade those exercise numbers below.

① ② ③ ④ ⑤ ⑥ ⑦ ⑧

Function Tables

What You'll Learn

Scan the lesson. List two headings you would use to make an outline of the lesson.

• _____
_____

• _____
_____

HOW are symbols, such as <, >, and =, useful?

Vocab **Vocabulary**

function
function rule
function table
independent variable
dependent variable

CCGPS **Common Core GPS**

Content Standards
MCC6.EE.2, MCC6.EE.2c, MCC6.EE.9

Mathematical Practices
1, 3, 4, 5

  ## Real-World Link

Science A ruby-throated hummingbird beats its wings about 52 beats per second.

1. Make a table showing show many times this bird beats its wings in 2 seconds.

Number of Seconds (s)	s · 52	Wing Beats
2	2 · 52	

2. Make a table to show how many times it beats its wings in 6 seconds.

Number of Seconds (s)	s · 52	Wing Beats
6		

3. Make a table to show how many times it beats its wings in 20 seconds.

Number of Seconds (s)	s · 52	Wing Beats

4. A Giant Hummingbird beats its wings about 10 times per second. Make a table to show how many times the Giant Hummingbird beats its wings in 3 seconds.

Number of Seconds (s)	s · 10	Wing Beats

Find the Output for a Function Table

A **function** is a relation that assigns exactly one output value to one input value. The number of wing beats (output) depends on the number of seconds (input). The **function rule** describes the relationship between each input and output. You can organize the input-output values and the function rule in a **function table**.

In a function, the input value is also known as the **independent variable**, since it can be any number you choose. The value of the output depends upon the input value, so the output value is known as the **dependent variable**.

STOP and Reflect

What values were used for the independent variable in Example 1? Answer below.

Examples

Tutor

1. **The output is 7 more than the input. Complete a function table for this relation.**

The function rule is $x + 7$. Add 7 to each input.

Input (x)	x + 7	Output
10		17
12		19
14		21

→

Input (x)	x + 7	Output
10	10 + 7	17
12	12 + 7	19
14	14 + 7	21

2. **The output is 5 times the input. Complete a function table for this relation.**

The function rule is $5x$. Multiply each input by 5.

Input (x)	5x	Output
8		40
10		50
12		60

→

Input (x)	5x	Output
8	5 ·	
10	5 ·	
12	5 ·	

Got It? Do these problems to find out.

a.

Input (x)	x − 4	Output
4		0
7		3
10		6

b.

Input (x)	3x	Output
0		
2		
5		

Find the Input for a Function Table

The input and output of a function table can be represented as a set of ordered pairs, or a *relation*. The input represents the *x*-values and the output represents the *y*-values.

Example

3. Find the input for the function table.

Use the *work backward* strategy to determine the input. If the output is found by multiplying by 3, then the input is found by dividing by 3.

Input (x)	3x	Output
2		6
5		15
7		21

The input values are 6 ÷ 3 or 2, 15 ÷ 3 or 5, and 21 ÷ 3 or 7.

Got It? Do these problems to find out.

c.

Input (x)	2x − 1	Output
1		1
2		3
3		5

d.

Input (x)	3x + 2	Output
5		17
6		20
9		29

Example

4. The Gomez family is traveling at a rate of 70 miles per hour. The function rule that represents this situation is 70x, where x is the number of hours. Make a table to find how many hours they have driven at 140 miles, 280 miles, and 350 miles. Then graph the function.

Input (x)	70x	Output (y)
2	70(2)	140
4	70(4)	280
5	70(5)	350

Use the *work backward* strategy. Divide each output by 70.

The missing input values are 140 ÷ 70 or 2, 280 ÷ 70 or 4, and 350 ÷ 70 or 5.

The input and output values are the ordered pairs (x, y). Plot each ordered pair on the graph.

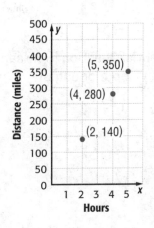

f.

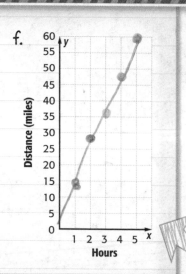

Got It? Do this problem to find out.

e. Briana bikes 12 miles per hour. The function rule that represents this situation is 12x, where is x is the number of hours. Make a table to find how many hours she has biked when she has gone 12, 36, and 48 miles. Then graph the function.

Input (x)	12x	Output (y)
1		12
2		24
3		36

Guided Practice

Check ✓

1. Isaiah is buying jelly beans. In bulk, they cost $3 per pound, and a candy dish costs $2. The function rule, 3x + 2 where x is the number of pounds, can be used to find the total cost of x pounds of jelly beans and 1 dish. Make a table that shows the total cost of buying 2, 3, or 4 pounds of jelly beans and 1 dish. (Examples 1 and 2)

Pounds (x)	3x + 2	Cost ($) (y)
2		8
3		11
4		14

2. Jasper hikes 4 miles per hour. The function rule that represents this situation is 4x, where x is the number of hours. Make a table to find how many hours he has hiked when he has gone 8, 12, and 20 miles. Then graph the function. (Examples 3 and 4)

Hours (x)	4x	Miles (y)
8		32
12		48
20		80

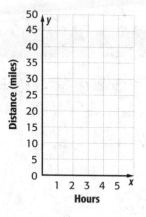

Rate Yourself!

Are you ready to move on?
Shade the section that applies.

I have a few questions. | I'm ready to move on.

I have a lot of questions.

3. ℮ **Building on the Essential Question** How can a function table help you find input or output?

It will help you
substitute.

For more help, go online to access a Personal Tutor.

Tutor 💬

FOLDABLES Time to update your Foldable!

Independent Practice

Go online for Step-by-Step Solutions

CCGPS **Use Math Tools** **Complete each function table.** (Examples 1–3)

1.

Input (x)	3x + 5	Output
0		5
3		14
9		32

2.

Input (x)	x − 4	Output
4		0
8		4
11		7

3.

Input (x)	x + 2	Output
0		2
1		3
6		8

4.

Input (x)	2x + 4	Output
7		18
9		22
15		34

5. Whitney has a total of 30 cupcakes for her guests. The function rule, $30 \div x$ where x is the number of guests, can be used to find the number of cupcakes per guest. Make a table of values that shows the number of cupcakes each guest will get if there are 6, 10, or 15 guests. Then graph the function. (Examples 1 and 2)

Number of Guests (x)	30 ÷ x	Cupcakes per Guest (y)
6	30 ÷ 6	5
10	30 ÷ 10	3
15	30 ÷ 15	2

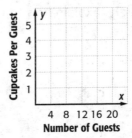

6. Bella rollerblades 8 miles in one hour. The function rule that represents this situation is $8x$, where x is the number of hours. Make a table to find how many hours she has skated when she has traveled 16, 24, and 32 miles. Then graph the function. (Examples 3 and 4)

Hours (x)	8x	Miles (y)
2		16
3		24
4		32

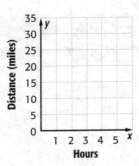

7. Refer to Exercise 6. How many miles would Bella travel if she skated for 7 hours? _____ 56 mi _____

8. **CCGPS** **Find the Error** Daniella is finding the output when the function rule is $10 \div x$ and the input is 2. Find her mistake and correct it.

Daniella is supposed to divide 10/2, which is 5.

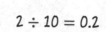
$2 \div 10 = 0.2$

9. **CCGPS** **Persevere with Problems** Around 223 million Americans keep containers filled with coins in their home. Suppose each of the 223 million people started putting their coins back into circulation at a rate of $10 per year. Create a function table that shows the amount of money that would be recirculated in 1, 2, and 3 years.

1	$10
2	$20
3	$30

10. **CCGPS** **Reason Inductively** Explain how to find the input given a function rule and output.

You just substitute "x" and compute.

11. Misu is making 28 muffins for his sister's class. Using the table as a guide, how many eggs will Misu need to make 28 muffins?

Eggs Needed for Muffins	
Number of Muffins	Number of Eggs
7	1
14	2

Ⓐ 3

Ⓑ 4

Ⓒ 5

Ⓓ 6

Extra Practice

CCGPS **Use Math Tools** Complete each function table.

12.

Homework Help →

Input (x)	x + 3	Output
0	0 + 3	3
2	2 + 3	5
4	4 + 3	7

13.

Input (x)	4x + 2	Output
1		6
3		14
6		26

14.

Input (x)	x − 1	Output
1		0
3		2
5		4

15.

Input (x)	2x − 6	Output
0		0
6		6
9		12

16. Ricardo weighs 2 pounds more than twice his sister's weight. The function rule, 2x + 2 where x is his sister's weight, can be used to find Ricardo's weight. Make a table of values that show Ricardo's weight when his sister is 20, 30, and 40 pounds. Then graph the function.

Ricardo's Sister's Weight (x)	2x + 2	Ricardo's Weight (y)
20		42
30		62
40		82

17. The Quinn family drove at a rate of 55 miles per hour. The function rule that represents this situation is 55x, where x is the number of hours. Make a table to find how many hours they have traveled when they have driven 165, 220, and 275 miles. Then graph the function.

Hours (x)	55x	Miles (y)
3		165
4		220
5		275

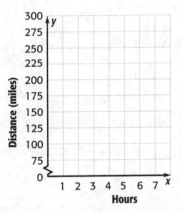

Georgia Test Practice

18. Which of the following sets of values completes the function table?

Input (x)	3x − 5	Output (y)
5	3(5) − 5	▪
6	3(6) − 5	▪
7	3(7) − 5	▪

Ⓐ 15, 16, 17   Ⓒ 10, 11, 12

Ⓑ 10, 13, 16   Ⓓ 0, 1, 2

19. Manuel has a total of 42 photos to place in an album. The function rule, $42 \div x$, where x is the number of pages in the album, can be used to find the number of photos per page. How many photos per page will there be if the album has 14 pages?

Ⓕ 3   Ⓗ 14

Ⓖ 6   Ⓘ 588

20. Short Response In football, a touchdown is worth 6 points. Complete the table that shows the point value after scoring 1, 2, and 3 touchdowns.

Number of Touchdowns (x)	6x	Points (y)
1		6
2		12
3		18

Common Core Review

Find the next number in the pattern using the given rule. MCC5.OA.3

21. Add 3: 2, 5, 8, 11, . . . __14__

22. Subtract 2: 10, 8, 6, 4, . . . __2__

23. Multiply by 2: 2, 4, 8, 16 . . . __32__

24. Subtract 7: 84, 77, 70, 63, . . . __56__

25. Multiply by 2: 3, 6, 12, 24, . . . __48__

26. Add 15: 12, 27, 42, 57, . . . __72__

27. Ms. Chen is buying pencils for her class. What is the cost if she buys 24 pencils? MCC5.NBT.7 __$4.80__

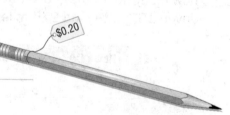

28. Gino and Abby both start a saving account in May. Gino saves $2 each month and Abby saves $4 each month. What do you notice about the amount in each account each month? MCC5.OA.3

__a = 4g__

Month	Gino's Account ($)	Abby's Account ($)
May	2	4
June	4	8
July	6	12

Need more practice? Download more Extra Practice at **connectED.mcgraw-hill.com.**

Function Rules

What You'll Learn

Scan the lesson. Predict two things you will learn about function rules.

- _____
- _____

Vocabulary

sequence
term
arithmetic sequence
geometric sequence

CCGPS **Common Core GPS**

Content Standards
MCC6.EE.2, MCC6.EE.2c, MCC6.EE.6, MCC6.EE.9

Mathematical Practices
1, 3, 4, 7

Vocabulary Start-Up

A **sequence** is a list of numbers in a specific order. Each number in the list is called a **term** of the sequence.

Arithmetic sequences can be found by adding the same number to the previous term. In a **geometric sequence**, each term is found by multiplying the previous term by the same number.

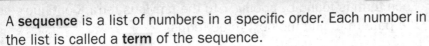
Compare arithmetic sequences and geometric sequences.

arithmetic sequence	geometric sequence
Definition: _____	Definition: _____
Example:	Example:

Real-World Link

Delivery The China Palace sells lunch specials for $6 with a delivery charge of $5 per order. Fill in the table with the next three numbers in the sequence.

Specials	1	2	3	4	5	6	7
Cost ($)	11	17	23	29			

Arithmetic and Geometric Sequences

Determining if a sequence is arithmetic or geometric can help you find the pattern. When you know the pattern, you can continue the sequence to find missing terms.

Examples

Tutor

1. Describe the relationship between the terms in the arithmetic sequence 7, 14, 21, 28, ... Then write the next three terms.

$$7, \quad 14, \quad 21, \quad 28, ...$$

+7 \quad +7 \quad +7

Each term is found by adding 7 to the previous term. Continue the pattern to find the next three terms.

$$28 + 7 = 35 \qquad 35 + 7 = 42 \qquad 42 + 7 = 49$$

The next three terms are 35, 42, and 49.

2. Describe the relationship between the terms in the geometric sequence 2, 4, 8, 16, ... Then write the next three terms.

$$2, \quad 4, \quad 8, \quad 16, ...$$

×2 \quad ×2 \quad ×2

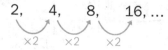
Show your work.

Each term is found by multiplying the previous term by two. Continue the pattern to find the next three terms.

$$16 \times 2 = 32 \qquad 32 \times 2 = 64 \qquad 64 \times 2 = 128$$

The next three terms are 32, 64, and 128.

Got It? Do these problems to find out.

a. 0, 15, 30, 45, ...   b. 4.5, 4, 3.5, 3, ...

c. 1, 3, 9, 27, ...   d. 3, 6, 12, 24, ...

a. ___60___

b. ___2.5___

c. ___81___

d. ___48___

Find a Rule

A sequence can also be shown in a table. The table gives both the position of each term in the list and the value of the term.

List

8, 16, 24, 32, ...

Table

Position	1	2	3	4
Value of Term	8	16	24	32

You can write an algebraic expression to describe a sequence. The value of each term can be described as a function of its position in the sequence.

In the table above, the position can be considered the input, and the value of the term as the output.

Example

3. **Use words and symbols to describe the value of each term as a function of its position. Then find the value of the tenth term.**

Position	1	2	3	4	n
Value of Term	3	6	9	12	■

Notice that the value of each term is 3 times its position number. So, the value of the term in position n is $3n$.

Now find the value of the tenth term.

$3n = 3 \cdot 10$ Replace n with 10.

$\quad = 30$ Multiply.

Position	Multiply by 3	Value of Term
1	1×3	3
2	2×3	6
3	3×3	9
4	4×3	12
n	$n \times 3$	$3n$

The value of the tenth term in the sequence is 30.

Got It? Do these problems to find out.

Work Backward
You can check your rule by working backward. Divide each term by 3 to check the position.

Use words and symbols to describe the value of each term as a function of its position. Then find the value of the eighth term.

e.

Position	2	3	4	5	n
Value of Term	12	18	24	30	■

f.

Position	3	4	5	6	n
Value of Term	7	8	9	10	■

Show your work.

e. ___48___

f. ___12___

Example

4. The table shows the number of necklaces Ari can make, based on the number of hours she works. Write a function rule to find the number of necklaces she can make in *x* hours.

To find the rule, determine the function.

Notice that the values 5, 7, 9, … increase by 2, so the rule includes 2*x*. If the rule were simply 2*x*, then the number of necklaces in 1 hour would be 2. But this value is 5, which is three more than 2*x*.

Hours (x)	Number of Necklaces
1	5
2	7
3	9
x	■

To test the rule $2x + 3$, use the *guess, check, and revise* strategy.

Row 1: $2x + 3 = 2(1) + 3 = 2 + 3$ or 5
Row 3: $2x + 3 = 2(3) + 3 = 6 + 3$ or 9

The rule $2x + 3$ represents the function table.

STOP and Reflect

Find the rule for the following sequence:
5, 9, 13, 17. . . .

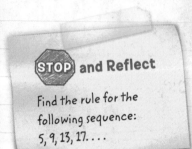

Guided Practice

Check ✓

1. Describe the relationship between the terms in the sequence 13, 26, 52, 104, … Then write the next three terms in the sequence. (Examples 1 and 2)

Geometric   3 terms: 208, 416, 832

2. Use words and symbols to describe the value of each term as a function of its position. Then find the value of the fifteenth term in the sequence. (Example 3)

Position	1	2	3	4	n
Value of Term	2	4	6	8	■

The value of term is 2 times its pos.

3. The table at the right shows the fee for overdue books at a library, based on the number of weeks the book is overdue. Write a function rule to find the fee for a book that is *x* weeks overdue. (Example 4)   X + 2

Weeks Overdue (x)	Fee ($)
1	3
2	5
3	7
4	9
x	■

4. **Building on the Essential Question** What is the difference between an arithmetic sequence and a geometric sequence?   Arithmetic sequences involve adding. Geometric involves multiplying.

Rate Yourself!

Are you ready to move on? Shade the section that applies.

YES   ?   NO

For more help, go online to access a Personal Tutor.

Tutor

Independent Practice

Go online for Step-by-Step Solutions

Use words and symbols to describe the value of each term as a function of its position. Then find the value of the twelfth term in the sequence. (Examples 1–3)

1.

Position	3	4	5	6	n
Value of Term	12	13	14	15	■

The value is 4 times the position.

2.

Position	2	3	4	5	n
Value of Term	24	36	48	60	■

The value is 12 times its position.

3. Describe the relationship between the terms in the sequence 6, 18, 54, 162, ... Then write the next three terms in the sequence. (Example 2)

It is a geometric sequence. The 3 terms are: 486, 1458, 4374.

4. The table shows the amount it costs to rock climb at an indoor rock climbing facility, based on the number of hours. What is the rule to find the amount charged to rock climb for x hours? (Example 4)

The rule is $ + 8.

Time (x)	Amount ($)
1	13
2	21
3	29
4	37
x	■

CCGPS Identify Structure Determine how the next term in each sequence can be found. Then find the next two terms in the sequence.

5. 4, 16, 28, 40, ...

 52, 84

6. 1.5, 3.9, 6.3, 8.7, ...

11.1, 13.5

$$\frac{\begin{matrix} 8 & 7 \\ 2 & 4 \end{matrix}}{11 \quad 1}$$

7. $2\frac{1}{4}, 2\frac{3}{4}, 3\frac{1}{4}, 3\frac{3}{4}, ...$

$4\frac{1}{4}, 4\ 3/4$

Find the missing number in each sequence.

8. 30, $24\frac{1}{2}$, 19, $13\frac{1}{2}$, ...

9. 43.8, 36.7, 31.6, 22.5, ...

State whether each sequence is arithmetic or geometric. Then find the next two terms in the sequence.

10. 1, 6, 36, 216

Geometric
1096, 6576

1096
536
6576

11. 0.75, 1.75, 2.75, 3.75

Arithmetic
4.75, 5.75

12. 0, 13, 26, 39

Arithmetic
52, 65

13. Jay is stacking cereal boxes to create a store display. The number of boxes in each row are shown in the table. Is the pattern an example of an arithmetic sequence or a geometric sequence? Explain. How many boxes will be in row 5?

12 boxes- since this is
an arithmetic seq.- which adds.

Row	Number of Boxes
1	4
2	6
3	8
4	10
5	■

H.O.T. Problems Higher Order Thinking

14. CCGPS **Reason Inductively** Create a sequence in which $1\frac{1}{4}$ is added to each number.

0, 1¼, 2½ 3¾, 5

15. CCGPS **Persevere with Problems** Use words and symbols to generalize the relationship of each term as a function of its position. Then determine the value of the term when $n = 100$.

Position	1	2	3	4	5	n
Value of Term	1	4	9	16	25	■

The value of the term
being increased by changes by 1.

Georgia Test Practice

16. What is the rule to find the value of the missing term in the sequence below?

A) $4x - 3$
B) $2x + 1$
C) $x + 4$
D) $3x$

Position, x	Value of Term
1	1
2	5
3	9
4	13
5	17
x	■

Extra Practice

Use words and symbols to describe the value of each term as a function of its position. Then find the value of the twelfth term in the sequence.

17.

Position	6	7	8	9	n
Value of Term	2	3	4	5	■

Homework Help

subtract 4 from the position number; $n - 4$; 8

Look at position 6 and the value of the term. 2 is 4 less than 6, so try subtracting 4 from the other position numbers listed. The function rule is $n - 4$. $12 - 4 = 8$

18.

Position	1	2	3	4	n
Value of Term	5	10	15	20	■

The value is 5 times the position. $y = 5x$

$$\begin{array}{r} 972 \\ \underline{\times\ 4} \\ 3888 \end{array}$$

$$\begin{array}{r} 108 \\ \underline{\times\ 3} \\ 324 \end{array}$$

19. Describe the relationship between the terms in the sequence 4, 12, 36, 108, ... Then write the next three terms in the sequence.

Geometric sequence. The 3 terms are: 324, 972, 3888.

20. The table shows the cost of a pizza based on the number of toppings. Write a function rule to find the cost for a pizza with x toppings.

Each time a topping is added, the cost increases by $2.

Number of Toppings (x)	Cost ($)
1	12
2	14
3	16
4	18

CCSS Identify Structure Determine how the next term in each sequence can be found. Then find the next two terms in the sequence.

21. 1, 4, 7, 10, ...
13, 16

22. 2.3, 3.2, 4.1, 5.0, ...
5.9, 6.8

23. $1\frac{1}{2}$, 3, $4\frac{1}{2}$, 6, ...
$7\frac{1}{2}$, 9

Find the missing number in each sequence.

24. 7, $11\frac{1}{2}$, 16, $20\frac{1}{2}$, ...

25. 14.6, 19.3, 24, 28.7, ...

Georgia Test Practice

26. In the fall, the number of cricket chirps in 5 seconds depends on the air temperature. The table below shows this relation. If the pattern continues, how many cricket chirps can be expected if the temperature is 65°F?

Cricket Chirps	
Temperature (°F)	Cricket Chirps in 5 Seconds
Less than 40	0
41–43	1
44–46	2
47–49	3
50–52	4

Ⓐ 8　　　　Ⓒ 10

Ⓑ 9　　　　Ⓓ 11

27. Which of the following statements is true about the sequence below?

8, 28, 48, 68...

Ⓕ This is a geometric sequence. Each term is found by multiplying the previous term by 3.

Ⓖ This is a geometric sequence. Each term is found by multiplying the previous term by 20.

Ⓗ This is an arithmetic sequence. Each term is found by adding 20 to the previous term.

Ⓘ This is an arithmetic sequence. Each term is found by adding 8 to the previous term.

28. Short Response The function table shows a relationship between the input *x* and the output. Write a function rule to represent the relation.

For the input adding by 1, the output adds by 4.

Input (x)	Output
0	1
1	5
2	9

ⒸⒸⒼⓅⓈ Common Core Review

Multiply. MCC5.NBT.5

29. 62 × 3 = 186

30. 12 × 7 = 84

31. 16 × 8 = 128

32. 11 × 23 = 243

33. 9 × 18 = 162

34. 5 × 22 = 120−10

35. The table shows the cost to rent from Ray's Rentals. How much would it cost to rent a video game for 3 weeks? MCC5.NBT.7 _____

$13.50

Rental	Cost per Week ($)
Movie	3.50
Video Game	4.50
Game System	20

36. Plot and label points K(3, 4), A(1, 3), and J(4, 2) on the graph. MCC5.G.2

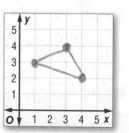

Functions and Equations

What You'll Learn

Scan the lesson. List two headings you would use to make an outline of the lesson.

• _____

   _____

• _____

   _____

Essential Question

HOW are symbols, such as <, >, and =, useful?

Vocabulary

linear function

Common Core GPS

Content Standards
MCC6.EE.9
Mathematical Practices
1, 3, 4, 8

Vocabulary Start-Up

A **linear function** is a function whose graph is a line.

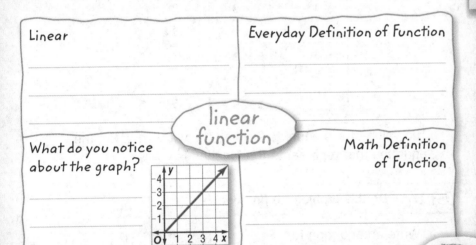

Linear	Everyday Definition of Function
_____	_____

linear function

What do you notice about the graph?	Math Definition of Function

Real-World Link

Babysitting The table shows the amount of money Carli earns based on the number of hours she babysits.

1. Write a sentence that describes the relationship between the number of hours she babysits and her earnings.

   _____

2. Does she earn the same amount each hour?

   Explain. _____

Hours Babysitting	Earnings ($)
1	6
2	12
3	18
4	24

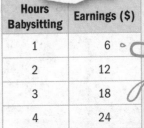

Write an Equation to Represent a Function

You can use an equation to represent a function. The input, or independent variable, represents the x-value, and the output, or dependent variable, represents the y-value. An equation expresses the dependent variable in terms of the independent variable.

Example

Tutor

1. Write an equation to represent the function shown in the table.

Input, x	1	2	3	4	5
Output, y	9	18	27	36	45

Input, x	Multiply by 9	Output, y
1	1 × 9	9
2	2 × 9	18
3	3 × 9	27
4	4 × 9	36
5	5 × 9	45

)+9
)+9
)+9
)+9

The value of y is equal to 9 times the value of x. So, the equation that represents the function is $y = 9x$.

Show your work.

Got It? Do this problem to find out.

a. Write an equation to represent the function shown in the table.

Input, x	1	2	3	4	5
Output, y	16	32	48	64	80

a. _____

Graph Linear Functions

You can also graph a function. If the graph is a line, the function is then called a *linear equation*. When graphing the function, the input is the x-coordinate and the output is the y-coordinate.

$$(\textbf{input}, \textit{output}) \longrightarrow (x, y)$$

Example

Tutor

2. Graph $y = 2x$.

| Step 1 | Make a table of ordered pairs. Select any three values for x. Substitute these values for x to find y. |

x	$2x$	y	(x, y)
0	2(0)	0	(0, 0)
1	2(1)	2	(1, 2)
2	2(2)	4	(2, 4)

| Step 2 | Graph each ordered pair. Draw a line through each point. |

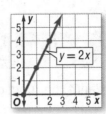

$y = 2x$

Show your work.

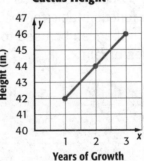

b.

c.

Got It? Do these problems to find out.

b. $y = x + 1$

c. $y = 3x + 2$

Tutor

Examples

Real World

Martino constructed the graph shown, which shows the height of his cactus after several years of growth.

Cactus Height

3. Make a function table for the input-output values.

The three input values are 1, 2, and 3. The corresponding output values are 42, 44, and 46.

Input (x)	Output (y)
1	42
2	44
3	46

4. Write an equation from the graph that could be used to find the height y of the cactus after x years.

Since the output values increase by 2, the equation includes $2x$. Each output value is 40 more than twice the input. So, the equation is $y = 2x + 40$.

Magazines (x)	Total (y)

Got It? Do this problem to find out.

d. The graph shows the total amount y that you spend if you buy one book and x magazines. Make a function table for the input-output values. Write an equation from the graph that could be used to find the total amount y if you buy one book and x magazines.

Total Amount

40
35
30
25
20

0 1 2 3 4 x

Number of Magazines

d. _____

Guided Practice

1. Write an equation to represent the function shown in the table. (Example 1)

Input (x)	0	1	2	3	4
Output (y)	0	4	8	12	16

_____

2. Graph the function $y = x + 3$. (Example 2)

y

8
7
6
5
4
3
2
1

O 1 2 3 4 5 6 7 8 x

3. The graph below shows the number of inches of rainfall x equivalent to inches of snow y. Make a function table for the input-output values. Write an equation from the graph that can be used to find the total inches of snow y equivalent to inches of rain x. (Examples 3 and 4)

50
40
30
20
10

Snowfall (in.)

0 1 2 3 4 x

Rainfall (in.)

Rain (x)	Snow (y)

_____

4. ⓔ **Building on the Essential Question** How are ordered pairs of a function used to create the graph of the function?

_____

_____

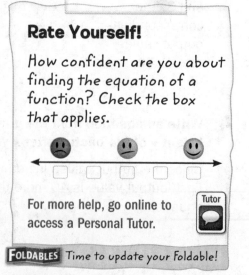

Rate Yourself!

How confident are you about finding the equation of a function? Check the box that applies.

☐ ☐ ☐ ☐ ☐

For more help, go online to access a Personal Tutor.

Tutor

FOLDABLES Time to update your Foldable!

Independent Practice

Go online for Step-by-Step Solutions

Write an equation to represent each function. (Example 1)

1.

Input (x)	1	2	3	4	5
Output (y)	6	12	18	24	30

_____

2.

Input (x)	0	1	2	3	4
Output (y)	0	15	30	45	60

_____

Graph each equation. (Example 2)

3. $y = x + 4$

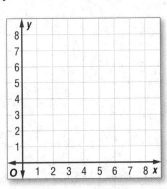

4. $y = 2x + 0.5$

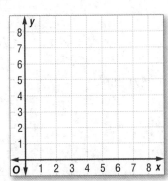

5. $y = 0.5x + 1$

6. The graph shows the charges for a health club in a month. Make a function table for the input-output values. Write an equation that can be used to find the total charge y for the number of x classes.
(Examples 3 and 4)

Input (x)			
Output (y)			

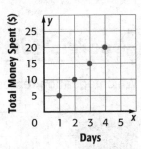

7. The graph shows the amount of money Pasha spent on lunch. Make a function table for the input-output values. Write an equation that can be used to find the money spent y for any number of days x. (Examples 3 and 4)

Input (x)			
Output (y)			

8. **CCGPS** **Multiple Representations** The table shows the area of a square with the given side length.

Side Length (x)	Area of Square (y)
1	1
2	4
3	9
4	16

a. **Variables** Write an equation that could represent the function table.

b. **Graphs** Graph the function.

c. **Words** Is this a linear function? Explain.

H.O.T. Problems Higher Order Thinking

9. **CCGPS** **Model with Mathematics** Write about a real-world situation that can be represented by the equation $y = 7x$. Be sure to explain what the variables represent in the situation.

10. **CCGPS** **Persevere with Problems** Write an equation to represent the function in the table.

Input (x)	6	8	10	12	14	16
Output (y)	0	1	2	3	4	5

Georgia Test Practice

11. Which equation represents the function?

Input (x)	1	2	3	4
Output (y)	4	5	6	7

Ⓐ $y = 2x + 1$ Ⓒ $y = 3x - 1$
Ⓑ $y = x + 3$ Ⓓ $y = 3x$

Extra Practice

 Identify Repeated Reasoning Write an equation to represent each function.

12.

Input (x)	0	1	2	3	4
Output (y)	0	11	22	33	44

13.

Input (x)	1	2	3	4	5
Output (y)	10	20	30	40	50

 $y = 11x$

Each output y is 11 times each input x.

_____

Graph each equation.

14. $y = 4x$

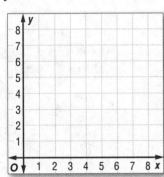

15. $y = 0.5x$

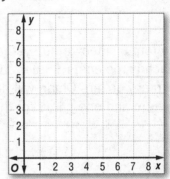

16. $y = x + 0.5$

17. A company charges $50 per month for satellite television service plus an additional $5 for each movie ordered. The equation $y = 50 + 5x$ describes the total amount y a customer will pay if they order x movies. Graph the function.

Show your work.

18. A fair charges an admission fee of $8. Each ride is an additional $2. The equation $t = 8 + 2r$ describes the total charge t for the number of rides r. Graph the function.

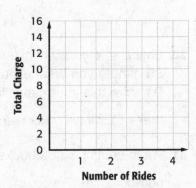

19. The table shows admission prices at a zoo based on the number of guests.

Number of Guests, x	Total Admission ($), y
1	7
2	14
3	21
4	28

Which equation can be used to find y, the total admission for x guests?

Ⓐ $x = 7y$ Ⓒ $y = 7x$

Ⓑ $y = 7 + x$ Ⓓ $x = 7 + y$

20. Which equation represents the function displayed in the table?

Input (x)	Output (y)
1	5
2	10
3	15
4	20

Ⓕ $y = 4x + 1$ Ⓗ $y = x + 5$

Ⓖ $y = 5x$ Ⓘ $y = 5x - 1$

21. Short Response Omari wants to rent a video game system that costs $8 to rent for four days. Each game costs $5 per day to rent. Complete the table to show how many dollars Omari will have to spend to rent the video game system and one game for the number of days given.

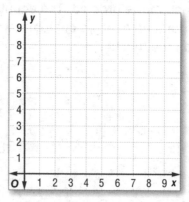

Number of Days	Total Cost
4	
8	
12	

Graph and label each point. MCC5.G.2

22. $A(3, 7)$ **23.** $B(4, 3)$

24. $C(8, 2)$ **25.** $D(6, 5)$

26. $E(3, 1)$ **27.** $F(9, 4)$

28. $G(4, 8)$ **29.** $H(2, 6)$

30. Shana studied 20 minutes on Monday, 45 minutes on Tuesday, 30 minutes on Wednesday, and 45 minutes on Thursday. Organize this information in the table. How long did she study these four days? MCC4.MD.2 _____

Day	Time Studied (min)

31. Pablo bought 3 notebooks for $5.85. How much did each notebook cost? MCC5.NBT.7 _____

Multiple Representations of Functions

Lesson 4

What You'll Learn

Scan the lesson. List two headings you would use to make an outline of the lesson.

- _____
- _____

Essential Question

HOW are symbols, such as <, >, and =, useful?

 Common Core GPS

Content Standards
MCC6.EE.9

Mathematical Practices
1, 2, 3, 4

 Real-World Link

Museum A group of friends are going to the museum. Each friend must pay an admission price of $9.

Total Cost of Admission

Number of Friends (n)	Total Cost ($)
1	9
2	
3	
4	

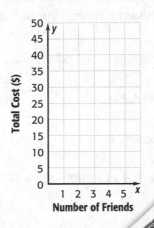

1. Complete the table and graph the ordered pairs (number of friends, total cost).

2. Describe the graph.

   _____

3. Write an equation to find the cost of *n* tickets.

   _____
   _____

4. List the ordered pair for the cost when 5 friends go to the museum. Describe the location.

   _____

connectED.mcgraw-hill.com

Lesson 4 Multiple Representations of Functions **519**

Copyright © The McGraw-Hill Companies, Inc.   Jason Edwards/National Geographic RF/Getty Images

Represent Functions Using Words and Equations

Words	A runner's distance in a marathon is equal to 8 miles per hour times the number of hours.
Equation	$d = 8t$

Words and equations can be used to describe functions. For example, when a rate is expressed in words, it can be written as an equation with variables. When you write an equation, determine what variables to use to represent different quantities.

 Examples

1. The drama club is holding a bake sale. They are charging $5 for each pie they sell. Write an equation to find the total amount earned *t* for selling *p* pies.

Words	Total earned equals $5 times the number of pies sold.
Variable	Let *t* represent the total earned and *p* represent the number of pies sold.
Equation	$t \quad = \quad 5 \quad \cdot \quad p$

So, the equation is $t = 5p$.

2. In a science report, Mia finds that the average adult breathes 14 times each minute when not active. Write an equation to find the total breaths *b* a non-active person takes in *m* minutes.

Let *b* represent the total breaths and *m* represent the number of minutes.

The number of total breaths equals 14 times the number of minutes.

So, the equation is $b = 14m$.

Got It? Do these problems to find out.

a. _____

a. A mouse can travel 8 miles per hour. Write an equation to find the total distance *d* a mouse can travel in *h* hours.

b. _____

b. Samantha can make 36 cookies each hour. Write an equation to find the total number of cookies *c* that she can make in *h* hours.

Represent Functions Using Tables and Graphs

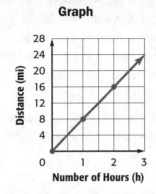

Time (h)	Distance (mi)
0	0
1	8
2	16

Table

Graph

Tables and graphs can also be used to represent functions.

 ## Examples

The Student Council is holding a car wash to raise money. They are charging $7 for each car they wash.

3. **Write an equation and make a function table to show the relationship between the number of cars washed c and the total amount earned t.**

Cars Washed, c	7c	Total Earned ($), t
1	1 × 7	7
2	2 × 7	14
3	3 × 7	21
4	4 × 7	28

Using the assigned variables, the total earned t equals $7 times the number of cars washed c. So, the equation is $t = 7c$.

The total earned (output) is equal to $7 times the number of cars washed (input).

Write $7c$ in the middle column of the table.

4. **Graph the ordered pairs. Analyze the graph.**

Find the ordered pairs (c, t). The ordered pairs are (1, 7), (2, 14), (3, 21), and (4, 28). Now graph the ordered pairs.

The graph is linear because the amount earned increases by $7 for each car washed.

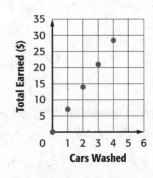

Show
your
Work.

Got It? Do these problems to find out.

While in normal flight, a bald eagle flies at an average speed of 30 miles per hour.

c. _____

d. _____

c. Write an equation and make a function table to show the relationship between the total distance d that a bald eagle can travel in h hours.

d. Graph the ordered pairs of the function. Analyze the graph.

$d = 30h$
$(y = mx)$

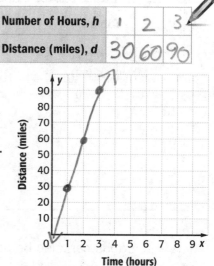

Number of Hours, h	1	2	3
Distance (miles), d	30	60	90

Guided Practice

Check ✓

1. The school cafeteria sells lunch passes that allow a student to purchase any number of lunches in advance for $3 per lunch. (Examples 1–4)

   a. Write an equation to find t, the total cost in dollars for a lunch pass with n lunches. ____ $t = 3n$ _____

   b. Make a function table to show the relationship between the number of lunches n and the cost t.

   c. Graph the ordered pairs. Analyze the graph.

Number of Lunches, n	1	2	3
Total Cost ($), t	3	6	9

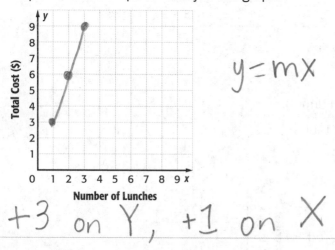

$y = mx$

$+3$ on Y, $+1$ on X

Rate Yourself!

How well do you understand the different ways to represent functions? Circle the image that applies.

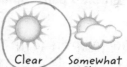

Clear   Somewhat   Not So
          Clear   Clear

2. **Building on the Essential Question** Why do you represent functions in different ways?

_____

_____

For more help, go online to access a Personal Tutor.

FOLDABLES Time to update your Foldable!

Independent Practice

Go online for Step-by-Step Solutions

1 An African elephant eats 400 pounds of vegetation each day. (Examples 1–4)

   a. Write an equation to find *v*, the number of pounds of vegetation an African elephant eats in *d* days. $v = 400d$

   b. Make a table to show the relationship between the number of pounds *v* an African elephant eats in days *d*.

Number of Days, d	1	2	3
Pounds Eaten, v	400	800	1200

   c. Graph the ordered pairs. Analyze the graph.

   _____

   _____

   _____

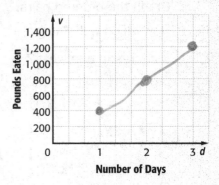

2. **CCGPS** **Model with Mathematics** Refer to the graphic novel frame below for Exercises a–c.

   a. Let *f* represent the cost of ordering each ticket online. Write an equation that could be used to find the cost of ordering each ticket online.

$$2f + 2(24.95) = 64.50$$

   b. Solve the equation from part a. $f = \$14.60/2 \text{ or } \$7.3$

   c. Another friend wants to go to the concert. What is the total cost of ordering three tickets online?

$$64.50 + 7.30 + 24.95 = \$96.75$$

$$\begin{array}{r} 7180 \\ 2495 \\ \hline 9675 \end{array}$$

3 Maurice receives $3 per week for allowance and earns an additional $1.75 for each chore he completes.

a. Write an equation to find t, the total amount earned for c chores in one week. _____

_____

b. Make a function table to show the relationship between the number of chores completed c and the total amount earned t in one week.

Number of Chores, c			
Total Earned ($), t			

c. Graph the ordered pairs.

d. How much will Maurice earn if he completes 5 chores in one week? _____

_____

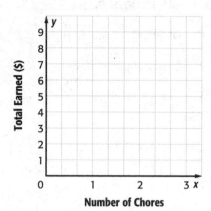

 H.O.T. Problems Higher Order Thinking

4. (CCGPS) **Reason Abstractly** What would the graph of $y = x$ look like? Name three ordered pairs that lie on the line. _____

_____

5. (CCGPS) **Persevere with Problems** Boards 4 U charges $10 per hour to rent a snowboard while Slopes charges $12 per hour. Will the cost to rent snowboards at each place ever be the same for the same number of hours after zero hours? If so, for what number of hours? _____

_____

6. (CCGPS) **Model with Mathematics** Write a real-world problem in which you could graph a function. _____

Georgia Test Practice

7. A movie rental club charges a one time fee of $25 to join and $2 for every movie rented. Which equation represents the cost of joining the club and renting any number of movies?

Ⓐ $c = 2 + 25m$ Ⓒ $c = 25 + 2m$

Ⓑ $c = 2m$ Ⓓ $c = 25m$

Extra Practice

8. In a video game, each player earns 5 points for reaching the next level and 15 points for each coin collected.

   a. Write an equation to find *p*, the total points for collecting *c* coins after reaching the next level. $p = 5 + 15c$

   Total points p equals 15 times the number of coins c collected plus 5 points for reaching the next level. So, the equation is p = 5 + 15c.

   b. Make a table to show the relationship between the number of coins collected *c* and the total points *p*.

   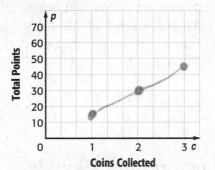

Number of Coins, *c*	1	2	3
Total Points, *p*	15	30	45

   c. Graph the ordered pairs. Analyze the graph.

   _____

   _____

   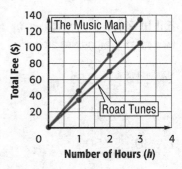

9. Two disc jockeys charge different rates. The Music Man charges $45 per hour and Road Tunes charges $35 per hour. Write equations to represent the total cost *t* of hiring either disc jockey for any number of hours *n*. _____

   $S = 80h$ (road tunes)

   $S = 45h$ (music man)

Copy and Solve **For Exercise 10, show your work on a separate piece of paper.**

10. **CCSS Construct an Argument** A catering service offers lasagna and chicken parmesan. Each pan of lasagna serves 24 people.

    a. Write an equation to represent the number of people *n* served by any number of pans *p* of lasagna.

    b. Make a function table to show the relationship between the number of pans *p* and the number of people served *n*.

    c. Graph the ordered pairs.

    d. The same catering company offers chicken parmesan that serves 16 people per pan. How many more people would 5 pans of lasagna serve than 5 pans of chicken parmesan? Explain your reasoning to a classmate.

11. The table shows a relationship between x and y. Which of the following equations is true for each of the ordered pairs in the table?

x	y
0	1
1	3.5
2	6
3	8.5
4	11

Ⓐ $y = 2x + 1$

Ⓑ $y = 3.5x$

Ⓒ $y = 2.5x + 1$

Ⓓ $y = 4x - 0.5$

12. For each table Ariella waits on at a restaurant, she is paid $4.00 plus 18% of the total bill. If x equals the total bill, which of the following equations could be used to represent the amount of money m Ariella is paid for any total bill?

Ⓕ $m = 0.18x - 4$

Ⓖ $m = 0.18x + 4$

Ⓗ $m = 4 - 0.18x$

Ⓘ $m = 0.18(x + 4)$

13. Short Response A science test has multiple choice questions and short answer questions. Each multiple choice question is worth 2 points and each short answer is worth 5 points. Write an equation to represent the total points possible for the test.

$$x(2 + 5) = y$$

(CCGPS) Common Core Review

Fill in each ◯ with < or > to make a true statement.
MCC4.NBT.2, MCC5.NBT.3b

14. 116 ◯< 161

15. 63 ◯> 61

16. 105 ◯< 115

17. 50 ◯< 500

18. 12 ◯> 1.2

19. 44 ◯< 49

20. The table shows the ticket sales for three days. On which day(s) were the ticket sales greater than 50? MCC4.NBT.2

Wed., Thu.

Day	Number of Tickets Sold
Wednesday	50
Thursday	56
Friday	41

Content Standards
MCC6.EE.9
Mathematical Practices
1, 3, 4

Case #1 Splitting Up

Blue-green algae is a type of bacteria that can double its population by splitting up to four times in one day.

If it grows at this rate, how many bacteria will be formed at the end of one day?

I know how to multiply.

 Understand *What are the facts?*

· Blue-green algae can double its population up to four times in one day.

 Plan *What is your strategy to solve this problem?*

Make a table to display and organize the information.

 Solve *How can you apply the strategy?*

Follow the pattern to find the total number of bacteria after 1 day.

Day Number	Number of Times Split	Total Number of Bacteria	
1	0	1	← ×2
1	1	2	← ×2
1	2		← ×2
1	3		← ×2
1	4		← ×2

 Check *Does the answer make sense?*

Use the equation $t = 2^n$ where n represents the number of times the bacteria split and t represents the total number of bacteria. $2^4 = 16$

Analyze the Strategy Tutor

Justify Conclusions If the bacteria continue to grow at this rate, would the number of bacteria be over 1,000 within a week? Explain.

Case #2 Game On!

Miguel and Lauren are testing two versions of a new video game. In Miguel's version he receives 25 points at the start of the game, plus 1 point for each level he completes. In Lauren's version she receives 20 points at the start of the game, and 2 points for each level she completes.

At what level will they both have the same number of points?

Understand

Read the problem. What are you being asked to find?

I need to find _____.

Underline key words and values in the problem.
What information do you know?

Miguel starts with ☐ points and earns ☐ point for each level.

Lauren starts with ☐ points and earns ☐ points for each level.

Plan

Choose a problem-solving strategy.

I will use the _____ strategy.

Solve

Use your problem-solving strategy to solve the problem.

	Start	Level 1	Level 2	Level 3	Level 4	Level 5
Miguel						
Lauren						

So, Miguel and Lauren will have the same score after completing

Level ☐.

Check

Place the level number answer in each box and evaluate to check your answer.

Miguel: $25 + \left(1 \times \boxed{}\right) = $ _____

Lauren: $20 + \left(2 \times \boxed{}\right) = $ _____

Collaborate Work with a small group to solve the following cases. Show your work on a separate piece of paper.

Case #3 Geometry

Determine how many cubes are used in each step.

Make a table to find the number of cubes in the seventh step.

_____

Case #4 Car Rental

Anne Marie needs to rent a car for 9 days to take on vacation. The cost of renting a car is $66 per day.

Make a table to find the total cost of her rental car.

_____

Case #5 Patterns

Make a table to find the number of toothpicks needed to create Figure 8 in the pattern below.

Figure 1   Figure 2   Figure 3

Circle a strategy below to solve the problem.

- Act it out.
- Solve a simpler problem.
- Guess, check, and revise.
- Look for a pattern.

Case #6 Money

The admission for a fair is $6 for adults, $4 for children, and $3 for senior citizens. Twelve people paid a total of $50 for admission.

If 8 children attended, how many adults and senior citizens attended?

_____

Mid-Chapter Check

Vocabulary Check

1. Define *sequence*. Give an example of an arithmetic and a geometric sequence. (Lesson 2)

_____

_____

2. Fill in the blank in the sentence below with the correct term. (Lesson 1)

A _____ is a relation that assigns exactly one output value to one input value.

Skills Check and Problem Solving

Complete each function table. (Lesson 1)

3.

Input (x)	2x + 6	Output
0		
1		
2		

4.

Input (x)	3x + 1	Output
0		
1		
2		

CCGPS **Identify Structure** **Find the rule for each function table.** (Lesson 2)

5.

Input (x)	Output
3	6
4	8
5	10

6.

Input (x)	Output
1	3
2	7
3	11

7.

Input (x)	Output
2	8
3	11
4	14

8. Arnold reads an average of 21 pages each day. Write an equation to represent the number of pages read after any number of days. (Lesson 4)

_____

9. **Georgia Test Practice** The table shows the cost of renting an inner tube to use at the Wave-a-Rama Water Park. Suppose an equation of the form $y = ax$ is written for the data in the table. What is the value of *a*? (Lesson 3)

Ⓐ 5

Ⓒ 6

Ⓑ 5.5

Ⓓ 6.5

Input (x)	Cost (y)
1	$5.50
2	$11.00
3	$16.50

HOW can bar diagrams help you to compare quantities?

 Content Standards MCC6.EE.5, MCC6.EE.8

Mathematical Practices 1, 3, 4

Fishing In saltwater fishing, any flounder that is caught may be kept if it is greater than or equal to 12 inches long. Any flounder shorter than that must be released back into the water. Pat caught a flounder that is 14 inches long. He wants to know if he can keep the fish.

Investigation

An *inequality* is a mathematical sentence that compares quantities. An inequality like $x < 7$ or $x > 5$ can be written to express how a variable compares to a number.

Step 1 Label the minimum length of flounders that may be kept.

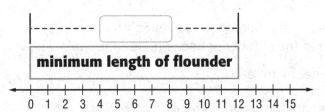

Step 2 Label the length of the flounder Pat caught on the top bar diagram.

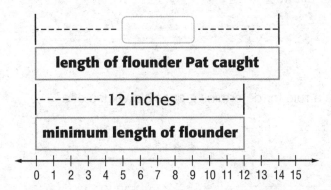

The bar representing Pat's fish is _____ than the bar representing the minimum length that can be kept.

So, Pat _____ keep the fish.

Collaborate

CCGPS **Model with Mathematics** Work with a partner. Draw bar diagrams to solve each problem.

1. In order to win a prize, Ephram needs to read at least 9 books. Ephram read 8 books. Will he win a prize? _____

 Show your work.

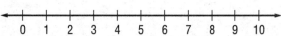

2. Eliza needs $4\frac{3}{4}$ cups of flour. The canister has 4 cups of flour. Will Eliza have enough flour? _____

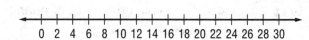

3. For flights within the United States, luggage must be no more than 50 pounds. Imelda's luggage weighs 53 pounds. Can she take the luggage on her flight? _____

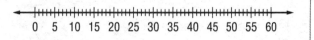

4. Byron needs at least 20 minutes between the end of his soccer practice and the start of his dentist appointment. His practice ends at 4:30 and his appointment is at 5:00.

Does he have enough time? _____

5. Refer to Exercise 1. If *b* represents the number of books Ephram read, write an inequality that compares the number of books he read to the minimum number of books he needs to read. _____

6. Refer to Exercise 3. If *w* represents the weight in pounds of Imelda's luggage, write an inequality that compares the weight of her luggage to the maximum weight of luggage allowed. _____

Reflect

7. CCGPS **Reason Inductively** Write a rule for determining possible values of a variable in an inequality. _____

_____

_____

8. (inquiry) HOW can bar diagrams help you to compare quantities?

_____

_____

Inequalities

What You'll Learn

Scan the lesson. Predict two things you will learn about inequalities.

- _____
  _____

- _____
  _____

 Essential Question

HOW are symbols, such as <, >, and =, useful?

 Vocabulary

inequality

 Common Core GPS

Content Standards
MCC6.EE.5, MCC6.EE.8

Mathematical Practices
1, 2, 3, 4, 6, 7

Vocabulary Start-Up

An **inequality** is a mathematical sentence that compares quantities.

Definition	Symbols
Example	Nonexample

inequality

Real-World Link

Compare the following using < or >.

1. the score after 2 goals is ◯ the score after 3 goals

2. the cost to download 10 songs is ◯ the cost to download 2 songs

3. the outside temperature in summer is ◯ the outside temperature in winter

4. the height of a 1st grade student is ◯ the height of a 6th grade student

5. the time to eat lunch is ◯ the time to brush your teeth

Inequalities

Symbols	<	>	≤	≥
Words	• is less than • is fewer than	• is greater than • is more than	• is less than or equal to • is at most	• is greater than or equal to • is at least
Examples	$3 < 5$	$8 > 4$	$7 \leq 10$	$12 \geq 9$

Work Zone

Inequalities can be solved by finding values of the variables that make the inequality true.

Example

1. **Of the numbers 6, 7, or 8, which is a solution of the inequality $f + 2 < 9$?**

Replace f with each of the numbers.

$f + 2 < 9$	Write the inequality.
$6 + 2 \overset{?}{<} 9$	Replace f with 6.
$8 < 9$ ✓	This is a true statement.

$f + 2 < 9$	Write the inequality.
$7 + 2 \overset{?}{<} 9$	Replace f with 7.
$9 < 9$ ✗	This is not a true statement.

$f + 2 < 9$	Write the inequality.
$8 + 2 \overset{?}{<} 9$	Replace f with 8.
$10 < 9$ ✗	This is not a true statement.

Since the number 6 is the only value that makes a true statement, 6 is a solution of the inequality.

Show your work.

Got It? Do this problem to find out.

a. Of the numbers 8, 9, or 10, which is a solution of the inequality $n - 3 > 6$?

a. _____

Determine Solutions of an Inequality

Since an inequality uses greater than and less than symbols, one-variable inequalities have infinitely many solutions. For example, any rational number greater than 4 will make the inequality $x > 4$ true.

Examples

Is the given value a solution of the inequality?

2. $x + 3 > 9$, $x = 4$

$x + 3 > 9$ Write the inequality.

$4 + 3 \overset{?}{>} 9$ Replace x with 4.

$7 \not> 9$ Simplify.

Since 7 is not greater than 9, 4 is not a solution.

3. $12 \leq 18 - y$, $y = 6$

$12 \leq 18 - y$ Write the inequality.

$12 \overset{?}{\leq} 18 - 6$ Replace y with 6.

$12 \leq 12$ Simplify.

Since $12 = 12$, 12 is a solution.

4. $17 \geq 11 + x$, $x = 8$

$17 \geq 11 + x$ Write the inequality.

$17 \overset{?}{\geq} 11 + \boxed{}$ Replace x with $\boxed{}$.

$17 \not\geq \boxed{}$ Simplify.

Since $\boxed{}$ is not greater than or equal to $\boxed{}$, $\boxed{}$ is not a solution.

Got It? Do these problems to find out.

b. $a + 7 > 15$, $a = 9$ **c.** $22 \leq 15 + b$, $b = 6$

d. $n - 4 < 6$, $n = 10$ **e.** $12 \geq 5 + g$, $g = 7$

STOP and Reflect

Name two solutions of the inequality $12 > 6 + y$.

Show your work.

b. _____

c. _____

d. _____

e. _____

Example

Tutor

5. Luisa works at a gift shop. She receives a bonus if she makes more than 20 balloon bouquets in a month. Which months did Luisa receive a bonus? Use the inequality $b > 20$, where b represents the number of balloon bouquets made each month, to solve.

Balloon Sales	
Month	Number Sold
July	25
August	12
September	18
October	32

Use the *guess, check, and revise* strategy.

Try 25.	Try 12.	Try 18.	Try 32.
$b > 20$	$b > 20$	$b > 20$	$b > 20$
$25 > 20$ Yes	$12 > 20$ No	$18 > 20$ No	$32 > 20$ Yes

So, Luisa received a bonus in July and October.

Guided Practice

Check

Determine which number is a solution of the inequality. (Example 1)

1. $9 + a < 17$; $7, 8, 9$ _____

 Show your work.

2. $b - 10 > 5$; $14, 15, 16$ _____

Is the given value a solution of the inequality? (Examples 2–4)

3. $x - 5 < 5$, $x = 15$

_____

4. $32 \geq 8n$, $n = 3$

_____

5. If the bakery sells more than 45 bagels in a day, they make a profit. Use the inequality $b > 45$ to determine which days the bakery makes a profit. (Example 5)

Day	Number of Bagels Sold
Monday	18
Tuesday	25
Wednesday	21
Thursday	36
Friday	50
Saturday	48
Sunday	40

_____

6. **Building on the Essential Question** How can mental math help you find solutions to inequalities?

_____

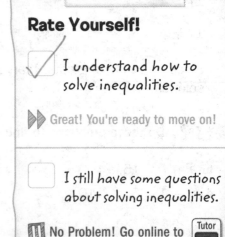

Rate Yourself!

✓ I understand how to solve inequalities.

▶▶ Great! You're ready to move on!

☐ I still have some questions about solving inequalities.

▮▮ No Problem! Go online to access a Personal Tutor. Tutor

Write and Graph Inequalities

What You'll Learn

Scan the lesson. List two headings you would use to make an outline of the lesson.

• _____

_____

• _____

_____

 Essential Question

HOW are symbols, such as <, >, and =, useful?

CCGPS **Common Core GPS**

Content Standards
MCC6.EE.6, MCC6.EE.8

Mathematical Practices
1, 3, 4, 5, 6

 Real-World Link

Fair Look at the situations below. Circle the numbers that are possible answers in each situation.

1. Jessica spent more than $5 at the arcade.

   1 2 3 4 5 6 7 8 9 10 11 12 13 14 15

2. Less than 6 people rang the bell on the mallet game.

   1 2 3 4 5 6 7 8 9 10 11 12 13 14 15

3. There were less than 10 people in line for the Ferris wheel.

   1 2 3 4 5 6 7 8 9 10 11 12 13 14 15

4. It costs more than 6 tokens to ride the bumper cars.

   1 2 3 4 5 6 7 8 9 10 11 12 13 14 15

5. There are less than 8 lemonade stands.

   1 2 3 4 5 6 7 8 9 10 11 12 13 14 15

6. There are more than 12 different flavors of taffy.

   1 2 3 4 5 6 7 8 9 10 11 12 13 14 15

7. Describe any patterns you see in Exercises 1–6.

   _____

ping!

Write Inequalities

You can write an inequality to represent a situation.

Examples

Tutor

Write an inequality for each sentence.

1. **You must be over 12 years old to ride the go-karts.**

Words	Your age	is over	12.
Variable		Let a = your age.	
Inequality	a	>	12

The inequality is $a > 12$.

2. **A pony is less than 14.2 hands tall.**

Words	A pony	is less than	14.2.
Variable		Let p = the height of the pony	
Inequality	p	<	14.2

The inequality is $p < 14.2$.

3. **You must be at least 16 years old to have a driver's license.**

Words	Your age	is at least	16 years.
Variable		Let a = your age.	
Inequality	a	$\geq$	16

The inequality is $a \geq 16$.

STOP and Reflect

Which inequality symbol represents "is at most"?

Got It? Do these problems to find out.

Write an inequality for each sentence.

a. You must be older than 13 to play in the basketball league.

b. To use one stamp, your domestic letter must weigh under 3.5 ounces.

c. You must be over 48 inches tall to ride the roller coaster.

d. You must be at least 18 years old to vote.

a. _____

b. _____

c. _____

d. _____

Show your work.

Graph an Inequality

Inequalities can be graphed on a number line. Sometimes, it is impossible to show all the values that make an inequality true. The graph helps you see the values that make the inequality true.

Examples

Tutor

Graph each inequality on a number line.

4. $n > 9$

Place an open dot at 9. Then draw a line and an arrow to the right.

The open dot means the number 9 is *not* included in the graph.

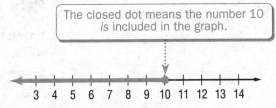

The values that lie on the line make the sentence true. All numbers greater than 9 make the sentence true.

Graphing Inequalities

When inequalities are graphed, an open dot means the number is not included ($<$ or $>$) and a closed dot means it is included ($\leq$ or $\geq$).

5. $n \leq 10$

Place a closed dot at 10. Then draw a line and an arrow to the left.

The closed dot means the number 10 *is* included in the graph.

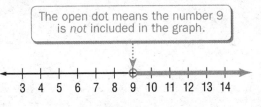

All numbers 10 and less make the sentence true.

Got It? Do these problems to find out.

e. $a < 15$

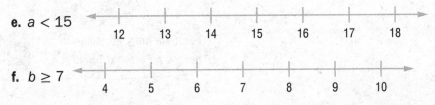

f. $b \geq 7$

Copyright © The McGraw-Hill Companies, Inc.

Lesson 6 Write and Graph Inequalities **543**

SPEED LIMIT 25

6. Traffic on a residential street can travel at speeds of no more than 25 miles per hour. Write and graph an inequality to describe the possible speeds on the street.

Let s represent the speed on the street.

The inequality is $s \leq 25$.

Place a closed dot at 25. Then draw a line and an arrow to the left. All numbers 25 and less make the sentence true.

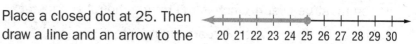
20 21 22 23 24 25 26 27 28 29 30

Guided Practice
 Check

Write an inequality for each sentence. (Examples 1–3)

1. The movie will be no more than 90 minutes in length. _____

2. The mountain is at least 985 feet tall. _____

Graph each inequality on a number line. (Examples 4 and 5)

3. $a \leq 6$

4. $b > 4$

5. Tasha can spend no more than $40 on new boots. Write and graph an inequality to describe how much she can spend. (Example 6) _____

6. **Building on the Essential Question** How can graphing an inequality help to solve it? _____

_____

Rate Yourself!

How confident are you about writing and graphing inequalities? Shade the ring on the target.

I'm on target.

I need help.

For more help, go online to access a Personal Tutor. Tutor

Independent Practice

Go online for Step-by-Step Solutions eHelp

Write an inequality for each sentence. (Examples 1–3)

1. Swim practice will be no more than 35 laps. _____ $S \leq 35$

2. Kevin ran for less than 5 miles. _____ $k < 5$

3. The occupancy of the room must be less than 437 people. $\emptyset < 437$

Graph each inequality on a number line. (Examples 4 and 5)

4. $f > 1$

1

5. $x \leq 5$

5

6. $y \geq 4$

4

7. A rewritable compact disc must have less than 20 songs on it. Write and graph an inequality to describe how many songs can be on the disc. (Example 6)

$r < 20$

20

8. **CCGPS** **Be Precise** Fill in the information in the table. The first is done for you.

Symbol	Words	Open or closed dot on number line?
>	greater than	open dot
≥	greater than or equal to	Closed dot
<	less than	open dot
≤	less than or equal to	closed dot

9. **CCGPS** **Find the Error** Mei is writing an inequality for the expression *at least 10 hours of community service.* Find her mistake and correct it.

$c \le 10$

10. **CCGPS** **Persevere with Problems** Name three solutions of the inequality $w \le \frac{4}{5}$. Then justify your response using a number line.

⟵—————————————————⟶

11. **CCGPS** **Justify Conclusions** Explain the difference between graphing an inequality with a closed dot and one with an open dot. Use examples to support your reasoning.

 Georgia Test Practice

12. To enter the school dance, you may not be older than 14. Which answer choice represents this inequality?

Ⓐ
```
10 11 12 13 14 15 16 17 18
```

Ⓑ
```
10 11 12 13 14 15 16 17 18
```

Ⓒ
```
10 11 12 13 14 15 16 17 18
```

Ⓓ
```
10 11 12 13 14 15 16 17 18
```

Extra Practice

Write an inequality for each sentence.

13. You cannot spend more than 50 dollars. $s \leq 50$

 Let's represent what you can spend. Cannot spend more means you can spend less than or equal to 50 dollars.

14. More than 800 fans attended the opening soccer game. _____

15. The heavyweight division is greater than 200 pounds. _____

Graph each inequality on a number line.

16. $g < 6$

17. $z > 18$

18. $h \geq 3$

19. On a certain day, the temperature in Bismarck, North Dakota, was below 4 °F. Write and graph an inequality to describe the possible temperatures.

_____

20. **CCGPS** **Use Math Tools** The graph shows the number of students who participate in some of the activities offered at Crestview Middle School.

  a. Which activities have more than 20 participants? at least 20? fewer than 19?

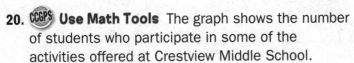

  b. Write an inequality comparing the number of orchestra participants and the number of tennis participants.

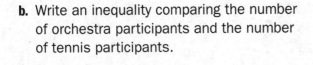

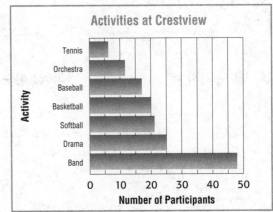

Activities at Crestview

Georgia Test Practice

21. Short Response The table below shows the number of different kinds of sports equipment sold in the City Sports Store.

Type	Number Sold in Store
Football	8
Basketball	n
Baseball	33
Hockey puck	3
Softball	21

The number of basketballs sold is greater than the total number of softballs sold. Write and graph an inequality to describe the number of basketballs that could have been sold.

22. Which of the following graphs represents the inequality?

$$x \geq 5$$

Ⓐ ← | | | | | ● | | | | | →
    0 1 2 3 4 5 6 7 8 9 10

Ⓑ ← | | | | | ⊕ | | | | | →
    0 1 2 3 4 5 6 7 8 9 10

Ⓒ ← | | | | | ⊕————————→
    0 1 2 3 4 5 6 7 8 9 10

Ⓓ ← | | | | | ●————————→
    0 1 2 3 4 5 6 7 8 9 10

23. Jason has less than 65 pages of his book left to read. Which inequality represents this situation?

Ⓕ $p > 65$ Ⓗ $p < 65$

Ⓖ $p \geq 65$ Ⓘ $p \leq 65$

Common Core Review

Evaluate each expression. MCC5.OA.1

24. $8(2) - 11 =$ _____

25. $7 + 2(2) =$ _____

26. $3(5) - 7 =$ _____

27. $19 - 2(3) =$ _____

28. $3(4) - 7 =$ _____

29. $28 - 4(4) =$ _____

Inquiry HOW can you use bar diagrams to solve one-step inequalities?

CCGPS Content Standards
MCC6.EE.5, MCC6.EE.8

Mathematical Practices
1, 3, 4

Jockeys In a recent Kentucky Derby, the total weight a horse could carry was less than 126 pounds. A jockey weighs a certain number of pounds and his equipment weighs 9 pounds. How much could the jockey weigh?

What do you know? _____

_____

What do you need to find? _____

_____

Investigation

You already learned that you can add or subtract the same quantity to each side of an equation when solving it. This is also true for inequalities.

Step 1 Solve the inequality $x + 9 < 126$ using a bar diagram. Place a dashed line on 126.

Step 2 The symbol is $<$, so a box is drawn to the left of 126.

Step 3 The bar represents $x +$ ☐. Label the bar diagram below.

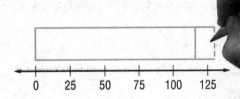

The section of the bar labeled x must be less than ☐ for the inequality to be true. So, $x <$ ☐.

Collaborate

Work with a partner to solve each problem by using a model.

1. Regina sent *x* text messages before lunch. She sent another 4 text messages after lunch. She sent less than 7 text messages today. How many text messages could she have sent before lunch? Write

   your answer as an inequality. _____

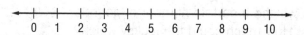

2. A player with five personal fouls cannot stay in the game. Dylan has already earned two personal fouls. How many more personal fouls *x* could he earn and still stay in the game? Write your answer as an inequality.

   _____

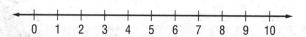

Work with a partner to solve by using the *guess, check, and revise* strategy. Find the least or greatest number that makes the inequality true.

3. $x - 5 \leq 1$ _____   4. $x + 3 \geq 8$ _____

Analyze

5. **CCGPS** **Reason Inductively** Explain how you could solve the inequality

   $x + 7 \leq 12$ using the *guess, check, and revise* strategy. Then solve. _____

   _____

Reflect

6. **CCGPS** **Model with Mathematics** Write and solve a word problem using the

   inequality $x + 6 \leq 25$. _____

   _____

7. **Inquiry** HOW can you use bar diagrams to solve one-step inequalities?

   _____

550   Chapter 7 Functions and Inequalities

Copyright © The McGraw-Hill Companies, Inc.

Solve One-Step Inequalities

What You'll Learn

Scan the lesson. Predict two things you will learn about solving one-step inequalities.

- _____
- _____

Essential Question

HOW are symbols, such as <, >, and =, useful?

CCGPS Common Core GPS

Content Standards
MCC6.EE.5, MCC6.EE.6, MCC6.EE.8

Mathematical Practices
1, 3, 4

🌎 Real-World Link

Baseball The graph shows the number of home runs that the top hitters on the baseball team hit last season.

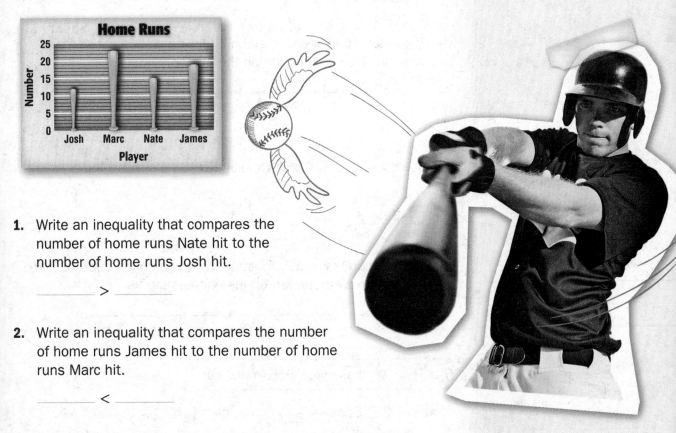

Home Runs

1. Write an inequality that compares the number of home runs Nate hit to the number of home runs Josh hit.

   _____ > _____

2. Write an inequality that compares the number of home runs James hit to the number of home runs Marc hit.

   _____ < _____

3. Suppose James and Marc each hit 3 more home runs. Write a new inequality that compares the number of home runs James and Marc hit.

   _____ < _____

Key Concept ▶ Use Addition and Subtraction Properties to Solve Inequalities

Words   When you add or subtract the same number from each side of an inequality, the inequality remains true.

Example

$5 < 9$	$11 > 6$
$+4 \quad +4$	$-3 \quad -3$
$9 < 13$	$8 > 3$

These properties are also true for $\leq$ and $\geq$.

Examples

Tutor

1. **Solve $x + 7 \geq 10$. Graph the solution on a number line.**

$x + 7 \geq 10$ Write the inequality.

$\underline{-7 \quad -7}$ Subtract 7 from each side.

$x \qquad \geq 3$ Simplify.

The solution is $x \geq 3$. To graph it, draw a closed dot at 3 and draw an arrow to the right on the number line.

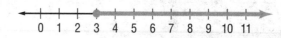

2. **Solve $x - 3 < 9$. Graph the solution on a number line.**

$x - 3 < 9$ Write the inequality.

$\underline{+3 \quad +3}$ Add 3 to each side.

$x \qquad < 12$ Simplify.

The solution is $x < 12$. To graph it, draw an open dot on 12 and draw an arrow to the left on the number line.

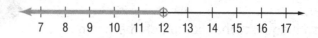

Got It?   Do these problems to find out.

Show your work.

a. $n + 2 \leq 5$

a. _____

b. $y - 3 > 9$

b. _____

Use Multiplication and Division Properties to Solve Inequalities

Key Concept

Words   When you multiply or divide each side of an inequality by the same *positive* number, the inequality remains true.

Example

$$5 < 10$$
$$5 \times 2 < 10 \times 2$$
$$10 < 20$$

$$16 > 12$$
$$\frac{16}{2} > \frac{12}{2}$$
$$8 > 6$$

These properties are also true for ≤ and ≥.

Examples

Tutor

3. **Solve 5x ≤ 45. Graph the solution on a number line.**

$$5x \le 45$$ Write the inequality.

$$\frac{5x}{5} \le \frac{45}{5}$$ Divide each side by 5.

$$x \le 9$$ Simplify.

The solution is $x \le 9$.

6   7   8   9   10   11   12

> **Checking Solutions**
> You can check your solutions by substituting numbers into the inequality and testing to verify that it holds true.

4. **Solve $\frac{x}{8} > 3$. Graph the solution on a number line.**

$$\frac{x}{8} > 3$$ Write the inequality.

$$\frac{x}{8}(8) > 3(8)$$ Multiply each side by 8.

$$x > 24$$ Simplify.

The solution is $x > 24$.

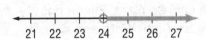
21   22   23   24   25   26   27

Got It?   Do these problems to find out.

Show your work.

c. $10x < 80$

5   6   7   8   9   10   11

c. _____

d. $\frac{x}{6} \ge 7$

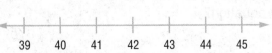
39   40   41   42   43   44   45

d. _____

Example

5. Laverne is making bags of party favors for each of the 7 friends attending her birthday party. She does not want to spend more than $42 on the party favors. Write and solve an inequality to find the maximum cost for each party favor bag.

Words to Symbols

Remember, at most translates to ≤, while at least translates to ≥.

Let c represent the cost for each bag of party favors.

7 times the cost of each bag must be no more than $42.

$$7c \leq 42 \qquad \text{Write the inequality.}$$
$$\frac{7c}{7} \leq \frac{42}{7} \qquad \text{Divide each side by 7.}$$
$$c \leq 6 \qquad \text{Simplify.}$$

Laverne can spend a maximum of $6 on each party favor bag.

Guided Practice

Check

Solve each inequality. Graph the solution on a number line. (Examples 1–4)

1. $h - 6 \geq 13$ _____

2. $5y > 30$ _____

3. Johanna's parents give her $10 per week for lunch money. She cannot decide whether she wants to buy or pack her lunch. If a hot lunch at school costs $2, write and solve an inequality to find the maximum number of times per week Johanna can buy her lunch. (Example 5)

_____

4. Tino's Pizza charges $9 for a cheese pizza. Eileen has $45 to buy pizza for the Spanish Club. Write and solve an inequality to find the maximum number of pizzas that

Eileen can buy. (Example 5) _____

5. ⓔ **Building on the Essential Question** How is solving an inequality similar to solving an equation?

_____

_____

Rate Yourself!

Are you ready to move on? Shade the section that applies.

YES   ?   NO

For more help, go online to access a Personal Tutor.

Tutor

Independent Practice

Go online for Step-by-Step Solutions

Solve each inequality. Graph the solution on a number line. (Examples 1–4)

1. $2 + y \leq 3$ _____

 Show your work.

2. $w - 1 < 4$ _____

3. $7x > 56$ _____

4. $\dfrac{d}{3} \leq 2$ _____

5. A company charges $0.10 for each letter engraved. Bobby plans to spend no more than $5.00 on the engraving on a jewelry box. Write and solve an inequality to find the maximum number of letters he can have engraved. (Example 5)

_____

6. **CCGPS** **Model with Mathematics** Refer to the graphic novel frame below for Exercises a–b.

a. Suppose David has $65 to spend on his ticket and some shirts. He already spent $32.25 on his ticket and fee. Write an inequality that could be used to find the maximum number of shirts he can buy.

_____

b. What is the maximum number of shirts he can buy?

_____

Solve each inequality. Graph the solution on a number line.

7 $p - \frac{7}{12} > \frac{3}{10}$ _____

8. $f + 0.3 < 1.7$ _____

H.O.T. Problems *Higher Order Thinking*

9. (CCGPS) **Model with Mathematics** Write a word problem that would have the solution $p \leq 21$.

_____

_____

_____

10. (CCGPS) **Persevere with Problems** In three math tests, you score 91, 95, and 88 points. How many points must you score on the fourth test to have an A average, or at least 90 points? _____

_____

11. (CCGPS) **Construct an Argument** Does the order of the quantities in an inequality matter? Explain.

_____

_____

_____

Georgia Test Practice

12. Which of the following number lines shows the solution to the inequality?

$$7x > 28$$

(A) number line with open circle at 4, arrow pointing left; labeled 1 2 3 4 5 6 7

(B) number line with open circle at 4, arrow pointing right; labeled 1 2 3 4 5 6 7

(C) number line with closed circle at 4, arrow pointing left; labeled 1 2 3 4 5 6 7

(D) number line with closed circle at 4, arrow pointing right; labeled 1 2 3 4 5 6 7

Extra Practice

Solve each inequality. Graph the solution on a number line.

13. $a + 4 < 9$ $a < 5$

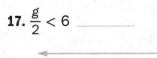

14. $x - 8 \geq 13$ _____

 Homework Help

$$a + 4 < 9$$
$$\underline{-4 \quad -4}$$
$$a < 5$$

15. $d + 13 \geq 22$ _____

16. $25t \leq 100$ _____

17. $\dfrac{g}{2} < 6$ _____

18. $\dfrac{r}{9} > 8$ _____

19. A community needs to raise at least \$5,000 to build a new skateboarding park. They are selling backpacks for \$25 each to raise the money. Write and solve an inequality to determine the minimum number of backpacks they need to sell in order to reach this goal.

_____

20. A sales associate at a computer store receives a bonus of \$100 for every computer he sells. He wants to make \$2,500 in bonuses next month. Write and solve an inequality to find the minimum number of computers

he must sell. _____

CCGPS **Model with Mathematics** Solve each inequality. Graph the solution on a number line.

21. $n + \dfrac{2}{7} \geq \dfrac{1}{2}$ _____

22. $0.2g > 1.8$ _____

23. The table shows a gym class's average results for boys and girls participating in the long jump.

Gender	Distance
Male	10 ft 6 in.
Female	8 ft 4 in.

Susan could jump no farther than 4 inches more than the average distance for females. If j represents the distance Susan could jump, which of the following best represents that sentence?

Ⓐ $j \leq 8$ ft 8 in.   Ⓒ $j \leq 8$ ft

Ⓑ $j \geq 8$ ft 8 in.   Ⓓ $j \geq 8$ ft

24. Which of the following values of x make the inequality a true statement?

$$x + 8 > 14$$

Ⓕ $x > 6$ Ⓗ $x \leq 22$

Ⓖ $x \geq 6$ Ⓘ $x < 22$

25. Which of the following inequalities represents the number line?

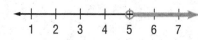

Ⓐ $y + 1 > 6$ Ⓒ $y + 1 \geq 5$

Ⓑ $y + 1 < 6$ Ⓓ $y + 1 \leq 5$

26. Short Response Look at the inequalities shown below. What value, to the hundredths place, could n represent to make both inequalities true statements?

$n > 0.45$ $n < 0.47$

Multiply. MCC4.NBT.5, MCC5.NBT.7

27. $12 \times 12 = $ _____

28. $9 \times 13 = $ _____

29. $16 \times 12 = $ _____

30. $8.5 \times 6 = $ _____

31. $13.2 \times 5 = $ _____

32. $7 \times 11.5 = $ _____

33. Mitchell is painting several boards for scenery for the school play.

What is the area of the board shown? MCC4.MD.3 _____

5 ft

3 ft

34. Daphne is painting her room. She knows that three of her bedroom walls are a total of 305 square feet. The fourth wall in her room measures 8 feet wide and 10 feet tall. How much total area will

Daphne need to paint? MCC4.MD.3 _____

21ST CENTURY CAREER
in Atmospheric Science

Meteorologist

Have you ever wondered how forecasters can predict severe storms such as hurricanes before they occur? Keeping track of changes in air pressure is one method that they use. Meteorologists study Earth's air pressure, temperature, humidity, and wind velocity. They use complex computer models to process and analyze weather data and to make accurate forecasts. In addition to understanding the processes of Earth's atmosphere, meteorologists must have a solid background in mathematics, computer science, and physics.

College & Career
R E A D I N E S S

Explore college and careers at ccr.mcgraw-hill.com

Is This the Career for You?

Are you interested in a career as a meteorologist? Take some of the following courses in high school.

◆ Algebra
◆ Calculus
◆ Earth and Its Environment
◆ Environmental Science
◆ Physics

Turn the page to find out how math relates to a career in Atmospheric Science.

The Pressure is On!

Use the information in the diagram and the table to solve each problem.

1. Write an inequality representing the temperature t of the ocean water during the formation of a hurricane. _____

2. Write an inequality representing the depth d of the water that must be greater than 80°F in order for a hurricane to form. _____

3. The air needs to be humid up to about 18,000 feet for a hurricane to form. Write an inequality to represent this altitude a of the air above the ocean. _____

4. Air pressure decreases during a storm. The difference between the normal air pressure n and the air pressure during the 1935 Florida Keys hurricane was greater than 121 millibars. Write and solve an inequality to find the normal air pressure in the Florida Keys before the hurricane.

5. The air pressure of Hurricane Katrina at landfall was greater than 17 millibars plus the air pressure p before landfall. Write and solve an inequality to find the air pressure of the storm before landfall.

_____

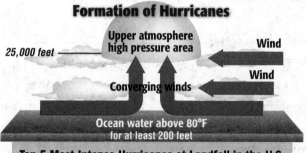

Formation of Hurricanes

Upper atmosphere high pressure area

25,000 feet

Wind

Wind

Converging winds

Ocean water above 80°F for at least 200 feet

Top 5 Most Intense Hurricanes at Landfall in the U.S.

Rank	Hurricane	Pressure (millibars)
1	Florida Keys, (Labor Day), 1935	892
2	Hurricane Camille, 1969	909
3	Hurricane Katrina, 2005	920
4	Hurricane Andrew, 1992	922
5	Texas (Indianola), 1886	925

Career Project

It's time to update your career portfolio! Interview a meteorologist at a local television station. Be sure to ask what he or she likes most about being a meteorologist and what is most challenging. Include all the interview questions and answers in your portfolio.

What skills would you need to improve to succeed in this career?

- _____
- _____
- _____
- _____
- _____

Vocabulary Check

Write the correct term for each clue in the crossword puzzle.

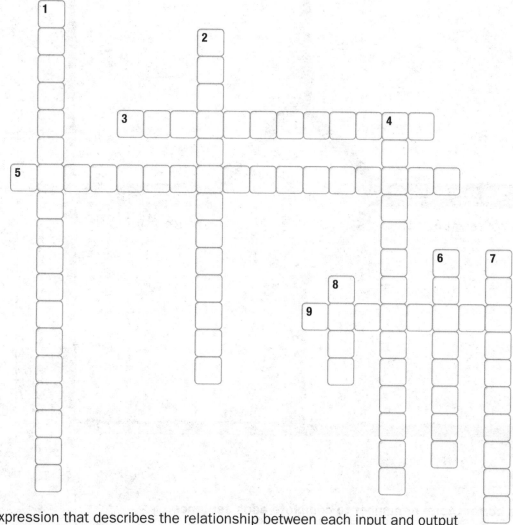

Across

3. an expression that describes the relationship between each input and output

5. found by multiplying the previous term by the same number

9. a list of numbers in a specific order

Down

1. found by adding the same number to the previous term

2. a table organizing the input, rule, and output of a function

4. a function that forms a line when graphed

6. a relationship that assigns exactly one output value to one input value

7. a mathematical sentence indicating that two quantities are not equal

8. each number in a sequence

Use Your FOLDABLES®

Use your Foldable to help review the chapter.

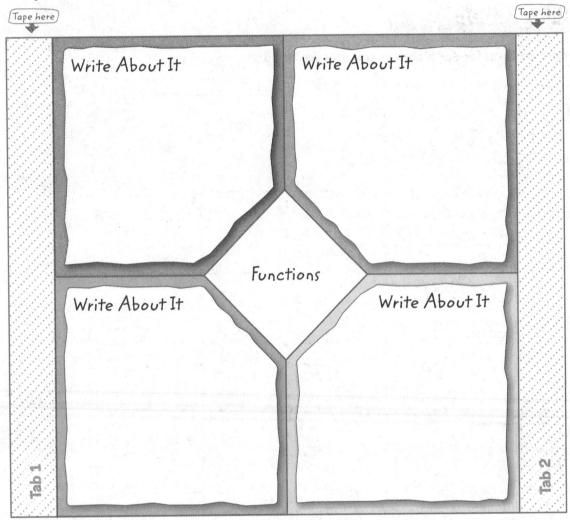

Tape here

Tape here

Write About It

Write About It

Functions

Write About It

Write About It

Tab 1

Tab 2

Got it?

Circle the correct term or number to complete each sentence.

1. The next number in the sequence 12, 15, 18, 21, . . . is (24, 27).

2. The output of a function is the (independent, dependent) variable.

3. A(n) (arithmetic, geometric) sequence can be found by multiplying each previous term by the same number.

4. The input of a function is the (independent, dependent) variable.

5. A(n)(inequality, function) is a relation that assigns exactly one output value to one input value.

Problem Solving

1. A bowling alley charges $4 per game. The function rule that represents this situation is $4n$, where n is the number of games. Make a table to find how much it would cost to bowl 1, 2, and 3 games. (Lesson 1)

Games (n)	4(n)	Cost (t)

2. Tina drove 60 miles per hour to Tucson. Write a function rule that relates the number of miles traveled to the hours driven. (Lesson 2) _____

_____

3. The Pizza Place is running a special for large pizzas. The cost of different numbers of pizzas is shown in the table. Write an equation to find the total cost t for a number of pizzas p. (Lesson 3) _____

Number of Pizzas, p	1	2	3	4
Total Cost, t ($)	10	20	30	40

_____

4. A baker used 16 ounces of butter for every batch of dough pretzels. Make a function table to show the relationship between the amount of butter b and the total batches of pretzels p. Write an equation to represent the situation. (Lesson 4)

Batches of Pretzels (p)	Butter (b)

_____

5. Valerie earns $25 a day plus $3 for each dog she washes. Make a function table to show the relationship between the number of dogs she washed d and the total amount earned t in one day. Write an equation to represent the situation. (Lesson 4)

Number of Dogs Washed (d)	Total Earned (t)

_____

6. In order for an entire class to fit into a certain theater, there must be less than 34 students in the class. Use the inequality $c < 34$, where c is the class size to determine which classes fit in the theater. (Lesson 5)

Homeroom	Size
101	34
102	30
103	32
104	35

_____

7. **CCGPS** **Reason Abstractly** Vincent spends $4 to play a ring toss game at the fair. If he has at most $12, write and solve an inequality to find how many games of ring toss he can play. (Lessons 6 and 7)

_____

Reflect

 Answering the Essential Question

Use what you learned about inequalities to complete the graphic organizer.

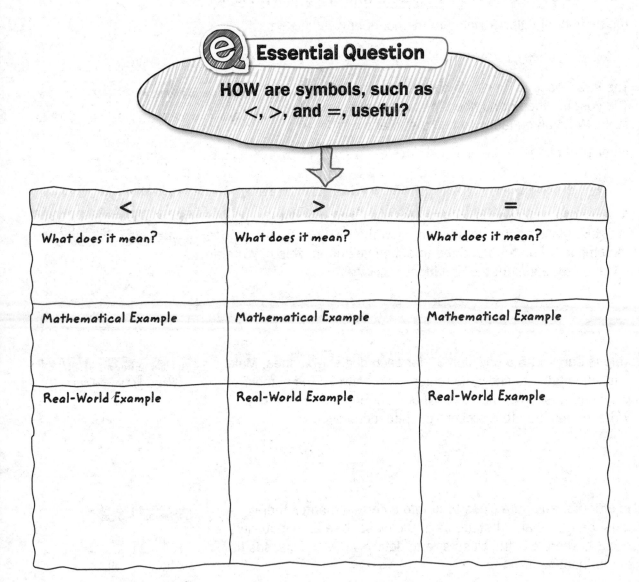

Essential Question

HOW are symbols, such as
<, >, and =, useful?

<	>	=
What does it mean?	What does it mean?	What does it mean?
Mathematical Example	Mathematical Example	Mathematical Example
Real-World Example	Real-World Example	Real-World Example

 Answer the Essential Question. HOW are symbols, such as <, >, and =, useful?

_____

_____

_____

UNIT 5

CCGPS Area and Volume

Essential Question

HOW can you use different measurements to solve real-life problems?

Chapter 8
Area

A composite figure can be decomposed into triangles and other shapes. In this chapter, you will find the area of triangles, quadrilaterals, and composite figures.

Chapter 9
Volume and Surface Area

Prisms and pyramids are examples of three-dimensional figures. In this chapter, you will find the volume and surface area of three-dimensional figures in the context of solving real-world and mathematical problems.

Chapter 8
Area

Paul Sutherland/National Geographic/Getty Images

 Essential Question

HOW does measurement help you solve problems in everyday life?

 Common Core GPS

Content Standards
MCC6.G.1, MCC6.G.3, MCC6.NS.8

Mathematical Practices
1, 2, 3, 4, 5, 6, 7, 8

 Math in the Real World

Gardens A garden designer plants dahlias in a 5 foot by 3 foot plot. What area of the garden do the dahlias cover? In the diagram below, shade the area covered by dahlias.

Area = _____

FOLDABLES
Study Organizer

 Cut out the correct Foldable from the FL pages in the back of this book.

 Place your Foldable on the Key Concept page toward the end of this chapter.

 Use the Foldable throughout this chapter to help you learn about area.

What Tools Do You Need?

Vocabulary

base

composite figure

congruent

formula

height

parallelogram

polygon

rhombus

Review Vocabulary

Using a graphic organizer can help you to remember important vocabulary terms. Fill in the graphic organizer below for the word *area*.

Area

Definition

Units of Measure

Real-World Examples

Try the Quick Check below.
Or, take the Online Readiness Quiz.

Check ✓

Example 1

Find the area of the rectangle.

6 ft

9 ft

$A = \ell w$ Area of a rectangle

$A = 9 \cdot 6$ Replace ℓ with 9 and w with 6.

$A = 54$ Multiply.

The area of the rectangle is 54 square feet.

Example 2

Find $\frac{1}{2} \times 16$.

$\frac{1}{2} \times 16 = \frac{1}{2} \times \frac{16}{1}$ Write 16 as $\frac{16}{1}$.

$= \frac{1 \times \overset{8}{\cancel{16}}}{\underset{1}{\cancel{2}} \times 1}$ Divide the numerator and the denominator by 2.

$= \frac{8}{1}$ or 8   Simplify.

Quick Check

Area **Find the area of each rectangle.**

1.   8 cm
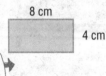
4 cm

Show your work.

2.   6 in.
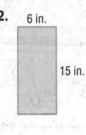
15 in.

3.   3 cm
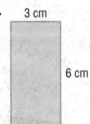
6 cm

4. The playing area of a board game is a rectangle with a length of 14 inches and a width of 20 inches. What is the area of the board game? _____

Fractions **Multiply. Write in simplest form.**

5. $\frac{1}{2} \times 28 =$ _____

6. $\frac{1}{3} \times 27 =$ _____

7. $\frac{1}{7} \times 84 =$ _____

How Did You Do?

Which problems did you answer correctly in the Quick Check?
Shade those exercise numbers below.

① ② ③ ④ ⑤ ⑥ ⑦

HOW does finding the area of a parallelogram relate to finding the area of a rectangle?

 Content Standards
MCC6.G.1

Mathematical Practices
1, 2, 3, 5

Banners Elise wants to make a banner in the shape of a parallelogram. Her parallelogram has a base of 2 feet and a height of 3 feet. What is the area of her parallelogram?

Investigation 1

Another type of quadrilateral is a *parallelogram*. A parallelogram has opposite sides parallel and congruent.

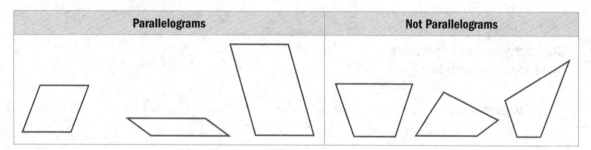

Parallelograms	Not Parallelograms

Make a parallelogram to represent Elise's banner.

Step 1　Start with a rectangle.
Trace the rectangle shown at the right.

3 feet

2 feet

Step 2　Cut a triangle from one side of the rectangle you traced and move it to the other side to form a parallelogram. Tape the parallelogram to the right.

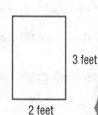

3 feet

2 feet

The rectangle was rearranged to form the parallelogram. Nothing was removed or added, so the parallelogram has _____ area as the rectangle.

Step 3　Find the base and height of the parallelogram to find the area.
The base of the parallelogram is 2 feet and the height is 3 feet.

☐ feet × ☐ feet = ☐ square feet

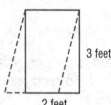
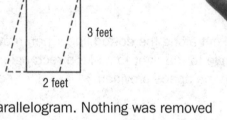

Investigation 2

Find the area of the parallelogram below.

Step 1 Trace the parallelogram on grid paper and cut it out.

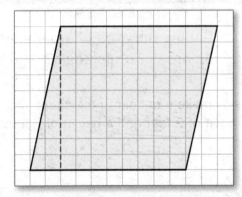

Step 2 Fold and cut along the dotted line.

Step 3 Move the triangle to the right to make a rectangle. Tape the rectangle in the space provided.

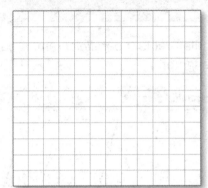

Step 4 Count the number of square units in the rectangle.

The area is ☐ square units.

Investigation 3

Find the area of the parallelogram below.

Step 1 Trace the parallelogram and cut it out.

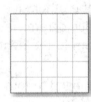

Step 2 Fold and cut along the dotted line. Then move the triangle to the right to make a rectangle. Tape it in the space provided.

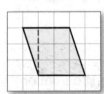

Step 3 Count the number of square units in the rectangle.

The area is ☐ square units.

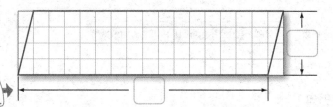
CCGPS Use Math Tools Work with a partner. Find the area of each parallelogram.

1. A = _____ square units

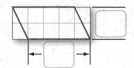
Show your work.

2. A = _____ square units

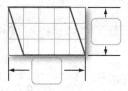

3. A = _____ square units

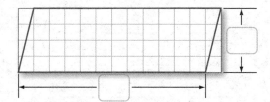

4. A = _____ square units

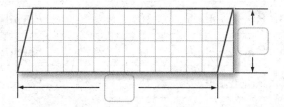

5. A = _____ square units

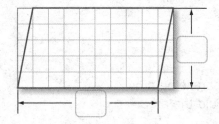

6. A = _____ square units

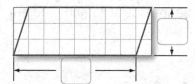

7. A = _____ square units

8. A = _____ square units

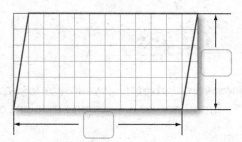

9. A = _____ square units

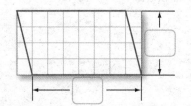

10. A = _____ square units

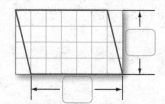

The table shows the dimensions of several rectangles and the corresponding dimensions of several parallelograms if each rectangle was rearranged to form a parallelogram. Work with a partner to complete the table. The first one is done for you.

	Rectangle	Length (ℓ)	Width (w)	Parallelogram	Base (b)	Height (h)	Area (units²)
	Rectangle 1	6	2	Parallelogram 1	6	2	12
11.	Rectangle 2	12	4	Parallelogram 2			
12.	Rectangle 3	7	3	Parallelogram 3			
13.	Rectangle 4	5	4	Parallelogram 4			
14.	Rectangle 5	10	6	Parallelogram 5			
15.	Rectangle 6	6	4	Parallelogram 6			
16.	Rectangle 7	15	9	Parallelogram 7			
17.	Rectangle 8	9	3	Parallelogram 8			

18. A rectangle was rearranged to form a parallelogram. How is the height of the parallelogram similar to and different from the width of the rectangle?

_____

_____

19. CCGPS **Reason Inductively** Write a rule that gives the area of a parallelogram.

_____

 Reflect

20. CCGPS **Reason Abstractly** If you were to draw three different parallelograms each with a base of 6 units and a height of 4 units, how would the areas

compare? _____

21. (inquiry) HOW does finding the area of a parallelogram relate to finding the area of a rectangle?

_____

_____

_____

Area of Parallelograms

What You'll Learn

Scan the lesson. List two headings you would use to make an outline of the lesson.

- _____
- _____

Essential Question

HOW does measurement help you solve problems in everyday life?

 Vocabulary

polygon
parallelogram
rhombus
base
height
formula

Common Core GPS

Content Standards
MCC6.G.1
Mathematical Practices
1, 3, 4, 7

Vocabulary Start-Up

A **polygon** is a closed figure formed by 3 or more straight lines. A **parallelogram** is a quadrilateral with opposite sides parallel and opposite sides the same length. A **rhombus** is a parallelogram with four equal sides. Fill in the lines in the diagram with polygon, parallelogram, or rhombus and draw an example of each.

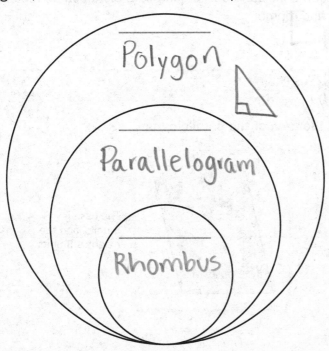

Polygon

Parallelogram

Rhombus

Real-World Link

Stairs Expert skateboarders can slide down the railings of stairs safely. A parallelogram is used to build a staircase. How many sets of parallel lines are shown in the parallelogram to the right?

_____

Area of a Parallelogram

Watch

Words   The area A of a parallelogram is the product of its base b and its height h.

Model

Symbols $A = bh$

The area of a parallelogram is related to the area of a rectangle as you discovered in the previous Inquiry Lab.

The **base** of a parallelogram can be any one of its sides.

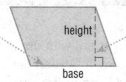

The **height** is the perpendicular distance from the base to the opposite side.

Parallelograms include special quadrilaterals, such as rectangles, squares, and rhombi.

Examples

Tutor

1. **Find the area of the parallelogram.**

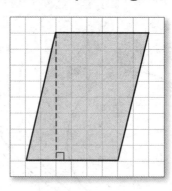

The base is 6 units, and the height is 8 units.

$A = bh$ Area of parallelogram

$A = 6 \cdot 8$ Replace b with 6 and h with 8.

$A = 48$ Multiply.

The area is 48 square units or 48 units^2.

Area Measurement

An area measurement can be written using abbreviations and an exponent of 2.

For example:

square units = units^2

square inches = in^2

square feet = ft^2

square meters = m^2

---

2. Find the area of the parallelogram.

Estimate $A \approx 20 \cdot 10$ or $200 \ cm^2$

11 cm   13 cm

20 cm

$A = bh$ Area of parallelogram

$A = 20 \cdot 11$ Replace b with 20 and h with 11.

$A = 220$ Check for Reasonableness $220 \approx 200$ ✓

The area is 220 square centimeters or 220 cm^2.

Got It? Do these problems to find out.

a.

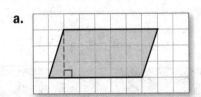

b.

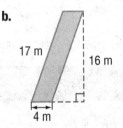

17 m   16 m

4 m

Show your work.

a. _____

b. _____

Find Missing Dimensions

A **formula** is an equation that shows a relationship among certain quantities. To find missing dimensions, use the formula for the area of a parallelogram. Replace the variables with the known measurements. Then solve the equation for the remaining variable.

Example

Tutor

3. Find the missing dimension of the parallelogram.

$A = bh$ Area of a parallelogram

$45 = 9 \cdot h$ Replace A with 45 and b with 9.

$\dfrac{45}{9} = \dfrac{9 \cdot h}{9}$ Divide each side by 9.

$5 = h$ Simplify.

So, the height is 5 inches.

9 in.

$A = 45 \ in^2$

Checking Your Work

To check your work, replace b and h in the formula with 9 and 5.

$A = bh$
$A = 9 \cdot 5$
$A = 45$ ✓

Got It? Do these problems to find out.

c.

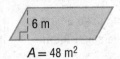

6 m

$A = 48 \ m^2$

d.

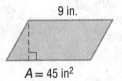

8 yd $A = 96 \ yd^2$

c. _____

d. _____

Height of Parallelograms

For the parallelogram formed by the area shaded black in Example 4, its height, 12 inches, is labeled outside the parallelogram.

 Example

4. Romilla is painting a replica of the national flag of Trinidad and Tobago for a research project. Find the area of the black stripe.

The black stripe is shaped like a parallelogram. So, use the formula $A = bh$.

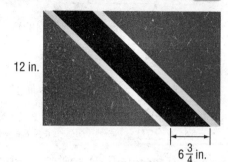

12 in.

$6\frac{3}{4}$ in.

$A = bh$ Area of parallelogram

$A = 6\frac{3}{4} \cdot 12$ Replace b with $6\frac{3}{4}$ and h with 12.

$A = 81$ $6\frac{3}{4} \cdot 12 = \frac{27}{4} \cdot 12$, or 81

The area of the flag that is black is 81 square inches.

Guided Practice

Check

Find the area of each parallelogram. (Examples 1 and 2)

1. 12 units

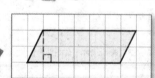

Show your work.

2. 50 ft

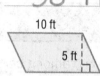

10 ft

5 ft

3. 88m

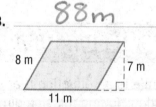

8 m

7 m

11 m

4. Find the height of a parallelogram if its base is 35 centimeters and its area is 700 square centimeters.

(Example 3)   20 cm

5. The size of the parallelogram piece in a set of tangrams is shown at the right. Find the area of the piece. (Example 4)

15.6 cm

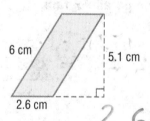

6 cm

5.1 cm

2.6 cm

6. **Building on the Essential Question** How are parallelograms related to triangles and rectangles?

$\begin{array}{r} 2\;\;6 \\ 3\;\;6 \\ \hline 15\;6 \end{array}$

Rate Yourself!

How confident are you about the area of parallelograms? Shade the ring on the target.

I'm on target.

I need help.

For more help, go online to access a Personal Tutor.

Tutor

FOLDABLES Time to update your Foldable!

Independent Practice

Go online for Step-by-Step Solutions

Find the area of each parallelogram. (Examples 1 and 2)

1. _____ 9 units _____

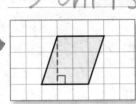

Show your work.

2. base, 6 millimeters; height, 4 millimeters

24 mm

3. _____ 96 cm _____

8 cm

9 cm | 12 cm

4. Find the base of a parallelogram with an area of 24 square feet and height 3 feet. (Example 3) _____ Base is 8 feet. _____

5. Find the area of the parking space shown to the right. (Example 4) 166.5 ft

6. **STEM** An architect designed three different parallelogram-shaped brick patios. Write the missing dimensions in the table.

Patio	Base (ft)	Height (ft)	Area (ft²)
1	$15\frac{3}{4}$	9 1/3	147
2	12 1/2	$11\frac{1}{4}$	$140\frac{5}{8}$
3	$10\frac{1}{4}$	14 3/4	$151\frac{3}{16}$

18 ft

$9\frac{1}{4}$ ft

Show your work.

7. The base of a building is shaped like a parallelogram. The first floor has an area of 20,000 square feet. If the base of this parallelogram is 250 feet, can its height be 70 feet? Explain.

No. 250 × 7 = 17500.
17500 < 20000.

8. **CCGPS Identify Structure** Draw and label a parallelogram with a base twice as long as the height and an area less than 60 square inches. Find the area. 54 in²

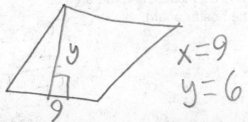

y

9

x=9
y=6

9. **CCGPS** **Multiple Representations** Draw five parallelograms that each have a height of 4 centimeters and different base measurements on centimeter grid paper.

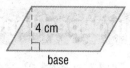
4 cm
base

a. **Table** Make a table with a column for base, height, and area.

Base (cm)	Height (cm)	Area (cm²)
1	4	4
2	4	8
3	4	12
4	4	16
5	4	20

b. **Graph** Graph the ordered pairs (base, area).

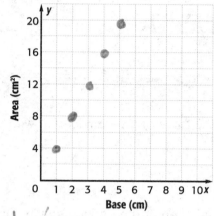

c. **Words** Describe the graph. The graph is a linear function of the form: y=mx

H.O.T. Problems Higher Order Thinking

10. **CCGPS** **Persevere with Problems** If $x = 5$ and $y < x$, which figure has the greater area? Explain your reasoning.

The rectangle has a greater area.

11. **CCGPS** **Reason Inductively** Explain how the formula for the area of a parallelogram is related to the formula for the area of a rectangle.

Both of them have the same formula, a=bh.

Georgia Test Practice

12. Robert used a piece of poster board shaped like a parallelogram to make a sign. The base of the poster board is 52 inches, and the area is 1,872 square inches. Find the height of the poster board.

Ⓐ 884 in.   Ⓒ 42 in.

Ⓑ 176 in.   Ⓓ 36 in.

Extra Practice

Find the area of each parallelogram.

13. 20 units²

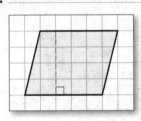

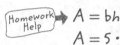

$A = bh$
$A = 5 \cdot 4$
$A = 20$

14. 48m²

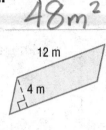

12 m

4 m

15. base, 12 inches; height, 15 inches

180 in²

16. Find the height of a parallelogram with base 6.75 meters and an area of 218.7 square meters.

32.4 m

17. Find the area of a parallelogram with base 15 yards and height $21\frac{2}{3}$ yards.

325 yd

18. What is the area of the region shown on the map? 2985.9375 mi²

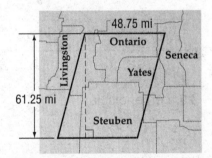

19. What is the height of the parallelogram-shaped pattern block shown below?

25 mm - height

$A = 525$ mm²

21 mm

Draw and label each figure. Then find the area.

20. a parallelogram with an equal base and height and an area greater than 64 square meters

9 = base
9 = height

21. a parallelogram with a base four times the height and an area less than 200 square feet

base = 16
height = 4

CCGPS Identify Structure Find the area of the shaded region in each figure.

22. 227 ft²

275
48
227

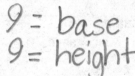

25 ft

4 ft

11 ft

12 ft

23. _____

120
36

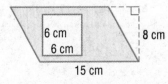

6 cm
6 cm

8 cm

15 cm

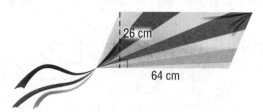

24. The kite is in the shape of a parallelogram. What is the area of the kite shown below?

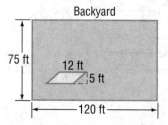

26 cm

64 cm

Ⓐ 8.32 cm²

Ⓑ 16.64 cm²

Ⓒ 832 cm²

Ⓓ 1,664 cm²

25. A family has a flower garden in the shape of a parallelogram in their backyard. They planted grass in the rest of the yard. What is the area of the backyard that is planted with grass?

Backyard

75 ft

12 ft

5 ft

120 ft

Ⓕ 390 sq ft

Ⓖ 8,940 sq ft

Ⓗ 9,060 sq ft

Ⓘ 9,144 sq ft

26. Short Response A wallpaper design uses 15 parallelogram-shaped pieces of paper, each with a base of 3 inches and a height of 2 inches. How much paper is used to make the 15 pieces?

90 pcs

Draw each pair of lines. MCC4.G.1

27. parallel

28. intersecting

29. perpendicular

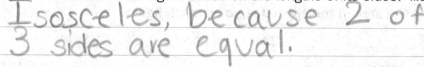

30. Rosa has 22 songs in her music library. Michael has half as many. How many songs does Michael have in his music library? MCC4.NBT.6

11 songs

31. Name and describe the figure based on the lengths of its sides. MCC5.G.4

Isosceles, because 2 of 3 sides are equal.

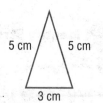

5 cm   5 cm

3 cm

Inquiry HOW can you use the area of a parallelogram to find the area of a triangle?

 Content Standards
MCC6.G.1
Mathematical Practices
1, 3, 7, 8

Art Yurri is making a mosaic and is cutting rectangular tiles to make triangular tiles. He wants to find the area of the triangular tiles he is cutting.

What do you know? _____

_____

What do you need to know? _____

_____

Investigation 1

 Watch ▶

Yurri starts with a rectangular piece that is 4 inches by 6 inches, similar to the size of an index card.

Step 1 Find the area of an index card.

A = length × width

A = ⬚ inches × ⬚ inches

A = ⬚ square inches

4 in.

6 in.

Step 2 Use an index card. Draw a diagonal line across your index card from one corner to another. Then cut across the line. Draw the resulting figures in the space below.

 Show your work. ➡

Step 3 Find the area of one of the remaining triangles. The triangle is exactly half the size of the related rectangle.

So, the area of the rectangle can be divided by 2 to find the area of one triangle.

The area is ⬚ ÷ 2, or ⬚ square inches.

You can also find the area of a triangle from the area of a related parallelogram.

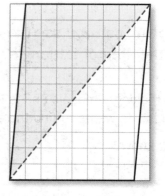

Step 1	Copy the parallelogram shown on grid paper.

Step 2	Draw a diagonal as shown by the dashed line. Cut out the parallelogram. The area of the parallelogram is _____ square units.

Step 3	Cut along the diagonal to form two triangles. Then find the area of one triangle. The triangle is half the size of the parallelogram. So, the area of the parallelogram can be divided by 2 to find the area of one triangle.

The area of one triangle is _____ ÷ 2 or _____ square units.

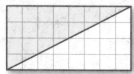 Collaborate

Work with a partner to find the area of each shaded triangle.

1.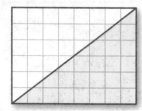

length: _____

width: _____

area: _____ × _____ = _____

area of triangle = _____ square units

2.

base: _____

height: _____

area: _____ × _____ = _____

area of triangle = _____ square units

3.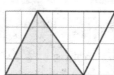

length: _____

width: _____

area: _____ × _____ = _____

area of triangle = _____ square units

4.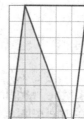

base: _____

height: _____

area: _____ × _____ = _____

area of triangle = _____ square units

Work with a partner to find the area of each shaded triangle.

5. $A =$ _____ square feet

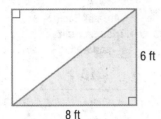

6 ft

8 ft

6. $A =$ _____ square meters

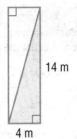

14 m

4 m

7. $A =$ _____ square centimeters

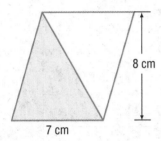

8 cm

7 cm

8. $A =$ _____ square feet

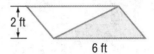

2 ft

6 ft

CCGPS **Identify Structure** Draw dotted lines to show the parallelogram or rectangle that can be used to find the area of each triangle. Then find the area of each triangle.

9. $A =$ _____ square inches

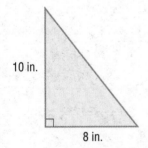

10 in.

8 in.

10. $A =$ _____ square yards

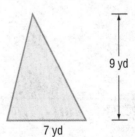

9 yd

7 yd

11. $A =$ _____ square centimeters

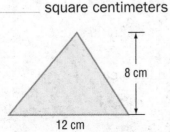

8 cm

12 cm

12. $A =$ _____ square feet

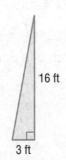

16 ft

3 ft

The table shows the dimensions of several parallelograms. Use the area of each parallelogram to find the missing information for each triangle. Work with a partner to complete the table. The first one is already done for you.

	Parallelogram	Base, b	Height, h	Area of Parallelogram (units squared)	Triangle created with diagonal	Base, b	Height, h	Area of Each Triangle (units squared)
	A	4	5	20	A	4	5	10
13.	B	4	6		B	4		12
14.	C	2	5		C	2	5	
15.	D	3	4		D	3	4	
16.	E	6	3		E		3	9
17.	F	8	5		F	8	5	
18.	G	5	7		G	5		17.5
19.	H	9	7		H	9	7	
20.	I	11	5		I	11	5	

21. CCGPS **Reason Inductively** How is the area of the parallelogram related to the area of a triangle with the same base and height?

_____

_____

_____

 **Reflect**

22. CCGPS **Identify Repeated Reasoning** Write a formula that relates the area A of a triangle to the lengths of its base b and height h.

_____

23. **Inquiry** HOW can you use the area of a parallelogram to find the area of a triangle?

_____

_____

_____

Area of Triangles

What You'll Learn

Scan the lesson. Predict two things you will learn about finding the area of triangles.

- _____

- _____

 Essential Question

HOW does measurement help you solve problems in everyday life?

 Vocabulary

congruent

 Common Core GPS

Content Standards
MCC6.G.1

Mathematical Practices
1, 3, 4, 8

 Real-World Link Watch ▶

Biosphere The Biosphere 2 complex in Tucson, Arizona, researches Earth and its living systems. Sections of the building are interlocking triangles of the same size.

1. There are two triangles that are outlined in the photo.

   They have the _____ size and the _____ shape.

2. Draw the figure formed by the two triangles.

 Show your work.

3. How many small triangles make up the outlined parallelogram? How many small triangles make

   up each outlined triangle? _____

4. Describe the relationship between the area of one outlined triangle and the area of the outlined parallelogram.

   _____

5. Draw another parallelogram like the one in the photo. Separate it into two triangles. Describe the relationship between the area of

   one triangle and the parallelogram. _____

   _____

Show your work.

Area of a Triangle

Work Zone

Words The area *A* of a triangle is one half the product of the base *b* and its height *h*.

Model

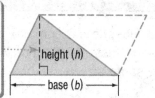

Symbols $A = \frac{1}{2}bh$ or $A = \frac{bh}{2}$

Congruent figures are figures that are the same shape and size.

A parallelogram can be formed by two congruent triangles. Since congruent triangles have the same area, the area of a triangle is one half the area of the parallelogram.

The base of a triangle can be any one of its sides. The height is the perpendicular distance from that base to the opposite vertex.

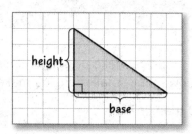

height (*h*)

base (*b*)

Examples

Watch Tutor

1. Find the area of the triangle.

height

base

By counting, you find that the measure of the base is 6 units and the height is 4 units.

$A = \frac{1}{2}bh$ Area of a triangle

$A = \frac{1}{2}(6)(4)$ Replace *b* with 6 and *h* with 4.

$A = \frac{1}{2}(24)$ Multiply.

$A = 12$ Multiply.

The area of the triangle is 12 square units.

Mental Math

You can use mental math to multiply $\frac{1}{2}(6)(4)$. Think: Half of 6 is 3, and 3×4 is 12.

2. Find the area of the triangle.

$$A = \frac{1}{2}bh \qquad \text{Area of a triangle}$$

$$A = \frac{1}{2}(12.1)(6.4) \qquad \text{Replace } b \text{ with 12.1 and } h \text{ with 6.4.}$$

$$A = \frac{1}{2}(77.44) \qquad \text{Multiply.}$$

$$A = 38.72 \qquad \text{Divide. } \frac{1}{2}(77.44) = 77.44 \div 2, \text{ or } 38.72$$

12.1 m

6.4 m

The area of the triangle is 38.72 square meters.

Got It? Do these problems to find out.

a.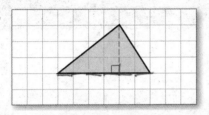

b.
9 ft

7 ft

a. $9 \; ft^2$

b. $31.5 \; ft^2$

Find Missing Dimensions

Use the formula for the area of a triangle to find missing dimensions.

Example

Tutor

3. Find the missing dimension of the triangle.

$$A = \frac{bh}{2} \qquad \text{Area of a triangle}$$

$$24 = \frac{b \cdot 6}{2} \qquad \text{Replace } A \text{ with 24 and } h \text{ with 6.}$$

$$24(2) = \frac{b \cdot 6}{2}(2) \qquad \text{Multiply each side by 2.}$$

$$48 = b \cdot 6 \qquad \text{Simplify.}$$

$$\frac{48}{6} = \frac{b \cdot 6}{6} \qquad \text{Divide each side by 6.}$$

$$8 = b \qquad \text{Simplify.}$$

6 cm

b

$A = 24 \; cm^2$

So, the base is 8 centimeters.

Check for Reasonableness
To check your work, replace b and h with the measurements and solve to find the area.

Got It? Do these problems to find out.

c.
$A = 40 \; m^2$

8 m

b

d.
$A = 72 \; yd^2$

h

12 yd

c. $10 \; in$

d. $12 \; in$

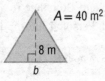

Example

4. The front of a camping tent has the dimensions shown. How much material was used to make the front of the tent?

3 ft
5 ft

$A = \frac{1}{2}bh$ Area of a triangle

$A = \frac{1}{2}(5)(3)$ Replace b with 5 and h with 3.

$A = \frac{1}{2}(15)$ or 7.5   Multiply.

The front of the tent has an area of 7.5 square feet.

Guided Practice

Check ✓

Find the area of each triangle. (Examples 1 and 2)

1. 6 units²

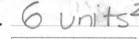

2. 48 ft²

8 ft
12 ft

3. 88 ft²

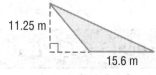

11.25 m
15.6 m

$2\overline{)176}$

Show your work.

4. Tayshan designs uniquely shaped ceramic floor tiles. What is the base of the tile shown? (Example 3)

7 in

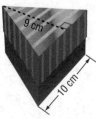

b
6 in.
$A = 21$ in²

5. Consuela made a triangular paper box as shown. What is the area of the top of the box? (Example 4)

45 cm²

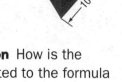

9 cm
10 cm

Rate Yourself!

✓ I understand how to find the area of a triangle.

▶▶ Great! You're ready to move on!

☐ I still have some questions about the area of a triangle.

6. **Building on the Essential Question** How is the formula for the area of a triangle related to the formula for the area of a parallelogram?

It is the same formula except divide by 2.

⫴ No Problem! Go online to access a Personal Tutor.

Tutor

FOLDABLES Time to update your Foldable!

Name _____ My Homework _____

Find the area of each triangle. (Examples 1 and 2)

1. __24 units²__

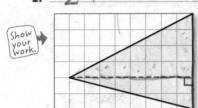

Show your work.

2. __200 cm²__

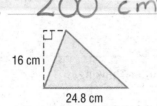

16 cm
24.8 cm

3. __1206 cm²__

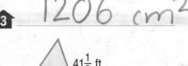

36 ft   41½ ft

(40×30)
1200
(1×6)
6

Find the missing dimension of each triangle described. (Example 3)

4. height: 14 in.
   area: 245 in²

   __37 in - base__

5. base: 27 cm
   area: 256.5 cm²

   __19 in - height__

6. Ansley is going to help his father shingle the roof of their house. What is the area of the triangular portion of one end of the roof? (Example 4)

   __14 sq. yd (14y²)__

4 yd
7 yd

7. CCPS **Multiple Representations** The table shows the areas of a triangle where the base of the triangle stays the same but the height changes.

a. **Algebra** Write an algebraic expression that can be used to find the area of a triangle that has a base of 5 units and a height of *n* units. __5 · n__

b. **Graph** Graph the ordered pairs (height, area).

Area of Triangles		
Base (units)	Height (units)	Area (units²)
5	2	5
5	4	10
5	6	15
5	8	20
5	*n*	?

(graph with y-axis marked 3, 6, 9, 12, 15, 18, 21, 24, 27, 30 and x-axis marked 1–10)

c. **Words** Describe the graph.

__As the height goes up by 2, the area is divided by 2.__

stop

8. What is the area of the triangle on the flag of the Philippines in inches? _45 square inches_

30 in.

3 ft

5 ft

9. CCGPS **Find the Error** Dwayne is finding the base of the triangle shown. Its area is 100 square meters. Find his mistake and correct it.

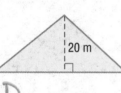

20 m

$$100 = (b)20$$
$$100 = 20b$$
$$5 = b$$

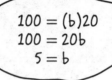

Dwayne should know that a = 1/2 bh.

10. CCGPS **Persevere with Problems** How can you use triangles to find the area of the hexagon shown? Draw a diagram to support your answer.

I can use 6 triangles.

11. CCGPS **Identify Repeated Reasoning** Draw a triangle and label its base and height. Draw another triangle that has the same base, but a height twice that of the first triangle. Find the area of each triangle. Then write a ratio that expresses the area of the first triangle to the area of the second triangle.

The 2 triangles make a rectangle.

12. A piece of metal is cut in the shape of the triangle below. What is the area of the piece of metal?

Ⓐ $3\frac{1}{4}$ ft^2

Ⓑ $4\frac{1}{2}$ ft^2

Ⓒ $6\frac{3}{8}$ ft^2

Ⓓ 9 ft^2

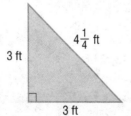

$4\frac{1}{4}$ ft

3 ft

3 ft

Extra Practice

Find the area of each triangle.

13. $7\frac{1}{2}$ units²

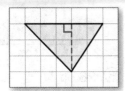

$A = \dfrac{bh}{2}$

$A = \dfrac{5 \cdot 3}{2}$

$A = \dfrac{15}{2}$ or $7\frac{1}{2}$

14. 45 sq in

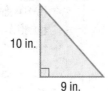

10 in.

9 in.

15. 87.5 m²

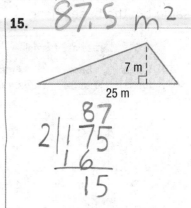

7 m

25 m

$$2\overline{\smash{\big)}\,\begin{array}{r}87\\175\\\underline{16}\\15\end{array}}$$

Find the missing dimension of each triangle described.

16. height: 7 in., area: 21 in²

6 – width

17. base: 11 m, area: 115.5 m²

21 m

18. base: 14.2 yd, area: 63.9 yd²

5 yds

19. height: 11 cm, area: 260.15 cm²

47.3 cm

20. **STEM** An architect is designing a building on a triangular plot of land. If the base of the triangle is 100.8 feet and the height is 96.3 feet, find the available floor area of the building.

4800 sq ft

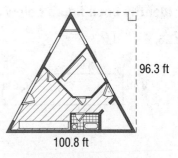

96.3 ft

100.8 ft

21. A flower bed in a parking lot is shaped like a triangle as shown.

   a. Find the area of the flower bed in square feet.

3 yd²

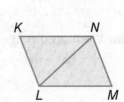

3 yd

2 yd

   b. If one bag of topsoil covers 10 square feet, how many bags are needed to cover this flower bed?

2.7 bags

22. **CCGPS** **Identify Repeated Reasoning** Refer to parallelogram *KLMN* at the right. If the area of parallelogram *KLMN* is 35 square inches, what is the area of triangle *KLN*?

—

K   N

L   M

Georgia Test Practice

23. The table shows the areas of a triangle where the height of the triangle stays the same but the base changes.

Areas of Triangles		
Height (units)	Base (units)	Area (square units)
7	2	7
7	3	$10\frac{1}{2}$
7	4	14
7	5	$17\frac{1}{2}$
7	x	?

Which expression can be used to find the area of a triangle that has a height of 7 units and a base of x units?

Ⓐ $7x$

Ⓑ $\frac{7x}{2}$

Ⓒ $\frac{7}{2}$

Ⓓ $\frac{x}{2}$

24. Norma cut a triangle out of construction paper for an art project. The area of the triangle is 84.5 square centimeters. What is the height of the triangle?

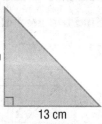
h cm
13 cm

Ⓕ 6.5 cm

Ⓖ 13 cm

Ⓗ 26 cm

Ⓙ 169 cm

25. Short Response The triangle has an area of 640 square millimeters. What is the base of the triangle? _____

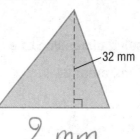
32 mm

9 mm

CCGPS Common Core Review

Identify each figure below as a *rectangle, rhombus,* or *trapezoid.* MCC5.G.4

26. _trapezoid_

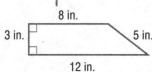
8 in.
3 in.
5 in.
12 in.

27. _rectangle_

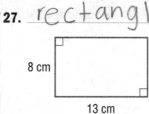
8 cm
13 cm

28. _rhombus_

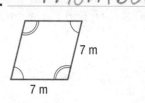
7 m
7 m

29. Jackson's floor rug has four 90° angles. All four sides are 18 inches long. The rug has two sets of parallel sides. What shape is Jackson's floor rug?

MCC5.G.4 _Square_

30. How many lines of symmetry can be drawn for the figure shown? Draw them on the figure. MCC4.G.3 _1 line_

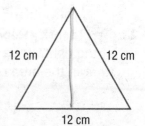
12 cm
12 cm
12 cm

inquiry HOW can you use the area of a parallelogram to find the area of a corresponding trapezoid?

CCGPS Content Standards
MCC6.G.1

Mathematical Practices
1, 3, 5, 7

Garden Lizette is building a garden in the shape of a trapezoid. The garden is 6 feet wide in the back, 10 feet wide in the front, and 5 feet from back to front. She wants to find the area of the garden.

Investigation 1

Find the area of a trapezoid by drawing the related parallelogram.

Step 1 Trace the trapezoid below on grid paper. Label the height h and label the bases b_1 and b_2.

A trapezoid has two bases, b_1 and b_2. The height h of a trapezoid is the perpendicular distance between the bases.

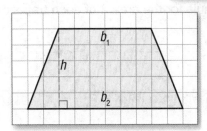

The shorter base b_1 represents the garden width of _back_.

The longer base b_2 represents the garden width of _front_.

The height h represents the garden dimension of _____.

Step 2 Cut out another trapezoid that is identical to the one in Step 1.

Step 3 Tape the trapezoids together as shown.

Step 4 Find the area of the parallelogram. Then divide by 2 to find the area of each trapezoid.

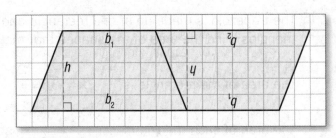

☐ × ☐ = ☐   ☐ ÷ 2 = ☐

So, the area of the garden is ☐ square feet.

Investigation 2

Discover the formula for the area of a trapezoid.

Step 1 What figure is formed by the two trapezoids in

Investigation 1? _____

Write an addition expression to represent the length of the base

of the entire figure. _____

Step 2 Write a formula for the area A of the parallelogram using b_1, b_2,

and h. _____

Step 3 How does the area of each trapezoid compare to the area of the

parallelogram? _____

_____

Step 4 Write a formula for the area A of each trapezoid using b_1, b_2, and h.

_____

Investigation 3

Another way to find the area of a trapezoid is to deconstruct it to determine
which figures form the trapezoid. Find the area of the trapezoid shown below.

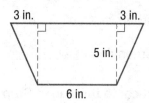

3 in.   3 in.

5 in.

6 in.

Step 1 The trapezoid is made up of one rectangle and two congruent
triangles. Find the area of the shapes that make up the trapezoid.

The area of the rectangle is ☐ × ☐ = ☐ square inches.

The area of each triangle is $\dfrac{☐ \times ☐}{☐}$ = ☐ square inches.

Step 2 Add the areas.

☐ + ☐ + ☐ = ☐ square inches

Collaborate

CCSS Use Math Tools Work with a partner. Find the area of each
trapezoid by drawing the related parallelogram.

1. $A = 40$ _____ square units

2. $A = 9$ _____ square units

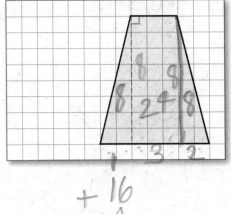

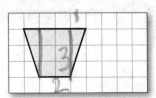

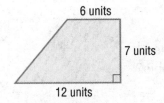

Work with a partner. Find the area of each trapezoid by using the formula.

3. $A = \dfrac{(\boxed{} + \boxed{})\boxed{}}{\boxed{}}$

$A =$ _____ square units

6 units
7 units
12 units

4. $A = \dfrac{(\boxed{} + \boxed{})\boxed{}}{\boxed{}}$

$A =$ _____ square units

11 units
8 units
14 units

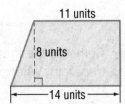

Work with a partner. Decompose each trapezoid to find the area.

5. $A =$ _____ square units

3 units
8 units
7 units

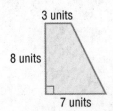

6. $A =$ _____ square units

10 units
9 units
6 units

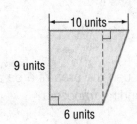

The table shows the dimensions of several parallelograms and corresponding trapezoids. Work with a partner to complete the table. The first one is done for you.

Dimensions of Parallelogram	Area of Parallelogram	Length of Trapezoid b_1	Length of Trapezoid b_2	Trapezoid Height	Area of Trapezoid
4 / 7	28	2	5	4	14
7. 6 / 11		5	6	6	
8. 5 / 12		8	4	5	
9. $b = 11$ $h = 3$		7	4	3	

10. CCGPS **Reason Inductively** Compare the dimensions of the parallelogram to the dimensions of the corresponding trapezoid. What pattern do you see in the table? _____

_____

11. CCGPS **Reason Inductively** Compare the area of the parallelogram to the area of the corresponding trapezoid. What pattern do you see in the table?

_____

_____

 Reflect

12. CCGPS **Identify Structure** Write the formula for the area A of a trapezoid with bases b_1 and b_2 and height h.

_____

_____

13. **inquiry** HOW can you use the area of a parallelogram to find the area of a corresponding trapezoid?

_____

_____

Area of Trapezoids

What You'll Learn

Scan the lesson. Predict two things you will learn about finding the area of trapezoids.

- _____
  _____

- _____
  _____

 Essential Question

HOW does measurement help you solve problems in everyday life?

CCGPS **Common Core GPS**

Content Standards
MCC6.G.1

Mathematical Practices
1, 2, 3, 4, 7, 8

 ## Real-World Link

Window Seat Kiana has a bay window in her room. The window seat is in the shape of a trapezoid. She needs to measure the seat in order to sew a cushion for the seat. The blue trapezoid in the diagram below represents the dimensions of the window seat.

Use the diagram below to describe the relationship between trapezoids and rectangles.

1. Find the dimensions of each figure.

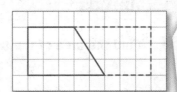

Trapezoid

base 1: ☐ units

base 2: ☐ units

height: ☐ units

Rectangle

length: ☐ units

height: ☐ units

2. What is the relationship between the measures of the rectangle and the measures of the trapezoid?

_____
_____

3. **CCGPS** **Make a Conjecture** How is the area of a trapezoid related to the area of a rectangle? _____

_____
_____

Area of a Trapezoid

Watch

Work Zone

Words   The area A of a trapezoid is one half the product of the height h and the sum of the bases b_1 and b_2.

Model

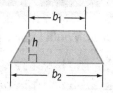

Symbols $A = \frac{1}{2}h(b_1 + b_2)$

A trapezoid has two bases, b_1 and b_2. The height of a trapezoid is the distance between the bases.

The height is the perpendicular distance between the bases.

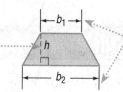

The two bases are parallel. They will always be the same distance apart.

When finding the area of a trapezoid, it is important to follow the order of operations. In the formula, the bases are to be added before multiplying by $\frac{1}{2}$ of the height h.

Examples

Tutor

1. **Find the area of the trapezoid.**

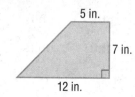

5 in.

7 in.

12 in.

The bases are 5 inches and 12 inches.
The height is 7 inches.

$A = \frac{1}{2}h(b_1 + b_2)$ Area of a trapezoid

$A = \frac{1}{2}(7)(5 + 12)$ Replace h with 7, b_1 with 5, and b_2 with 12.

$A = \frac{1}{2}(7)(17)$ Add 5 and 12.

$A = 59.5$ Multiply.

The area of the trapezoid is 59.5 square inches.

2. Find the area of the trapezoid.

7 m
9.8 m
12 m

$A = \frac{1}{2}h(b_1 + b_2)$ Area of a trapezoid

$A = \frac{1}{2}(9.8)(7 + 12)$ Replace h with 9.8, b_1 with 7, and b_2 with 12.

$A = \frac{1}{2}(9.8)(19)$ Add 7 and 12.

$A = 93.1$ Multiply.

So, the area of the trapezoid is 93.1 square meters.

12.5
24.8
100 0

Got It? Do these problems to find out.

a.
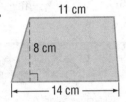
11 cm
8 cm
14 cm

b.
2.5 m
4 m
4.8 m

c.
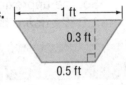
1 ft
0.3 ft
0.5 ft

a. $\underline{100 \ cm^2}$

b. $\underline{14.6 \ m^2}$

c. $\underline{0.2 \ ft^2}$

Find the Missing Height

Use the related formula, $h = \dfrac{2A}{b_1 + b_2}$, to find the height of a trapezoid.

$35\overline{)210}$
6

Example

Tutor

3. The trapezoid has an area of 108 square feet. Find the height.

12 ft
h
15 ft

$h = \dfrac{2A}{b_1 + b_2}$ Height of a trapezoid

$h = \dfrac{2(108)}{12 + 15}$ Replace A with 108, b_1 with 12, and b_2 with 15.

$h = \dfrac{216}{27}$ Multiply 2 and 108. Add 12 and 15.

$h = 8$ Divide.

So, the height of the trapezoid is 8 feet.

Be Precise
Check your answer by using the formula for the area of a trapezoid.

365
224
1460

Got It? Do these problems to find out.

d. $A = 24 \ cm^2$
$b_1 = 4 \ cm$
$b_2 = 12 \ cm$
$h = ?$

e. $A = 21 \ yd^2$
$b_1 = 2 \ yd$
$b_2 = 5 \ yd$
$h = ?$

d. $\underline{3 \ cm}$

e. $\underline{4.2 \ cm}$

Example

Watch | Tutor

4. The shape of Osceola County, Florida, resembles a trapezoid. Find the approximate area of this county.

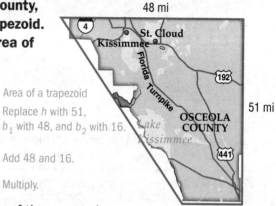

48 mi

51 mi

16 mi

$A = \frac{1}{2}h(b_1 + b_2)$ Area of a trapezoid

$A = \frac{1}{2}(51)(48 + 16)$ Replace h with 51, b_1 with 48, and b_2 with 16.

$A = \frac{1}{2}(51)(64)$ Add 48 and 16.

$A = 1,632$ Multiply.

So, the approximate area of the county is 1,632 square miles.

Mental Math

To multiply $\frac{1}{2}(51)(64)$, it is easier to use the Commutative Property to reorder the factors as $\frac{1}{2}(64)(51)$ and take half of 64 instead of half of 51.

$$\begin{array}{r} 68 \\ 2\overline{)136} \end{array}$$

226
248
1208

Guided Practice

Check ✓

Find the area of each trapezoid. Round to the nearest tenth if necessary. (Examples 1 and 2)

1. **68 m²**

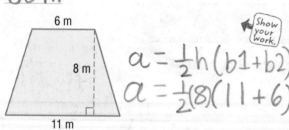

6 m

8 m

11 m

Show your work.

$a = \frac{1}{2}h(b1+b2)$
$a = \frac{1}{2}(8)(11+6)$

2. **6.04 ft²**

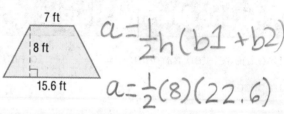

7 ft

8 ft

15.6 ft

$a = \frac{1}{2}h(b1+b2)$
$a = \frac{1}{2}(8)(22.6)$

3. A trapezoid has an area of 15 square feet. If the bases are 4 feet and 6 feet, what is the height of the trapezoid? (Example 3)   **3 feet**

$\frac{1}{2}(46)(11)$

4. In the National Hockey League, goaltenders can play the puck behind the goal line only in a trapezoid-shaped area, as shown at the right. Find the area of the trapezoid. (Example 4)   **253 ft²**

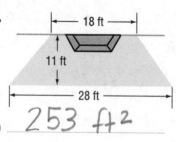

18 ft

11 ft

28 ft

$\frac{1}{2}h(b_1+b_2)$

5.  **Building on the Essential Question** How is the formula for the area of a trapezoid related to the formula for the area of a parallelogram?

Rate Yourself!

Are you ready to move on? Shade the section that applies.

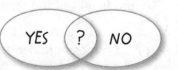

YES   ?   NO

For more help, go online to access a Personal Tutor.

Tutor

FOLDABLES Time to update your Foldable!

Independent Practice

Go online for Step-by-Step Solutions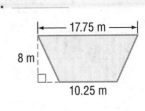

Find the area of each trapezoid. Round to the nearest tenth if necessary. (Examples 1 and 2)

1 168 yd^2

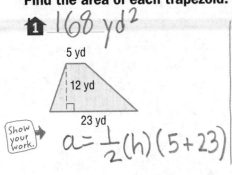

5 yd
12 yd
23 yd

Show your work.

$a = \frac{1}{2}(h)(5+23)$

2. 4.5 cm^2

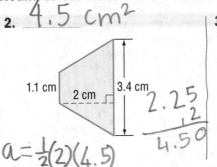

1.1 cm   2 cm   3.4 cm

$a = \frac{1}{2}(2)(4.5)$

$\begin{array}{r} 2.25 \\ \times \ 2 \\ \hline 4.50 \end{array}$

3. _____

17.75 m
8 m
10.25 m

4. A trapezoid has an area of 150 square meters. If the bases are 14 meters and 16 meters, what is the height of the trapezoid? (Example 3)

_____

5. A trapezoid has an area of 400 square millimeters. The bases are 14 millimeters and 36 millimeters. What is the height of the trapezoid? (Example 3)

_____

6. Find the area of the patio shown. (Example 4)

_____

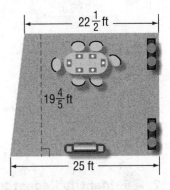

$22\frac{1}{2}$ ft

$19\frac{4}{5}$ ft

25 ft

7 Use the diagram that shows the lawn that surrounds an office building.

a. What is the area of the lawn? _____

_____

b. If one bag of grass seed covers 2,000 square feet, how many bags are needed to seed the lawn?

_____

_____

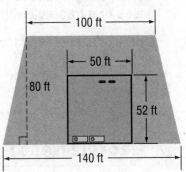

100 ft
50 ft
80 ft
52 ft
140 ft

8. **CCGPS** **Reason Abstractly** Tiles are being placed in front of a fireplace to create a trapezoidal hearth. The hearth will have a height of 24 inches and bases that are 48 inches and 60 inches. If the tiles cover 16 square inches, how many tiles will be needed?

Draw and label each figure. Then find the area.

9. a trapezoid with no right angles and an area less than 12 square centimeters

10. a trapezoid with a right angle and an area greater than 40 square inches

Show your work.

H.O.T. Problems Higher Order Thinking

11. **Persevere with Problems** Apply what you know about rounding to explain how to estimate the height *h* of the trapezoid shown if the area is 235.5 m².

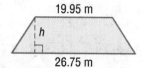

19.95 m

h

26.75 m

$$\begin{array}{r} 4 \\ 6 38 \\ 8.5 \\ \hline 190 \\ 304 \\ \hline 323.0 \end{array}$$

12. 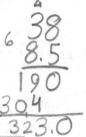 **Identify Repeated Reasoning** Find two possible lengths of the bases of a trapezoid with a height of 1 foot and an area of 9 square feet. Explain how you found your answer.

Georgia Test Practice

13. Barrington cuts a piece of wood in the shape of a trapezoid. The height is 4 feet. The top is 3 feet across and the bottom is 10 feet across. Which equation could be used to find the area of the piece of wood?

Ⓐ $10 = \frac{1}{2} \times h(4 + 3)$

Ⓑ $A = \frac{1}{2} \times 10(4 + 3)$

Ⓒ $A = \frac{1}{2} \times 3(4 + 10)$

Ⓓ $A = \frac{1}{2} \times 4(3 + 10)$

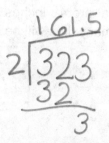
$$\begin{array}{r} 161.5 \\ 2\overline{)323} \\ \underline{32} \\ 3 \end{array}$$

Extra Practice

Find the area of each figure. Round to the nearest tenth if necessary.

14. 121 cm² _____

13 cm

11 cm

9 cm

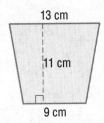

15. 161.5 ft²

15 ft

$8\frac{1}{2}$ ft   10 ft

23 ft

16. _____

17.3 ft

13.4 ft

10.7 ft

$A = \frac{1}{2}h(b_1 + b_2)$

$A = \frac{1}{2}(11)(13 + 9)$

$A = \frac{1}{2}(11)(22)$

$A = 121$

$\frac{1}{2}(8.5)(38)$

17. A trapezoid has an area of 50 square inches. The bases are 3 inches and 7 inches. What is the height of the trapezoid?

_____

18. A trapezoid has an area of 18 square miles. The bases are 5 miles and 7 miles. What is the height of the trapezoid?

_____

19. A county is shaped like a trapezoid. Its northern border is about 9.6 miles across, and the southern border is approximately 25 miles across. The distance from the southern border to the northern border is about 90 miles. Find the approximate area of the county.

_____

20. A play tent is shown. How much fabric was used to make the front and back of the play tent?

_____

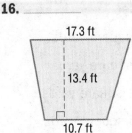

23 in.

32 in.

36.5 in.

Identify Structure Each figure below is made up of congruent trapezoids. Find the area of each figure.

21. _____

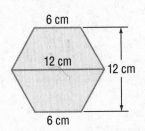

6 cm

12 cm

12 cm

6 cm

22. _____

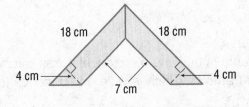

18 cm   18 cm

4 cm   4 cm

7 cm

Georgia Test Practice

23. Find the area of a trapezoid with a height of 4 yards and bases of $5\frac{1}{2}$ yards and $6\frac{1}{2}$ yards.

   Ⓐ 16 square yards

   Ⓑ 24 square yards

   Ⓒ $28\frac{1}{2}$ square yards

   Ⓓ 143 square yards

24. Short Response Serina designed the bag shown. How much fabric will be needed to make the front of the bag?

25. Short Response A piece of sod is shaped like a trapezoid as shown. What is the area of the piece of sod?

_____

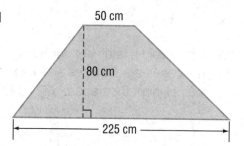

CCGPS **Common Core Review**

Add or multiply. MCC5.NBT.7

26. $5 + 6.2 + 8.8 =$ _____

27. $8 \times 8 \times 4 =$ _____

28. $725 + 315 + 4 =$ _____

29. Find the perimeter of the rectangle. MCC4.MD.3

_____

_____

_____

30. Delanie is building a rectangular frame for her favorite photograph. The frame is 7 inches wide and 5 inches long. What is the perimeter of the frame? MCC4.MD.3 _____

CCGPS Content Standards
MCC6.G.1
Mathematical Practices
1, 4, 7

Case #1 Amazing Array

A designer wants to arrange 12 mosaic tiles into a rectangular shape with the least perimeter possible.

What are the dimensions of the rectangle?

 Understand *What are the facts?*

Twelve tiles will be arranged with the least perimeter possible.

  Plan *What is your strategy to solve this problem?*

Use graph paper. Make diagrams of 12 squares to represent 12 tiles.

 Solve *How can you apply the strategy?*

A rectangle with dimensions of 12 and 1 has a perimeter of _____.

A rectangle with dimensions of 3 and 4 has a perimeter of _____.

A rectangle with dimensions of 2 and 6 has a perimeter of _____.

So, the least perimeter has dimensions of _____.

Check *Does the answer make sense?*

Use addition to check your answer.

$3 + 4 + 3 + 4 = 14$ $2 + 6 + 2 + 6 = 16$ $12 + 1 + 12 + 1 = 26$

Analyze the Strategy

CCGPS **Identify Structure** Describe a design with a perimeter and an area of 16.

_____

_____

Case #2 Dynamic Dimensions

For a school assignment, Santiago has to give three different possibilities for the dimensions of a rectangle that has a perimeter of 28 feet and an area greater than 30 square feet. One of the diagrams he drew is shown at the right.

What are two other possibilities for the dimensions of the rectangle?

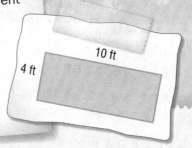

Understand

Read the problem. What are you being asked to find?

I need to find _____.

Underline key words and values in the problem. What information do you know?

The perimeter of the rectangle is ☐ feet, and the area is

greater than _____.

Plan

Choose a problem-solving strategy.

I will use the _____ strategy.

Solve

Use your problem-solving strategy to solve the problem.

Draw rectangles with perimeters of ☐ feet.
Then, multiply length times width to find the area.

The product must be greater than ☐.

_____

_____

So, the dimensions of two possible rectangles are

_____

11 ft
3 ft

12 ft
2 ft

8 ft
6 ft

Check

Use information from the problem to check your answer.

Reread the problem. Check that both conditions have been met.

Perimeter: ☐ = 28   Area: ☐ > 30 and ☐ > 30

Case #3 Decorations

A rectangular table that is placed lengthwise against a wall is 8 feet long and 3 feet wide. Balloons will be attached 1 foot apart along the three exposed sides, with one balloon at each of the four corners.

How many balloons are needed?

_____

Case #4 Geography

The mall is 10 miles from your home. Your school is one half of the way from your home to the mall. The library is two fifths of the way from your school to the mall.

How many miles is it from your home to the library?

_____

Case #5 Painting

Van is going to paint a mural in his home. The mural is in the shape of a parallelogram with a base of 8 feet and a height of 15 feet.

a. *What is the area of the mural?* _____

b. *If one quart of paint will cover 70 square feet, how*
many quarts of paint does Van need to buy? _____

Circle a strategy below
to solve the problem.
- *Look for a pattern.*
- *Work backward.*
- *Guess, check, and*
  revise.
- *Make a table.*

Case #6 Geometry

The base and height of each successive triangle are each half the length of the previous triangle.

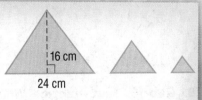

16 cm

24 cm

What will be the area of the fourth triangle?

_____

Mid-Chapter Check

Vocabulary Check

1. **CCGPS** **Be Precise** Define *polygon*. Give an example of a figure that is a polygon and an example of a figure that is not a polygon. (Lesson 1)

_____

_____

2. Fill in the blank in the sentence below with the correct term(s). (Lesson 2)

   Congruent figures have the _____ size and the _____ shape.

Skills Check and Problem Solving

Find the area of each figure. (Lessons 1 and 2)

3. _____

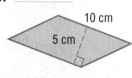

10 cm
5 cm

4. _____

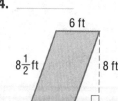

6 ft
$8\frac{1}{2}$ ft
8 ft

5. _____

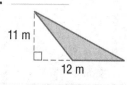

11 m
12 m

Find the missing dimension of each figure. (Lessons 1 and 3)

6. parallelogram: $h = 5\frac{1}{4}$ ft; $A = 12$ ft^2

_____

7. trapezoid: $b_1 = 3$ m; $b_2 = 4$ m; $A = 7$ m^2

_____

8. **CCGPS** **Model with Mathematics** A corner table is in the shape of a trapezoid. Find the area of the tabletop. (Lesson 3) _____

45 in.
28 in.
30 in.

9. **Georgia Test Practice** What is the height of a triangle with a base of 14 centimeters and an area of 56 square centimeters? (Lesson 2)

   Ⓐ 112 centimeters   Ⓒ 8 centimeters

   Ⓑ 56 centimeters   Ⓓ 7 centimeters

Changes in Dimension

What You'll Learn

Scan the lesson. Predict two things you will learn about changes in dimension.

- _____
_____

- _____
_____

Essential Question

HOW does measurement help you solve problems in everyday life?

CCGPS Common Core GPS

Content Standards
MCC6.G.1

Mathematical Practices
1, 2, 3, 4, 7

🌐 Real-World Link

Construction Mr. Blackwell is building a rectangular dog house. The floor of the dog house is 4 feet long and 2 feet wide.

1. Draw the floor of the dog house on the graph paper below.

2. Add the lengths of the sides to find the perimeter.

_____

3. Multiply the length and width to find the area.

_____

4. Mr. Blackwell doubles the width of the dog house. Draw the new floor below.

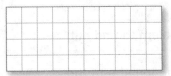

5. How did the perimeter and area of the floors change from the first to the second dog house? _____

_____

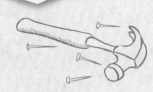

Changing Dimensions: Effect on Perimeter

Work Zone

Words   If the dimensions of a polygon are multiplied by x, then the perimeter of the polygon changes by a factor of x.

Model

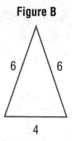

Figure A

Figure B

3   3

2

6   6

4

Example   The dimensions of Figure A are multiplied by 2 to produce Figure B.

perimeter of Figure A • 2 = perimeter of Figure B

8   • 2 =   16

Notice that all the dimensions of the figure must change using the same factor, x.

Example

1. Suppose the side lengths of the parallelogram at the right are tripled. What effect would this have on the perimeter? Justify your answer.

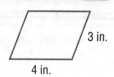

3 in.

4 in.

Show your work.

The dimensions are 3 times greater.

original perimeter: $2(4) + 2(3) = 14$ in.

new perimeter: $2(12) + 2(9) = 42$ in.

compare perimeters: 42 in. ÷ 14 in. = 3

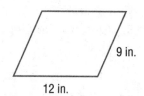

9 in.

12 in.

So, the perimeter is 3 times the perimeter of the original figure.

Got It?   Do this problem to find out.

a. Suppose the side lengths of the trapezoid at the right are multiplied by $\frac{1}{2}$. What effect would this have on the perimeter? Justify your answer.

a. _____

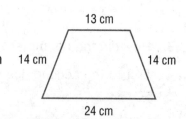

13 cm

14 cm   14 cm

24 cm

Changing Dimensions: Effect on Area

Key Concept

Words If the dimensions of a polygon are multiplied by x, then the area of the polygon changes by $x \cdot x$ or x^2.

Model

Figure A

Figure B

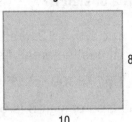

Example The dimensions of Figure A are multiplied by 2 to produce Figure B.

$$\underbrace{\text{area of Figure A}}_{20} \cdot 2^2 = \underbrace{\text{area of Figure B}}_{80}$$

$$20 \quad \cdot 4 = \quad 80$$

Notice that all the dimensions of the figure must change using the same factor, x.

Example

Tutor

2. **The side lengths of the triangle at the right are multiplied by 5. What effect would this have on the area? Justify your answer.**

1 cm
2 cm

The dimensions are 5 times greater.

original area: $\frac{1}{2} \cdot 2 \cdot 1 = 1 \text{ cm}^2$

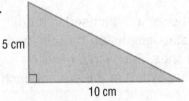
5 cm
10 cm

new area: $\frac{1}{2} \cdot 10 \cdot 5 = 25 \text{ cm}^2$

compare areas:
$25 \text{ cm}^2 \div 1 \text{ cm}^2 = 25$ or 5^2.

So, the area is 5^2 or 25 times the area of the original figure.

Got It? Do this problem to find out.

Show your work.

b. A rectangle measures 2 feet by 4 feet. Suppose the side lengths are multiplied by 2.5. What effect would this have on the area? Justify your answer.

b. _____

Example

Tutor

3. A stop sign is in the shape of a regular octagon. Sign A shown at the right has an area of 309 square inches. What is the area of sign B?

A   B

8 in.   12 in.

Since $8 \times 1.5 = 12$, the area of sign B is 1.5^2 times the area of sign A.

$309 \cdot 1.5^2 = 309 \cdot 2.25$ or 695.25

So, the area of sign B is 695.25 square inches.

Guided Practice

Check ✓

Refer to the figure at the right for Exercises 1 and 2. Justify your answers. (Examples 1–2)

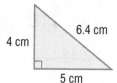

6.4 cm

4 cm

5 cm

1. Each side length is doubled. Describe the change in the perimeter.

_____

_____

2. Each side length is tripled. Describe the change in the area.

_____

_____

3. Different sizes of regular hexagons are used in a quilt. Each small hexagon has side lengths of 4 inches and an area of 41.6 square inches. Each large hexagon has side lengths of 8 inches. What is the area of each

large hexagon? (Example 3) _____

_____

4. **Building on the Essential Question** How can exponents help you find the area of a rectangle if each

side length is multiplied by x? _____

_____

_____

Rate Yourself!

How confident are you about changes in dimension? Check the box that applies.

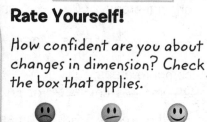

For more help, go online to access a Personal Tutor.

Tutor

Independent Practice

Go online for Step-by-Step Solutions

1. Each side length of the parallelogram at the right is multiplied by 4. Describe the change in the perimeter. Justify your answer. (Example 1)

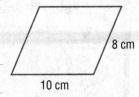

_____

_____

_____

2. The base and height of the triangle at the right are multiplied by 4. Describe the change in the area. Justify your answer. (Example 2)

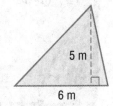

_____

_____

_____

3. Each side length of the rectangle is multiplied by $\frac{1}{3}$. Describe the change in the area. Justify your answer. (Example 2)

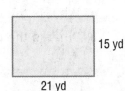

_____

_____

_____

4. Different sizes of regular pentagons are used in a stained glass window. Each small pentagon has side lengths of 4 inches and an area of 27.5 square inches. Each large pentagon has side lengths of 8 inches. What is the area of each large pentagon? (Example 3)

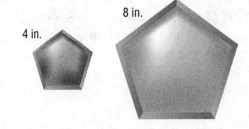

_____

_____

5. **Justify Conclusions** A dollhouse has a bed with dimensions $\frac{1}{12}$ the size of a queen-size bed. A queen-size bed has an area of 4,800 square inches, and a length of 80 inches. What are the side lengths of the dollhouse bed? Justify your answer. _____

_____

_____

_____

6. CCGPS **Reason Abstractly** Refer to the graphic novel frame below for Exercises a–b.

a. What is the original area of the triangle? _____

b. What is the new area if the sides are all two times longer?

_____

H.O.T. Problems Higher Order Thinking

7. CCGPS **Identify Structure** Sketch a triangle with the side lengths labeled. Sketch and label another triangle that has a perimeter two times greater than the perimeter of the first triangle.

8. CCGPS **Persevere with Problems** The corresponding side lengths of two figures have a ratio of $\frac{a}{b}$. What is the ratio of the perimeters? the ratio of the areas?

_____

Georgia Test Practice

9. The regular pentagon shown at the right is enlarged so that its sides are four times longer. What effect does this have on the perimeter?

Ⓐ The perimeter is 4 times greater.

Ⓑ The perimeter is 12 times greater.

Ⓒ The perimeter is 16 times greater.

Ⓓ The perimeter is 20 times greater.

3 cm

Extra Practice

Refer to the parallelogram at the right for Exercises 10–12. Justify your answers.

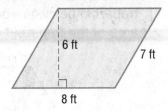

6 ft

7 ft

8 ft

10. Suppose the base and height are each multiplied by $\frac{1}{2}$. What effect would this have on the area?

original area: 8 · 6 or 48 square feet

new dimensions: base = 8 · $\frac{1}{2}$ or 4 ft, height = 6 · $\frac{1}{2}$ or 3 ft

new area: 4 · 3 or 12 square feet; 12 ft² ÷ 48 ft² = $\frac{1}{4}$;

So, the area is $\frac{1}{2}$ · $\frac{1}{2}$ or $\frac{1}{4}$ times the area of the original figure.

11. Suppose the side lengths are multiplied by 6. Describe the change in the

perimeter. _____

_____

_____

12. Suppose the base and height are each multiplied by 3.5. Describe the

change in the area. _____

_____

_____

13. Refer to the triangle at the right. Suppose the side lengths and height of the triangle were divided by 4. What effect would this have on the perimeter? the area? Justify your answer.

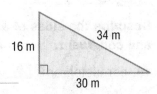

34 m

16 m

30 m

_____

_____

_____

_____

14. **CCGPS** **Justify Conclusions** A model car has a windshield with dimensions $\frac{1}{18}$ the size of a real car windshield. The rectangular windshield of the real car has an area of about 2,318 square inches, with a width of 61 inches. What are the side lengths of the model car's windshield? Round to the nearest hundredth. Justify your answer.

_____

_____

15. The lengths of the bases and height of the trapezoid below are doubled. How does the area of the trapezoid change?

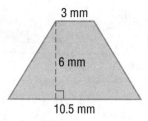

3 mm

6 mm

10.5 mm

Ⓐ The area doubles.

Ⓑ The area triples.

Ⓒ The area is 4 times greater.

Ⓓ The area is 6 times greater.

16. Short Response Two regular pentagons have side lengths of 1 centimeter and 7 centimeters, respectively. How many times greater is the perimeter of the larger pentagon?

17. Two regular hexagons are shown below. How many times greater is the area of the larger hexagon than the smaller hexagon?

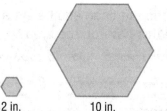

2 in.   10 in.

Ⓕ 2 times   Ⓗ 10 times

Ⓖ 5 times   Ⓘ 25 times

18. Two equilateral triangles have perimeters of 9 meters and 27 meters, respectively. How many times greater is the area of the larger triangle?

Ⓐ 2 times   Ⓒ 9 times

Ⓑ 3 times   Ⓓ 27 times

 Common Core Review

Describe the sides of each figure using the terms *parallel*, *perpendicular*, **and** *congruent*. MCC5.G.4

19. parallelogram _____

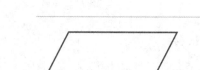

20. trapezoid _____

21. Mr. Macy's garden is surrounded by a fence. The fence makes four right angles at each corner. All four sides of the fence are 14 meters long. What shape best describes Mr. Macy's garden? MCC5.G.4

_____

_____

22. Gary drew the logo to the right. The blue figure has two pairs of parallel sides, two pairs of congruent sides, and four right angles. What is the shape of the blue figure? MCC5.G.4

_____

Inquiry HOW can you estimate the area of an irregular figure?

 **Content Standards**
MCC6.G.1
Mathematical Practices
1, 3, 4, 5

Ponds The Ramirez family is putting a koi pond in their backyard. They need to estimate the area of the pond to know how many fish they can put in the pond. A scale drawing of the pond is shown below. In the drawing, each square represents one square foot.

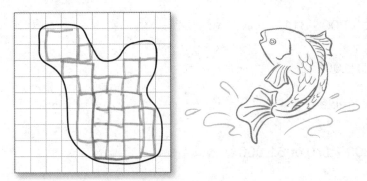

What do you know? _____

_____

What do you need to know? $\text{The area of the pond}$

_____

Investigation 1

Step 1 Shade and count the number of whole squares the pond covers.
$\boxed{35}$

Step 2 Estimate the number of whole squares covered by the partial squares altogether. $\boxed{10}$

Step 3 Add your answers from Steps 1 and 2.
$\boxed{35} + \boxed{10} = \boxed{45}$

So, the area of the pond is about $\boxed{45}$ square feet.

Investigation 2

Another way to estimate the area of an irregular figure is to separate the figure into simpler shapes. Then find the sum of these areas.

Step 1 First, separate the figure into a triangle and a rectangle.

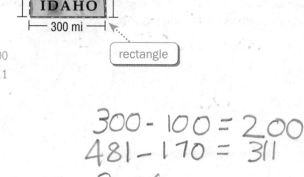

triangle

481 mi   100 mi

170 mi

IDAHO

300 mi

rectangle

Step 2 Find the area of each figure.

Area of a triangle

$A = \frac{1}{2}bh$

$= \frac{1}{2} \cdot 200 \cdot 311$ $b = 300 - 100$ or 200
$h = 481 - 170$ or 311

$= 31{,}100$ Simplify.

Area of rectangle

$A = \ell w$

$= 300 \cdot 170$ or $51{,}000$ $\ell = 300$ and $w = 170$

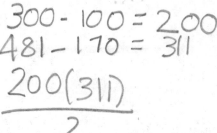

$300 - 100 = 200$
$481 - 170 = 311$

$\dfrac{200(311)}{2}$

Step 3 Add to find the total area.

$\boxed{51000} + \boxed{31100} = \boxed{82100}$

The area of Idaho is about $\boxed{82100}$ square miles.

Collaborate

CCGPS **Use Math Tools** Work with a partner to estimate the area of each irregular figure.

1. $A \approx$ _____

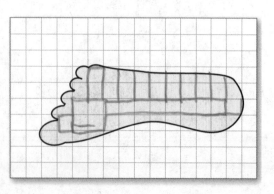

2. $A \approx$ _____

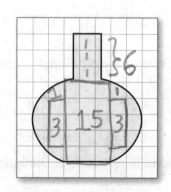

Collaborate

Work with a partner to estimate the area of each irregular figure.

3. A ≈ $\underline{51,475 \text{ sq. mi (mi}^2)}$ 4. A ≈ $\underline{9 \text{ sq in}}$

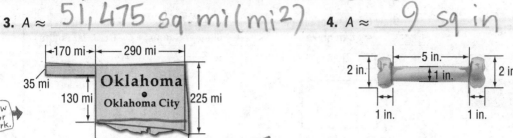

Show your work.

$a = \frac{1}{2}(290)(355)$

$\begin{array}{r} 225 \\ 130 \\ \hline 355 \end{array}$

5. A ≈ $\underline{35 \text{ in}^2}$ 6. A ≈ $\underline{14 \text{ sq cm (cm}^2)}$

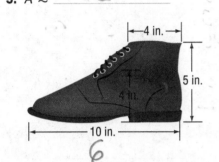

6

7. A ≈ $\underline{10 \text{ in}^2}$ 8. A ≈ $\underline{32 \text{ cm}^2}$

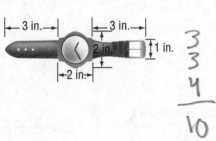

$\begin{array}{c} 3 \\ 3 \\ \underline{4} \\ 10 \end{array}$

9. A ≈ $\underline{22 \text{ cm}^2}$ 10. A ≈ $\underline{14.5 \text{ sq in}}$

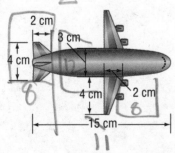

11

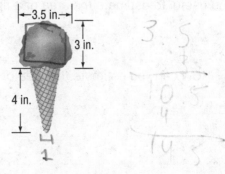

$\begin{array}{r} 3.5 \\ + \\ \hline 10.5 \\ 4 \\ \hline 14.5 \end{array}$

Analyze

Work with a partner to complete the table. The first one is done for you.

Irregular Figure	Draw the simpler shapes you can make.	Area of Each Simpler Shape	Estimated Area of Irregular Figure
8 cm, 3 cm, 4 cm, 12 cm		$8 \times 3 = 24$ $12 \times 4 = 48$	72 square centimeters
11. 15 in., 6 in., 20 in., USA ★		$15 * 6 = 90$ $5 * 6 = 30$ $30/2 = 15$	105 sq. in
12. 4 cm, 4 cm, 7 cm, 5 cm, 9 cm		28 28 45	157 sq cm
13. 1 in., 2 in., 1 in., 2 in., 3 in., 2 5, 6 in.		12 0.5 5	17.5 sq in.

14. **CCGPS** **Reason Inductively** Heather solves Exercise 11 by subtracting the area of two triangles from the area of a large rectangle and finds the answer 105 square inches. How does Heather's answer compare to your answer for Exercise 11?

_____

_____

Reflect

15. **CCGPS** **Model with Mathematics** Describe a real-world example of when it would be useful to estimate the area of a figure.

_____

16. **Inquiry** HOW can you estimate the area of an irregular figure?

_____

_____

_____

Area of Composite Figures

What You'll Learn

Scan the lesson. List two things real-world scenarios in which you would use the area of composite figures.

- _____
- _____

 Essential Question

HOW does measurement help you solve problems in everyday life?

 Vocabulary

composite figure

Common Core GPS

Content Standards
MCC6.G.1

Mathematical Practices
1, 2, 3, 4, 6, 7

Vocabulary Start-Up

A **composite figure** is a figure made of two or more two-dimensional figures. The composite figure shown to the right is made of two rectangles.

Draw a composite figure made of a rectangle and a right triangle on the graph paper below.

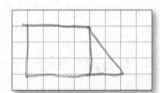

$$\frac{b1 + b2 + h}{2}$$

$$a = \frac{1}{2}(2)(4+6)$$
$$a = \frac{1}{2}(20)$$

Real-World Link

Pools The dimensions of the city pool are shown.

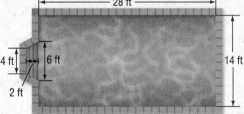

1. What two-dimensional figures are used to make the shape of the pool?

   Rectangle, Trapezoid

2. How could you determine the area of the pool floor?

   28 * 14 and 10

Find the Area of a Composite Figure

You can decompose some trapezoids into a square and a triangle to find the area.

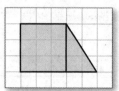

Area of Square

$A = \ell \cdot w$

$A = 3 \cdot 3$, or 9

Area of Triangle

$A = \frac{1}{2}bh$

$A = \frac{1}{2}(2)(3)$, or 3

Then add the area of the square and the area of the triangle to find the area of the trapezoid. The area of the trapezoid is $9 + 3$ or 12 square units.

You can find the area of a composite figure using the same strategy. To find the area of a composite figure, separate it into figures with areas you know how to find. Then add those areas.

Example

Tutor

1. Find the area of the figure at the right.

The figure can be separated into a rectangle and a triangle. Find the area of each.

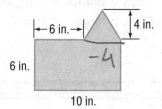

Area of Rectangle

6 in.

10 in.

Area of Triangle

4 in.

4 in.

$A = \ell w$

$A = 10 \cdot 6$ or 60

$A = \frac{1}{2}bh$

$A = \frac{1}{2}(4)(4)$ or 8

The base of the triangle is $10 - 6$ or 4 inches.

The area is $60 + 8$ or 68 square inches.

Got It? Do these problems to find out.

Find the area of each figure.

a.

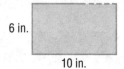

10 ft   6   4   ← 8 ft →   48   4 ft   12 ft

b.

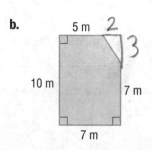

5 m   2   3   10 m   7 m   7 m

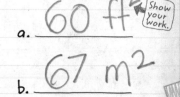

a. ___60 ft²___

b. ___67 m²___

Show your work.

Example

 Tutor

2. **Find the area of the pool's floor.**

Separate the figure
into a rectangle and
a trapezoid.

Rectangle: 28 × 14 or 392

Trapezoid: $\frac{1}{2}$(2)(4 + 6) or 10

So, the area of the pool's
floor is 392 + 10 or 402 square feet.

Got It? **Do this problem to find out.**

Show
your
work.

c.

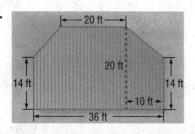

c. $\underline{672\ ft^2}$

Find the Area of Overlapping Figures

To find the area of overlapping figures, decompose the figures.

Example

 Tutor

3. **Find the area of the figure at the right.**

Square: 12 × 12 or 144

$12-6=6$

Rectangle: 15 × 12 or 180

The sum of the areas: 144 + 180 or 324

Overlapping area: 6 × 7 or 42

Subtract the overlapping area. 324 − 42 = 282

So, the area of the figure is 282 square centimeters.

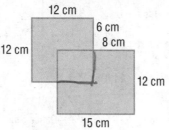

Be Precise

It is important not to count
the area of the overlapping
portion twice when finding
the area of overlapping
figures.

Got It? **Do this problem to find out.**

d.

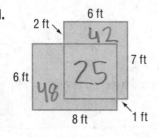

90
− 25
⟨65⟩

d. $\underline{65\ ft^2}$

Copyright © ...cGraw-Hill Companies, Inc.

Lesson 5 Area of Composite Figures **625**

Example

4. Charlie and his brother Matthew are neighbors in an apartment complex where they share a patio. What is the area of both apartments and the patio?

Matthew's Apartment
55 ft
45 ft
22 ft
32 ft
45 ft
Charlie's Apartment
55 ft

Each apartment:
55 × 45 or 2,475

The sum of the areas:
2,475 + 2,475 or 4,950

Patio: 23 × 23 or 529

Subtract the overlapping area. 4,950 − 529 = 4,421

So, the total area is 4,421 square feet.

Guided Practice

Check ✓

1. The manager of an apartment complex will install new carpeting in a studio apartment. The floor plan is shown at the right. What is the total area that needs to be carpeted? (Example 1 and 2)

|← 12 ft →| 8 ft |
5 ft
10 ft
|← 25 ft →|

Show your work.

2. Finn Fitness has an entrance to the locker room from both the dance studio and the weight room. What is the total area of Finn Fitness? (Examples 3 and 4)

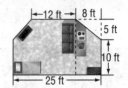
28 ft
Weight Room
16 ft
30 ft
Locker Room
14 ft
42 ft
Dance Studio
33 ft

Rate Yourself!

Are you ready to move on? Shade the section that applies.

I have a few questions. | I'm ready to move on.
I have a lot of questions.

For more help, go online to access a Personal Tutor. **Tutor**

3. 🄰 **Building on the Essential Question** How can you decompose figures to find area?

Name _____ My Homework _____

Find the area of each figure. Round to the nearest tenth if necessary. (Example 1)

1 58.6

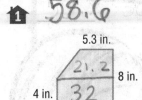

5.3 in.

21.2

8 in.

4 in.

32

8 in.

Show your work.

2. 87.5 cm²

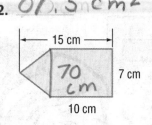

15 cm

70 cm

7 cm

10 cm

3. The floor plan of a kitchen is shown at the right. If the entire kitchen floor is to be tiled, how many square feet of tile are needed? (Example 2)

189 sq ft

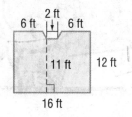

2 ft
6 ft   6 ft

11 ft   12 ft

16 ft

4. Ms. Friedman and Mrs. Elliot both teach sixth grade math. They share a storage closet. What is the total area of both rooms and the storage closet? (Examples 3 and 4)

2844 ft²

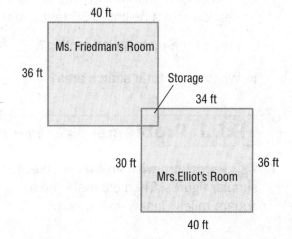

40 ft

Ms. Friedman's Room

36 ft

Storage

34 ft

30 ft   36 ft

Mrs. Elliot's Room

40 ft

5 The diagram shows one side of a storage barn.

a. This side needs to be painted. Find the total area to be painted. 467.4 ft²

Show your work.

b. Each gallon of paint costs $20 and covers 350 square feet. Find the total cost to paint this side once. Justify your answer.

_____

_____

_____

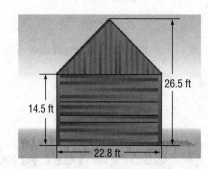

26.5 ft

14.5 ft

22.8 ft

6. **Reason Abstractly** Refer to the graphic novel frame below for Exercises a–b.

Watch ▶ Replay it online!

We need to find the total area we searched.

a. The first clue was hidden in a triangular section of the park with an area of 600 square feet. The second clue was hidden in a rectangular section with a height of 30 feet and a width of 24 feet. What was the area of the rectangular section? _____

b. What is the total search area? _____

H.O.T. Problems Higher Order Thinking

7. **CCGPS Persevere with Problems** Describe how to separate the figure into simpler figures. Then estimate the area. One square unit equals 2,400 square miles. Justify your answer.

_____

_____

_____

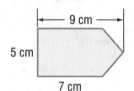

NEVADA

8. **CCGPS Identify Structure** Describe how you would find the area of the figure shown at the right. _____

_____

9 cm

5 cm

7 cm

Georgia Test Practice

9. The diagram gives the dimensions of the geodome climber on the playground. What is the total area of the geodome?

Ⓐ 82.8 ft²

Ⓒ 331.2 ft²

Ⓑ 165.6 ft²

Ⓓ 883.2 ft²

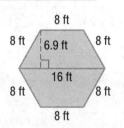

8 ft

8 ft / 6.9 ft \ 8 ft

16 ft

8 ft \ / 8 ft

8 ft

Extra Practice

Find the area of each figure. Round to the nearest tenth if necessary.

10. $\underline{69.5 \text{ ft}^2}$

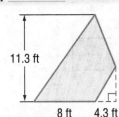

$A = \frac{1}{2}(8)(11.3) = 45.2$

$A = \frac{1}{2}(4.3)(11.3) \approx 24.3$

$45.2 + 24.3 = 69.5$

11. 76.24 m^2

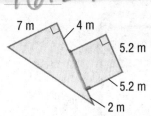

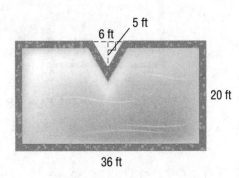

39.2
27.04
$+ 76.24$

12. The diagram gives the dimensions of a swimming pool. If a cover is needed for the pool, what will be the approximate area of the cover? $\underline{705 \text{ ft}^2}$

720
$- 15$
705

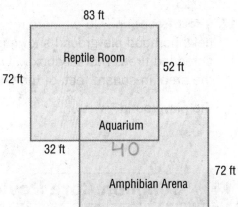

13. At the local zoo, the aquarium can be seen from the Reptile Room and the Amphibian Arena. What is the total area of both rooms and the aquarium?

$\underline{10{,}932 \text{ ft}^2}$

14. **CCGPS Persevere with Problems**
The diagram shows one wall of Sadie's living room.

a. This wall needs to be painted. Find the total area to be painted.

$\underline{144 \text{ ft}^2}$

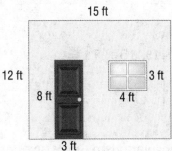

180
24
156
$- 12$
144

b. Each quart of paint costs $8 and covers 90 square feet. Find the total cost to paint this wall once. Justify your answer.

$\underline{1.6 \text{ quarts} (2)}$

15. What is the area of the window shown?

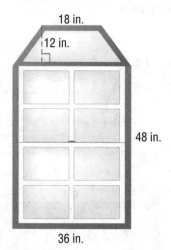

18 in.

12 in.

48 in.

36 in.

- (A) 2,052 in²
- (C) 508.68 in²
- (B) 1,728 in²
- (D) 324 in²

16. The shaded part of the grid represents the plans for a fish pond.

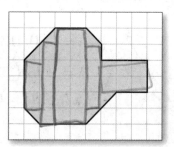

If each square on the grid represents 5 square feet, what is the approximate area of the fish pond?

- (F) 175 square feet
- (G) 165 square feet
- (H) 150 square feet
- (I) 33 square feet

17. Short Response To promote recycling, the ground of the neighborhood playground shown is being covered by shredded tires. The sandbox will *not* be covered. What is the area, in square feet, of the shredded tire portion of the playground? 3150

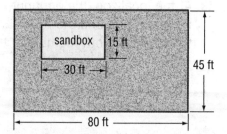

sandbox 15 ft

30 ft

45 ft

80 ft

Common Core Review

Multiply. MCC5.NBT.5

18. 36 × 12 = _____

19. 15 × 71 = _____

20. 72 × 200 = _____

21. Find the volume of the rectangular prism. MCC5.MD.5b

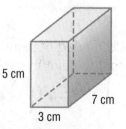

5 cm

7 cm

3 cm

22. Hiking burns about 144 Calories each half hour. About how many Calories can be burned if someone hikes 3 days a week for an hour?

MCC4.OA.3 _____

21ST CENTURY CAREER
in Community Planning

Parks and Recreation Planner

Do you enjoy thinking about how your community might look 10 years in the future? If so, a career in parks and recreation planning might be a perfect fit for you. Most planners are employed by local governments. They assess the best use for the land and create short and long term plans for various parks and recreation areas. They make recommendations based on the location of roads, schools, and residential areas. A parks and recreation planner uses mathematics, science, and computer software to complete their work.

College & Career
R E A D I N E S S

Explore college and careers at ccr.mcgraw-hill.com

Is This the Career for You?

Are you interested in a career as a parks and recreation planner? Take some of the following courses in high school.

◆ Economics
◆ Environmental Design
◆ Geometry

Turn the page to find out how math relates to a career in Community Planning.

You be the Parks and Recreation Planner!

For each problem, use the information in the designs.

1. What is the area of the playground in Design 2? _____

2. In Design 2, how much larger is the area of the soccer field than the area of the playground? _____

3. In Design 1, the amphitheater has a stage. What is the area of the amphitheater without the stage? _____

4. The cost of building the amphitheater including the stage is $225 a square yard. The budget provided to build the amphitheater is $65,000. Are they within budget? Explain.

_____

_____

_____

_____

Design 1

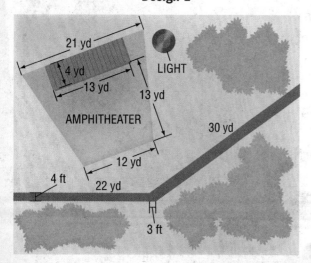

Design 2

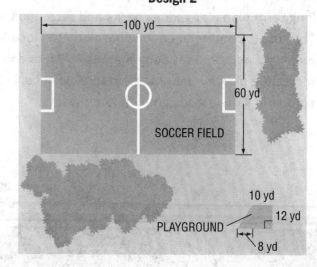

Career Project

It's time to update your career portfolio! The New York City Department of Parks and Recreation has a free "Park Planner Game" online. Go to the Website to create your own park with trees, sports fields, and paths, while trying to stay under budget.

_____

_____

_____

_____

> What is something you really want to do in the next ten years?
>
> • _____
> • _____
> • _____
> • _____
> • _____

Vocabulary Check

Unscramble each of the clue words.

SEBA

☐☐☐☐

HGEHTI

☐☐☐☐☐☐

LYNPOOG

☐☐☐☐☐☐☐

LAEGARLAPLORM

☐☐☐☐☐☐☐☐☐☐☐☐☐

MHOBRUS

☐☐☐☐☐☐☐

NETRUGNOC

☐☐☐☐☐☐☐☐☐

POMECSOTI ERFUGI

☐☐☐☐☐☐☐☐☐ ☐☐☐☐☐☐

AROMLUF

☐☐☐☐☐☐☐

Complete each sentence using one of the unscrambled words above.

1. A _____ is a simple closed figure formed by three or more straight line segments.

2. The shortest distance from the base of a parallelogram to its opposite side is

   the _____ .

3. A _____ is a quadrilateral with opposite sides parallel and opposite sides congruent.

4. Any side of a parallelogram is a _____ .

5. A parallelogram with four congruent sides is a _____ .

6. If two shapes have the same measure they are _____ .

7. A figure made of triangles, quadrilaterals, and other two dimensional figures

   is a _____ .

8. A _____ is an equation that shows a relationship among certain quantities.

Use Your FOLDABLES

Use your Foldable to help review the chapter.

Tape here ⬇

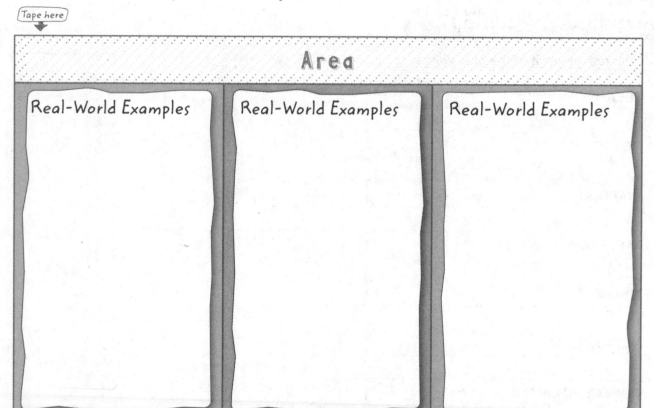

Area

Real-World Examples

Real-World Examples

Real-World Examples

Got it?

Match each expression with correct steps used to find the area of the trapezoid.

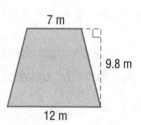

7 m

9.8 m

12 m

1. Write the correct area formula.

2. Replace h with 9.8.

3. Replace b_1 with 7 and replace b_2 with 12.

4. Add.

5. Multiply.

a. $A = \frac{1}{2}(9.8)(b_1 + b_2)$

b. $A = \frac{1}{2}bh$

c. $A = \frac{1}{2}(9.8)(19)$

d. $A = \frac{1}{2}h(b_1 + b_2)$

e. $A = 93.1$

f. $A = \frac{1}{2}(9.8)(7 + 12)$

Problem Solving

1. Find the height of a deck if it is a parallelogram with base $8\frac{1}{4}$ feet and an area of $49\frac{1}{2}$ square feet. (Lesson 1) _____

2. How much material is needed to make a triangular flag with base $2\frac{1}{4}$ feet and height $8\frac{1}{2}$ feet? (Lesson 2) _____

3. One room in Franco's room is in the shape of a trapezoid with the dimensions shown. Find the area of the wall to be painted. (Lesson 3)

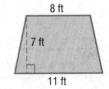

$$66.5 \; ft^2$$

4. **CCGPS Reason Abstractly** A window is shaped like a trapezoid. The bases are 30 inches and 40 inches. The height of the window is 24 inches. Find the area of the window. (Lesson 3)

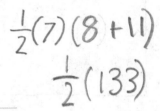

$\frac{1}{2}(7)(8+11)$

$\frac{1}{2}(133)$

5. A bricklayer wants to arrange 16 bricks into a rectangular shape with the greatest perimeter possible. How many bricks will be in each row? (PSI)

6. **CCGPS Identify Structure** Each side of a rectangle with a length of 10 centimeters, and a width of 8 centimeters is multiplied by 0.5. Describe the change in the perimeter. (Lesson 4) _____

7. The side of a four season room is being constructed with the dimensions shown. Find the area of the side being built of glass windows. (Lesson 5)

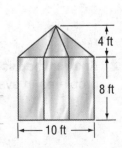

Reflect

 Answering the Essential Question

Use what you learned about area to complete the graphic organizer. List several real-world examples for each figure.

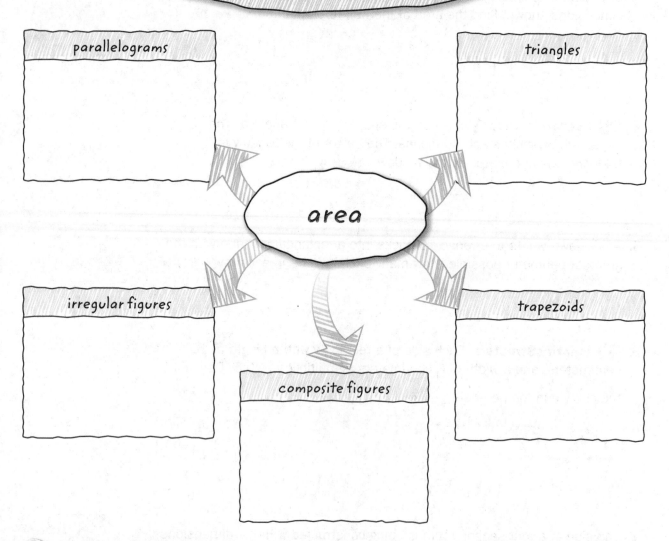

Essential Question

HOW does measurement help you solve problems in everyday life?

parallelograms

triangles

area

irregular figures

trapezoids

composite figures

 Answer the Essential Question. HOW does measurement help you solve problems in everyday life?

Chapter 9
Volume and Surface Area

Essential Question

HOW is shape important when measuring a figure?

Common Core GPS

Content Standards
MCC6.G.2, MCC6.G.4

Mathematical Practices
1, 2, 3, 4, 5, 6, 7, 8

Math in the Real World

Aquariums Two-dimensional figures have area, while three-dimensional figures have volume and surface area.

A 20-gallon aquarium can measure 24 inches wide, 12 inches deep, and 16 inches high. What is the area of the bottom of the aquarium?

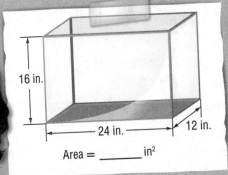

16 in.

24 in.

12 in.

Area = _____ in²

FOLDABLES
Study Organizer

1 Cut out the correct Foldable from the FL pages in the back of this book.

2 Place your Foldable on the Key Concept page toward the end of this chapter.

3 Use the Foldable throughout this chapter to help you learn about volume and surface area.

What Tools Do You Need?

 Vocabulary

base

cubic units

lateral face

prism

pyramid

rectangular prism

slant height

surface area

three-dimensional figure

triangular prism

vertex

volume

Review Vocabulary

Using a graphic organizer can help you to remember important vocabulary terms. Fill in the graphic organizer below for the phrase *two-dimensional figure*.

two-dimensional figure

Definition

Real-World Examples

Drawings

The number of square units needed to cover the surface of a closed figure is the _____.

Try the Quick Check below.
Or, take the Online Readiness Quiz.

 **Quick Review**

Common Core Review MCC5.OA.1, MCC5.NBT.5, MCC5.NBT.7

Example 1

Find 16 × 2.5 × 8.

16 × 2.5 = 40   Multiply 16 and 2.5.
40 × 8 = 320   Multiply the product by 8.

Example 2

Evaluate (6 × 4) + (3 × 5).

(6 × 4) + (3 × 5) = 24 + 15   Multiply.
                  = 39   Add.

Quick Check

Decimals Multiply.

 Show your work.

1. 3 × 5.5 × 13 = _____

2. 9.8 × 4 × 15 = _____

3. 18 × 1.6 × 6 = _____

4. Dante earned $7.25 for each hour he worked. If he worked 8 hours a week for 4 weeks, how much did he earn?

_____

Numerical Expressions Evaluate each expression.

5. (3 × 12) + (4 × 2) = _____

6. (9 × 7) + (6 × 4) = _____

7. (15 × 3) + (8 × 7) = _____

How Did You Do?

Which problems did you answer correctly in the Quick Check?
Shade those exercise numbers below.

1 2 3 4 5 6 7

Inquiry **HOW can you use models to find volume?**

CCGPS
Content
Standards
MCC6.G.2

Mathematical
Practices
1, 3, 4

Storage Desmond is purchasing a storage cabinet. The cabinet is 2 feet wide, 3 feet long, and 6 feet tall. What is the volume of the cabinet?

Investigation 1

You can use centimeter cubes to find the *volume* of the cabinet. Volume is the amount of space inside a three-dimensional figure. Volume is measured in *cubic units.* Each cube of your model represents 1 cubic foot.

Step 1 Build a model that is 2 cubes wide, 3 cubes long, and 6 cubes tall.

Step 2 Count the number of cubes used to build the model. The model uses ☐ cubes.

So, the volume of the cabinet is ☐ cubic feet.

Find the product of the dimensions of the cabinet.

☐ × ☐ × ☐ = ☐

The product is _____ as the volume.

Collaborate

Work with a partner. Use 36 cubes. Build all the possible prisms with a volume of 36 cubic units. List the dimensions below. Use each set of factors only once.

☐ × ☐ × ☐ = 36   ☐ × ☐ × ☐ = 36

☐ × ☐ × ☐ = 36   ☐ × ☐ × ☐ = 36

☐ × ☐ × ☐ = 36   ☐ × ☐ × ☐ = 36

☐ × ☐ × ☐ = 36   ☐ × ☐ × ☐ = 36

Investigation 2

You can find the volume of rectangular prisms with fractional side lengths.

Step 1 The model to the right is _____ cubes long,

_____ cube wide, and _____ cube tall.

Step 2 Count the number of cubes used to build the model.

The model uses _____ cubes.

So, the volume of the model is _____ cubic feet.

Compare the product of the dimensions of the prism with its volume.

_____ × _____ × _____ = _____

They are _____ .

Investigation 3

You can use cubes of candy to find the volume of rectangular prisms with fractional sides.

Step 1 Cut one piece of candy into two halves.

Step 2 Make a model that is $2\frac{1}{2}$ cubes long, 2 cubes wide, and 1 cube tall. Draw a picture of your model.

Step 3 Count the number of cubes used to build the model. The

model uses _____ whole cubes and _____ half-cubes.

Two halves equal one whole. So, a total of _____ cubes were used.

So, the volume of the prism is _____ cubic units.

Compare the product of the dimensions of the prism with its volume.

_____ × _____ × _____ = _____

They are _____ .

Collaborate

CCGPS **Model with Mathematics** Work with a partner. Use models to determine the volume of each prism. Draw a diagram of each model in the space provided.

1. length: 1
height: 1
width: 1
volume: _____

Show your work.

2. length: 2
height: 4
width: 1
volume: _____

3. length: 3
height: 4
width: 2
volume: _____

4. length: $\frac{1}{2}$
height: 1
width: 1
volume: _____

5. length: $2\frac{1}{2}$
height: 4
width: 1
volume: _____

6. length: $3\frac{1}{2}$
height: 2
width: 2
volume: _____

Work with a partner to complete the table. Use models, if needed. The first one is done for you.

Prism	Height	Length	Width	Volume
A	6	3	2	36
7. B	$2\frac{1}{2}$	$1\frac{1}{2}$	2	
8. C	5	$1\frac{1}{2}$	2	
9. D	2	5	$1\frac{1}{2}$	
10. E	5	3	4	

11. Compare the dimensions for prism C to the dimensions of prism D. Compare the volume of the two prisms. What do you notice?

_____

12. The length and width of prisms B and C are equal. Compare the height of the two prisms. How does the change in height affect the change in volume?

_____

13. Compare the dimensions for prism B to the dimensions of prism E. Compare the volume of the two prisms. What do you notice?

_____

14. CCGPS **Reason Inductively** Describe the relationship between the number of cubes needed and the dimensions of the prism.

_____

_____

 Reflect

15. CCGPS **Model with Mathematics** Write a real-world problem that involves volume of rectangular prisms. Include the dimensions and the volume of the rectangular prism in your response. _____

_____

16. (Inquiry) HOW can you use models to find volume?

_____

_____

Volume of Rectangular Prisms

What You'll Learn

Scan the lesson. Predict two things you will learn about finding the volume of rectangular prisms.

- _____
- _____

Vocabulary Start-Up

Define Volume	When would you use volume?

volume

Example	Nonexample

 Essential Question

HOW is shape important when measuring a figure?

 Vocabulary

three-dimensional figure
prism
rectangular prism
volume
cubic units

Common Core GPS

Content Standards
MCC6.G.2
Mathematical Practices
1, 3, 4, 5, 6, 7

 **Real-World Link**   Watch

Aquarium The dimensions of an aquarium are shown.

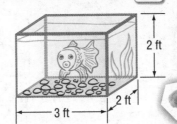
2 ft
3 ft
2 ft

1. What is the area of the base of the aquarium? _____

2. What is the height of the aquarium? _____

3. Fill in the blanks to find the volume.

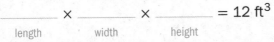

_____ × _____ × _____ = 12 ft³
  length   width   height

Words The volume V of a rectangular prism is the product of its length ℓ, width w, and height h.

Model

Symbols $V = \ell wh$ or $V = Bh$

A **three-dimensional figure** has length, width, and height. A **prism** is a three-dimensional figure with two parallel bases that are congruent polygons. In a **rectangular prism**, the bases are congruent rectangles.

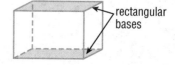

rectangular bases

Volume is the amount of space inside a three-dimensional figure. It is measured in **cubic units**, which can be written using abbreviations and an exponent of 3, such as units^3 or in^3.

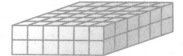

Decomposing the prism tells you the number of cubes of a given size it will take to fill the prism. The volume of a rectangular prism is related to its dimensions, length, width, and height.

Another method to decompose a rectangular prism is to find the area of the base (B) and multiply it by the height (h).

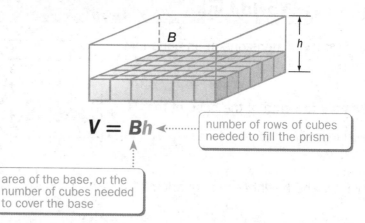

$$V = Bh$$ ◂······· number of rows of cubes needed to fill the prism

area of the base, or the number of cubes needed to cover the base

---

Work Zone

Cubes

Cubes are special rectangular prisms. All three side lengths are equal. So, the volume of a cube can be written using the formula $V = s^3$.

Example

Tutor

1. Find the volume of the rectangular prism.

B, or the area of the base, is 10 × 12 or 120 square centimeters. The height of the prism is 6 centimeters.

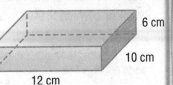

6 cm

10 cm

12 cm

$V = Bh$	Volume of rectangular prism
$V = 120 \times 6$	Replace *B* with 120 and *h* with 6.
$V = 720$	Multiply.

The volume is 720 cubic centimeters.

Decomposing Figures

You can think of the volume of the prism as consisting of six congruent slices. Each slice contains the area of the base, 120 cm², multiplied by a height of 1 cm.

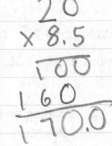

Got It? Do these problems to find out.

a.
5 in.

5 in.

5 in.

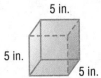

b.
6 ft

4 ft

10 ft

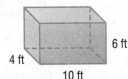

Show your work.

a. ___125___

b. ___240___

Example

Tutor

2. A cereal box has the dimensions shown. What is the volume of the cereal box?

8 in.

$12\frac{1}{2}$ in.

$3\frac{1}{4}$ in.

Estimate 10 × 3 × 10 = 300

$V = \ell wh$ Volume of a rectangular prism.

$V = 8 \times 3\frac{1}{4} \times 12\frac{1}{2}$ Replace ℓ with 8, *w* with $3\frac{1}{4}$, and *h* with $12\frac{1}{2}$.

$V = \frac{\overset{1}{\cancel{8}}}{1} \times \frac{13}{\underset{1}{\cancel{4}}} \times \frac{25}{\underset{1}{\cancel{2}}}$ Write as improper fractions. Then divide out common factors.

$V = \frac{325}{1}$ or 325   Multiply.

The volume of the cereal box is 325 cubic inches.

Check for Reasonableness 325 ≈ 300 ✓

20
× 8.5
——
100
160
——
170.0

Got It? Do this problem to find out.

c. Find the volume of a container measures 4 inches as its length, 5 inches high, and $8\frac{1}{2}$ inches wide.

c. ___170___

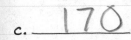

To find missing dimensions of a rectangular prism, replace the variables with known measurements. Then solve for the unknown measurement.

Example

3. Find the missing dimension of the prism.

$V = \ell wh$	Volume of rectangular prism
$84 = 6 \times 4 \times h$	Replace V with 84, ℓ with 6, and w with 4.
$84 = 24h$	Multiply.
$\dfrac{84}{24} = \dfrac{24h}{24}$	Divide each side by 24.
$3.5 = h$	Simplify.

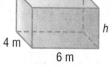

The height of the prism is 3.5 meters.

Check $6 \times 4 \times 3.5 = 84$ ✔

Got It? Do these problems to find out.

d. $V = 94.5$ km^3, $\ell = 7$ km, $h = 3$ km, $w = ?$

Handwritten (left margin):

4 2 3 1
4 . 7 5
36
2850
1425
171.00

4.5
21) 94.5
84
10.5

d. _____
d = 4.5

Guided Practice

1. A rectangular kitchen sink is 25.25 inches long, 19.75 inches wide, and 10 inches deep. Find the amount of water that can be contained in the

   sink. (Examples 1 and 2) *4986. 785*

2. Find the missing dimension of a rectangular prism with a volume of 126 cubic centimeters, a width of $7\frac{7}{8}$ centimeters, and a height of 2 centimeters. (Example 3) *6*

3. **🅠 Building on the Essential Question** Why can you use either the formula $V = \ell wh$ or $V = Bh$ to find the volume of a rectangular prism?

_____

_____

_____

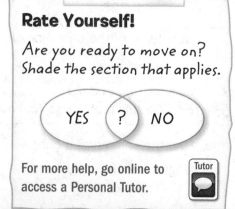

Rate Yourself!

Are you ready to move on? Shade the section that applies.

YES   ?   NO

For more help, go online to access a Personal Tutor.

FOLDABLES *Time to update your Foldable!*

Independent Practice

Go online for Step-by-Step Solutions

Find the volume of each prism. (Example 1)

1. 132

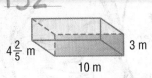

$4\frac{2}{5}$ m   3 m   10 m

Show your work.

44 × 3   132

2. 61.875

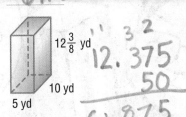

$12\frac{3}{8}$ yd   10 yd   5 yd

$\overset{3\ 2}{12.375}$
$\times\ 50$
61.875

3. 171

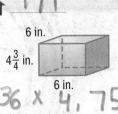

6 in. $4\frac{3}{4}$ in.   6 in.

36 × 4.75

4. A fishing tackle box is 13 inches long, 6 inches wide, and $2\frac{1}{2}$ inches high. What is the volume of the tackle box? (Example 2)

195

5. Find the length of a rectangular prism having a volume of 2,830.5 cubic meters, width of 18.5 meters, and height of 9 meters. (Example 3)

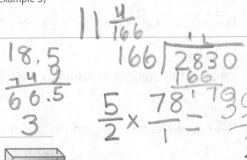

18.5
× 9
166.5

$11\frac{4}{166}$
166) 2830
166

$\frac{5}{2} \times \frac{78}{1} = \frac{390}{2}$

Find the missing dimension of each prism. (Example 3)

6. 6

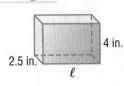

4 in.   2.5 in. ℓ

$V = 60$ in³

7. 3

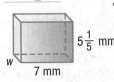

$5\frac{1}{5}$ mm   w   7 mm

$V = 109\frac{1}{5}$ mm³

8. **CCGPS** **Be Precise** In Japan, farmers have created watermelons in the shape of rectangular prisms. Find the volume of a prism-shaped watermelon in cubic inches if its length is 10 inches, its width is $\frac{2}{3}$ foot, and its height is 9 inches.

$90 \times \frac{2}{3}$

60

9. The glass container shown is filled to a height of 2.25 inches.

a. How much sand is currently in the container?

67.5 in

b. How much more sand could the container hold before it overflows? —

c. What percent of the container is filled with sand? 60

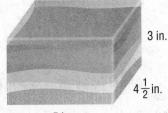

3 in. $4\frac{1}{2}$ in.   5 in.

$\overset{2}{4.5}$
$\times 15$
225
$w45$
675

10. **CCGPS** **Identify Structure** Refer to the graphic novel frame below for Exercises a–c.

a. What is the volume of the short box Pilar chose on the left?

$$512 \text{ in}^2$$

b. What is the volume of Amanda's tall popcorn box on the right?

$$480 \text{ in}^2$$

c. Who received more popcorn, Pilar or Amanda? How much more?

32 inches more– Pilar

 H.O.T. Problems Higher Order Thinking

11. **CCGPS** **Persevere with Problems** Refer to the prism at the right. If all the dimensions of the prism doubled, would the volume double? Explain your reasoning.

No. Instead, it would multiply by 8 – since $27 \times 8 = 216$.

12. **CCGPS** **Justify Conclusions** Which has the greater volume: a prism with a length of 5 inches, a width of 4 inches, and a height of 10 inches, or a prism with a length of 10 inches, a width of 5 inches, and a height of 4 inches? Justify your selection. Both are the same– but with different dimensions w. same numbers.

Georgia Test Practice

13. Don used the shoebox to create a home for the toad he caught. Find the volume of the shoebox.

Ⓐ 222 in³

Ⓒ 1,620 in³

Ⓑ 864 in³

Ⓓ 1,710 in³

10 in.

9 in.

18 in.

Extra Practice

Find the volume of each prism.

14. <u>105.84 cm³</u>

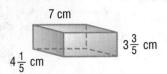

7 cm

$3\frac{3}{5}$ cm

$4\frac{1}{5}$ cm

15. _____

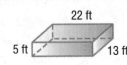

22 ft

5 ft   13 ft

16. _____

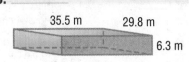

35.5 m   29.8 m

6.3 m

Homework Help

$V = \ell wh$

$V = 7 \times 4\frac{1}{5} \times 3\frac{3}{5}$

$V = \frac{7}{1} \times \frac{21}{5} \times \frac{18}{5}$

$V = \frac{2{,}646}{25}$

$V = 105.84$

17. Find the volume of the pet carrier shown at the right.

_____

18. What is the width of a rectangular prism with a length of 13 feet, volume of 11,232 cubic feet, and height of 36 feet?

_____

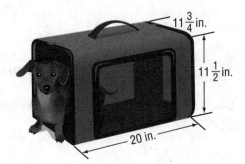

$11\frac{3}{4}$ in.

$11\frac{1}{2}$ in.

20 in.

19. The Palo Duro Canyon is 120 miles long, as much as 20 miles wide, and has a maximum depth of more than 0.15 mile. What is the approximate volume of this canyon?

_____

20. **CCGPS** **Use Math Tools** Use the table at the right.

a. What is the approximate volume of the small truck?

_____

b. The Davis family is moving, and they estimate that they will need a truck with about 1,250 cubic feet. Which truck would be best for them to rent?

_____

c. About how many cubic feet greater is the volume of the Mega Moving Truck than the 2-bedroom moving truck?

_____

_____

Inside Dimensions of Moving Trucks			
Truck	**Length (ft)**	**Width (ft)**	**Height (ft)**
Van	10	$6\frac{1}{2}$	6
Small Truck	$11\frac{1}{13}$	$7\frac{5}{12}$	$6\frac{3}{4}$
2-Bedroom Moving Truck	$14\frac{1}{2}$	$7\frac{7}{12}$	$7\frac{1}{6}$
3-Bedroom Moving Truck	$20\frac{5}{6}$	$7\frac{1}{2}$	$8\frac{1}{12}$
Mega Moving Truck	$22\frac{1}{4}$	$7\frac{7}{12}$	$8\frac{5}{12}$

Georgia Test Practice

21. Poppy's Pasta comes in the rectangular box shown. What is the volume of the box?

21.4 cm

6.8 cm

13.7 cm

Ⓐ 41.9 cm³

Ⓑ 93.16 cm³

Ⓒ 1,993.624 cm³

Ⓓ 2,058 cm³

22. A pet carrier company is creating a new size carrier. It has a width of 27 centimeters, a length of 7 centimeters, and a volume of 6,426 cubic centimeters. Find the height.

← 27 cm →

7 cm

Ⓕ 34 centimeters

Ⓖ 38 centimeters

Ⓗ 42 centimeters

Ⓘ 46 centimeters

23. Short Response The volume of the rectangular prism shown is 2,520 cubic inches. Find the width of the prism.

9 in.

w

14 in.

 Common Core Review

Classify each triangle by the measure of the angles. MCC5.G.4

24. _____

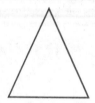

25. _____

26. _____

27. Draw the next figure in the pattern below. MCC4.OA.5, MCC4.G.2

28. Triangles are often used in designing bridges. Classify the triangle shown by the measure of its sides. Explain. MCC5.G.4

_____

_____

Volume of Triangular Prisms

What You'll Learn

Scan the lesson. Predict two things you will learn about finding the volume of triangular prisms.

- _____
  _____

- _____
  _____

 Essential Question

HOW is shape important when measuring a figure?

 Vocabulary

triangular prism

CCGPS **Common Core GPS**

Content Standards
Extension of MCC6.G.2

Mathematical Practices
1, 3, 4, 6, 8

Real-World Link

Camping Ari has a pup tent like the one shown. The opening of the tent has a base and a height of 6 feet. The length of the tent is 8 feet.

What is the area of the front

triangular face? _____

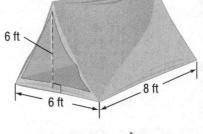

6 ft

8 ft

6 ft

Collaborate On a piece of grid paper, draw a right triangle with a base and height of 4 units as shown.

1. What is the area of the triangle?

   _____

2. Suppose you cover the triangle with cubes the size of one square on the grid paper. How many cubes would you use? (*Hint*: You can cut and reassemble the cubes.) _____

3. How many cubes would you use if you had 4 layers? _____

4. **CCGPS** **Make a Conjecture** Write a formula to find the volume of a triangular prism. _____

Volume of a Triangular Prism

Words	The volume V of a triangular prism is the area of the base B times the height h.	**Model**
Symbols	$V = Bh$, where B is the area of the base	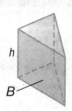

In a **triangular prism**, the bases are congruent triangles. The diagram below shows that the volume of a triangular prism is also the product of the area of the base B and the height h of the prism.

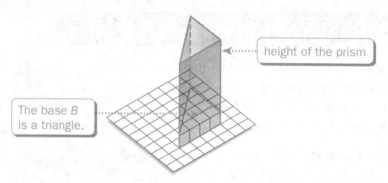

height of the prism

The base B is a triangle.

Example

1. Find the volume of the triangular prism.

The area of the triangle is $\frac{1}{2} \cdot 8 \cdot 10$, so B is $\frac{1}{2} \cdot 8 \cdot 10$.

$V = Bh$ Volume of a prism

$V = \left(\frac{1}{2} \cdot 8 \cdot 10\right)h$ Replace B with $\frac{1}{2} \cdot 8 \cdot 10$.

$V = \left(\frac{1}{2} \cdot 8 \cdot 10\right)13$ Replace h with 13, the height of the prism.

$V = 520$ Multiply.

The volume is 520 cubic meters or 520 m³.

8 m   13 m

10 m

12.8 m

Base

Before finding the volume of a triangular prism, identify the base. In Exercise b, the base is not on the "bottom." The base is one of the parallel faces.

Show your work.

Got It? Do these problems to find out.

a.

3.5 m   4 m

7 m

4 m   4 m

b.

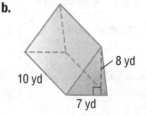

8 yd

10 yd

7 yd

a. _____

b. _____

Example

Tutor

2. **A large skateboard ramp is shown. Find the volume of the triangular prism.**

The base is a triangle with a base length of 10 feet and a height of 7 feet. The height of the prism is 4 feet.

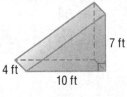

$V = Bh$	Volume of a prism
$V = \left(\frac{1}{2} \cdot 10 \cdot 7\right)h$	Replace B with $\frac{1}{2} \cdot 10 \cdot 7$.
$V = \left(\frac{1}{2} \cdot 10 \cdot 7\right)4$	Replace h with 4, the height of the prism.
$V = 140$	Multiply.

The volume is 140 cubic feet or 140 ft^3.

Got It? Do this problem to find out.

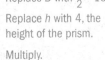
Show your work.

c. Find the volume of a triangular prism-shaped model with a base of 32 square centimeters and a height of 6 centimeters.

c. _____

Find Missing Dimensions

To find missing dimensions of a triangular prism, replace the variables with known measurements. Then solve for the unknown measurement.

Example

Tutor

3. **Find the height of the triangular prism.**

$V = Bh$	Volume of a triangular prism
$V = \left(\frac{1}{2} \cdot 1 \cdot 0.3\right)h$	Replace B with $\frac{1}{2} \cdot 1 \cdot 0.3$.
$12 = \left(\frac{1}{2} \cdot 1 \cdot 0.3\right)h$	Replace V with 12.
$12 = 0.15h$	Multiply.
$\frac{12}{0.15} = \frac{0.15h}{0.15}$	Divide each side by 0.15.
$80 = h$	Simplify.

So, the height of the prism is 80 cm.

Got It? Do these problems to find out.

Find the missing dimension of the triangular prism.

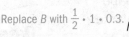

d. $V = 55$ km^3, base length = 2 km, base height = 5 km, $h = ?$

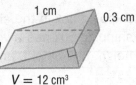

d. _____

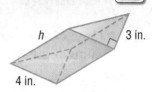

Example

Tutor

4. Dwane bought a cheese wedge for his March Madness party. The cheese wedge has the dimensions shown. The volume of the cheese wedge is 54 cubic inches. What is the height of the cheese wedge?

h 3 in.

4 in.

$V = Bh$	Volume of a triangular prism
$54 = \left(\dfrac{1}{2} \cdot 3 \cdot 4\right)h$	Replace V with 54, and B with $\dfrac{1}{2} \cdot 3 \cdot 4$.
$54 = 6h$	Multiply.
$\dfrac{54}{6} = \dfrac{6h}{6}$	Divide each side by 6.
$9 = h$	Simplify.

So, the height of the cheese wedge is 9 inches.

Guided Practice

Check ✓

Find the volume of each prism. Round to the nearest tenth if necessary. (Example 1)

1. _____

3 ft   5 ft

6 ft

Show your work.

2. _____

4 m

2 m

3 m

3.6 m

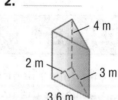

3. Dirk has a triangular-shaped piece of cheesecake in his lunch. Find the volume of the piece of cheesecake. (Example 2)

4 in.

3 in.

6 in.

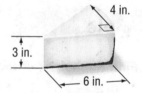

4. Find the base length of a shipping box in the shape of a triangular prism. The shipping box has a volume of 276 cubic feet, a base height of 6.9 feet, and a height of 10 feet. (Examples 3 and 4)

_____

5. **Building on the Essential Question** How is the area of a triangle related to the volume of a triangular prism?

_____

_____

Rate Yourself!

How well do you understand volume of triangular prisms? Circle the image that applies.

Clear   Somewhat Clear   Not So Clear

For more help, go online to access a Personal Tutor.

Tutor

FOLDABLES *Time to update your Foldable!*

Independent Practice

Go online for Step-by-Step Solutions

Find the volume of each prism. Round to the nearest tenth if necessary. (Example 1)

1. _____

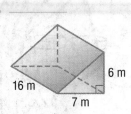

16 m
6 m
7 m

2. _____

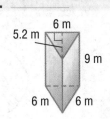

5.2 m
6 m
9 m
6 m   6 m

3 _____

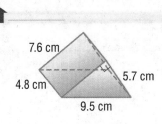

7.6 cm
4.8 cm
5.7 cm
9.5 cm

4. A wheelchair ramp is in the shape of a triangular prism. It has a base area of 37.4 square yards and a height of 5 yards. Find the volume of the ramp. (Example 2)

_____

5 A triangular prism has a height of 9 inches. The triangular base has a base of 3 inches and a height of 8 inches. Find the volume of the prism. (Example 2)

_____

Find the missing dimension of each triangular prism. (Example 3)

6. x = _____

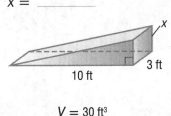

10 ft
3 ft
x

V = 30 ft³

7. x = _____

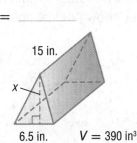

15 in.
x
6.5 in.

V = 390 in³

8. x = _____

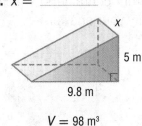

x
5 m
9.8 m

V = 98 m³

9. Mr. Standford's greenhouse has the dimensions shown. The volume of the greenhouse is 90 cubic yards. Find the missing dimension of the greenhouse. (Example 4)

_____

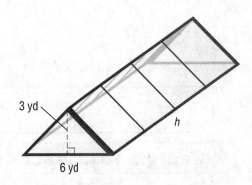

3 yd
6 yd
h

10. **CCGPS** **Be Precise** Darcy built the dollhouse shown.

a. What is the volume of the first floor?

_____

b. What is the volume of the attic space?

_____

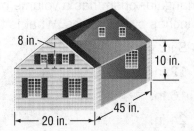

8 in.
10 in.
45 in.
20 in.

11. CCGPS **Find the Error** Amanda is finding the volume of the triangular prism. Find her mistake and correct it.

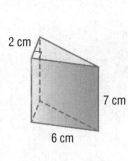

$$V = Bh$$
$$V = 12 \times 7$$
$$V = 84 \text{ cm}^3$$

12. CCGPS **Identify Repeated Reasoning** A rectangular prism and a triangular prism each have a volume of 210 cubic meters. Find possible sets of dimensions for each prism.

13. CCGPS **Persevere with Problems** A candy company sells mints in two different containers. Which container shown below holds more mints? Justify your answer.

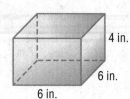

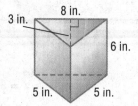

Georgia Test Practice

14. A triangular prism has a volume of 1,560 cubic inches and a base of 13 inches by 15 inches. What is the height of the prism?

Ⓐ 8 in.

Ⓑ 12 in.

Ⓒ 16 in.

Ⓓ 24 in.

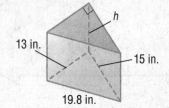

Extra Practice

Find the volume of each prism. Round to the nearest tenth if necessary.

15. 346.5 ft^3

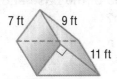

7 ft 9 ft
11 ft

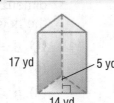

16. _____

17 yd   5 yd
14 yd

17. _____

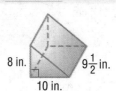

8 in. $9\frac{1}{2}$ in.
10 in.

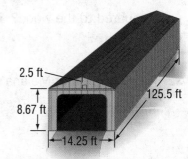

Homework Help →

$V = Bh$

$V = \left(\frac{1}{2} \cdot 7 \cdot 9\right)(11)$

$V = 346.5$

18. A candle is in the shape of a triangular prism. The base has an area of 30 square inches. The candle has a height of 6 inches. Find the volume of the candle.

_____

_____

19. A cabinet is in the shape of a triangular prism. The triangular base has a base length of 14 inches and a base height of 22 inches. The cabinet is 67.5 inches tall. What is the volume of the cabinet?

_____

_____

Find the missing dimension of each triangular prism.

20. $x =$ _____

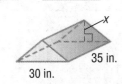

x
35 in.
30 in.

$V = 6{,}300 \text{ in}^3$

21. $x =$ _____

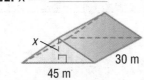

x
30 m
45 m

$V = 10{,}125 \text{ m}^3$

22. $x =$ _____

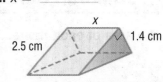

x
1.4 cm
2.5 cm

$V = 3.5 \text{ cm}^3$

23. What is the volume of the A-frame tent shown?

_____

_____

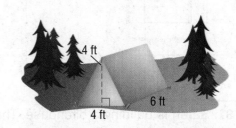

4 ft
6 ft
4 ft

24. CCSS **Be Precise** A covered bridge in Vermont has the dimensions shown.

a. What is the volume of the bottom section rounded to the nearest tenth? _____

_____

b. What is the volume of the roof, rounded to the nearest tenth? _____

_____

2.5 ft
125.5 ft
8.67 ft
14.25 ft

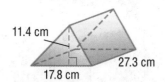

25. Find the volume of the triangular prism shown, rounded to the nearest tenth.

11.4 cm

27.3 cm

17.8 cm

Ⓐ 5,539.7 cm³   Ⓒ 2,769.9 cm³

Ⓑ 2,867.3 cm³   Ⓓ 1,846.6 cm³

26. A triangular prism has a volume of 240 cubic meters. Which of the measurements below are *not* possible dimensions for the area of the base and the height of the prism?

Ⓕ $B = 48$ m², $h = 5$ m

Ⓖ $B = 24$ m², $h = 10$ m

Ⓗ $B = 12$ m², $h = 20$ m

Ⓘ $B = 20$ m², $h = 4$ m

27. Short Response Tia wants to purchase the corner kitchen cabinet with the greater volume. Find the volume of each cabinet to determine which one Tia should buy.

_____

_____

_____

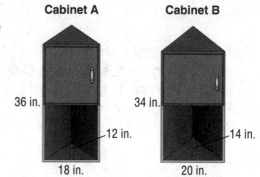

Cabinet A   **Cabinet B**

36 in.   34 in.

12 in.   14 in.

18 in.   20 in.

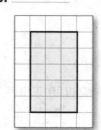

CCGPS Common Core Review

Find the area of each figure. MCC4.MD.3

28. _____

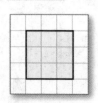

29. _____

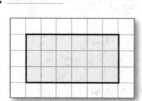

30. _____

31. Sarah is building a birdhouse. The nails she uses are one inch long. The wood board is 1 foot long. How many times smaller are the nails compared to the wood? MCC4.MD.1 _____

32. The floor area of Melana's rectangular closet is 18 square feet. The closet is 6 feet long. How wide is the closet? MCC4.MD.3 _____

Content Standards
MCC6.G.2, MCC6.G.4
Mathematical Practices
1, 3, 4

Case #1 Scooter Storage

Nick works for a sporting goods store. He is stacking boxes of scooters in the storage space at the back of the store. The first layer has 9 boxes.

If the storage area will hold 6 layers of boxes, how many boxes will the storage space hold?

Understand *What are the facts?*

· The first layer has 9 boxes.

· The storage space will hold 6 layers.

Plan *What is your strategy to solve this problem?*

Make a model using centimeter cubes.

Solve *How can you apply the strategy?*

Make a model of one layer of the box by arranging 9 cubes in a 3 × 3 array.

Continue stacking the cubes until there are 6 layers.

So, the storage space will hold 54 boxes.

Check *Does the answer make sense?*

Use the volume formula to check your answer.
$V = 3 \times 3 \times 6$ or 54

So, the storage space will hold a total of 54 boxes.

Analyze the Strategy

Justify Conclusions Suppose the boxes are a different size and the first layer has 6 boxes instead. How many boxes can be stored if the storage space will hold 5 layers? Explain.

_____

_____

_____

Case #2 Contain Your Fun

A storage container is made from plastic that measures $1\frac{1}{2}$ feet long, 2 feet wide, and $2\frac{1}{2}$ feet high.

Find the surface area of the plastic container, including the lid.

Understand

Read the problem. What are you being asked to find?

I need to find _____.

Underline key words and values in the problem.
What information do you know?

The storage container measures _____ long, _____ wide,

and _____ high.

Plan

Choose a problem-solving strategy.

I will use the _____ strategy.

Solve

Use your problem-solving strategy to solve the problem.

Make a model of the container using a net. Then find the area of each rectangle to find the total surface area.

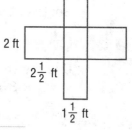

2 ft

$2\frac{1}{2}$ ft

$1\frac{1}{2}$ ft

front and back: 2(_____ × _____) = _____

left and right: 2(_____ × _____) = _____

top and bottom: 2(_____ × _____) = _____

Sum of 6 sides: _____ + _____ + _____ = _____

So, the surface area of the container is _____ square feet.

Check

Use information from the problem to check your answer.

Substitute known values into the surface area formula to check your answer.

S.A. = (_____) + (_____) + (_____) = _____ ft^2

Collaborate Work with a small group to solve the following cases. Show your work on a separate piece of paper.

Case #3 Assembly

DJ is helping set up 7 rows of chairs for a school assembly. There are eight chairs in the first row. Each row after that has two more chairs than the previous row.

If he has 100 chairs, can he set up enough rows? Explain.

_____

_____

Case #4 Paper

Timothy took a piece of notebook paper and cut it in half. Then he placed the 2 pieces on top of each other and cut them in half again to have 4 pieces of paper.

If he could keep cutting the paper in this manner, how many pieces of paper would he have after 6 cuts?

_____

Case #5 Sports

Rosario is packing a crate with boxes of miniature golf putters. Each box has a height of 1 foot, a width of 1 foot, and a length of 3 feet.

How many boxes can Rosario fit in a crate that is 4 feet high, 4 feet wide, and 3 feet long?

_____

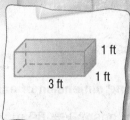

Case #6 Patterns

Circle a strategy below to solve the problem.
- Look for a pattern.
- Act it out.
- Work backward.
- Guess, check and revise.

Draw the seventeenth figure in the pattern.

Show your work.

Mid-Chapter Check

Vocabulary Check

1. **CCGPS** **Be Precise** Define *three-dimensional figure*. Give an example of a figure that is a three-dimensional figure and an example of a figure that is not a three-dimensional figure. (Lesson 1)

   A 3-Dimensional figure is a shape which has length, width, height.

Fill in the blanks in the sentences below with the correct terms. (Lesson 1)

2. Volume is the amount of ___space___ inside a three-dimensional figure.

3. Volume is measured in ___cubic___ units.

Skills Check and Problem Solving

Find the volume of each prism. Round to the nearest tenth if necessary. (Lessons 1 and 2)

4. 4 1/5

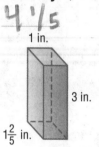
1 in.
3 in.
$1\frac{2}{5}$ in.

5. _____

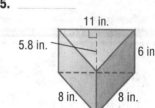
11 in.
5.8 in.
6 in.
8 in.   8 in.

6. _____

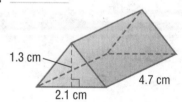
1.3 cm
2.1 cm
4.7 cm

Find the missing dimension of each figure. (Lessons 1 and 2)

7. rectangular prism: $V = 80$ m^3; length = 5 m; width = 4 m

   $h = $ 4 m

8. triangular prism: $V = 42$ cm^3; base length = 2 cm; base height = 6 cm

   $h = $ 7

9. A storage unit is in the shape of a rectangular prism. Find the volume of the storage unit. (Lesson 1) ___15/16 sq. in___

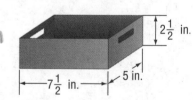
$2\frac{1}{2}$ in.
$7\frac{1}{2}$ in.
5 in.

10. **Georgia Test Practice** What is the height of a rectangular prism with a volume of 63 cubic feet and a base area of 15 square feet? (Lesson 1)

    Ⓐ 945 feet   Ⓒ 48 feet

    Ⓑ 78 feet   Ⓓ 4.2 feet

Inquiry HOW can you use nets to find surface area?

CCGPS Content Standards MCC6.G.4

Mathematical Practices 1, 3, 4

Cereal If you want to know the amount of cereal that can fit in the box, you would find the volume. But if you want to know how much cardboard is needed to make the box, you would find the *surface area.*

Investigation 1

One way to find the surface area is to use a *net.* Nets are two-dimensional patterns of three-dimensional figures. When you construct a net, you are decomposing the three-dimensional figure into separate shapes.

Step 1 Use a cereal box in the shape of a rectangular prism. Measure and record the length, width, and height of the box on the lines below.

Length: _____

Width: _____

Height: _____

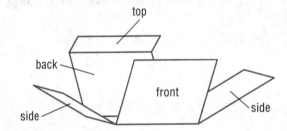

Step 2 Using a marker, label the top, bottom, front, back and side faces of the box.

Step 3 Using scissors, carefully cut along three edges of the top face and then cut down each vertical edge.

Step 4 Measure and record the area of each face, using the dimensions of the box shown in the table.

Step 5 Add the areas of each face to find the surface area of the box.

Face	Length	Width	Area of Face
Front			
Back			
Side 1			
Side 2			
Top			
Bottom			

☐ + ☐ + ☐ + ☐ + ☐ + ☐ = ☐

So, the surface area of the box is ☐ square inches.

Orthogonal drawings consist of separate views of an object taken from different angles. You can make a net from orthogonal drawings.

Step 1 Find the dimensions of each side of a rectangular prism from the orthogonal drawing.

Orthogonal Drawing		
View	**Drawing**	**Dimensions**
Front and Back		×
Sides		×
Top and Bottom		×

Step 2 Use grid paper to draw a net from the orthogonal drawing. Trace and cut out your drawing and tape it in the space below. Check the dimensions of each face using the information in the table.

Show your work.

Step 3 Fold the net into a three-dimensional figure. Draw the resulting figure in the space provided.

So, the figure is a _____.

It has a surface area of ☐ square units.

Collaborate

Model with Mathematics Work with a partner. Use a net to determine the surface area of each prism. Draw a net of each prism on the provided grid.

1. _____ mm²

2 mm
2 mm 2 mm

2. _____ in²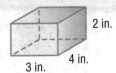

2 in.
3 in. 4 in.

Show your work.

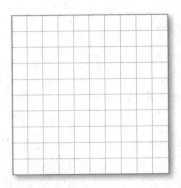

3. _____ ft²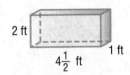

2 ft
4½ ft 1 ft

4. _____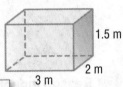

1.5 m
3 m 2 m

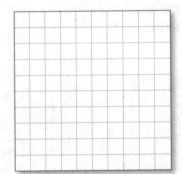

Draw a net on the grid from the orthogonal drawing. Then find the surface area of the prism.

5. _____ square units

Orthogonal Drawing	
View	**Drawing**
Front and Back	
Sides	
Top and Bottom	

Work with a partner to complete the table. The first one is done for you.

Dimensions of Rectangular Prism	Area of Top (units²)	Area of Bottom (units²)	Area of Side 1 (units²)	Area of Side 2 (units²)	Area of Front (units²)	Area of Back (units²)	Surface Area (units²)
1 × 2 × 3	2	2	6	6	3	3	22
6. 2 × 2 × 3							
7. 3 × 3 × 3							
8. 3 × 2 × 8							
9. 6 × 6 × 6							

10. Compare the surface area for Exercise 7 to the surface area for Exercise 9. How does doubling each dimension affect the surface area?

_____

_____

_____

11. CCGPS **Reason Inductively** Write a formula to find the surface area of a rectangular prism. Use your formula to find the surface area of the prism

in Investigation 2. _____

 Reflect

12. CCGPS **Model with Mathematics** Write a real-world problem that involves the surface area of rectangular prisms. Provide the dimensions and the surface

area. _____

_____

13. Will the surface area of a cube ever have the same numerical value as the volume of the cube?

_____

_____

14. (Inquiry) HOW can you use nets to find surface area?

_____

_____

Surface Area of Rectangular Prisms

What You'll Learn

Scan the lesson. Predict two things you will learn about finding the surface area of rectangular prisms.

- _____
  _____
- _____
  _____

Essential Question

HOW is shape important when measuring a figure?

Vocab
Vocabulary

surface area

Common Core GPS

Content Standards
MCC6.G.4

Mathematical Practices
1, 3, 4, 8

Vocabulary Start-Up

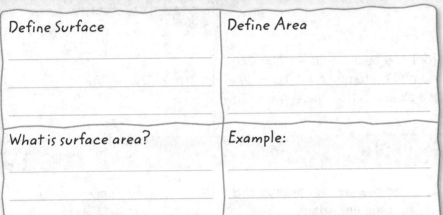

Define Surface	Define Area
_____	_____
_____	_____
_____	_____
What is surface area?	**Example:**
_____	_____
_____	_____
_____	_____

Real-World Link

Gifts Roberta is wrapping a gift for her sister's quinceañera. She places it in a box with the measurements shown below.

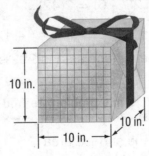

10 in.

10 in.

10 in.

1. What is the area of one face of the box?

_____

2. How many faces does the box have? ⬚

3. What operations would you use to find the surface area of the box?

_____

Surface Area of a Rectangular Prism

Words The surface area S.A. of a rectangular prism with length ℓ, width w, and height h is the sum of the areas of the faces.

Model

Symbols S.A. $= 2\ell h + 2\ell w + 2hw$

The surface area of a prism is the sum of the areas of its faces.

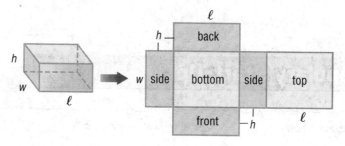

front and back: $\ell h + \ell h = 2\ell h$
top and bottom: $\ell w + \ell w = 2\ell w$ $\Big\}$ $2\ell h + 2\ell w + 2hw$
two sides: $hw + hw = 2hw$

Example

Watch   Tutor

1. **Find the surface area of the rectangular prism.**

Find the area of each pair of faces.

front and back: $2(8 \cdot 6) = 2(48)$

top and bottom: $2(7 \cdot 8) = 2(56)$

sides: $2(7 \cdot 6) = 2(42)$

$48 + 48 + 56 + 56 + 42 + 42 = 292$ Add the area of each face.

So, the surface area is 292 square meters.

Got It? Do this problem to find out.

a. Find the surface area of the rectangular prism.

a. _____

Nets

The net shows that a rectangular prism has six faces. The faces can be grouped as three pairs of congruent sides. The colors indicate which faces are congruent.

Show your work.

Find Surface Area Using a Formula

You can use nets or models to find the surface area of a rectangular prism. You can also use the surface area formula,
S.A. $= 2\ell h + 2\ell w + 2hw$.

Examples

Tutor

2. **Find the surface area of the rectangular prism.**

Find the area of each face.

front and back:
$2\ell h = 2(7)(4)$ or 56

top and bottom:
$2\ell w = 2(7)(5)$ or 70

left and right sides:
$2hw = 2(4)(5)$ or 40

Add to find the surface area.

The surface area is $56 + 70 + 40$ or 166 square feet.

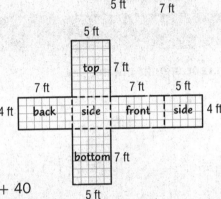

3. **Find the surface area of the rectangular prism.**

To find the area of each face determine the dimensions.

$\ell = 7, w = 4.8, h = 6$

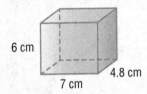
6 cm
7 cm
4.8 cm

front and back: $2\ell h = 2\left(\right)\left(\right)$ or $\boxed{}$

top and bottom: $2\ell w = 2\left(\right)\left(\right)$ or $\boxed{}$

two sides: $2hw = 2\left(\right)\left(\right)$ or $\boxed{}$

Add to find the surface area.

$\boxed{} + \boxed{} + \boxed{}$ or $\boxed{}$ square centimeters

Got It? Do this problem to find out.

Show your work.

b. Find the surface area of the rectangular prism.

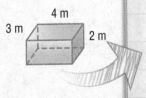
4 m
3 m
2 m

b. _____

Tutor

4. **STEM** A geode is being sent as a gift. It is packed in a box that measures 7 inches long, 3 inches wide, and 16 inches tall. What is the surface area of the box?

$S.A. = 2\ell h + 2\ell w + 2hw$	Surface area of a prism
$S.A. = 2(7)(16) + 2(7)(3) + 2(16)(3)$	$\ell = 7, w = 3, h = 16$
$S.A. = 14(16) + 14(3) + 32(3)$	Multiply.
$S.A. = 224 + 42 + 96$	Multiply.
$S.A. = 362$	Add.

The surface area of the box is 362 square inches.

Guided Practice

Check ✓

Find the surface area of each rectangular prism. (Examples 1–3)

1.

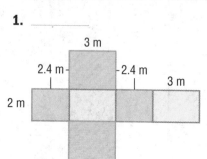

3 m
2.4 m — 2.4 m
3 m
2 m

2.

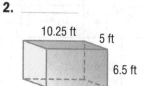

10.25 ft   5 ft
6.5 ft

3.

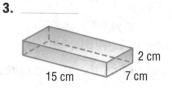

2 cm
15 cm   7 cm

 Show your work.

4. Tomás keeps his diecast car in a glass display case as shown. What is the surface area of the glass, including the bottom? (Example 4)

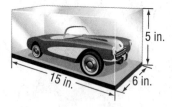

5 in.
15 in.   6 in.

5. **Building on the Essential Question** What is the relationship between area and surface area?

Rate Yourself!

Are you ready to move on? Shade the section that applies.

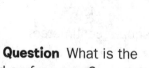

I have a few questions.
I'm ready to move on.
I have a lot of questions.

For more help, go online to access a Personal Tutor.

Tutor

FOLDABLES *Time to update your Foldable!*

Name _____ My Homework _____

Find the surface area of each rectangular prism. (Examples 1–3)

1. _____

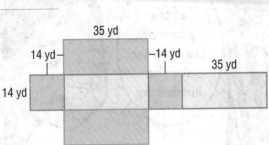

35 yd
14 yd— —14 yd
35 yd
14 yd

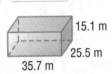
Show your work.

2. _____

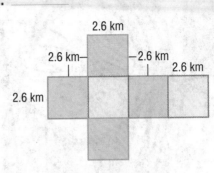

2.6 km
2.6 km— —2.6 km
2.6 km
2.6 km

3

15.1 m
25.5 m
35.7 m

4. _____

12 in.
5 in.
4 in.

5. **STEM** A game box for video games is shaped like a rectangular prism. What is the surface area of the game box? (Example 4)

15 cm
11 cm
16 cm

_____

6. **CCGPS** **Justify Conclusions** Martina estimates that the surface area of a rectangular prism with a length of 13.2 feet, a width of 6 feet, and a height of 8 feet is about 460 square feet. Is her estimate reasonable? Explain your reasoning.

_____

_____

7 **CCGPS** **Justify Conclusions** Find the surface area of each shipping package. Which package has the greater surface area? Does the same package have a greater volume? Explain your reasoning to a classmate.

Package A 3 in.
MAIL
12 in.
FREIGHT
14 in.

Package B 8 in.
MAIL
6 in.
FREIGHT
11 in.

_____

_____

8. **Model with Mathematics** Refer to the graphic novel frame below for Exercises a–c. (*Hint:* The boxes are missing the top face.)

  a. What is the surface area of the short box on the left? _____

  b. What is the surface area of the tall box on the right? _____

  c. How much more surface area does the larger container have?

  _____

 H.O.T. Problems Higher Order Thinking

CCGPS **Persevere with Problems** All of the triangular faces of the figure are congruent.

9. What is the area of one of the triangular faces? the square face?

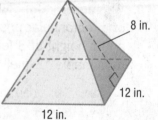

  _____

10. Use what you know about finding the surface area of a rectangular prism to find the surface area of the square pyramid.

  _____

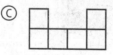 **Georgia Test Practice**

11. Which net can be used to make and find the surface area of a cube?

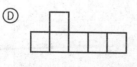

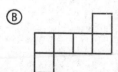

Extra Practice

Find the surface area of each rectangular prism.

12. 150 ft²

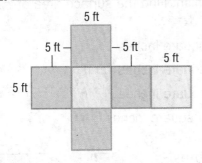

5 ft
5 ft — — 5 ft
5 ft
5 ft

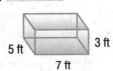

$2(5)(5) + 2(5)(5) + 2(5)(5)$
$= 50 + 50 + 50$
$= 150$

13. _____

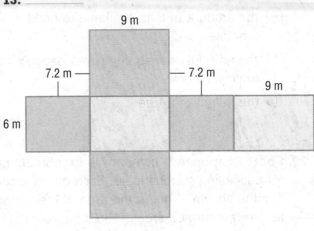

9 m
7.2 m — — 7.2 m
6 m
9 m

14. _____

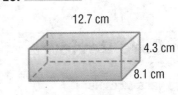

5 ft
3 ft
7 ft

15. _____

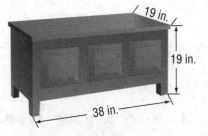

12.7 cm
4.3 cm
8.1 cm

16. Nadine is going to paint her younger sister's toy chest, including the bottom. What is the approximate surface area that she will paint? _____

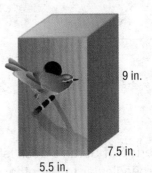

19 in.
19 in.
38 in.

_____

17. **CCGPS** **Identify Repeated Reasoning** Chrissy is making a bird nesting box for her backyard.

a. What is the surface area of the nesting box, including the hole? _____

9 in.
7.5 in.
5.5 in.

b. What is the surface area if the width is doubled?

_____

_____

c. What is the surface area if the width is half as great?

_____

_____

18. Which measure can be classified as surface area?

Ⓐ the amount of water in a lake

Ⓑ the amount of land available to build a house

Ⓒ the amount of wrapping paper needed to cover a box

Ⓓ the height of a tree

19. Dilip is going to paint a shoebox to use for storage of his trading cards. The shoebox is 23 inches long, 10 inches wide, and 8 inches high. Find the surface area of the shoebox.

Ⓕ 246 square inches

Ⓖ 828 square inches

Ⓗ 988 square inches

Ⓘ 1,840 square inches

20. Short Response A company is experimenting with two new boxes for packaging merchandise. Each box is a cube with the side lengths shown. What is the ratio of the surface area of the smaller box to the surface area of the larger box?

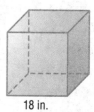

12 in.

18 in.

Common Core Review

Add or multiply. MCC5.NBT.5, MCC4.NBT.4

21. 14 × 16 = _____

22. 72 + 62 + 84 = _____

23. 27 × 63 = _____

24. Classify the triangle by the measure of its sides. Explain. MCC5.G.4

15 in.   15 in.

15 in.

25. The top of Sarah's desk is a hexagon. One side of the desk is perpendicular to the other side. Angle x is created where the sides meet. What type of angle is angle x? MCC4.G.2

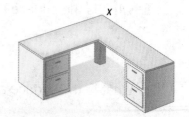

Inquiry HOW is the area of a triangle related to the surface area of a triangular prism?

 Content Standards
MCC6.G.4

Mathematical Practices
1, 3, 4, 7

Packaging A computer hardware company packages batteries and cords in boxes shaped like triangular prisms. You can use nets and drawings to determine the surface area of the box.

Investigation

Use orthogonal drawings to find the surface area of a triangular prism. A *triangular prism* is a prism that has triangular bases.

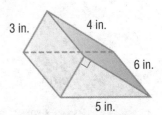

3 in.   4 in.   6 in.   5 in.

Step 1 Find the dimensions of each side of the triangular prism from the orthogonal drawing.

View	**Drawing**	**Dimensions (in.)**	**Area of Face (in²)**	**View**	**Drawing**	**Dimensions (in.)**	**Area of Face (in²)**
Bases		base = 3 height = 4	$\frac{1}{2}(3 \times 4) = 6$	Bottom		length = 6 width = 5	$6 \times 5 = 30$
Left		length = 6 width = 3	$6 \times 3 = 18$	Right		length = 6 width = 4	$6 \times 4 = 24$

Step 2 Use grid paper to draw a net. Check the dimensions of each face using the information in the table.

Step 3 Add the area of each face to find the surface area of the figure. Remember, there are two bases.

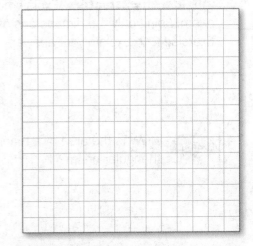

☐ + ☐ + ☐ + ☐ + ☐ = ☐

So, the surface area is ☐ square units.

Model with Mathematics Work with a partner. Use nets to determine the surface area of each prism. Draw a net of each prism on the provided grid paper.

1. _____ m²

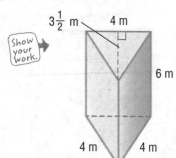

2. _____ cm²

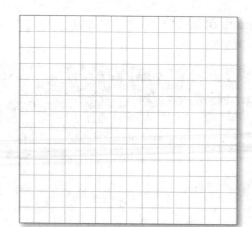

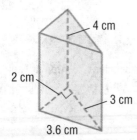

3. **Identify Structure** Explain how to find the surface area of a triangular prism, using only the dimensions of the figure. Use the dimensions in Exercise 2 to explain your answer.

_____

_____

4. **Inquiry** HOW is the area of a triangle related to the surface area of a triangular prism?

_____

_____

Surface Area of Triangular Prisms

What You'll Learn

Scan the lesson. Predict two things you will learn about finding the surface area of triangular prisms.

- _____
- _____

Essential Question

HOW is shape important when measuring a figure?

Common Core GPS

Content Standards
MCC6.G.4

Mathematical Practices
1, 2, 3, 4, 6

Real-World Link

Ramp Raj and his dad are building a ramp to move his dirt bike onto a trailer.

24 ft

2 ft   3 ft

24 ft

Fill in the table by drawing the sides of the ramp and naming the shape of each face.

	Face	Draw the Face	Shape of the Face
1.	Front		
2.	Back		
3.	Top		
4.	Bottom		
5.	Side		

Surface Area of a Triangular Prism

Words

The surface area of a triangular prism is the sum of the areas of the two triangular bases and the three rectangular faces.

Model

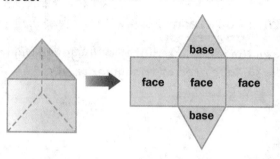

A triangular prism is a prism that has triangular bases. When the bases are equilateral triangles, the areas of the three rectangular faces are equal. You can use a net to find the surface area of a triangular prism.

Example

1. **Find the surface area of the triangular prism.**

To find the surface area of the triangular prism, find the area of each face and add.

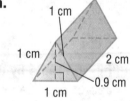

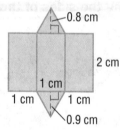

area of each triangular base: $\frac{1}{2}(1)(0.9) = 0.45$

area of each rectangular face: $1(2) = 2$

Add to find the surface area.

$0.45 + 0.45 + 2 + 2 + 2 = 6.9$ square centimeters

Got It? Do this problem to find out.

a. _____

a. Find the surface area of the triangular prism.

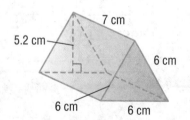

Surface Area of Other Triangular Prisms

You can also find the surface area of any triangular prism by adding the areas of all the sides of the prism using an orthogonal drawing.

Example

Tutor

2. **Find the surface area of the triangular prism.**

Find the area of each face and add. For this prism, each rectangular face has a different area.

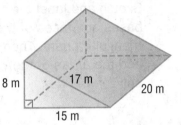
8 m   17 m   20 m   15 m

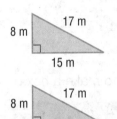
8 m   17 m   15 m

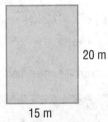
20 m   15 m

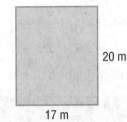
20 m   17 m

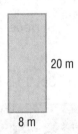
20 m   8 m

8 m   17 m   15 m   8 m   17 m   15 m

area of each triangular base: $\frac{1}{2}(15)(8) = 60$

area of the rectangular faces: $15(20) = 300$

$$17(20) = 340$$
$$8(20) = 160$$

Add to find the surface area.

$60 + 60 + 300 + 340 + 160 = 920$ square meters

Got It? Do this problem to find out.

Show your work.

Find the surface area of each triangular prism.

b.

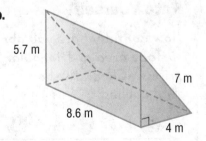
5.7 m   7 m   8.6 m   4 m

c.

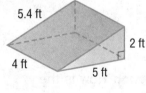
5.4 ft   2 ft   4 ft   5 ft

b. _____

c. _____

 Example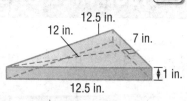

3. A bakery boxes pie pieces in a triangular prism box, as shown. Find the amount of cardboard used to make a box for a slice of pie.

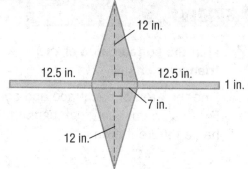

Sketch and label the bases and faces of the triangular prism. Then add the areas of the polygons.

Surface area $= 2\left(\dfrac{1}{2} \cdot 7 \cdot 12\right) + 2(1 \cdot 12.5) + (1 \cdot 7)$

$ = 84 + 25 + 7 \text{ or } 116$

So, 116 square inches of cardboard is needed to make a box.

Guided Practice

Check ✓

1. Find the surface area of the triangular prism. (Examples 1–2) _____

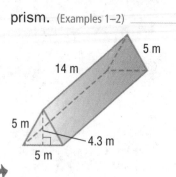

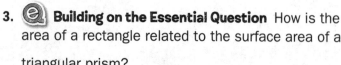

2. A skateboarding ramp is in the shape of a triangular prism. If the entire ramp is to be painted, what is the surface area to be painted? (Example 3) _____

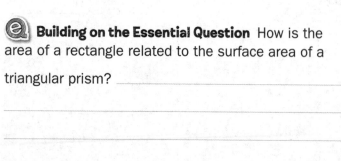

3. 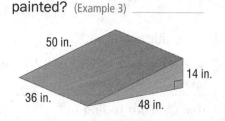 **Building on the Essential Question** How is the area of a rectangle related to the surface area of a triangular prism? _____

_____

_____

Rate Yourself!

How confident are you about surface area of triangular prisms? Check the box that applies.

For more help, go online to access a Personal Tutor.

FOLDABLES Time to update your Foldable!

Independent Practice

Go online for Step-by-Step Solutions

Find the surface area of each triangular prism. (Examples 1–2)

1. _____

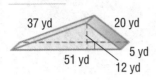

37 yd   20 yd
51 yd   5 yd
12 yd

2. _____

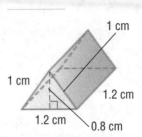

1 cm
1 cm
1.2 cm
1.2 cm
0.8 cm

3. _____

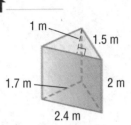

1 m   1.5 m
1.7 m   2 m
2.4 m

4. _____

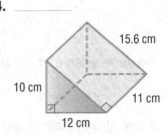

15.6 cm
10 cm
11 cm
12 cm

5. A tent is in the shape of a triangular prism. About how much canvas, including the floor, is used to make the tent? (Example 3)

_____

Show your work.

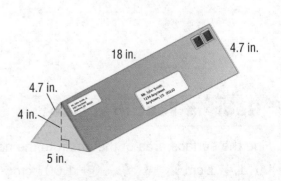

1.7 yd
2 yd   2 yd
3 yd
1 yd   1 yd

6. A decorative gift box is in the shape of a triangular prism as shown. What is the surface area of the box? (Example 3)

_____

12.5 in.
10 in.
5 in.
7.5 in.

7. A mailer for posters is a triangular prism as shown. Find the surface area of the mailer. (Example 3)

_____

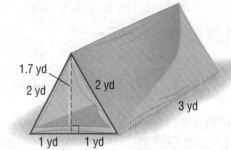

18 in.   4.7 in.
4.7 in.
4 in.
5 in.

8. **Multiple Representations** The figure shows the dimensions of a triangular prism.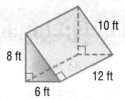

   a. Models Draw a model of the faces and bases of the triangular prism.

Show your work.

   b. Words Describe the triangular prism. _____

_____

_____

   c. Numbers Find the surface area of the triangular prism using addition.

_____

9. The surface area of a right triangular prism is 228 square inches. The base is a right triangle with a base height of 6 inches and a base length of 8 inches. The length of the third side of the base is 10 inches. Find the height of the prism. _____

 H.O.T. Problems Higher Order Thinking

10. **Reason Abstractly** Describe the dimensions of a triangular prism that has a surface area between 550 square inches and 700 square inches.

_____

_____

11. **Persevere with Problems** Sketch and label two triangular prisms such that one has a greater volume and the other has a greater surface area.

_____

_____

_____

_____

_____

✏️ **Georgia Test Practice**

12. Find the surface area of the prism to the nearest whole number.

   Ⓐ 1,471 cm²   Ⓒ 1,007 cm²

   Ⓑ 945 cm²   Ⓓ 777 cm²

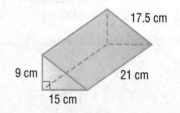

Extra Practice

CCGPS **Be precise** Find the surface area of each triangular prism. Round to the nearest tenth if necessary.

13. 537 ft²

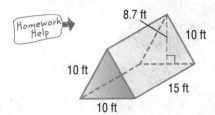

Homework Help

area of each base: $\frac{1}{2} \cdot 10 \cdot 8.7 = 43.5$ ft²

area of each face: $15 \cdot 10 = 150$ ft²

surface area $= 2(43.5) + 3(150)$
$= 537$ ft²

14. 331.9 m²

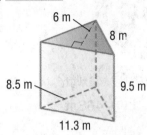

area of each base: $\frac{1}{2} \cdot 11.3 \cdot 6 = 33.9$ m²

areas of faces: $11.3 \cdot 9.5 = 107.35$ m²
$8.5 \cdot 9.5 = 80.75$ m²
$8 \cdot 9.5 = 76$ m²

surface area $= 33.9 + 33.9 + 107.35 +$
$80.75 + 76$ or 331.9 m²

15. _____

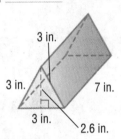

16. _____

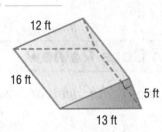

17. _____

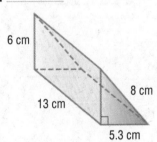

18. _____

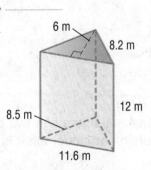

Copy and Solve Find the surface area of each triangular prism using the base triangles shown. Show your work on a separate piece of paper.

19.

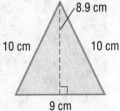

height of prism: 12 cm

20.

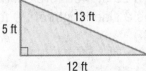

height of prism: 15 ft

Lesson 4 Surface Area of Triangular Prisms **685**

Georgia Test Practice

21. What is the surface area of the prism shown below?

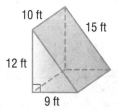

10 ft
15 ft
12 ft
9 ft

Ⓐ 348 ft²   Ⓒ 414 ft²

Ⓑ 360 ft²   Ⓓ 468 ft²

22. **Short Response** A triangular prism has bases that each have an approximate area of 173 square centimeters. The triangles measure 20 centimeters on each side and the prism is 4 centimeters high. What is the surface area of the prism?

_____

23. The attic of the house is a wooden surface. How many square meters of wood are needed to build the roof and floor of the attic?

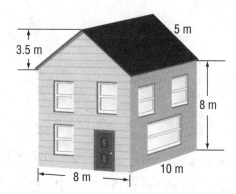

5 m
3.5 m
8 m
10 m
8 m

Ⓕ 140 m²

Ⓖ 158 m²

Ⓗ 180 m²

Ⓘ 640 m²

CCGPS # Common Core Review

Identify each triangle as *acute*, *right*, or *obtuse*. MCC5.G.4

24. _____

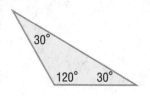

30°
120° 30°

25. _____

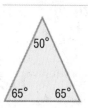

50°
65° 65°

26. _____

20° 70°

27. A certain two-dimensional figure has two pairs of parallel lines, four right angles, and four congruent sides. What is the figure? MCC4.G.2

_____

28. The showcase floor at Murphy Motors is divided into four equal sections. Find the area of Motorcycle Madness if the square showcase floor has a side length of 20 feet. MCC4.MD.3

Sports Stars

Motorcycle Madness   SUV Showcase

Water Wonderland

Inquiry HOW is the area of a triangle related to the surface area of a square pyramid?

CCGPS Content Standards MCC6.G.4

Mathematical Practices 1, 3, 4

Art Anderson Art is designing a paper weight that is shaped like a square pyramid.

Investigation

Use orthogonal drawings to find the surface area of a square pyramid. A *square pyramid* is a three-dimensional figure with a square base and four triangular faces.

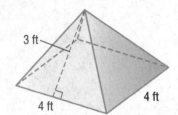

Step 1 Find the dimensions of each side of the square pyramid from the orthogonal drawing.

Orthogonal Drawing			
View	**Drawing**	**Dimensions (ft)**	**Area of Face (ft²)**
Bases	4 ft / 4 ft (square)	length = 4 height = 4	4 × 4 = 16
Triangular Faces	3 ft / 4 ft (triangle)	height = 3 base = 4	$\frac{1}{2}(3 \times 4) = 6$

Step 2 Use grid paper to draw a net. Check the dimensions of each face using the information in the table.

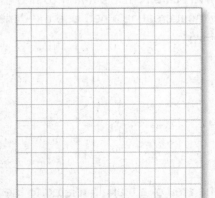

Step 3 Add the area of each face to find the surface area of the figure. Remember, there are four triangular faces.

☐ + ☐ × ☐ = ☐

So, the surface area is ☐ square units.

Collaborate

CCGPS **Model with Mathematics** Work with a partner. Use nets to determine the surface area of each pyramid. Draw a net of each pyramid on the provided grid paper.

1. _____ cm²

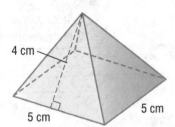

4 cm

5 cm

5 cm

Show your work.

2. _____ m²

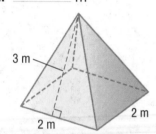

3 m

2 m

2 m

Reflect

3. **CCGPS** **Construct an Argument** Explain how to find the surface area of a square pyramid, without creating a net. Use the dimensions in Exercise 1 to explain your answer.

_____

_____

_____

_____

4. **inquiry** HOW is the area of a triangle related to the surface area of a square pyramid? _____

_____

Surface Area of Pyramids

What You'll Learn

Scan the lesson. Predict two things you will learn about finding the surface area of pyramids.

• _____

_____

• _____

_____

Essential Question

HOW is shape important when measuring a figure?

 Vocabulary

pyramid
vertex
base
lateral face
slant height

 Common Core GPS

Content Standards
MCC6.G.4

Mathematical Practices
1, 3, 4, 6, 7

Vocabulary Start-Up

A **pyramid** is a three-dimensional figure with at least three triangular sides that meet at a common **vertex** and only one **base** that is a polygon. The triangular sides of a square pyramid are called the **lateral faces**. The **slant height** is the height of each lateral face.

Fill in the blanks on the diagram below with vocabulary words.

Real-World Link

Museum Claude made a model of the large pyramid in front of the Louvre museum. His model is shown.

3.5 in.

5 in.   5 in.

1. Draw the faces of the pyramid.

____ ____ ____ ____ ____
base lateral face lateral face lateral face lateral face

Surface Area of a Pyramid

Work Zone

Words The surface area of a pyramid is the sum of the area of the base and the areas of the lateral faces.

Model

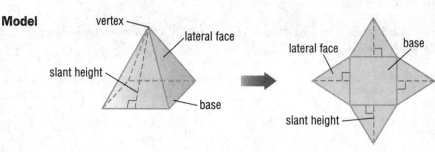

Some pyramids have square or rectangular bases. You can use a net to find the surface area of a pyramid.

Example

1. **Find the surface area of the pyramid.**

Use a net to find the area of each face and then add.

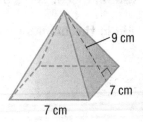

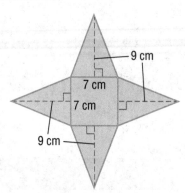

area of base: $7(7) = 49$

area of each triangular side: $\frac{1}{2}(7)(9) = 31.5$

Add to find the surface area.
$49 + 31.5 + 31.5 + 31.5 + 31.5 = 175$ square centimeters

 Show your work.

Got It? Do these problems to find out.

a. _____

b. _____

a.

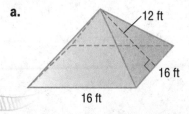

b.

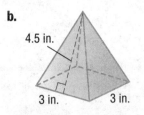

Surface Area of Pyramids with Triangular Bases

A triangular pyramid has one triangular base, and three triangular faces. If the base is an equilateral triangle, all three lateral faces are congruent. If the sides of the base triangle are different lengths, the areas of the lateral faces will also vary.

Example

2. **Find the surface area of the pyramid.**

Find the area of each face and add. The triangular base is an equilateral triangle because all three sides are 4 feet long.

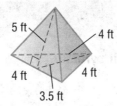

base **lateral faces**

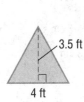 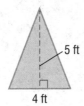 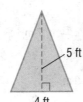 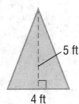

area of base: $\frac{1}{2}(4)(3.5) = 7$

area of each lateral face: $\frac{1}{2}(4)(5) = 10$

Add to find the surface area.
$7 + 10 + 10 + 10 = 37$ square feet

Got It? Do these problems to find out.

c.

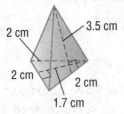

d.

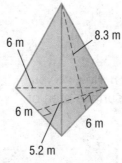

Show your work.

c. _____

d. _____

Example

3. A pyramid puzzle has all sides that are equilateral triangles. Each triangle has side lengths of 8 centimeters. The slant height is 6.9 centimeters. Find the surface area of the puzzle.

Create a net and then use it to find the surface area of the pyramid.

Each face has an area of $\frac{1}{2}(8)(6.9)$ or 27.6 square centimeters. So, the surface area of the puzzle is 4 · 27.6 or 110.4 square centimeters.

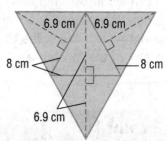

Guided Practice

Find the surface area of each pyramid. (Examples 1–2)

1. _____

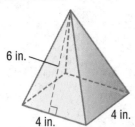

6 in.

4 in.   4 in.

Show your work.

2. _____

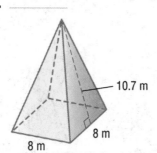

10.7 m

8 m   8 m

3. _____

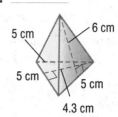

5 cm   6 cm

5 cm   5 cm

4.3 cm

4. Pyramid-shaped gift boxes have square bases that measure 5 inches on each side. The slant height is 6.5 inches. How much cardboard is used to make each box? (Example 3)

_____

5. **Building on the Essential Question** How do you use the area of a triangle to find the surface area of a triangular pyramid?

_____

_____

_____

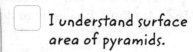

Rate Yourself!

☐ I understand surface area of pyramids.

▶▶ Great! You're ready to move on!

☐ I still have questions about surface area of pyramids.

▮▮ No Problem! Go online to access a Personal Tutor.

 Tutor

FOLDABLES Time to update your Foldable!

Independent Practice

Go online for Step-by-Step Solutions

Find the surface area of each pyramid. (Examples 1–2)

1. _____

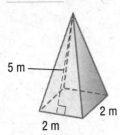

5 m
2 m
2 m

2. _____

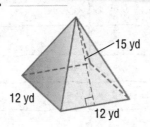

15 yd
12 yd
12 yd

3 _____

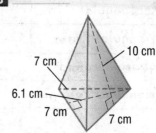

10 cm
7 cm
6.1 cm
7 cm
7 cm

4. _____

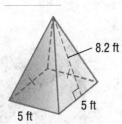

8.2 ft
5 ft
5 ft

5. _____

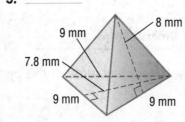

9 mm
8 mm
7.8 mm
9 mm
9 mm

6. _____

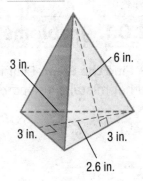

3 in.
6 in.
3 in.
3 in.
2.6 in.

7 A tea bag is shaped like a square pyramid with the base measuring 4 centimeters on each side. The slant height is 4.5 centimeters. How much mesh is used to create the tea bag? (Example 3)

Show your work.

8. An earring design is shaped like a triangular pyramid. All the faces are equilateral triangles with side lengths of 14 millimeters. The slant height is 12.1 millimeters. What is the surface area of the earring? (Example 3)

9. An acting award is a square pyramid with a base that measures 6 inches on each side. The slant height is 8 inches. What is the surface area of the award? (Example 3)

10. **Identify Structure** Refer to the figures listed in the table. Determine the number of faces the figure has of each two-dimensional shape. Explain.

Figure	Rectangular Faces	Triangular Faces
Rectangular Prism		
Triangular Prism		
Square Pyramid		
Triangular Pyramid		

_____

_____

_____

🔥 H.O.T. Problems Higher Order Thinking

11. <img_ccgps> **Find the Error** Pilar is finding the surface area of the pyramid shown. Find her mistake and correct it.

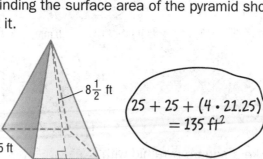

$$25 + 25 + (4 \cdot 21.25) = 135 \text{ ft}^2$$

12. <img_ccgps> **Persevere with Problems** The *lateral surface area L.A.* of a pyramid is the area of its lateral faces. Use the square pyramid at the right to complete each step to find the lateral surface area of any pyramid.

$L.A. = \frac{1}{2} s\ell +$ _____   Lateral surface area

$\quad = \frac{1}{2} ($ _____ $)\ell$ Distributive Property

$\quad =$ _____   Perimeter of base: $P = s + s + s + s$

✏️ Georgia Test Practice

13. Find the surface area of the pyramid.

  Ⓐ 360 cm²   Ⓒ 765 cm²

  Ⓑ 540 cm²   Ⓓ 1,305 cm²

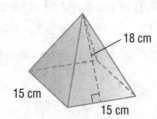

Extra Practice

Find the surface area of each pyramid.

14. <u>55 m²</u>

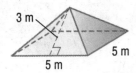

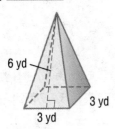

Homework Help

area of base: $5 \cdot 5 = 25 \text{ m}^2$

area of each face: $\frac{1}{2} \cdot 5 \cdot 3 = 7.5 \text{ m}^2$

surface area $= 25 + (4 \cdot 7.5)$
$= 25 + 30 \text{ or } 55 \text{ m}^2$

15. 223.5 ft²

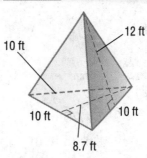

area of base: $\frac{1}{2} \cdot 10 \cdot 8.7 = 43.5 \text{ ft}^2$

area of each face: $\frac{1}{2} \cdot 10 \cdot 12 = 60 \text{ ft}^2$

surface area $= 43.5 + (3 \cdot 60)$
$= 43.5 + 180 \text{ or } 223.5 \text{ ft}^2$

16. _____

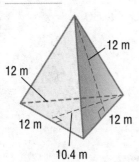

17. _____

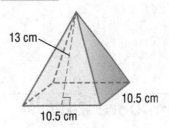

18. _____

19. _____

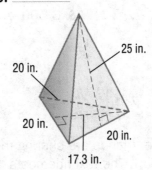

20. A paper model of the Khafre pyramid in Egypt has a square base 7.2 centimeters on each side. The slant height is 6 centimeters. How much paper was used to make the model?

21. CCGPS **Be Precise** A triangular pyramid has a surface area of 336 square inches. It is made up of equilateral triangles with side lengths of 12 inches. What is the slant height?

Georgia Test Practice

22. What is the surface area of the pyramid shown below?

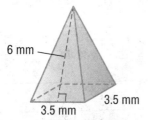

6 mm

3.5 mm
3.5 mm
3.5 mm

Ⓐ 24.5 mm²   Ⓒ 54.25 mm²

Ⓑ 42 mm²   Ⓓ 96.25 mm²

23. Short Response A pyramid has a base that is an equilateral triangle. The area of the base is 209.6 square inches and the sides measure 22 inches. The slant height of the pyramid is 14 inches. What is the surface area?

24. A salt shaker is in the shape of a square pyramid. The net is shown below. What is the surface area of the salt shaker?

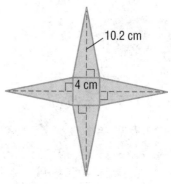

10.2 cm

4 cm

Ⓕ 36.4 cm²

Ⓖ 40.8 cm²

Ⓗ 81.6 cm²

Ⓘ 97.6 cm²

Common Core Review

Divide. MCC5.NBT.6

25. 240 ÷ 10 = _____

26. 3,600 ÷ 36 = _____

27. 4,800 ÷ 80 = _____

28. Jalisa and two of her friends are sharing the cost of a taxi ride to the airport. The taxi ride costs $24.75. How much will each person pay? MCC5.NBT.7

29. How many centimeters are equal to 0.05 meters? MCC5.MD.1

21ST CENTURY CAREER
in Design

Interior Designer

Do you like coming up with new ways to decorate your room, or are you always rearranging the furniture? You could have a career doing just that by becoming an interior designer. Interior designers plan the interior space and furnishings of homes, offices, and other places. Their designs are based on the client's specifications, tastes, and budget. Interior designers are responsible for recommending color schemes, furniture, lighting, and remodeling options. Many interior designers also develop their own product lines such as furniture, bedding, and accessories.

College & Career
READINESS

Explore college and careers at ccr.mcgraw-hill.com

Is This the Career for You?

Are you interested in a career as an interior designer? Take some of the following courses in high school.

◆ Algebra
◆ Geometry
◆ Interior Design
◆ Intro to CAD

Turn the page to find out how math relates to a career in Design.

697

You be the Designer!

Use the labeled figures to solve each problem. Round to the nearest tenth if necessary.

1. A client wants to buy the rectangular ottoman with the most storage area inside. Which one should she choose? Explain your reasoning. _____

_____

2. Find the volume of the paisley blanket chest. _____

3. What is the volume of the toy chest? How does it compare to the volume of the paisley blanket chest?

paisley blanket chest? _____

4. A designer is having the red ottoman reupholstered. Find the surface area to estimate the amount of fabric needed.

_____

5. What is the surface area of the purple ottoman? _____

6. How much greater is the surface area of the paisley blanket chest than the surface area of the toy chest? _____

Red Ottoman

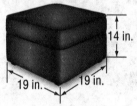

14 in.

19 in.   19 in.

Purple Ottoman

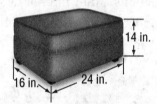

14 in.

16 in.   24 in.

Blanket Chest

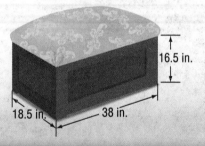

16.5 in.

18.5 in.   38 in.

Toy Chest

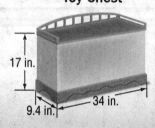

17 in.

9.4 in.   34 in.

Career Project

It's time to update your career portfolio! Use grid paper to make a scale drawing of a room in your home. Model the furniture using squares, rectangles, and triangles drawn to scale. Cut out each shape and use them to create different room arrangements. Then, tape the pieces onto the grid paper. Describe the room's color scheme and style.

_____

_____

_____

_____

Do you think you would enjoy a career as an interior designer? Why or why not?

_____

_____

_____

Vocabulary Check

Complete each sentence using the vocabulary list at the beginning of the chapter. Then circle the word that completes the sentence in the word search.

1. A figure with length, width, and height is

a _____.

2. _____ is the sum of the area of all the faces of a three-dimensional figure.

3. The amount of space inside a three-dimensional figure is its _____.

4. A prism that has triangular bases is

a _____.

5. A _____ is a prism that has rectangular bases.

6. Volume is measured in _____.

7. The point where three or more faces

intersect is the _____.

8. The _____ is the height of each lateral face.

9. Any face that is not a base is

a _____.

```
V R O D I S X W A J A K S M K H N Y P K F V T
G T N G B Z W G E Q J U R E A G K T C B G S R
X T O E X L A T E R A L F A C E T E A P D T I
E G H I E H Y L I T J S T I N U C I B U C X A
F M H G F G C H H V F O T V E X K X Z U I E N
E R U G I F L A N O I S N E M I D E E R H T G
A K J L B E L M A E R A E C A F R U S F K R U
U G U K O H H U K D K L P N T J K Q Y H E E L
V F O M Q V S T K I L N I O Y S B R Z Q K V A
R Y J S H U W D N M B T P B O T S U L F C J R
R E C T A N G U L A R P R I S M U D V C C Y P
H K I A D Z V G M U L W W Q R I K R A K D M R
P Z T B Y U X B S F N S O K E D X G C F G N I
N I W Y Q A Z K E D V U O L U L H N B J O S S
I A H P V J A K O W N Z W E I U D Q Q H V I M
```

Use Your FOLDABLES

Use your Foldable to help review the chapter.

Tape here

Tab 1

Real-World Examples

Formulas   Model

Tab 2

Tape here

Got it?

Use the figure provided to complete the cross number puzzle.

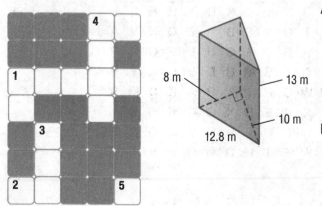

Across

1. surface area of the prism
2. height of the base triangle
4. height of the prism
5. length of the base triangle

Down

1. area of the base
3. volume of the prism
4. length of one side of the base triangle

1. An office building is built in the shape of a rectangular prism. It has a length of 168 yards, a width of 115 yards, and a height 96 yards. What is the volume of the building? (Lesson 1) _____

2. Liza is researching packaging options for her shop. She wants to know the volume of a triangular prism 9 inches tall with a triangular base that is 3 inches by 2 inches. (Lesson 2) _____

3. **CCGPS** **Use Math Tools** Justin is building a storage trunk like the one shown. How much wood is needed to make the trunk? (Lesson 3) _____

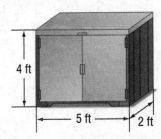
4 ft 5 ft 2 ft

4. A baker needs to put icing on a rectangular cake. The cake is 14 inches long, 12 inches wide, and 4 inches tall. What is the surface area of the cake, not including the bottom? (Lesson 3) _____

5. Stephanie was making a tent like the one shown. How much fabric does she need to make the tent? (Lesson 4) _____

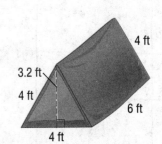
4 ft 3.2 ft 4 ft 6 ft 4 ft

6. **CCGPS** **Reason Abstractly** A paper die has sides that are all equilateral triangles. Each triangle has a side length of 1.5 cm. The slant height is 1.3 cm. Find the surface area of the die. (Lesson 5)

Reflect

 Answering the Essential Question

Use what you learned about volume and surface area to complete the graphic organizer.

 Essential Question

HOW is shape important when measuring a figure?

	Draw it.	How do you find the volume?	How do you find the surface area?
rectangular prism			
triangular prism			

 Answer the Essential Question. HOW is shape important when measuring a figure?

_____

_____

UNIT 6

 Statistics

 Essential Question

WHY is learning mathematics important?

Chapter 10
Statistical Measures

Statistical data has a distribution that can be described by its center or by its spread. In this chapter, you will find and use measures of center and measures of variation to describe sets of data.

Chapter 11
Statistical Displays

Statistical data can be represented in a variety of ways. In this chapter, you will represent and analyze data using line plots, histograms, and box plots.

Chapter 10

Statistical Measures

Essential Question

HOW are the mean, median, and mode helpful in describing data?

Common Core GPS

Content Standards
MCC6.SP.1, MCC6.SP.3, MCC6.SP.5, MCC6.SP.5b, MCC6.SP.5c, MCC6.SP.5d

Mathematical Practices
1, 2, 3, 4, 5, 6

Math in the Real World

Sports A baseball team scored 9, 6, 8, 16, and 5 points in 5 games. Plot the scores on the number line.

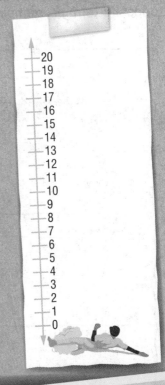

FOLDABLES
Study Organizer

1 Cut out the correct Foldable from the FL pages in the back of this book.

2 Place your Foldable on the Key Concept page toward the end of this chapter.

3 Use the Foldable throughout this chapter to help you learn about statistical measures.

705

Vocabulary

average	median
first quartile	mode
interquartile range	outliers
mean	quartiles
mean absolute deviation	range
measure of center	statistical question
measures of variation	third quartile

Review Vocabulary

Graphic Organizer One way to remember vocabulary terms is to connect them to an opposite term or example. Use this information to complete the graphic organizer.

quotient

⬇

Definition

Opposite

Example

Are You Ready?

Try the Quick Check below.
Or, take the Online Readiness Quiz.

Check ✓

CCGPS **Quick Review**

Common Core Review MCC5.NBT.7

Example 1

Find **12.53 + 9.87 + 16.24 + 22.12.**

```
 2 1 1
  12.53
   9.87      Add.
  16.24
 +22.12
  60.76
```

Example 2

Michelle read 56.5 pages of her book on Monday and Tuesday. If she read the same amount of pages each day, how many pages did she average each day?

56.5 ÷ 2 = 28.25 Divide the total number of pages by the number of days.

Michelle averaged 28.25 pages per day.

Quick Check

Add Decimals Find each sum.

1. 6.20 + 31.59 + 11.11 + 19.85 =

2. 22.69 + 15.45 + 9.87 + 26.79 =

 Show your work.

3. Sonya went to the baseball game. She paid $10.50 for admission. She bought a drink for $2.75, a bag of popcorn for $4.60, and a hot dog for $3.75. How much did she spend in total?

Divide Decimals Find each quotient.

4. 79.2 ÷ 6 =

5. 72.60 ÷ 3 =

6. 240.5 ÷ 13 =

7. The Chen family drove 345.6 miles on their vacation. They drove the same amount each of the 3 days. How many miles did they drive each day?

How Did You Do?

Which problems did you answer correctly in the Quick Check? Shade those exercise numbers below.

 ① ② ③ ④ ⑤ ⑥ ⑦

Content Standards
MCC6.SP.1,
MCC6.SP.3

Mathematical Practices
1, 3, 4

 HOW are surveys created to collect and analyze data?

Marketing Anderson Advertising is collecting information for a pizza shop. They want to know the number of toppings most customers prefer on their pizza. They will use this information to determine the weekly special.

Investigation 1

Statistics deals with collecting, organizing, and interpreting pieces of information, or *data*. One way to collect data is by asking statistical questions. A **statistical question** is a question that anticipates and accounts for a variety of answers.

The table below gives some examples of statistical questions and questions that are *not* statistical questions.

Statistical Questions	Not Statistical Questions
How many text messages do you send each day?	What is the height in feet of the tallest mountain in Colorado?
What is the minimum driving age for each state in the United States?	How many people attended last night's jazz concert?

Create a survey similar to the one Anderson Advertising would use to survey your classmates. Consider a cheese pizza with no additional toppings as a pizza with one topping.

Step 1	Write a statistical question. *How many toppings do you like on your pizza?*
Step 2	Survey your classmates.
Step 3	Record the results in the table to the right. Add additional numbers of toppings to the table as necessary.

How Many Toppings Do Your Like on Your Pizza?	
Number of Toppings	**Number of Responses**

Why is *How many toppings do you like on your pizza?* a statistical question?

_____

Investigation 2

Sometimes a set of data can be organized into intervals to more easily organize it. This often happens when the set of data has a wide range of values.

Suppose you want to determine the number of video games each of your math classmates has at home.

Step 1 Write the statistical question. *How many different video games do you own?*

Step 2 Survey your classmates.

Step 3 Record the results in the table to the right.

How Many Different Video Games Do You Own?	
Number of Video Games	**Number of Responses**
less than 5	
5–9	
10–14	
15 or more	

Investigation 3

Tools

You can use surveys to provide information about patterns in the responses.

Suppose you surveyed five students using the statistical question, *How many Web sites did you visit before school this morning?* The students said 4, 3, 5, 1, and 2 Web sites. If the total amount was equally distributed among all five students, how many Web sites did each student visit?

Step 1 Make a stack of centimeter cubes to represent the number of Web sites visited by each student as shown.

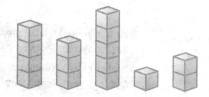

Step 2 Move the cubes so that each stack has the same number of cubes. Draw your models in the space below.

There are five stacks with ☐ cubes in each stack. So, if the responses were equally distributed, each student visited ☐ Web sites before school.

Collaborate

Work with a partner. State whether each question is a statistical question. Explain your reasoning.

1. Who was the first president of the United States?

   _____

2. How much time do the students in my school spend on the Internet each night?

   _____

3. What is the height of the tallest waterslide at Wild Rides Water Park?

   _____

4. What are the cabin rental prices for each of the state parks in Kentucky?

   _____

Work with a partner. Determine the equal share if the total number of centimeter cubes were equally distributed among the groups. Draw your models in the space provided.

5.

6.

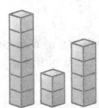

7.

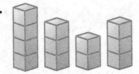

8.

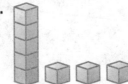

Analyze

Work with a partner to determine the equal share for each exercise. Use centimeter cubes or counters if needed. The first one is done for you.

Scenario	Responses	Response Total	Number of Responses	Equal Share
Rainfall (inches)	7, 5, 2, 6	$7 + 5 + 2 + 6 = 20$	4	5
9. Books Read	8, 7, 3			
10. Eggs Hatched	5, 2, 3, 6			
11. States Visited	1, 4, 2, 5, 3			
12. Photos Taken	5, 3, 7, 2, 4, 3			
13. Miles Hiked	11, 12, 8, 9			

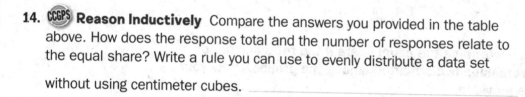

14. **CCGPS** **Reason Inductively** Compare the answers you provided in the table above. How does the response total and the number of responses relate to the equal share? Write a rule you can use to evenly distribute a data set without using centimeter cubes. _____

_____

15. One week, the high temperatures in Muncie, Indiana, were 90°F, 88°F, 86°F, 89°F, 91°F, 88°F, and 91°F. What is the equal share of the data? Explain.

_____

Reflect

16. **CCGPS** **Model with Mathematics** Write a real-world problem that involves equal shares. Find the equal share of your data set.

_____

_____

_____

17. **Inquiry** HOW are surveys created to collect and analyze data?

_____

_____

What You'll Learn

Scan the lesson. Predict two things you will learn about mean.

- _____
  _____

- _____
  _____

 Essential Question

HOW are the mean, median, and mode helpful in describing data?

 Vocabulary

mean
average

 Common Core GPS

Content Standards
MCC6.SP.3

Mathematical Practices
1, 2, 3, 4, 6

Real-World Link

Music Tina and her friends downloaded songs for 6 weeks, as shown in the table below.

Number of Songs Downloaded Each Week					
12	6	10	9	4	1

1. How many total songs were downloaded? _____

2. On average, how many songs did they download each week?

   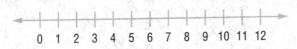

   ⬜ ÷ ⬜ = ⬜
   total   number   average
         of weeks   per week

3. On the number line below, draw an arrow that points to the average. Plot the number of songs downloaded on the number line.

   ```
   ←──┬──┬──┬──┬──┬──┬──┬──┬──┬──┬──┬──┬──→
      0  1  2  3  4  5  6  7  8  9 10 11 12
   ```

4. How far below the average is 1? 4? 6? How far above the average is 9? 10? 12? _____

5. What is the sum of the distances between the average and the points below the average? above the average? _____

6. Explain why the average is the balance point of the data.

   _____
   _____

| **Mean**

The **mean** of a data set is the sum of the data divided by the number of pieces of data. It is the balance point for the data set.

On the previous page, you found a single number to describe the number of songs downloaded each week. The **average**, or mean, summarizes the data using a single number.

You can find the mean of a set of data shown in different displays such as pictographs and dot plots.

Work Zone

Real World

Example

1. **Find the mean number of representatives for the four states shown in the pictograph.**

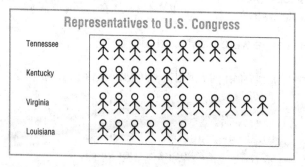

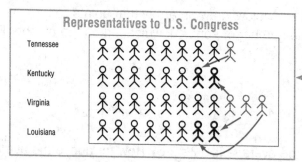

Move the figures to equally distribute the total number of representatives among the four states.

Each state has a mean or average of 8 representatives.

Including Data
Even if a data value is 0, it still should be counted in the total number of pieces of data.

Show your work.

a. _____

Got It? Do this problem to find out.

a. The table shows the number of CDs a group of friends bought. Find the mean number of CDs the group bought.

Number of CDs Purchased		
3	4	6
	0	2

Examples

Tutor

2. The dot plot shows the recorded high temperatures for six days in Little Rock, Arkansas. Find the mean temperature.

High Temperatures

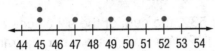

44 45 46 47 48 49 50 51 52 53 54

mean $= \dfrac{45 + 45 + 47 + 49 + 50 + 52}{6}$ ◄···· sum of the data
◄···· number of data items

$= \dfrac{288}{6}$ or 48   Simplify.

The mean is 48 degrees. So, all of the data values can be summarized with a single number, 48.

· ·

3. The dot plot shows the number of runs a baseball team had for each game of a 4 game series. Find the mean number of runs for the series.

Number of Runs

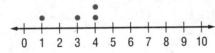

0 1 2 3 4 5 6 7 8 9 10

mean $= \dfrac{\boxed{}}{\boxed{}}$ ◄···· sum of the data
◄···· number of data items

$= \dfrac{\boxed{}}{\boxed{}}$ or $\boxed{}$ Simplify.

The mean number of runs for the series is $\boxed{}$.

Got It? Do this problem to find out.

b. The dot plot shows the number of books Deanna read each week of a month-long reading challenge. Find the mean number of books she read:

Books Read

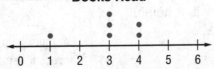

0 1 2 3 4 5 6

Copyright © McGraw-Hill Companies, Inc.

Show your work.

b. _____

The mean is sometimes described as the balance point. Explain below what this means using the data set {2, 2, 3, 8, 10}.

266
+260
———
526   87
      6⟌526
        48
        ——
        46

Example

Tutor

4. The number of minutes Mary Anne spent talking on her cell phone each month for the past five months were 494, 502, 486, 690, and 478. Suppose the mean for six months was 532 minutes. How many minutes did she talk on her cell phone during the sixth month?

If the mean is 532, the sum of the six pieces of data must be 532 × 6 or 3,192. You can create a bar diagram.

	---------------3,192---------------	
494	502	486	690	478	?

$3{,}192 - (494 + 502 + 486 + 690 + 478) = 3{,}192 - 2{,}650$
$= 542$

Mary Anne talked 542 minutes during the sixth month.

Guided Practice

Check ✓

1. The dot plot shows the number of beads sold. Find the mean number of beads. (Examples 1–3)

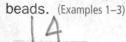 14

Number of Beads

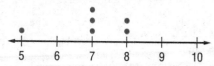

5 6 7 8 9 10

$\dfrac{21 + 16 + 5}{3}$

2. The table shows the greatest depths of four of the five oceans in the world. If the average greatest depth is 8.094 kilometers, what is the greatest depth of the Southern Ocean? (Example 4) _____

Ocean	Greatest Depth (km)
Pacific	10.92
Atlantic	9.22
Indian	7.46
Arctic	5.63
Southern	■

Rate Yourself!

How confident are you about finding the mean of a data set? Check the box that applies.

☹ 😐 🙂

☐ ☐ ☐ ☐ ☐

For more help, go online to access a Personal Tutor.

Tutor

3. **Building on the Essential Question** Why is it helpful to find the mean of a data set?

_____

_____

 FOLDABLES Time to update your Foldable!

Independent Practice

Go online for Step-by-Step Solutions
eHelp

Find the mean for each data set. (Examples 1–3)

1 *88*

87.66

Show your work.

87 + 93 + 86

Pablo's Chapter Test Scores

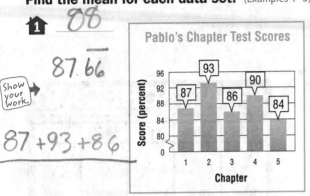

2. *14*

Number of Flowers

10 11 12 13 14 15 16 17 18

12 + 12 + 14 + 15 + 15 + 16

3 **Financial Literacy** Jamila babysat nine times. She earned $15, $20, $10, $12, $20, $16, $80, and $18 for eight babysitting jobs. How much did she earn the ninth time if the mean of the data set is $24?

(Example 4) _____ $25 _____

4. **CCGPS** **Model with Mathematics** Refer to the graphic novel frame below for Exercises a–b.

a. What is the mean number of wins for the Cranes? for the Panthers?

40 wins- Cranes
40 wins- Panthers

b. Based on your answer for part **a**, is the mean a good measure for determining which team has the better record? Explain.

Yes. this totally compares.

5. A stem-and-leaf plot is a display that organizes data from least to greatest. The digits of the least place value form the leaves, and the next place-value digits form the stems. The stem and leaf plot shows Marcia's scores on several tests. Find the mean test score.

Stem	Leaf
7	8
8	5 8 9
9	2 6

7|8 = 78

_____

6. CCGPS **Multiple Representations** The graphic shows the 5-day forecast.

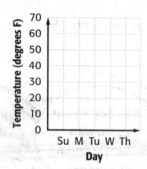

5-DAY FORECAST

SUN	MON	TUE	WED	THU
Sunny	Partly Cloudy	Showers	Scattered Showers	Sunny
Hi: 63°F	Hi: 60°F	Hi: 55°F	Hi: 57°F	Hi: 65°F
Lo: 45°F	Lo: 38°F	Lo: 40°F	Lo: 39°F	Lo: 42°F

   a. Numbers What is the difference between the mean high and mean low temperature for this 5-day period? Justify your answer.

   _____

   _____

   b. Graph Make a double-line graph of the high and low temperatures for the 5-day period.

(Graph with y-axis "Temperature (degrees F)" marked 0, 10, 20, 30, 40, 50, 60, 70 and x-axis "Day" marked Su M Tu W Th)

H.O.T. Problems Higher Order Thinking

7. CCGPS **Reason Abstractly** Create a data set that has five values. The mean of the data set should be 34. _____

8. CCGPS **Persevere with Problems** The mean of a set of data is 45 years. Find the missing numbers in the data set {40, 45, 48, ?, 54, ?, 45}. Explain the method or strategy you used.

_____

Georgia Test Practice

9. Which of the following data sets does *not* have a mean of 12?
   Ⓐ 12, 11, 13   Ⓒ 12, 12, 12, 8
   Ⓑ 8, 16, 10, 14   Ⓓ 7, 12, 17

Extra Practice

Find the mean for each data set.

10. _8 bags_

Number of Popcorn Bags Sold

Pilar

Marisa

Gary

Irene

🍿 = 2 Popcorn Bags

11. _56_

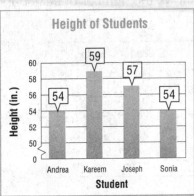

Height of Students

Homework Help → $\frac{8 + 5 + 7 + 12}{4} = 8$

12. _9_

Number of Cards Decorated

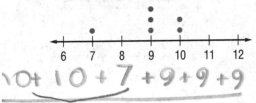

ı0+ 10 + 7 + 9 + 9 + 9

13. _26_

Number of Tickets Sold

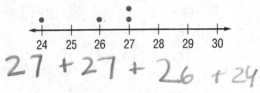

$27 + 27 + 26 + 24$

4

14. 🅒🅒🅒🅟🅢 **Be Precise** The table shows the approximate heights of some of the tallest U.S. trees.

a. Find the mean of the data. _185 ft_

b. Find the mean if the Coast Redwood is not included in the data set. _158 ft_

c. How does the height of the Coast Redwood affect the mean of the data? _The coast redwood increases the mean._

Tallest Trees in U.S.	
Tree	**Height (ft)**
Western Red Cedar	160
Coast Redwood	320
Monterey Cypress	100
California Laurel	110
Sitka Spruce	200
Port-Orford-Cedar	220

d. Suppose Blue Spruce was included in the list and the mean decreased to 165 feet. What is the height of the Blue Spruce?

_55 ft_

Georgia Test Practice

15. The Student Council sells school calendars each year as a fundraiser. Eric was on the Student Council from 2007 to 2010. The bar graph shows the number of calendars he sold over the 4 years.

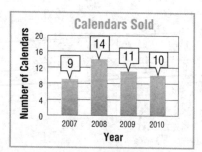

What is the mean number of calendars Eric sold each year?

Ⓐ 9   Ⓒ 11

Ⓑ 10   Ⓓ 14

17. Find the mean number of points scored in three games.

Ⓕ 9   Ⓗ 30

Ⓖ 25   Ⓘ 75

Game	Points Scored
1	24
2	30
3	21

16. Short Response The table shows the money raised by each booth at a craft sale.

Northside Craft Sale	
Booth	**Money Raised ($)**
Artwork	58
Candles	47
Holiday decorations	54
Jewelry	70
Picture frames	45
T-shirts	?

How much money, in dollars, was raised by the T-shirt booth if the mean amount raised was $59? ___50___

(CCGPS) **Common Core Review**

Compare the numbers using < or >. MCC4.NBT.2

18. 18 ⊘ 16

19. 65 ⊘ 63

20. 22 ⊘ 28

21. 34 ⊘ 31

22. 75 ⊘ 79

23. 67 ⊘ 57

24. The table shows the distances from Louisville to several cities.

  a. How much farther is it from Louisville to Charlotte than from Louisville to Lexington? MCC4.NBT.4 ___185 mi___

  b. Which city is the greatest distance from Louisville? MCC4.NBT.2
    ___Lexington___

City	Distance (miles)
Charlotte	474
Cincinnati	100
Indianapolis	114
Lexington	75
St. Louis	265

Median and Mode

What You'll Learn

Scan the lesson. List two headings you would use to make an outline of the lesson.

• _____

_____

• _____

_____

 Essential Question

HOW are the mean, median, and mode helpful in describing data?

Vocab
Vocabulary

measures of center
median
mode

CCGPS **Common Core GPS**

Content Standards
MCC6.SP.3, MCC6.SP.5, MCC6.SP.5b, MCC6.SP.5c

Mathematical Practices
1, 3, 4, 5, 6

Vocabulary Start-Up

A data set can also be described by its median or its mode. The mean, median, and mode are called **measures of center** because they describe the center of a set of data.

Find the definition of each term in the glossary. Then complete the graphic organizer.

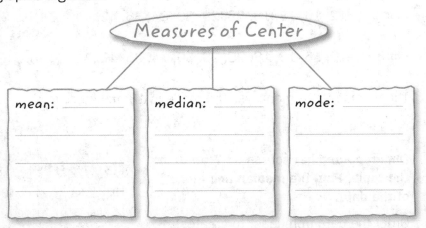

Measures of Center

mean: _____

_____

_____

median: _____

_____

_____

mode: _____

_____

_____

Real-World Link

Hurricanes The table shows the number of Atlantic hurricanes in different years.

Atlantic Hurricanes						
5	15	9	7	4	9	8

1. Order the data from least to greatest. Circle the number in the middle of your list. _____8_____

2. Find the mean. Compare the middle number to the mean of the data. Round to the nearest hundredth if necessary.

    8 = mean

Key Concept

Median and Mode

The **median** of a list of values is the value appearing at the center of a sorted version of the list, or the mean of the two central values, if the list contains an even number of values.

The **mode** is the number or numbers that occur most often.

Just as mean is one value used to summarize a data set, the median and mode also summarize a data set with a single number. If there is more than one number that occurs with the same frequency, a data set may have more than one mode.

Examples

1. The table shows the number of monkeys at eleven different zoos. Find the median and mode of the data.

Number of Monkeys					
28	36	18	25	12	44
	18	42	34	16	30

Order the data from least to greatest.

Median   12, 16, 18, 18, 25, (28) 30, 34, 36, 42, 44   28 is in the center.

Mode   12, 16, [18, 18,] 25, 28, 30, 34, 36, 42, 44   18 occurs most often.

The median is 28 monkeys. The mode is 18 monkeys.

- -

2. Dina recorded her scores on 7 tests in the table. Find the median and mode of the data.

Test Scores			
93	88	94	93
	85	97	90

Order the data from least to greatest.

_____

(Circle) the number in the center. This is the median.

(Circle) the most frequently occurring numbers. This value is the mode.

The median is a score of [   ]. The mode is a score of [   ].

Got It?   Do this problem to find out.

Show your work.

a. The list shows the number of stories in the 11 tallest buildings in Springfield. Find the median and mode of the data.

40, 38, 40, 37, 33, 30, 20, 24, 21, 17, 19

a. 27, 40

17, 19, 20, 21, 24, 30, 33, 37, 38, 40, 4

2

Work Zone

Examples

Tutor

3. Find the median and mode of the temperatures displayed in the graph.

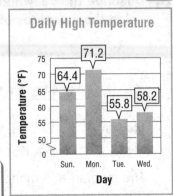

Daily High Temperature

Median   55.8, 58.2, 64.4, 71.2

$$\frac{58.2 + 64.4}{2} = \frac{122.6}{2}$$
$$= 61.3°$$

There are an even number of data values. So, to find the median, find the mean of the two central values.

Mode   There is no mode.

. . . .

4. Miguel researched the average precipitation in several states. Find and compare the median and mode of the average precipitation.

State	Precipitation (in.)	State	Precipitation (in.)
Alabama	58.3	Louisiana	60.1
Florida	54.5	Maine	42.2
Georgia	50.7	Michigan	32.8
Kentucky	48.9	Missouri	42.2

Median   32.8, 42.2, 42.2, 48.9, 50.7, 54.5, 58.3, 60.1

$$\frac{48.9 + 50.7}{2} = \frac{99.6}{2}$$
$$= 49.8$$

Mode   32.8, 42.2, 42.2, 48.9, 50.7, 54.5, 58.3, 60.1

The median is 49.8 inches and the mode is 42.2 inches. The median is 7.6 inches greater than the mode.

Got It?   Do these problems to find out.

Show your work.

b. Find the median and mode of the costs in the table.

Cost of Backpacks ($)			
16.78	48.75	31.42	18.38
22.89	51.25	28.54	26.79

b. _No Mode_

c. _2.87_

c. Find and compare the median and mode of the costs in the table.

Cost of Juice ($)			
1.65	1.97	2.45	2.87
2.35	3.75	2.49	2.87

16.78, 48.75, 31.42, 18.38, 22.89, 51.25, 28.54, 26.79

2

Example

Tutor

5. Describe the daily high temperatures using the measures of center.

Daily High Temperature (°F)			
72	73	67	65
71	64	71	

Mean $\dfrac{72 + 73 + 67 + 65 + 71 + 64 + 71}{7} = \dfrac{483}{7}$ or 69°

Median 64, 65, 67, (71) 71, 72, 73

Mode 64, 65, 67, (71, 71) 72, 73

The median and mode are equal, 71 degrees. They are both 2 degrees greater than the mean. The data follows the measures of center in that the temperatures are close to the measures of center.

Got It? Do this problem to find out.

d. Describe the cost of CDs using the measures of center.

Cost of CDs ($)		
11.95	12.89	19.99
19.99	12.59	18.49

Handwritten left margin:

7̶, 3̶1̶, 38, 42, 4̶8̶, 5̶0̶
―――――――――――
2

d. _____

36, 40, 40, 40, ... Show your work.
―――――――――――
2

89
2)178
16
18

Guided Practice

Check

1. Find and compare the median and mode for the following set of data.
monthly spending: $46, $62, $62, $57, $50, $42, $56, $40 (Examples 1–4)

_____

2. Describe the daily high temperatures using the measures of center. (Example 5)

Daily High Temperature (°F)			
34	35	31	36
31	24	33	

_____
_____
_____
_____

3.  **Building on the Essential Question** How are mean and median similar? _____

_____
_____

Rate Yourself!

Are you ready to move on?
Shade the section that applies.

I have a few questions. | I'm ready to move on.

I have a lot of questions.

For more help, go online to access a Personal Tutor.

Tutor

FOLDABLES *Time to update your Foldable!*

Independent Practice

Go online for Step-by-Step Solutions

Find and compare median and mode for each set of data. (Examples 1–4)

1. math test scores: 97, 85, 92, 86 _____ 89, no mode

the mode is 89
_____

85, 86, 92, 97
——————————
      2

2.

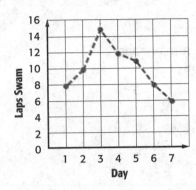

8, 10, 15, 12, 11, 8, 6

3. Describe the average speeds using the measures of center. (Example 5)

The mode and median
are the same when
being compared.

Average Speeds (mph)			
40	52	44	46
52	40	44	50
41	44	44	50

4. **CCGPS** **Model with Mathematics** Refer to the graphic novel frame below for Exercises a–b.

40, 41, 44, 44, 44, (44) 46, 50, 50, 52, 52

Let's check other measures to really see which team is better.

CRANES

Season	Wins
1	38
2	42
3	31
4	50
5	31
6	48

PANTHERS

Season	Wins
1	36
2	42
3	40
4	40
5	42
6	40

a. Find the median and mode for each team's wins.

40 - median (cranes), 31 - mode (panthers)
40 - median (panthers), 40 - mode

b. Which team had the better record? Justify your response.

Panthers - most values are
steady.

5 A Louisville newspaper claims that during seven days, the high temperature in Lexington was typically 6° warmer than the high temperature in Louisville. What measure was used to make this claim?

Justify your answer. _____

Daily High Temperatures (°F)							
Louisville				**Lexington**			
75	50	80	72	80	73	75	74
	70	84	70		71	76	76

_____

6. **CCGPS** **Use Math Tools** Use the Internet to find the high temperatures for each of the last seven days in a city near you. Then find the median high temperature.

_____

 H.O.T. Problems Higher Order Thinking

7. **CCGPS** **Persevere with Problems** The ticket prices for a concert series were $12, $37, $45, $18, $8, $25, and $18. What was the ticket price of the eighth and final concert in this series if the set of 8 prices had a mean of $23, a mode of $18, a median of $19.50? _____

8. **CCGPS** **Construct an Argument** One evening at a local pizzeria, the following number of toppings were ordered on each large pizza.

   3, 0, 1, 1, 2, 5, 4, 3, 1, 0, 0, 1, 1, 2, 2, 3, 6, 4, 3, 2, 0, 2, 1, 3

Determine whether each statement is *true* or *false*. Explain your reasoning.

a. The greatest number of people ordered a pizza with 1 topping.

_____

b. Half the customers ordered pizzas with 3 or more toppings, and half the customers ordered pizzas with less than 3 toppings.

_____

9. **CCGPS** **Justify Conclusions** In the data set {3, 7, 4, 2, 31, 5, 4}, which measure best describes the set of data: mean, median, or mode? Explain your reasoning. _____

_____

Georgia Test Practice

10. The lengths of the 5 long jumps at track practice were 14.5 feet, 13.7 feet, 14.1 feet, 14.9 feet, and 13.8 feet. What would the sixth length have to be to have a mean length of 14.1 feet?

ⓐ 14.8 feet   ⓒ 13.6 feet

ⓑ 14.1 feet   ⓓ 12.9 feet

Name _____ My Homework _____

Extra Practice

Find and compare median and mode for each set of data.

11. age of employees: 23, 22, 15, 44, 44 *median: 23; mode: 44; The mode is 21 years more than the median.*

> Homework Help →

Median: 15, 22, ⃝23, 44, 44

Mode: 15, 22, 23, ⃝44, 44⃝

12. minutes spent on homework: 18, 20, 22, 11, 19, 18, 18

No difference, 18=18

13.

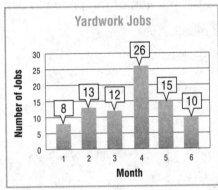

12.5 = median
no mode

11 16 18 18 19 20 22

8 10 12 13 15 26
        2
              12.5

14. Describe the test grades using the measures of center.

_____

_____

65 75

Test Grades			
100	77	80	65
87	85	85	82
100	97	95	75

15. CCGPS **Be Precise** Fill in the graphic organizer with the description. The first one is done for you.

measures of center ⇒ numbers used to describe the center of data

mean ⇒

median ⇒

mode ⇒

16. The table shows the number of concerts performed by The Quest. What is the difference between the median number of concerts and the mode number of concerts for 2003–2010?

The Quest			
Year	Number of Concerts	Year	Number of Concerts
2003	142	2007	124
2004	142	2008	138
2005	136	2009	136
2006	136	2010	150

Ⓐ 0   Ⓒ 4

Ⓑ 1   Ⓓ 5

17. Short Response The prices of some dinners at the Town Diner are shown in the table.

Dinner	Price($)
Turkey	9.90
Cheeseburger	6.75
Chicken Salad	5.29
Spaghetti	8.15

What is the median of the prices in dollars for the meals? _____

18. The table shows the number of schools in 12 different counties. What is the median of the data?

Ⓕ 4   Ⓗ 7

Ⓖ 6   Ⓘ 8

Number of Schools					
4	3	6	10	3	14
8	5	7	11	7	8

 ## Common Core Review

Find the greatest number in the data set. MCC4.NBT.2

19. {23, 35, 31, 28, 26, 34}

_____

20. {56, 58, 49, 50, 56, 57}

_____

21. {78, 81, 79, 84, 82, 83}

_____

Find the least number in the data set. MCC4.NBT.2

22. {62, 58, 56, 61, 59, 57}

_____

23. {24, 29, 22, 26, 23, 24}

_____

24. {56, 58, 52, 54, 53, 57}

_____

25. The table shows the distances Mari biked each day. What is the greatest distance she biked during the week? MCC5.NBT.3b

_____

26. It is 143 miles from Columbus to Cleveland and 107 miles from Columbus to Cincinnati. How much further is it from Columbus to Cleveland than Columbus to Cincinnati? MCC4.NBT.4

Day	Distance (miles)
Monday	5.2
Tuesday	3.5
Wednesday	4.9
Thursday	3.8
Friday	3.2

Need more practice? Download more Extra Practice at **connectED.mcgraw-hill.com.**

Content Standards
MCC6.SP.1

Mathematical Practices
1, 3, 4

Case #1 Speak to Me

Amy surveyed 15 students with the statistical question, "Do you speak Spanish, French, both languages, or neither language?" Four students speak French, seven students speak Spanish, and two students speak both languages.

Use a Venn diagram to find how many students speak neither Spanish nor French.

 ## Understand *What are the facts?*

- You know ☐ classmates speak Spanish and ☐ classmates speak French.

- You know that ☐ students speak both languages.

 ## Plan *What is your strategy to solve this problem?*

Make a Venn diagram to organize the information. Use logical reasoning to find the answer.

 ## Solve *How can you apply the strategy?*

Draw and label two overlapping circles to represent the two languages. Since 2 students speak both languages, place a 2 in the section that is part of both circles. Use subtraction to determine the number for each of the other sections.

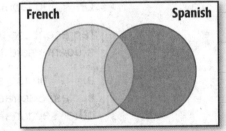

French   Spanish

only French: 4 − ☐ = ☐

only Spanish: 7 − ☐ = ☐

neither: 15 − ☐ − ☐ − ☐ = ☐

So, ☐ students speak neither French nor Spanish.

 ## Check *Does the answer make sense?*

Check each circle to see if the appropriate number of students is represented.

Analyze the Strategy

Reason Inductively Explain why Amy's question, "Do you speak Spanish, French, both languages, or neither language?" is a statistical question.

Case #2 Battle of the Mascots

Nick conducted a survey of 85 students about a new school mascot. The results showed that 40 students liked Tigers, and 31 students liked Bears. Of those students, 12 liked both Tigers and Bears.

How many students liked neither Tigers nor Bears?

Understand

Read the problem. What are you being asked to find?

I need to find _____

Underline key words and values in the problem. What information do you know?

☐ students were surveyed. In the survey, ☐ students said they liked Tigers, ☐ said they liked Bears, and ☐ said they liked both.

Plan

Choose a problem-solving strategy.

I will use the _____ strategy.

Solve

Use your problem-solving strategy and a Venn diagram to solve the problem.

Draw and label two overlapping circles to represent the two mascots. Since ☐ students said they liked both mascots, place a ☐ in the section that is part of both circles. Subtract to find the numbers for the other sections.

only tigers: _____   only bears: _____

neither tigers nor bears: _____

So, ☐ students liked neither tigers nor bears as the school mascot.

Check

Use information from the problem to check your answer.

_____

_____

_____

Case #3 Marketing

A survey showed that 70 customers bought white bread, 63 bought wheat bread, and 35 bought rye bread. Of those who bought exactly two types of bread, 12 bought wheat and white, 5 bought white and rye, and 7 bought wheat and rye. Two customers bought all three.

How many customers bought only wheat bread?

_____

Case #4 Pets

Dr. Poston is a veterinarian. One week she treated 20 dogs, 16 cats, and 11 birds. Some owners had more than one pet, as shown in the table.

How many owners had only a dog as a pet?

Pet	Number of Owners
dog and cat	7
dog and bird	5
cat and bird	3
dog, cat, and bird	2

Case #5 Sports

The Student Council surveyed a group of 24 students by asking the statistical question, "Do you like softball, basketball, both, or neither?" The results showed that 14 students liked softball, and 18 liked basketball. Of these, 8 liked both.

How many students liked just softball and how many liked just basketball?

_____

Circle a strategy below to solve the problem.
- Act it out.
- Guess, check, and revise.
- Solve a simpler problem.
- Look for a pattern.

Case #6 Money

Jorge has $125 in his savings account. He deposits $20 every week and withdraws $25 every four weeks.

What will his balance be in 8 weeks?

_____

Mid-Chapter Check

Vocabulary Check

1. Define *mean*. Then determine the mean of the following data set {22, 18, 38, 6, 24, 18}. (Lesson 1)

   Mean: Arithmetic Average

2. Fill in the blank in the sentence below with the correct term. (Lesson 2)

   The _____ is the number or numbers that occur most often in a set.

Skills Check and Problem Solving

Find the mean of each data set. (Lesson 1)

3. number of home runs by baseball players in a season: 43, 21, 35, 15, 35

4. number of different birds spotted: 7, 10, 13, 9, 12, 3

Find the median and mode for each set of data. (Lesson 2)

5. hours spent studying: 4, 2, 5, 7, 1

6. heights of buildings in feet: 35, 42, 40, 25, 42, 54, 50

7. **CCGPS Use Math Tools** Use the table that shows the lengths of different lizards. Find and compare the median and mode of the data. (Lesson 2)

Lizard Length (cm)			
14	12	14	14
19	18	11	16
30	12	19	15

8. **Georgia Test Practice** The table shows the number of minutes spent doing different exercises. Which is the median? (Lesson 2)

   Ⓐ 12.5   Ⓒ 18.2
   Ⓑ 15   Ⓓ 38

Daily Exercises	
Exercise	Time (min)
Pull-ups	8
Push-ups	10
Running	38
Sit-ups	15
Weight lifting	20

What You'll Learn

Scan the lesson. Predict two things you will learn about measures of variation.

- _____
  _____

- _____
  _____

Vocabulary Start-Up

Measures of variation are used to describe the distribution, or spread, of the data. They describe how the values of a data set vary with a single number. A *quartile* is one measure of variation.

Look in a dictionary and find words that begin with *quar-*. Write two of the words and their definitions.

Word beginning with *quar-*	Definition

Based on the definitions you found, fill in the blank below.

Quartiles are values that divide a set of data into _____ equal parts.

Real-World Link

Surveys James asked his classmates how many hours of TV they watch on a typical day.

Hours of TV Watched

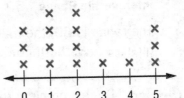

1. Divide the data into 4 equal parts. Draw a circle around each part.

2. How many data values are in each group? _____

Essential Question

HOW are the mean, median, and mode helpful in describing data?

Vocabulary

measures of variation
quartiles
first quartile
third quartile
interquartile range
range
outliers

Common Core GPS

Content Standards
MCC6.SP.3, MCC6.SP.5, MCC6.SP.5c

Mathematical Practices
1, 2, 3, 4, 5

Measures of Variation

Quartiles are values that divide the data set into four equal parts.

First and Third Quartiles

The first and third quartiles are the medians of the data values less than the median and the data values greater than the median, respectively.

Interquartile Range (IQR)

The distance between the first and third quartiles of the data set.

Range

The difference between the greatest and least data values.

Measures of variation of a data set are shown below.

$$Q_1 \qquad \text{median} \qquad Q_3$$

$$0, \ 0, \ 1, \ 1, \ 2, \ 2, \ 2, \ 3, \ 4, \ 5, \ 6, \ 6, \ 7, \ 7, \ 7, \ 8$$

The median of the data values less than the median is the first quartile or Q_1; in this case, 1.5.

The median of the data values greater than the median is the third quartile or Q_3; in this case, 6.5.

One fourth of the data lie below the first quartile and one fourth of the data lie above the third quartile. So, one half of the data lie between the first quartile and third quartile.

Example

1. **Find the measures of variation for the data.**

Range   70 − 1 or 69 mph

Quartiles   Order the numbers.

$$Q_1 \qquad \text{median} = 27.5 \qquad Q_3$$

$$1 \quad 8 \quad 25 \quad 30 \quad 50 \quad 70$$

Interquartile Range   50 − 8 or 42 $Q_3 - Q_1$

The range is 69, the median is 27.5, the first quartile is 8, the third quartile is 50, and the IQR is 42.

Animal	Speed (mph)
cheetah	70
lion	50
cat	30
elephant	25
mouse	8
spider	1

Interquartile Range
If the interquartile range is low, the middle data are grouped closely together.

Show your work.

Got It?   Do this problem to find out.

a. Determine the measures of variation for the data 64, 61, 67, 59, 60, 58, 57, 71, 56, and 62.

a. _____

Work Zone

Find Outliers and Analyze Data

An **outlier** is a data value that is either much *greater* or much *less* than the median. If a data value is more than 1.5 times the value of the interquartile range beyond the quartiles, it is an outlier.

Example

2. The ages of candidates in an election are 23, 48, 49, 55, 57, 63, and 72. Name any outliers in the data.

Find the interquartile range: $63 - 48 = 15$

Multiply the interquartile range by 1.5: $15 \times 1.5 = 22.5$

Subtract 22.5 from the first quartile and add 22.5 to the third quartile to find the limits for the outliers.

$$48 - 22.5 = 25.5 \qquad\qquad 63 + 22.5 = 85.5$$

The only age beyond the limits is 23. So, it is the only outlier.

Got It? Do this problem to find out.

b. The lengths, in feet, of various bridges are 88, 251, 275, 354, and 1,121. Name any outliers in the data set.

Example

3. The table shows a set of scores on a science test in two different classrooms. Compare and contrast their measures of variation.

Find the measures of variation for both rooms.

	Room A	Room B
Range	$100 - 65 = 35$	$98 - 63 = 35$
Median	80	81
Q_3	$\dfrac{87 + 92}{2} = 89.5$	$\dfrac{87 + 93}{2} = 90$
Q_1	$\dfrac{67 + 72}{2} = 69.5$	$\dfrac{65 + 73}{2} = 69$
IQR	$89.5 - 69.5 = 20$	$90 - 69 = 21$

Room A	Room B
72	63
100	93
67	79
84	83
65	98
78	87
92	73
87	81
80	65

Both classrooms have a range of 35 points, but Room B has an interquartile range of 21 points while Room A's interquartile range is 20 points. There are slight differences in the medians as well as the third and first quartiles.

STOP and Reflect

Which measure of center would most likely be affected by an outlier? Explain below.

Show your work.

$$\begin{array}{r} 354 \\ +154.5 \\ \hline 508.5 \end{array}$$

b. ___1121___

$$\begin{array}{r} 354 \\ -251 \\ \hline 103 \end{array}$$

$$\begin{array}{r} 103 \\ \times 1.5 \\ \hline 515 \\ 103 \\ \hline 154.5 \end{array}$$

$$\begin{array}{r} 251 \\ -154.5 \\ \hline 96.5 \end{array}$$

Show your work.

c. _____

Got It? Do this problem to find out.

c. Temperatures for the first half of the year are given for Antelope, Montana, and Augusta, Maine. Compare and contrast the measures of variation of the two cities.

Month	Antelope, MT	Augusta, ME
January	21	28
February	30	32
March	42	41
April	58	53
May	70	66
June	79	75

Guided Practice

1. The average wind speeds for several cities in Pennsylvania are given in the table. (Examples 1 and 2)

   a. Find the range of the data. _____

   b. Find the median and the first and third quartiles.

   _____

   c. Find the interquartile range. _____

   d. Identify any outliers in the data. _____

Wind Speed	
Pennsylvania City	Speed (mph)
Allentown	8.9
Erie	11.0
Harrisburg	7.5
Middletown	7.7
Philadelphia	9.5
Pittsburgh	9.0
Williamsport	7.6

2. The heights of several types of palm trees, in feet, are 40, 25, 15, 22, 50, and 30. The heights of several types of pine trees, in feet, are 60, 75, 45, 80, 75, and 70. Compare and contrast the measures of variation of both kinds of trees. (Example 3)

_____

_____

_____

_____

3. **Building on the Essential Question** Describe the difference between measure of center and measure of variation. _____

_____

_____

_____

Rate Yourself!

Are you ready to move on?
Shade the section that applies.

YES (?) NO

For more help, go online to access a Personal Tutor.

FOLDABLES Time to update your Foldable!

Independent Practice

Go online for Step-by-Step Solutions

1 The table shows the number of golf courses in various states. (Examples 1 and 2)

Number of Golf Courses			
California	1,117	New York	954
Florida	1,465	North Carolina	650
Georgia	513	Ohio	893
Iowa	437	South Carolina	456
Michigan	1,038	Texas	1,018

a. Find the range of the data. _____

b. Find the median and the first and third quartiles.

_____

c. Find the interquartile range. _____

d. Name any outliers in the data. _____

For each data set, find the median, the first and third quartiles, and the interquartile range. (Example 1)

2. texts per day: 24, 53, 38, 12, 31, 19, 26

_____

_____

3 daily attendance at the water park: 346, 250, 433, 369, 422, 298

_____

_____

4. The table shows the number of minutes of exercise for each person. Compare and contrast the measures of variation for both weeks. (Example 3) _____

_____

_____

_____

Minutes of Exercise		
	Week 1	Week 2
Tanika	45	30
Tasha	40	55
Tyrone	45	35
Uniqua	55	60
Videl	60	45
Wesley	90	75

5. **STEM** The table shows the number of known moons for each planet in our solar system. Use the measures of variation to describe the data. _____

_____

_____

_____

Known Moons of Planets			
Mercury	0	Jupiter	63
Venus	0	Saturn	34
Earth	1	Uranus	27
Mars	2	Neptune	13

6. **CCGPS Use Math Tools** The double stem-and-leaf plot, where the stem is in the middle and the leaves are on either side, shows the high temperatures for two cities in the same week. Use the measures of variation to describe the data in the stem-and-leaf plot.

Minneapolis		Columbus
5 3 1 0	2	5 7 9 9
6 4	3	7
3	4	8
	5	
	6	2

6|3 = 36°   2|5 = 25°

_____

_____

_____

_____

H.O.T. Problems Higher Order Thinking

7. **CCGPS Find the Error** Hiroshi was finding the measures of variation of the following set of data: 89, 93, 99, 110, 128, 135, 144, 152, and 159. Find his mistake and correct it.

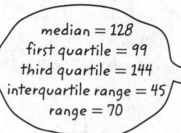

median = 128
first quartile = 99
third quartile = 144
interquartile range = 45
range = 70

_____

_____

_____

_____

8. **CCGPS Reason Abstractly** Create a list of data with at least six numbers that has an interquartile range of 15 and two outliers.

_____

_____

9. **CCGPS Persevere with Problems** How is finding the first and third quartiles similar to finding the median? _____

_____

_____

10. **CCGPS Reason Inductively** Explain why the median is not affected by very high or very low values in the data. _____

_____

_____

Georgia Test Practice

11. Which of the following sets of data has an interquartile range of 10?

  (A) 3, 4, 9, 16, 17, 24, 31   (C) 12, 14, 17, 19, 19, 20, 21

  (B) 41, 43, 49, 49, 50, 53, 55   (D) 55, 56, 56, 57, 58, 59, 62

Extra Practice

12. The table shows the countries with the most Internet users.

Millions of Internet Users	
China	99.8
Germany	41.88
India	36.97
Japan	78.05
South Korea	31.67
United Kingdom	33.11
United States	185.55

a. Find the range of the data.

153,880,000   185,550,000 − 31,670,000 = 153,880,000

Homework Help

b. Find the median and the first and third quartiles.

41,880,000; 33,110,000; 99,800,000

31.67   33.11   36.97   41.88   78.05   99.8   185.55
Q_1 Median Q_3

c. Find the interquartile range.

66,690,000   99,800,000 − 33,110,000 = 66,690,000

d. Name any outliers in the data. none

13. CCGPS **Use Math Tools** The table shows the top teams in the National Football Conference (NFC) and the American Football Conference (AFC).

Penalties By NFL Teams			
NFC		**AFC**	
Dallas Cowboys	104	New England Patriots	78
Arizona Cardinals	137	Indianapolis Colts	67
Green Bay Packers	113	Jacksonville Jaguars	76
New Orleans Saints	68	San Diego Chargers	94
New York Giants	77	Cleveland Browns	114
Seattle Seahawks	59	Pittsburgh Steelers	80
Minnesota Vikings	86	Houston Texans	82

a. Which conference had a greater range of penalties? _____

_____

b. Find the measures of variation for each conference. _____

_____

_____

c. Compare and contrast the measures of variation for each conference.

_____

_____

_____

14. Find the median, the first and third quartiles, and the interquartile range for the cost of admission: $13.95, $24.59, $19.99, $29.98, $23.95, $28.99.

_____

_____

_____

15. The number of games won by 10 chess players is given.

$$\{13, 15, 2, 7, 5, 9, 11, 10, 12, 11\}$$

Which of the following statements is *not* supported by these data?

Ⓐ Half of the players won more than 10.5 games and half won less than 10.5 games.

Ⓑ The range of the data is 13 games.

Ⓒ There are no outliers.

Ⓓ Only one fourth of the players won more than 7 games.

16. The normal monthly rainfall in inches for a city are given in the table.

Jan	Feb	Mar	Apr	May	June
0.65	1.39	0.63	2.16	2.82	4.21

July	Aug	Sept	Oct	Nov	Dec
3.22	1.20	9.31	11.25	0.70	0.80

What values, if any, are outliers?

Ⓕ 9.31 only

Ⓖ 11.25 only

Ⓗ both 9.31 and 11.25

Ⓘ There are no outliers.

17. Short Response The ages in months of dogs enrolled in obedience class are: 8, 12, 20, 10, 6, 15, 12, 9, and 10. Find the range, median, first and third quartiles, and interquartile range of the dogs' ages.

Common Core Review

Divide. MCC5.NBT.6, MCC5.NBT.7

18. 160 ÷ 5 = _____

19. 188 ÷ 8 = _____

20. 133 ÷ 7 = _____

21. 87.5 ÷ 5 = _____

22. 136.5 ÷ 7 = _____

23. 74.4 ÷ 6 = _____

24. Refer to the table. How much farther did the Sing family drive on Friday than on Saturday? MCC4.NBT.4

Day	Distance (miles)
Thursday	68
Friday	193
Saturday	26
Sunday	95

25. Refer to the table. How many more hours did Koli work in week 2 than in week 3? MCC4.NBT.4

Week	Hours Worked
1	12
2	16
3	9

Mean Absolute Deviation

What You'll Learn

Scan the lesson. List two headings you would use to make an outline of the lesson.

- _____

- _____

Essential Question

HOW are the mean, median, and mode helpful in describing data?

Vocabulary

mean absolute deviation

Common Core GPS

Content Standards
MCC6.SP.5, MCC6.SP.5b, MCC6.SP.5c

Mathematical Practices
1, 2, 3, 4, 5, 6

Real-World Link

Basketball The tables show the number of points two teams scored.

Ally's Team			
52	48	60	50
56	54	58	62

Lena's Team			
51	48	60	49
59	50	62	61

1. Plot each set of data on a number line.

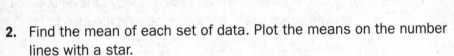

Ally's Team   46 48 50 52 54 56 58 60 62 64

Lena's Team   46 48 50 52 54 56 58 60 62 64

2. Find the mean of each set of data. Plot the means on the number lines with a star.

3. Find the range of each set of data. _____

_____

4. Refer to the number lines. Compare and contrast each set of data.

_____

_____

_____

Find Mean Absolute Deviation

You have used the interquartile range to describe the spread of a set of data. You can also use the mean absolute deviation. The **mean absolute deviation** of a set of data is the average distance between each data value and the mean.

 Example

 Tutor

1. The table shows the maximum speeds of eight roller coasters. Find the mean absolute deviation of the set of data. Describe what the mean absolute deviation represents.

Maximum Speeds of Roller Coasters (mph)			
58	88	40	60
72	66	80	48

Step 1 Find the mean.

$$\frac{58 + 88 + 40 + 60 + 72 + 66 + 80 + 48}{8} = 64$$

Step 2 Find the absolute value of the differences between each value in the data set and the mean. Each data value is represented by an "x".

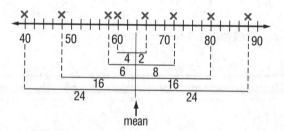

Step 3 Find the average of the absolute values of the differences between each value in the data set and the mean.

$$\frac{24 + 16 + 6 + 4 + 2 + 8 + 16 + 24}{8} = 12.5$$

The mean absolute deviation is 12.5. This means that the average distance each data value is from the mean is 12.5 miles per hour.

Got It? Do this problem to find out.

 Show your work.

a. The table shows speeds of ten birds. Find the mean absolute deviation of the data. Round to the nearest hundredth. Describe what the mean absolute deviation represents.

Speeds of Top Ten Fastest Birds (mph)				
88	77	65	70	65
72	95	80	106	68

a. _____

Compare Variation

You can compare the mean absolute deviations for two data sets. A data set with a smaller mean absolute deviation has data values that are closer to the mean than a data set with a greater mean absolute deviation.

Example

Tutor

2. **The top five salaries and the bottom five salaries for the 2010 New York Yankees are shown in the table below. Salaries are in millions of dollars and are rounded to the nearest hundredth.**

2010 New York Yankees Salaries (millions of $)										
Top Five Salaries					Bottom Five Salaries				
33.00	24.29	22.60	20.63	16.50	0.45	0.44	0.43	0.41	0.41

a. **Find the mean absolute deviation for each set of data. Round to the nearest hundredth.**

Find the mean of the top five salaries.

$$\frac{33.00 + 24.29 + 22.60 + 20.63 + 16.50}{5} \approx 23.40$$

The mean is about $23.40 million.

Find the mean absolute deviation of the top five salaries.

$$\frac{9.60 + 0.89 + 0.80 + 2.77 + 6.90}{5} \approx 4.19$$

The mean absolute deviation is about $4.19 million.

Find the mean of the bottom five salaries.

$$\frac{0.45 + 0.44 + 0.43 + 0.41 + 0.41}{5} \approx 0.43$$

The mean is about $0.43 million.

Find the mean absolute deviation of the bottom five salaries.

$$\frac{0.02 + 0.01 + 0 + 0.02 + 0.02}{5} \approx 0.01$$

The mean absolute deviation is about $0.01 million.

b. **Write a few sentences comparing their variation.**

The mean absolute deviation for the bottom five salaries is much less than that for the top five salaries. The data for the bottom five salaries are closer together than the data for the top five salaries.

> **Mean Absolute Deviation**
>
> The absolute values of the differences between each data value and the mean for the top five salaries are calculated below.
>
> $|33.00 - 23.40| = 9.60$
>
> $|24.29 - 23.40| = 0.89$
>
> $|22.60 - 23.40| = 0.80$
>
> $|20.63 - 23.40| = 2.77$
>
> $|16.50 - 23.40| = 6.90$

Got It? Do this problem to find out.

b. The table shows the running time in minutes for two kinds of movies. Find the mean absolute deviation for each set of data. Round to the nearest hundredth. Then write a few sentences comparing their variation.

Running Time for Movies (min)									
Comedy					**Drama**				
90	95	88	100	98	115	120	150	135	144

Guided Practice

1. Find the mean absolute deviation for the set of data. Round to the nearest hundredth if necessary. Then describe what the mean absolute deviation represents. (Example 1)

Number of Daily Visitors to a Web Site				
112	145	108	160	122

_____

_____

2. The table shows the height of waterslides at two different water parks. Find the mean absolute deviation for each set of data. Round to the nearest hundredth. Then write a few sentences comparing their variation. (Example 2)

Height of Waterslides (ft)									
Splash Lagoon					**Wild Water Bay**				
75	95	80	110	88	120	108	94	135	126

_____

_____

_____

_____

3. **Building on the Essential Question** What does the mean absolute deviation tell you about a set of data?

_____

_____

_____

Rate Yourself!

☐ I understand how to find the mean absolute deviation.

▶▶ Great! You're ready to move on!

☐ I still have questions about finding the mean absolute deviation.

▥ No Problem! Go online to access a Personal Tutor. [Tutor]

FOLDABLES Time to update your Foldable!

Independent Practice

Go online for Step-by-Step Solutions

Find the mean absolute deviation for each set of data. Round to the nearest hundredth if necessary. Then describe what the mean absolute deviation represents. (Example 1)

Known Moons of Planets			
0	0	1	2
63	34	27	13

2.

Hard Drive (gigabytes)			
640	250	500	640
720	640	250	720

_____

_____

3. The table shows the lengths of the longest bridges in the United States and in Europe. Find the mean absolute deviation for each set of data. Round to the nearest hundredth if necessary. Then write a few sentences comparing their variation.

Longest Bridges (kilometers)									
United States					Europe				
38.4	36.7	29.3	24.1	17.7	17.2	11.7	7.8	6.8	6.6
12.9	11.3	10.9	8.9	8.9	6.1	5.1	5.0	4.3	3.9

_____

_____

For Exercises 4–7, refer to the table that shows the recent population, in millions, of the ten largest U.S. cities.

Population of Largest U.S. Cities (millions)				
1.5	3.8	1.3	1.6	2.9
1.4	0.9	2.3	8.4	1.3

4. Find the mean absolute deviation. Round to the nearest hundredth.

_____

5. How many data values are closer than one mean absolute deviation away from the mean? _____

6. Which population is farthest from the mean? How far away from the mean is that population? Round to the nearest hundredth.

_____

7. Are there any populations that are more than twice the mean absolute deviation from the mean? Explain. _____

_____

CCGPS **Be Precise** For Exercises 8 and 9, look up the word *deviate* in a dictionary or online.

8. What does the word *deviate* mean? How can it help you remember what the mean absolute deviation refers to? _____

_____

9. How does the word *absolute* help you to remember how to calculate the mean absolute deviation? _____

_____

H.O.T. Problems   Higher Order Thinking

10. **CCGPS** **Reason Abstractly** Create two sets of data, each with five values, that satisfy the following conditions.

   The mean absolute deviation of Set A is less than the mean absolute deviation of Set B.

   The mean of Set A is greater than the mean of Set B.

_____

CCGPS **Persevere with Problems** For Exercises 11 and 12, refer to the table that shows the recorded speeds of several cars on a busy street.

Recorded Speeds (mph)					
35	38	41	35	36	55

11. Calculate the mean absolute deviation both with and without the data value of 55. Round to the nearest hundredth if necessary.

_____

_____

12. Explain how including the value of 55 affects the mean absolute deviation.

_____

_____

_____

13. **CCGPS** **Construct an Argument** Explain why the mean absolute deviation is calculated using absolute value. _____

_____

_____

Georgia Test Practice

14. The table shows the high temperature for 6 days. Which of the following is the mean absolute deviation for the set of data?

   Ⓐ 4°F   Ⓑ 4.8°F   Ⓒ 10°F   Ⓓ 68°F

High Temperature (°F)					
75	58	72	68	69	66

Extra Practice

Use Math Tools Find the mean absolute deviation for each set of data. Round to the nearest hundredth if necessary. Then describe what the mean absolute deviation represents.

15.

Digital Camera Prices ($)				
140	125	190	148	156
212	178	188	196	224

$26.76; The average distance each data value is from the mean is $26.76.

mean: $\dfrac{140 + 125 + 190 + 148 + 156 + 212 + 178 + 188 + 196 + 224}{10} = \$175.70$

mean absolute deviation: $\dfrac{35.7 + 50.7 + 14.3 + 27.7 + 19.7 + 36.3 + 2.3 + 12.3 + 20.3 + 48.3}{10} = 26.76$

16.

Grand Slam Singles Titles Won				
14	8	7	6	5
10	11	8	8	6

Copy and Solve Find the mean absolute deviation for each set of data. Round to the nearest hundredth. Then write a few sentences comparing their variation.

17. The table shows the amount of money raised by the homerooms for two grade levels at a middle school.

Money Raised ($)											
Sixth Grade						**Seventh Grade**					
88	116	94	108	112	124	144	91	97	122	128	132

18. The table shows the number of points scored each game for two different basketball teams.

Number of Points Scored											
Lakeside Panthers						**Jefferson Eagles**					
44	38	54	48	26	36	58	42	64	62	70	40

19. The table shows the prices for parking at various beaches along the same coastline.

Beach Parking ($)				
2.50	3.75	1.25	2.25	3.00

Which of the following is the mean absolute deviation for the set of data?

Ⓐ $0.25

Ⓒ $2.50

Ⓑ $0.66

Ⓓ $2.55

20. Which of the following is true concerning the mean absolute deviation of a set of data?

Ⓕ It describes the variation of the data values around the median.

Ⓖ It describes the absolute value of the mean.

Ⓗ It describes the average distance between each data value and the mean.

Ⓘ It describes the variation of the data values around the mode.

21. Short Response The table shows the number of Calories in several sandwiches at a restaurant. Find the mean absolute deviation for the set of data. Round to the nearest hundredth.

Number of Calories per Sandwich					
477	660	572	561	527	605

Common Core Review

Divide. MCC5.NBT.6, MCC5.NBT.7

22. 86 ÷ 5 = _____

23. 95 ÷ 4 = _____

24. 105 ÷ 6 = _____

25. 94.5 ÷ 15 = _____

26. 72 ÷ 5 = _____

27. 40.6 ÷ 7 = _____

28. 59.5 ÷ 7 = _____

29. 126 ÷ 8 = _____

30. 146 ÷ 5 = _____

31. The table shows the number of different cones Delightful Dips ice cream shop sold in one afternoon. What is the total number of cones sold? MCC4.NBT.4 _____

Flavor	Number of Cones
Chocolate	57
Cookie Crunch	49
Fudge Swirl	41
Strawberry	37
Vanilla	51

32. The hiking club wanted to cover a different trail each day for a week. On Monday they hiked 2.3 miles, on Tuesday they hiked 1.8 miles, on Wednesday they hiked 3.2 miles, on Thursday they hiked 1.4 miles and on Friday they hiked 2.8 miles. What is the total distance they hiked? MCC5.NBT.7

Appropriate Measures

What You'll Learn

Scan the lesson. Predict two things you will learn about appropriate measures.

- _____
  _____

- _____
  _____

Essential Question

HOW are the mean, median, and mode helpful in describing data?

CCGPS Common Core GPS

Content Standards
MCC6.SP.5, MCC6.SP.5c, MCC6.SP.5d

Mathematical Practices
1, 3, 4

 ## Real-World Link [Watch ▶]

Recycling The green committee had a recycling drive where they collected aluminum cans, plastic bottles, newspapers, and batteries. The weights collected on the first day are shown.

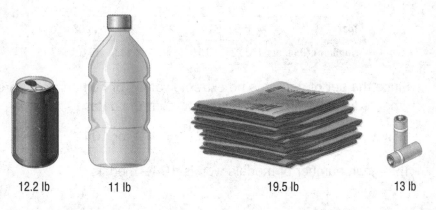

12.2 lb   11 lb   19.5 lb   13 lb

1. Find the mean weight collected. _____

2. If the newspapers are not included, find the mean weight of the

   remaining items. _____

3. How does the weight of the newspapers affect the mean?

   _____

   _____

4. What is the median for the data set? How does the median differ if the newspapers are not included?

   _____

   _____

Using Mean, Median, and Mode

Measure	Most appropriate when...
mean	• the data have no extreme values.
median	• the data have extreme values. • there are no big gaps in the middle of the data.
mode	• data have many repeated numbers.

Outlier=

Mean= No extreme values

Work Zone

Sometimes, one measure is more appropriate than others to use to summarize a data set.

Examples

Tutor

1. The table shows the number of medals won by the U.S. Which measure of center best represents the data? Then find the measure of center.

Year	1992	1996	2000	2004	2008
Number of Medals	112	101	97	103	110

Since the set of data has no extreme values or numbers that are repeated, the mean would best represent the data.

Mean $\dfrac{112 + 101 + 97 + 103 + 110}{5} = \dfrac{523}{5}$ or $104\frac{3}{5}$

The mean number of medals won is $104\frac{3}{5}$ medals.

2. The table shows the water temperature over several days. Which measure of center best represents the data? Then find the measure of center.

Water Temperature (°F)			
82	85	82	81
	82	82	78

In the set of data, there are no extreme values. There is a temperature repeated four times, so the mode 82° is the measure of center that best represents the data.

Show your work.

Got It? Do this problem to find out.

a. _____

a. The prices of several DVDs are $22.50, $21.95, $25.00, $21.95, $19.95, $21.95, and $21.50. Which measure of center best represents the data? Justify your selection. Then find the measure of center.

Outliers and Appropriate Measure

Sometimes data sets contain outliers. Outliers are deviations from the majority of the data set. The outlier may affect the measures of center.

Examples

The table shows average life spans of some animals.

3. Identify the outlier in the data set.

Compared to the other values, 200 years is extremely high. So, it is an outlier.

Average Life Span	
Animal	**Life Span (years)**
African elephant	35
Bottlenose dolphin	30
Chimpanzee	50
Galapagos tortoise	200
Gorilla	30
Gray whale	70
Horse	20

4. Determine how the outlier affects the mean, median, and mode of the data.

Find the mean, median, and mode with and without the outlier.

With the outlier

Mean $\dfrac{35 + 30 + 50 + 200 + 30 + 70 + 20}{7} \approx 62$

Median 35

Mode 30

Without the outlier

Mean $\dfrac{35 + 30 + 50 + 30 + 70 + 20}{6} \approx 39$

Median 32.5

Mode 30

The mean life span decreased by 62 − 39 or 23 years. The median life span decreased by 35 − 32.5 or 2.5 years. The mode did not change.

5. Which measure of center best describes the data with and without the outlier? Justify your selection.

The mean was affected the most with the outlier. The median life span changed very little with and without the outlier, so it best describes the data in both cases. The mode does not describe the data very well since there were only two repeated numbers.

Outliers

In Example 3, 200 is an outlier.

IQR = 40

40 • 1.5 = 60

200 − 70 = 130

130 > 60

So, 200 is an outlier.

STOP and Reflect

If a data set has an outlier, why might you use the median instead of the mean?

Got It? Do these problems to find out.

The prices of some new athletic shoes are shown in the table.

Price of Athletic Shoes			
$51.95	$47.50	$46.50	$48.50
	$52.95	$78.95	$39.95

b. _____

    b. Identify the outlier in the data set.

    c. Determine how the outlier affects the mean, median, and mode of the data. _____

_____

_____

    d. Tell which measure of center best describes the data with and without the outlier. _____

_____

_____

Guided Practice

1. The table shows the required temperatures for different recipes. (Examples 1–5)

Cooking Temperature (°F)			
175	325	325	350
350	350	400	450

    a. Identify the outlier in the data set. _____

    b. Determine how the outlier affects the mean, median, and mode of the data. _____

_____

_____

    c. Tell which measure of center best describes the data with and without the outlier. Justify your selection.

_____

_____

_____

Rate Yourself!

How well do you understand choosing the appropriate measure of center for a data set? Circle the image that applies.

2. **Building on the Essential Question** How does an outlier affect the mean, median, and mode of a data set?

_____

_____

_____

_____

Clear   Somewhat   Not So
        Clear   Clear

For more help, go online to access a Personal Tutor.

Tutor

Independent Practice

Go online for Step-by-Step Solutions

1 The number of minutes spent studying are: 60, 70, 45, 60, 80, 35, and 45.
Find the measure of center that best represents the data. Justify your
selection and then find the measure of center. (Examples 1 and 2)

_____

_____

2. The table shows monthly rainfall in inches for
five months. Identify the outlier in the data set.
Determine how the outlier affects the mean,
median, and mode of the data. Then tell which
measure of center best describes the data with
and without the outlier. Round to the nearest
hundredth. Justify your selection. (Examples 3–5)

Month	June	July	Aug	Sept	Oct	Nov
Rainfall (in.)	6.14	7.19	8.63	8.38	6.47	2.43

_____

_____

_____

_____

3 The table shows the average depth of several lakes.

a. Identify the outlier in the data set. _____

b. Determine how the outlier affects the mean, median, mode, and

range of the data. _____

_____

_____

Lake	Depth (ft)
Crater Lake	1,148
East Okoboji	10
Lake Gilead	43
Lake Erie	62
Great Salt Lake	14
Medicine Lake	24

c. Tell which measure of center best describes the data with and without

the outlier. _____

_____

4. **CCGPS** **Construct an Argument** Fill in the graphic organizer below.

Measure of Center	How can an outlier affect it?
mean	
median	
mode	

5. 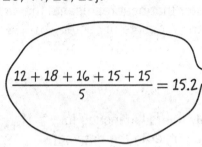 **Find the Error** Pilar is determining which measure of center best describes the data set {12, 18, 16, 44, 15, 15}. Find her mistake and correct it.

$$\frac{12 + 18 + 16 + 15 + 15}{5} = 15.2$$

6. **CCGPS Justify Conclusions** Determine whether the following statement is *true* or *false*. If true, explain your reasoning. If false, give a counterexample.

> *Of mean, median, and mode, the median will always be most affected by outliers.*

7. **CCGPS Persevere with Problems** Add three data values to the following data set so the mean increases by 10 and the median does not change.

42, 37, 32, 29, 20

Georgia Test Practice

8. The table shows the greatest recorded weights of fish.

Record Fish Weights	
Fish	**Weight (lb)**
King Mackerel	90
Red Snapper	46.5
Snook	44
Swordfish	612.75
Tarpon	243
Yellowfin Grouper	34.38

Which measure is most affected by the outlier?

Ⓐ mean   Ⓒ mode

Ⓑ median   Ⓓ range

Extra Practice

9. The number of songs downloaded per month by a group of friends were 8, 12, 6, 4, 2, 0, and 10. Find the measure of center that best represents the data. Justify your selection then find the measure of center. <u>Since the</u> <u>set of data has no extreme values or numbers that are identical, the mean</u> <u>or median, 6 songs, would best represent the data.</u>

 There are no extreme values and no repeated numbers.

mean: $\dfrac{0 + 2 + 4 + 6 + 8 + 10 + 12}{7} = 6$

median: 0, 2, 4, ⑥ 8, 10, 12

10. The ages of participants in a relay race are 12, 15, 14, 13, 15, 12, 22, 16, and 11. Identify the outlier in the data set. Determine how the outlier affects the mean, median, and mode of the data. Then tell which measure of center best describes the data with and without the outlier. <u>The</u> <u>mean is the best measure</u>

_____

_____

_____

11. **CCGPS** **Justify Conclusions** The table shows the high temperatures during one week. Round to the nearest hundredth if necessary.

High Temperatures			
29°	27°	29°	25°
28°	29°	62°	

a. Identify the outlier in the data set. _____

b. Determine how the outlier affects the mean, median, mode, and range of the data. _____

_____

_____

_____

c. Tell which measure of center best describes the data with and without the outlier. Explain your reasoning to a classmate. _____

_____

_____

_____

Georgia Test Practice

12. Find the measures of center for the set of data.

 17, 36, 45, 98, 25, 34, 19, 45, 36

Ⓐ mean: 41, median: 36,
modes: 45 and 36, outlier: none

Ⓑ mean: 41, median: 36,
modes: 45 and 36, outliers: 98 and 19

Ⓒ mean: 39.4, median: 36,
modes: 45 and 36, outlier: 98

Ⓓ mean: 39.4, median: 36,
mode: 45, outlier: 98

13. Short Response Refer to Exercise 12. Which measure best describes the set of data? Explain.

Median, since there is an outlier.

14. The table shows the points a basketball team scored in different games.

Points Scored		
79	83	79
85	41	77

Which measure is most affected by the outlier?

Ⓕ mean   Ⓗ mode

Ⓖ median   Ⓘ range

15. Short Response The times from a 100 meter race in seconds were: 12.5, 13.1, 11.9, 12.4, 12.7, 13.1, 12.6, and 12.2. What measure of center best represents the data? Explain.

The mean, since there are no extreme values.

Find the total of each set of numbers. MCC4.NBT.4

16. {19, 16, 24, 22, 18} _____

17. {54, 48, 52, 57, 49} _____

18. {9, 5, 6, 7, 4, 11, 7} _____

19. {31, 36, 28, 34, 25} _____

20. The table shows the number of tickets sold to the school musical on three days. How many total tickets were sold? MCC4.NBT.4

_____

Day	Number of Tickets Sold
Wednesday	56
Thursday	79
Friday	68

21ST CENTURY CAREER
in Marine Biology

Marine Biologist

Do all the unusual and amazing creatures in the ocean fascinate you? Do you think you would be good at coming up with your own experiments to test theories about them? If so, a career in marine biology might be something to think about! A marine biologist studies plants and animals that live in the ocean. These include everything from microscopic plankton to multi-ton whales. Marine biologists study organisms that live in the tiny layers of the surface and those that live thousands of meters below the surface.

College & Career
R E A D I N E S S

Explore college and careers at ccr.mcgraw-hill.com

Is This the Career for You?

If you would like to be a marine biologist, you may want to take some of the following courses in high school.

- ◆ Biology
- ◆ Calculus
- ◆ Chemistry
- ◆ Marine Science
- ◆ Statistics

Turn the page to find out how math relates to a career in Marine Biology.

Ready to Make Waves?

Use the information in the line plot and the table to solve each problem. Round to the nearest tenth if necessary.

1. Find the mean of the pipefish data. _____

2. Find the median and mode of the pipefish data. _____

3. What is the range of the pipefish data? Would you describe the data as spread out or close in value? Explain. _____

4. Identify the outlier in the artificial reef data. Find the mean with and without the outlier. _____

5. Describe how the outlier affects the mean in Exercise 4. _____

6. Find the median and mode of the artificial reef data. Which better represents the data? Explain. _____

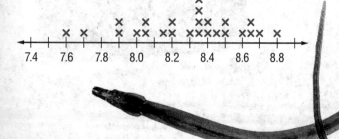

Pipefish Specimens (cm)

Number of Artificial Reefs in Florida Counties						
198	62	108	34	29	73	173
96	97	9	46	21	22	69
8	83	31	79	67	61	15
105	63	34	351	13	126	36
25	12	82	35	4		

Career Project

It's time to update your career portfolio! Use the Internet or another source to research several careers in marine biology. Write a brief summary comparing and contrasting the careers.

_____

_____

_____

_____

_____

What subject in school is the most important to you? How would you use that subject in this career?

_____

_____

_____

_____

Vocabulary Check

Reconstruct the vocabulary word and definition from the letters under the grid. The letters for each column are scrambled directly under that column.

Complete each sentence using the vocabulary list at the beginning of the chapter.

1. The _____ is the number(s) or item(s) that appear most often in a set of data.

2. Numbers that are used to describe the center of a set of data are _____.

3. The difference between the greatest number and the least number in a set of data is the _____.

4. The _____ of a list of values is the value appearing at the center of a sorted version of the list, or the mean of the two central values, if the list contains an even number of values.

5. The _____ is the distance between the first and third quartiles of a data set.

6. A value that is much higher or much lower than the other values of a data set is a(n) _____.

Use Your FOLDABLES

Use your Foldable to help review the chapter.

Tape here

Tape here

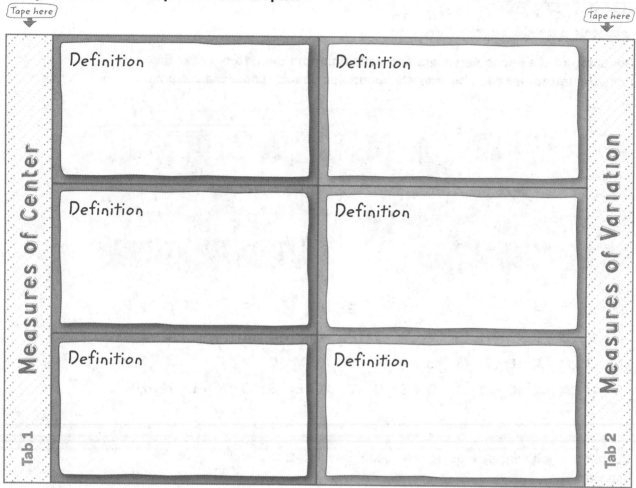

Measures of Center

Tab 1

Definition

Definition

Definition

Definition

Definition

Definition

Measures of Variation

Tab 2

Got it?

Complete the cross number puzzle by finding the mean of each data set.

Across

1. {563, 462, 490}
3. {260, 231, 248, 257}
5. {140, 163, 133, 116}
6. {21, 9, 18}
8. {145, 158, 182, 171}
9. {113, 82, 98, 91}
11. {7960, 8624, 8298, 8366}
12. {4625, 3989, 5465}

Down

1. {62, 58, 51, 41}
2. {5326, 5048, 4968}
3. {269, 293, 281}
4. {103, 89, 98, 98}
7. {720, 597, 756}
8. {142, 169, 150, 155}
10. {588, 615, 652, 653}
11. {70, 89, 90}

Problem Solving

1. The speeds of six cheetahs are shown in the table. What is the mean speed? (Lesson 1) _____

   72 mph

Cheetah Speeds (mph)					
68	72	74	72	71	75

2. 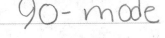 **Be Precise** The minutes spent doing homework for one week were 30, 60, 77, 90, 88, 76, and 90. Find the median and mode of these times. (Lesson 2) **77 – median, 90 – mode**

3. The table shows the high temperatures for one week in July. Find the median and mode for these temperatures. (Lesson 2) **82 – md.**

July Temperatures (°F)						
78	82	85	84	82	79	83

4. The table shows the number of books read in a reading challenge. Use the measures of variation to describe the data and identify any outliers. (Lesson 3) _____

Books Read						
12	15	12	2	18	20	14
15	13	15	16	10	15	17

   Outlier = 2

5. The table shows the museum admission price for several museums. Find the mean absolute deviation. Round to the nearest hundredth if necessary. Then describe what the mean absolute deviation represents. (Lesson 4) **MAD = 1.2**

Museum Admission ($)		
14.25	11.00	15.00
12.25	12.50	13.50

6. The number of points scored in volleyball games are 15, 11, 14, 15, 9, 12, 10, 15, 3, and 15. Find the measure of center that best represents the data. Justify you selection and then find the measure of center. (Lesson 5)

   Median – there is an outlier
   Mode

7. The table shows scores on an English test. Which measure of center best describes the data with and without the outlier. (Lesson 5)

   Median – there is outlier
   W/o the outlier, grade increases

Test Scores (%)			
87	89	94	95
98	88	92	94
89	52	94	96

Reflect

 Answering the Essential Question

Use what you learned about mean, median, and mode to complete the graphic organizer.

 Essential Question

HOW are the mean, median, and mode helpful in describing data?

	mean	median	mode
definition			
When is it appropriate to use?			
How does an outlier affect it?			

Answer the Essential Question. HOW are the mean, median, and mode helpful in describing data?

_____

_____

Chapter 11
Statistical Displays

Essential Question

WHY is it important to carefully evaluate graphs?

Common Core GPS

CCGPS

Content Standards
MCC6.SP.2, MCC6.SP.4, MCC6.SP.5, MCC6.SP.5a, MCC6.SP.5b, MCC6.SP.5c, MCC6.SP.5d

Mathematical Practices
1, 2, 3, 4, 5, 6, 7

Math in the Real World

Roller Coaster The table shows the drop of several different roller coasters.

Roller Coaster	Drop (ft)
Anaconda	144
Mind Eraser	95
Scorpion	60
Thunderbolt	70

Draw bars to represent the drop of each roller coaster.

FOLDABLES®
Study Organizer

1 Cut out the correct Foldable from the FL pages in the back of this book.

2 Place your Foldable on the Key Concept page toward the end of this chapter.

3 Use the Foldable throughout this chapter to help you learn about statistical displays.

Vocabulary

box plot	gap	symmetric
cluster	histogram	
distribution	line graph	
dot plot	line plot	
frequency distribution	peak	

Review Vocabulary

Using a graphic organizer can help you remember important vocabulary terms. Fill in the graphic organizer for the word *graph*.

graph

⬇

Definition

Example

Picture

Your Turn! You will solve this problem in the chapter.

Are You Ready?

Try the Quick Check below.
Or, take the Online Readiness Quiz.

Check ✓

CCGPS **Quick Review**

Common Core Review MCC6.SP.4c

Example 1

Find the mean of the data set.

$$\{15, 30, 20, 25, 30\}$$

$15 + 30 + 20 + 25 + 30 = 120$ Add.

$$\frac{120}{5} = 24$$ Divide.

The mean is 24.

Example 2

Find the median of the data set.

$$\{65, 57, 33, 41, 49\}$$

33 41 (49) 57 65   Order the numbers.

The number in the middle is 49, so 49 is the median.

Quick Check

Mean **Find the mean of each data set.**

1. {8, 13, 21, 12, 29, 13}

2. {52, 76, 61, 58, 68}

3. {35, 18, 22, 20, 36, 31}

Show your work.

4. Jackson's social studies grades during one quarter are shown in the table. What is his mean score for the quarter?

Social Studies Grades (%)					
94	89	96	93	90	99
87	97	95	93	98	97

Median **Find the median of each data set.**

5. {56, 61, 54, 54, 58, 59}

6. {124, 131, 114, 148, 126}

7. {85, 79, 82, 90, 84, 87}

8. The table shows the high temperatures in a certain city for a week. What is the median temperature?

High Temperature (°F)						
71	64	56	52	62	62	66

How Did You Do?

Which problems did you answer correctly in the Quick Check?
Shade those exercise numbers below.

① ② ③ ④ ⑤ ⑥ ⑦ ⑧

What You'll Learn

Scan the lesson. List two headings you would use to make an outline of the lesson.

- _____
- _____

Essential Question

WHY is it important to carefully evaluate graphs?

Vocabulary

line plot
dot plot

Common Core GPS

Content Standards
MCC6.SP.4, MCC6.SP.5, MCC6.SP.5a, MCC6.SP.5b, MCC6.SP.5c

Mathematical Practices
1, 3, 4

Real-World Link

Activities Students in Mr. Cotter's class were asked how many after-school activities they have. Their responses are shown in the table.

Step 1 Use the data to fill in the frequency table.

Number of Activities

0	2	1	3
1	1	3	4
2	1	0	1
2	3	2	1

→

Number of Activities

Number	Tally
0	||
1	|||| |
2	|||
3	|||
4	

Step 2 Turn the table so the number of activities is along the bottom on a number line. Instead of tally marks, place Xs above the number line. The Xs for 0 activities have been placed for you.

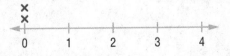

```
  X
  X
  └───┴───┴───┴───┴───
  0   1   2   3   4
```

The data is now represented in a *line plot*.

Make a Line Plot

One way to give a picture of data is to make a line plot. A **line plot** is a visual display of a distribution of data values where each data value is shown as a dot or other mark, usually an X, above a number line. A line plot is also known as a **dot plot**.

Example

Tutor

1. Jasmine asked her class how many pets they had. The results are shown in the table. Make a line plot of the data. Then describe the data presented in the graph.

Number of Pets					
3	2	2	1	3	1
0	1	0	2	3	4
0	1	1	4	2	2
1	2	2	3	0	2

Step 1 Draw and label a number line.

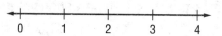

Step 2 Place as many Xs above each number as there are responses for that number. Include a title.

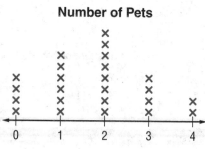
Number of Pets

Step 3 Describe the data. 24 students responded to the question. No one has more than 4 pets. Four students have no pets. Include a title. The response given most is 2 pets. This represents the mode.

Show your work.

Got It? Do this problem to find out.

a. _____

a. Javier asked the members of his 4-H club how many projects they were taking. The results are shown in the table. Make a line plot of the data. Then describe the data in the graph.

Number of Projects				
2	4	3	3	1
0	5	4	2	2
1	3	2	1	2

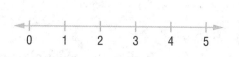

Analyze Line Plots

You can describe a set of data using measures of center as well as measures of variability. The range of the data and any outliers are also useful in describing the data.

 Real World

Examples

 Tutor

The line plot shows the prices of cowboy hats.

Prices of Cowboy Hats

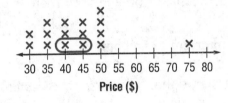

Price ($)

2. **Find the median and mode of the data. Then describe the data using them.**

There are 16 hat prices, in dollars, represented in the line plot. The median is between the 8th and 9th pieces of data.

The two middle numbers, shown on the line plot, are 40 and 45. So, the median is $42.50. This means that half of the cowboy hats cost more than $42.50 and half cost less than $42.50.

The number that appears most often is 50. So, the mode of the data is 50. This means that more cowboy hats cost $50 than any other price.

3. **Find the range and any outliers of the data. Then describe the data using them.**

The range of the prices is $75 − $30 or $45. The limits for the outlier are $12.50 and $72.50. So, $75 is an outlier.

Got It? Do this problem to find out.

b. The line plot shows the number of magazines each member of the student council sold. Find the median, mode, range, and any outliers of the data. Then describe the data using them.

Number of Magazines Sold

STOP and Reflect

Suppose two sets of data have the same median but different ranges. What can you conclude about the sets? Explain below.

Show your work.

b. _____

Example

4. The line plot shows the amount James deposited in his savings account each month. Describe the data. Include measures of center and variability.

Amount Saved ($)

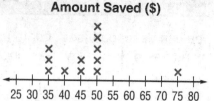

The mean is $46.67. The median is $47.50, and the mode is $50. So, the majority of the data are close to the measures of center.

The range of the data is $75 − $35 or $40. The interquartile range is $Q_3 − Q_1$, or $50 − $37.50 = $12.50. So, half of the amounts are between $37.50 and $50. There is one outlier at $75.

Got It? Do this problem to find out.

c. _____

c. The line plot shows the prices of sweaters in a store. Describe the data. Include measures of center and variability.

Sweater Prices ($)

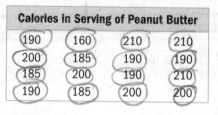

Guided Practice

1. Make a line plot for the set of data. Describe the data. Include measures of center and variability. (Examples 1–4)

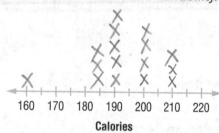

Calories in Serving of Peanut Butter

190	160	210	210
200	185	190	190
185	200	190	210
190	185	200	200

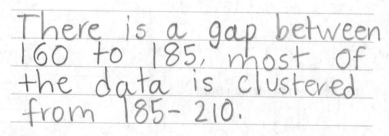

There is a gap between 160 to 185, most of the data is clustered from 185− 210.

2. 🅔 **Building on the Essential Question** How is using a line plot useful to analyze data? _____

Rate Yourself!

How confident are you about line plots? Check the box that applies.

For more help, go online to access a Personal Tutor.

FOLDABLES Time to update your Foldable!

Independent Practice

Go online for Step-by-Step Solutions eHelp

Make a line plot for each set of data. Find the median, mode, range, and any outliers of the data shown in the line plot. Then describe the data using them. (Examples 1–3)

1 Length of summer camps in days:
7, 7, 12, 10, 5, 10, 5, 7, 10, 9, 7, 9, 6, 10, 5, 8, 7, and 8

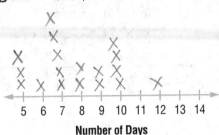

Number of Days

The peak is 7 days. The data is clustered from 5-10 days.

2.

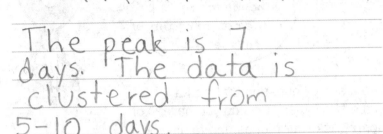

Students' Estimates of Room Length (m)				
10	11	12	12	13
13	13	14	14	14
15	15	15	15	15
16	16	16	17	17
17	17	18	18	25

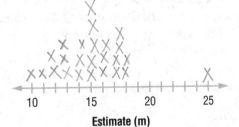

Estimate (m)

The data is clustered from 10-18 m. There is a gap from 18-25 m.

Number of Songs in Play Lists

3 The line plot shows the number of songs in play lists. Describe the data. Include measures of center and variability. (Example 4)

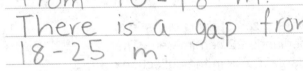

The data is clustered from 36-48 songs. There is an outlier at 26.

CCGPS **Inductive Reasoning** The number of runs a softball team scored in their last five games is shown in the line plot. How many runs would the team need to score in the next game so that each statement is true?

4. The range is 10. __2__

5. Another mode is 11. __1__

6. The median is 9.5. __1/2__

Runs Scored

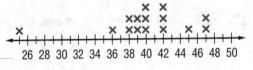

H.O.T. Problems Higher Order Thinking

7. **CCGPS** **Find the Error** Dwayne is analyzing the data in the line plot. Find his mistake and correct it.

High Temperature (°F)

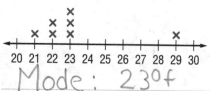

Mode: 23°f

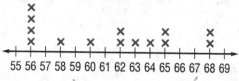

The median and the mode are 23°F. The outlier of the data set is 20°F.

8. **CCGPS** **Model with Mathematics** Write a survey question that has a numerical answer. Some examples are "How many CDs do you have?" or "How many feet long is your bedroom?" Ask your friends and family the question. Record the results and organize the data in a line plot. Use the line plot to make conclusions about your data. For example, describe the data using the measures of center and variability.

The data has a mean of 23.5.

Show your work.

9. **CCGPS** **Persevere with Problems** There are several sizes of flying disks in a collection. The range is 8 centimeters. The median is 22 centimeters. The smallest size is 16 centimeters. What is the largest disk in the collection?

Median

10. **CCGPS** **Construct an Argument** Determine whether the statement is *true* or *false*. Explain.

Line plots display individual data.

No. Line plots have lots of data.

Georgia Test Practice

11. The line plot shows the number of student visitors to the National Wildlife Refuge each day for two weeks. Which is the median of the data?

Ⓐ 56
Ⓒ 62
Ⓑ 61.4
Ⓓ 65

Number of Visitors

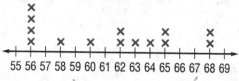

56, 56, 56, 56, 58, 60, 62, 62, 63, 64, 65, 65, 6

Extra Practice

Make a line plot for each set of data. Find the median, mode, range, and any outliers of the data shown in the line plot. Then describe the data using them.

12. Daily high temperatures in degrees Fahrenheit:
71, 72, 74, 72, 72, 68, 71, 67, 68, 71, 68, 72, 76, 75, 72, 73, 68, 69, 69, 73, 74, 76, 72, and 74

Daily High Temperatures

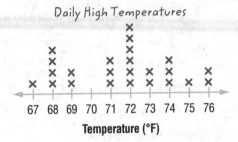

median: 72°F; mode: 72°F; range: 9°F; no outliers; The number of temperatures, in °F, represented is 24. The median means half the daily high temperatures are greater than 72°F and half are less. More days had a high of 72°F than any other temperature.

> Homework Help

13.

Number of Tornadoes				
0	1	1	1	6
0	0	0	0	0
2	1	2	0	0

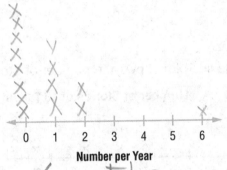

Number per Year

Outlier is at 6. The mode is 0.

Copy and Solve Describe the data in the line plots. Show your work on a separate piece of paper.

14. The line plot shows the number of hours students spend watching TV each night. Describe the data. Include measures of center and variability. Round to the nearest tenth if necessary.

Hours Spent Watching TV

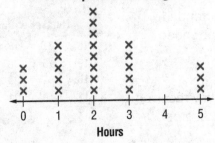

Hours

15. **CCGPS Justify Conclusions** The line plot shows students' favorite pizza toppings. Which can you find using the line plot: the median, mode, range, or outlier(s)? Explain. Then write a sentence or two to describe the data set. Explain your reasoning to a classmate.

Favorite Pizza Toppings

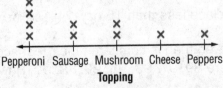

Topping

Georgia Test Practice

16. The table shows the speeds of the world's fastest roller coasters. Which roller coaster in the table represents the median speed?

Roller coaster	Speed (mi per h)
Dodonpa, Japan	107
Kingda Ka, USA	128
Superman the Escape, USA	100
Top Thrill Dragster, USA	120
Tower of Terror, Australia	100

Ⓐ Dodonpa

100, 100, 107,

Ⓑ Kingda

Ⓒ Top Thrill Dragster

Ⓓ Tower of Terror

17. The line plot shows the number of weekly chores that fifth graders have.

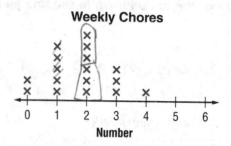

Weekly Chores

Which represents the interquartile range of the data?

Ⓕ 0   Ⓗ 2

Ⓖ 1.5   Ⓘ 4

18. Short Response The line plot shows the number of stories of the tallest buildings.

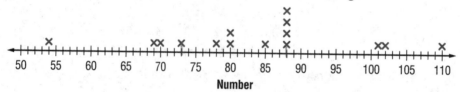

Number of Stories of 15 Tallest Buildings

What is the median, first quartile, third quartile, and interquartile range of the data?

Md: 88, Q1: 71.5, Q3: 94.5, IQR: 23

(CCGPS) **Common Core Review**

Fill in each ◯ with >, <, or = to make a true statement.   MCC4.NBT.2, MCC5.NBT.3b

19. 26 ⟩ 19

20. 89 ⟨ 92

21. 5.6 ⟨ 6.5

22. 11.5 ⟨ 105

23. 47 ⟩ 44

24. 1.52 ⟨ 14.8

25. The table shows the number of days several students attended an exercise class during a month. How many students attended a class less than 15 days? MCC4.NBT.2   5 students

Number of Days			
16	21	18	6
19	15	8	11
16	4	20	22
12	19	21	9

26. Seven friends compared their test scores. The scores they received were 89, 97, 93, 95, 90, 88, 91. How many people had scores greater than 90? MCC4.NBT.2   4

Histograms

What You'll Learn

Scan the lesson. List two headings you would use to make an outline of the lesson.

• _____

_____

• _____

_____

 Essential Question

WHY is it important to carefully evaluate graphs?

 Vocabulary

histogram
frequency distribution

 Common Core GPS

Content Standards
MCC6.SP.4, MCC6.SP.5, MCC6.SP.5a, MCC6.SP.5b

Mathematical Practices
1, 3, 4, 5, 6

Real-World Link

Concerts Alicia researched the average price of concert tickets. The table shows the results.

Average Ticket Prices of Top 10 Money Earning Concerts				
$83.87	$68.54	$51.53	$62.10	$59.58
$47.22	$66.58	$88.49	$50.63	$68.98

1. Fill in the tally column and frequency column on the frequency table.

Average Ticket Prices of Top 10 Money Earning Concerts		
Price	**Tally**	**Frequency**
$25.00–$49.99		
$50.00–$74.99		
$75.00–$99.99		

2. What does each tally mark represent? _____

3. What is one advantage of using the frequency table?

_____

_____

4. What is one advantage of using the first table?

_____

_____

Interpret Data

Data from a frequency table can be displayed as a histogram. A **histogram** is a type of bar graph used to display numerical data that have been organized into equal intervals. These intervals allow you to see the **frequency distribution** of the data, or how many pieces of data are in each interval.

There is no space between bars.

Because all of the intervals are equal, all of the bars have the same width.

Intervals with a frequency of 0 have a bar height of 0.

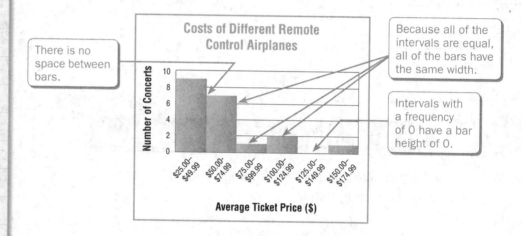

Costs of Different Remote Control Airplanes

Example

1. **Refer to the histogram above. Describe the histogram. How many remote control airplanes cost at least $100?**

There are 9 + 7 + 1 + 2 + 1 or 20 prices, in dollars, recorded. More remote control airplanes had prices between $25.00 and $49.99 than any other range. There were no airplanes recorded with a price between $125.00 and $149.99.

Two remote control airplanes had prices between $100.00–$124.99 and one remote control airplane had a price between $150.00–$174.99. So, 2 + 1, or 3 remote control airplanes had prices that were at least $100.

Show your work.

Got It? Do this problem to find out.

a. _____

a. Refer to the histogram above. How many remote control airplanes cost less than $75?

Construct a Histogram

You can use data from a table to construct a histogram.

Example

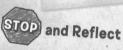

2. The table shows the number of daily visitors to selected state parks. Draw a histogram to represent the data.

Daily Visitors to Selected State Parks				
108	209	171	152	236
165	244	263	212	161
327	185	192	226	137
193	235	207	382	241

Step 1 Make a frequency table to organize the data. Use a scale from 100 through 399 with an interval of 50.

Daily Visitors to Selected State Parks		
Visitors	**Tally**	**Frequency**
100–149	||	2
150–199	ⅢⅠ ||	7
200–249	ⅢⅠ |||	8
250–299	|	1
300–349	|	1
350–399	|	1

Step 2 Draw and label a horizontal and vertical axis. Include a title. Show the intervals from the frequency table on the horizontal axis. Label the vertical axis to show the frequencies.

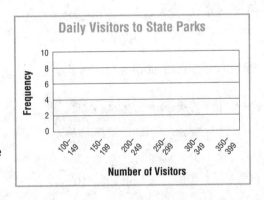

Step 3 For each interval, draw a bar whose height is given by the frequencies.

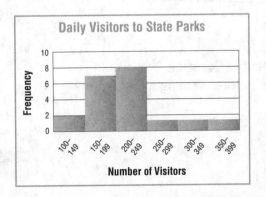

Scales and Intervals

It is important to choose a scale that includes all of the numbers in the data set. The interval should organize the data to make it easy to compare.

STOP and Reflect

When is a histogram more useful than a table with individual data? Explain below.

Got It? Do this problem to find out.

b. The list at the right shows a
set of test scores. Choose
intervals, make a frequency
table, and construct a histogram
to represent the data.

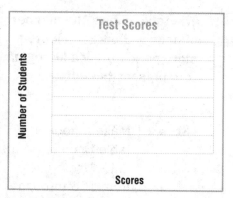

Test Scores						
72	97	80	86	92	98	88
76	79	82	91	83	90	76
81	94	96	92	72	83	85
65	91	92	68	86	89	97

Test Scores

Score	Tally	Frequency

Test Scores

Number of Students

Scores

Guided Practice

1. The frequency table shows the number of books read on vacation by the
   students in Mrs. Angello's class. (Examples 1 and 2)

   a. Draw a histogram to represent the data.

   b. Describe the histogram. _____

   _____

   c. How many students read six or more books? _____

Number of Books Read

Books	Tally	Frequency
0-2	ⅣⅡ	6
3-5	ⅣⅣ	10
6-8	ⅣⅡ	7
9-11	|||	3
12-14	||||	4

Rate Yourself!

Are you ready to move on?
Shade the section that applies.

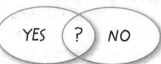

YES   ?   NO

2.  **Building on the Essential Question** Why would you
   create a frequency table before creating a histogram?

   _____

   _____

For more help, go online to
access a Personal Tutor.

FOLDABLES Time to update your Foldable!

Independent Practice

Go online for Step-by-Step Solutions eHelp

For Exercises 1–4, use the histogram at the right. (Example 1)

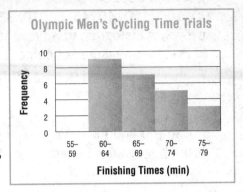

1. Describe the histogram. _This is_ _a stairstep histogram._

2. Which interval has 7 cyclists? _65-69_

3. Which interval represents the greatest number of cyclists?
   _60-64_

4. How many cyclists had a time less than 70 minutes?
   _16_

Draw a histogram to represent the set of data. (Example 2)

5.

Number of States Visited by Students in Marty's Class		
Number of States	Tally	Frequency
0-4	IIII IIII	9
5-9	III	3
10-14	IIII	5
15-19	III	3
20-24	IIII I	6
25-29	I	1

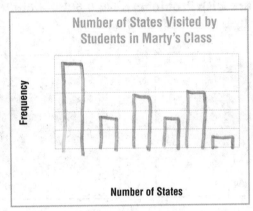

Use Math Tools For Exercises 6 and 7, refer to the histograms below.

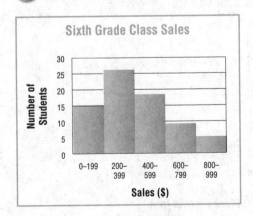

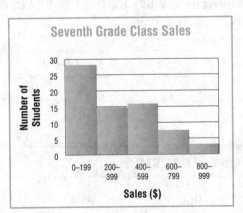

6. About how many students from both grades earned $600 or more?
   22 students

7. Which grade had more students earn between $400 and $599?
   Grade 6

8. **CCGPS Be Precise** The following data provides the number of Calories of various types of frozen bars. {25, 35, 200, 280, 80, 80, 90, 40, 45, 50, 50, 60, 90, 100, 120, 40, 45, 60, 70, 350}
   a. Draw a histogram to represent the data.
   b. Find the measures of center.

   Mean, Median

   c. Can you find the measures of center only from the histogram? Explain.

   _No._

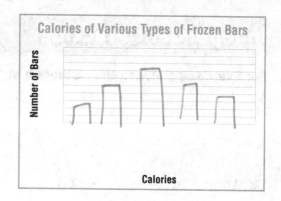

H.O.T. Problems Higher Order Thinking

9. **CCGPS Persevere with Problems** Give a set of data that could be represented by both histograms below.

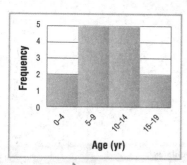 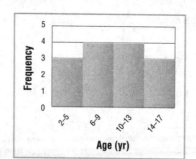

   Age

10. **CCGPS Justify Conclusions** Identify the interval that is not equal to the other three. Explain your reasoning.

| 15–19 | 30–34 | (40–45) | 45–49 |

   _45 – 40 = 5_

Georgia Test Practice

11. The table shows a set of plant heights. What would be an appropriate scale to use if you were making a histogram from the list?

   (A) 0 to 30   (C) 10 to 45
   (B) 20 to 50   (D) 0 to 45

Plant Heights (in.)		
12	7	15
8	24	41
16	18	27
43	33	11
24	10	22

Extra Practice

For Exercises 12–16, use the histogram.

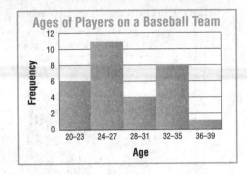

Ages of Players on a Baseball Team

12. Describe the histogram. _The ages of 30 players were collected. One player is older than 35, the rest are 35 or younger._

Homework Help ➡ Add each of the frequencies to find the total players.
6 + 11 + 4 + 8 + 1 = 30

13. Which interval represents the greatest number of players?
24-27 yrs

14. Which interval has 4 players? _28-31_

15. How many players are younger than 28? _17_

16. How many players have ages in the interval 32–35? _8_

CCGPS Model with Mathematics Draw a histogram to represent the set of data.

17.

Number of Homeruns in a Season		
Homeruns	**Tally**	**Frequency**
0-9	Ц||| Ц||| ||	12
10-19	Ц||| Ц|||	10
20-29	Ц||| ||||	9
30-39	Ц||| ||||	9
40-49	Ц|||		6

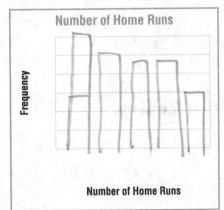

Number of Home Runs

18. **CCGPS Find the Error** Pilar is analyzing the frequency table below. Find her mistake and correct it.

Distances from Home to School (mi)	Tally	Frequency
0.1-0.5	Ц||| ||	7
0.6-1.0	|||	3
1.1-1.5	Ц|||	5
1.6-2.0	|||	3

15 people live less than 1.5 miles from school.

Actually, 10 since < 1.5 mi

19. How many more people travel 11–20 miles than 1–10 miles to get to work?

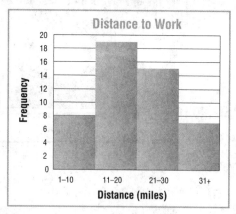

Ⓐ 11

Ⓒ 7

Ⓑ 12

Ⓓ 4

20. Short Response Explain why there is not a bar for the interval of 30–44 goals.

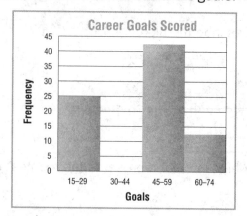

No one scored.

21. The table shows the number of sit-ups each member of a gym class completed in one minute. What would be an appropriate scale to use if you were making a histogram from the list?

Ⓕ 0 to 30

Ⓗ 0 to 40

Ⓖ 20 to 40

Ⓘ 10 to 30

Number of Sit-Ups in One Minute				
30	15	34	22	28
20	25	26	31	29
27	30	19	22	28
32	31	27	23	26

Common Core Review

Divide. MCC4.NBT.6

22. $126 \div 3 =$ _42_

23. $477 \div 9 =$ _53_

24. $162 \div 6 =$ _27_

25. $327 \div 5 =$ _65.4_

26. $195 \div 2 =$ _97.5_

27. $842 \div 4 =$ _210.5_

28. Jamie, Tucker, and Lucinda bought a bag of apples.
Jamie kept 0.25 of the apples, and Lucinda kept 0.5 of the apples.

Who kept more of the apples? MCC5.NBT.3b _Lucinda_

What You'll Learn

Scan the lesson. Predict two things you will learn about box plots.

* _____
  _____
  _____

* _____
  _____

Essential Question

WHY is it important to carefully evaluate graphs?

Vocab
Vocabulary

box plot

CCGPS **Common Core GPS**

Content Standards
MCC6.SP.2, MCC6.SP.4,
MCC6.SP.5, MCC6.SP.5b,
MCC6.SP.5c

Mathematical Practices
1, 2, 3, 4, 7

Real-World Link

Football The table shows the number of touchdowns scored by each of the 16 teams in the National Football Conference in a recent year.

47	41	35	38	28	54	49	24
49	44	27	34	37	44	26	36

1. Plot the scores on a line plot.

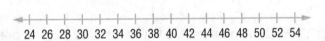

24 26 28 30 32 34 36 38 40 42 44 46 48 50 52 54

2. Find the median, lower extreme, upper extreme, first quartile and third quartile of the data. Place a star on the number line above for each value.

median: _____   first quartile: _____

lower extreme: _____   third quartile: _____

upper extreme: _____

3. What percent of the teams scored less than 31 touchdowns?

_____

4. What percent of the teams scored more than 37.5 touchdowns?

_____

Construct a Box Plot

Watch

A **box plot**, or box-and-whisker plot, uses a number line to show the distribution of a set of data by using the median, quartiles, and extreme values. A *box* is drawn around the quartile values, and the *whiskers* extend from each quartile to the extreme data points that are not outliers. The median is marked with a vertical line. The figure below is a box plot.

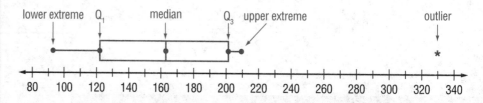

Box plots separate data into four parts. Even though the parts may differ in length, each contains 25% of the data. The box shows the middle 50% of the data.

Example

Watch | Tutor

1. **Draw a box plot of the car speed data.**

25   35   27   22   34   40   20   19   23   25   30

Step 1 | Order the numbers from least to greatest. Then draw a number line that covers the range of the data.

Step 2 | Find the median, the extremes, and the first and third quartiles. Mark these points above the number line.

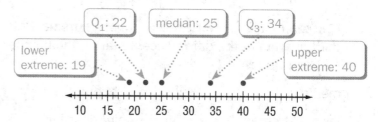

Step 3 | Draw the box so that it includes the quartile values. Draw a vertical line through the box at the median value. Extend the whiskers from each quartile to the extreme data points. Include a title.

Car Speeds

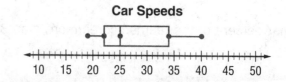

Got It? Do this problem to find out.

  a. Draw a box plot of the data set below.

   {$20, $25, $22, $30, $15, $18, $20, $17, $30, $27, $15}

a. _____

Interpret Data

Show your work.

Though a box plot does not show individual data, you can use it to interpret data.

Examples

Tutor

Refer to the box plot in Example 1.

2. **Half of the drivers were driving faster than what speed?**

Half of the 11 drivers were driving faster than 25 miles per hour.

3. **What does the box plot's length tell about the data?**

The length of the left half of the box plot is short. This means that the speeds of the slowest half of the cars are concentrated. The speeds of the fastest half of the cars are spread out.

Got It? Do this problem to find out.

  b. What percent were driving faster than 34 miles per hour?

b. _____ **25%**

Example

Tutor

4. **The box plot below shows the daily attendance at a fitness club. Find the median and the measures of variability. Then describe the data.**

Fitness Club Attendance

45 50 55 60 65 70 75 80 85 90 95 100 105 110

The median is 72.5. The first quartile is 65 and the third quartile is 80. The range is 54 and the interquartile range is 15. There is an outlier at 110. Both whiskers are approximately the same size so the data, without the outlier, is spread evenly below and above the quartiles.

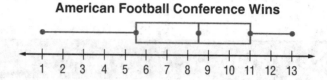

Got It? Do this problem to find out.

Show your work.

c. _____

c. The number of games won in the American Football Conference in a recent year is displayed below. Find the median and the measures of variability. Then describe the data.

American Football Conference Wins

Guided Practice

Check ✓

1. Use the table. (Examples 1–3)

   a. Make a box plot of the data.

Depth of Recent Earthquakes (km)						
5	15	1	11	2	7	3
9	5	4	9	10	5	7

   b. What percent of the earthquakes were between 4 and 9 kilometers deep? _____

   c. Write a sentence explaining what the length of the box plot means. _____

   _____

2. Find the median and the measures of variability for the box plot shown. Then describe the data. (Example 4)

   Average Gas Mileage for Various Sedans

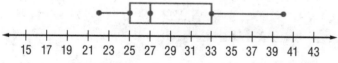

   _____

   _____

   _____

3. **Building on the Essential Question** How is the information you can learn from a box plot different from what you can learn from the same set of data shown in a line plot?

   _____

   _____

Rate Yourself!

How confident are you about making and interpreting box plots? Check the box that applies.

☐ ☐ ☐ ☐ ☐

For more help, go online to access a Personal Tutor.

Tutor

FOLDABLES Time to update your Foldable!

786 Chapter 11 Statistical Displays

Copyright © The McGraw-Hill Companies, Inc.

Name _____ My Homework _____

Go online for Step-by-Step Solutions

Draw a box plot for each set of data. (Example 1)

1 {65, 92, 74, 61, 55, 35, 88, 99, 97, 100, 96}

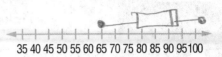

35 40 45 50 55 60 65 70 75 80 85 90 95 100

2.

Cost of MP3 Players ($)	
95	55
105	100
85	158
122	174
165	162

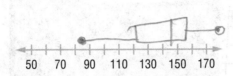

50 70 90 110 130 150 170

3 The table shows the length of coastline for the 13 states along the Atlantic Coast. (Examples 1–3)

Length of Coastline (mi)	
28	130
580	127
100	301
228	40
31	187
192	112
13	

a. Make a box plot of the data.

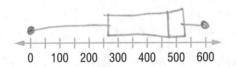

0   100   200   300   400   500   600

b. Half of the states have a coastline less than how many miles?

300 mi

c. Write a sentence describing what the length of the box plot tells about the number of miles of coastline for states along the Atlantic coast.

There are values from 13 to 580 miles.

4. The amount of Calories for a serving of certain fruits is displayed. Find the median and the measures of variability. Then describe the data. (Example 4)

Number of Calories

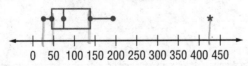

0   50 100 150 200 250 300 350 400 450

There is an outlier at 425. The extreme values r 25 and 200. The median is 75. The IQR is 85.

5. **CCGPS** **Model with Mathematics** Refer to the graphic novel frame below for Exercises a–b.

Watch ▷ Replay it online!

Ticket Sales

6th Grade

50 51 52 53 54 55 56 57 58 59 60 61 62 63 64 65

Grade 7	
Homeroom	Tickets Sold
701	60
702	50
703	54
704	52

How can I display the data for Grade 7?

a. Draw a box plot using the data for Grade 7.

b. Compare the box plots. Which grade sold the most tickets? Explain.

Grade 6, their highest value is 64.

H.O.T. Problems Higher Order Thinking

6. **CCGPS** **Persevere with Problems** Write a set of data that contains 12 values for which the box plot has no whiskers. State the median, first and third quartiles, and lower and upper extremes.

Md: 26

7. **CCGPS** **Reason Abstractly** Write a set of data that, when displayed in a box plot, will result in a long box and short whiskers. Draw the box plot.

Georgia Test Practice

8. The box plot shows distances traveled by vacationers. Half of the drivers traveled farther than what distance?

Ⓐ 68 miles   Ⓒ 86 miles

Ⓑ 75 miles   Ⓓ 99 miles

Miles Traveled

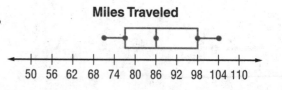

50 56 62 68 74 80 86 92 98 104 110

Name _____ My Homework _____

Extra Practice

Draw a box plot for each set of data.

9. {26, 22, 31, 36, 22, 27, 15, 36, 32, 29, 30}

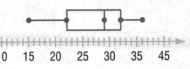

15, 22, ⟨22⟩, 26, 27, ⟨29⟩ 30, 31, ⟨32⟩ 36, 36

median: 29; Q₁: 22; Q₃: 32

Mark the median, Q₁, Q₃, and extremes above the number line. Draw a box around the quartiles and a line through the center of the median. Connect the extremes to the box with a line.

Homework Help →

10.

Height of Waves (in.)		
80	51	77
72	55	65
42	78	67
40	81	68
63	73	59

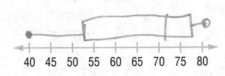

11. The box plot below summarizes math test scores.

Math Test Scores

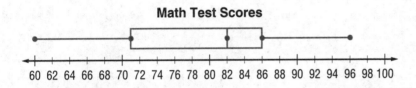

a. What was the greatest test score? _____96_____

b. Explain why the median is not in the middle of the box.

It is not symmetrical.

c. What percent of the scores were between 71 and 96? __75%__

d. Half of the scores were higher than what score? ___82___

12. **CCGPS Identify Structure** Find the median, first and third quartiles, and the interquartile range for the set of data in the table. Create a box plot of the data.

Words Typed Per Minute		
80	42	65
72	63	81
67	73	40
51	68	59
77	55	78

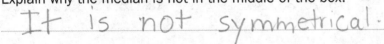

13. Which box plot represents the data set 14, 18, 21, 24, and 29?

Ⓐ
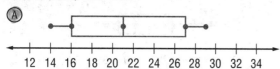

Ⓑ
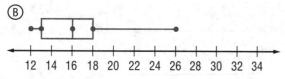

Ⓒ
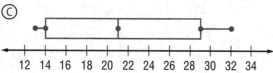

Ⓓ
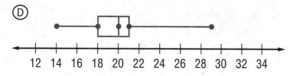

14. Which of the following statements is *not* true concerning the box plot below?

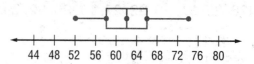

Ⓕ The value 74 is an extreme value.

Ⓖ Half of the data are above 62.

Ⓗ Half of the data are in the interval 62–74.

Ⓘ There are more data values in the interval 52–62 than there are in the interval 62–74.

15. Short Response Construct a box plot with the data set 35, 42, 44, 47, and 54.

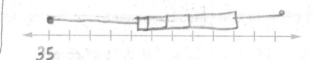

35

Find the total of each set of numbers. MCC4.NBT.4

16. {6, 8, 7, 9, 2, 4}

17. {15, 20, 35, 24, 31}

18. {16, 25, 35, 28, 31, 27}

19. {56, 58, 63, 51, 52}

20. {84, 106, 98, 88}

21. {34, 68, 23, 18, 57}

22. The table shows the number of raffle tickets each member of the drama club sold. How many members sold more than 50 raffle tickets?
MCC4.NBT.2

Raffle Tickets Sold				
26	32	18	53	28
35	42	29	38	50
49	51	21	34	46
42	52	50	36	20

Content Standards
MCC6.SP.4, MCC6.SP.5,
MCC6.SP.5c

Mathematical Practices
1, 3, 4

Case #1 Football

Finn's brother is on the football team and he is making a display of the number of points the team scored in each game last year. He uses the information in the table to make a line plot.

What score occurred most frequently?

Number of Points Scored			
35	35	43	21
49	35	21	24
34	35	21	

Understand *What are the facts?*

The range of the points is 49 – 21, or 28.

Plan *What is your strategy to solve this problem?*

Make a line plot to see which score occurs most frequently. Use the range to label the line plot from 20 to 50.

Solve *How can you apply the strategy?*

Plot each score on the line plot.

Number of Points Scored

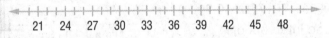

```
21   24   27   30   33   36   39   42   45   48
```

The score occurring most frequently is ☐.

Check *Does the answer make sense?*

The team scored 35 points four times. No other score occurred four or more times. So, the answer is reasonable.

Analyze the Strategy

Reason Inductively How would the results change if the team played a twelfth game and scored 21 points?

_____

_____

Case #2 Life Span

Different animals have different average life spans. The average life spans of several animals are shown in the table.

How many more animals have an average life span between 11 and 15 years than those that have an average life span between 1 and 5 years?

Average Life Span (years)	
Camel	12
Deer	10
Dog	12
Fox	9
Gorilla	20
Horse	20
Kangaroo	7
Lion	15
Lobster	15
Mouse	2
Pig	10
Polar Bear	20
Rabbit	5

Understand

Read the problem. What are you being asked to find?

I need to find _____

_____.

What information do you know?

Animals with 11–15 year life span: _____

Animals with 1–5 year life span: _____

Plan

Choose a problem-solving strategy.

I will use the _____ strategy.

Solve

Use your problem-solving strategy to solve the problem.

Make a histogram. Use intervals of

1–5 years, _____ years,

_____ years, and 16–20 years.

So, there are ☐ more animals with an average life span between 11–15 years than with an average life span between 1–5 years.

Check

Use information from the problem to check your answer.

There are four animals with an average life span between 11 and 15 years and two animals, mice and rabbits, with an average life span between 1 and 5 years.

Case #3 Lawn Mowing

DeShawn mowed lawns over the summer to earn extra money. The number of lawns he mowed each week is shown in the line plot.

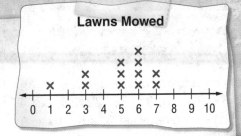

Lawns Mowed

What is the mean number of lawns he mowed?

Case #4 Magazines

The box plot shows the number of magazines sold for a club fundraiser.

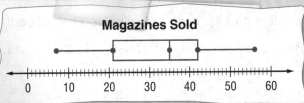

Magazines Sold

What is the difference between the median number of magazines sold and the most magazines sold? _____

Case #5 Quiz Scores

A teacher recorded quiz scores for a class in the table.

Make a line plot to determine the median quiz score.

_____

89	88	95	100
78	89	92	92
95	85	88	90
100	95	98	88
100	90	76	94

Case #6 Exercise

Circle a strategy below to solve the problem.
• Guess, check, and revise.
• Solve a simpler problem.
• Act it out.
• Look for a pattern.

To train for a marathon, Colleen plans to run four miles the first week and 150% the number of miles next week.

How many miles will Colleen run the next week?

Mid-Chapter Check

Vocabulary Check

1. **CCGPS** **Be Precise** Define *histogram*. Use the data set {26, 37, 35, 49, 54, 53, 30, 36, 31, 28, 29, 33, 38, 47, 54, 50, 37, 26, 35, 51} to make a histogram. (Lesson 2)

   Histogram is a bar graph which the bars r intervals.

Skills Check and Problem Solving

Make a line plot for each set of data. Then describe the data. (Lesson 1)

2. {36, 43, 39, 47, 34, 43, 47, 39, 34, 43}

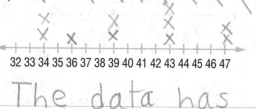

32 33 34 35 36 37 38 39 40 41 42 43 44 45 46 47

The data has lots of gaps.

3. {63, 54, 57, 63, 52, 59, 52, 63, 61, 54}

52 53 54 55 56 57 58 59 60 61 62 63

There are gaps between the data points.

4. The histogram shows a movie theater's attendance each time a move is shown. Describe the data in the histogram. (Lesson 2) The mode is 1-20 people.

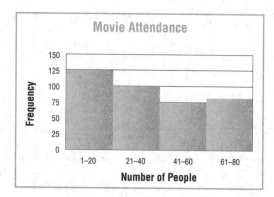

5. **Georgia Test Practice** What is the median in the box plot? (Lesson 3)

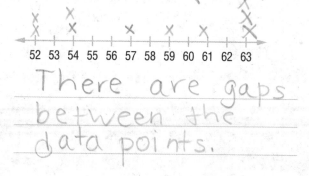

28 30 32 34 36 38 40 42 44 46 48 50 52 54

   (A) 28   (B) 33   (C) 39   (D) 47

Shape of Data Distributions

What You'll Learn

Scan the lesson. Predict two things you will learn about the shape of data distributions.

• _____

   _____

• _____

Essential Question

WHY is it important to carefully evaluate graphs?

Vocabulary

distribution
symmetric distribution
cluster
gap
peak

Common Core GPS

Content Standards
MCC6.SP.2, MCC6.SP.5, MCC6.SP.5d

Mathematical Practices
1, 3, 4, 5, 7

Vocabulary Start-Up

The **distribution** of a set of data shows the arrangement of data values. The words below show some of the ways the distribution of data can be described. Match the words below to their definitions.

cluster	The left side of the distribution looks like the right side.
gap	The numbers that have no data value.
peak	The most frequently occurring values, or mode.
symmetry	Data that grouped closely together.

 ### Real-World Link

Parasailing The line plot shows the costs in dollars for parasailing for different companies on a certain beach.

1. Draw a vertical line through the middle of the data. What do you notice?

   Both sides =

2. Use one of the words shown above to write a sentence about the data.

   Symmetry

Parasailing Costs ($)

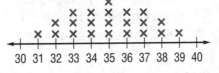

Describe the Shape of a Distribution

Data that are evenly distributed between the left side and the right side, have a **symmetric distribution**. The distribution shown has a **cluster** of several data values within the interval 10–12. The **gaps** 9 and 13 have no data values. The value 10 is a **peak** because it is the most frequently occurring value.

 ## Examples

Tutor

Describe the shape of each distribution.

1. The line plot shows the temperature in degrees Fahrenheit in a city over several days.

Temperature (°F)

You can use clusters, gaps, peaks, outliers and symmetry to describe the shape. The shape of the distribution is not symmetric because the left side of the data does not look like the right side of the data. There is a gap from 19–21. There are clusters from 16–18 and 22–25. The distribution has a peak at 22. There are no outliers.

2. The box plot shows the number of visitors to a gift shop in one month.

Number of Visitors to a Gift Shop

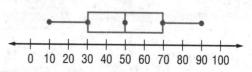

You cannot identify gaps, peaks, and clusters.
Each box and whisker has the same length. So, the data is evenly distributed. The distribution is symmetric since the left side of the data looks like the right side. There are no outliers.

Show your work.

Got It? Do this problem to find out.

a. _____

a. Use clusters, gaps, peaks, outliers, and symmetry to describe the shape of the distribution at the right.

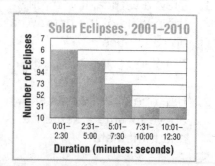

Solar Eclipses, 2001–2010

Key Concept

Use the following flow chart to decide which measures of center and spread are most appropriate to describe a data distribution.

Is the data distribution symmetric?

Yes   No

Use the **mean** to describe the center. Use the **mean absolute deviation** to describe the spread.

Use the **median** to describe the center. Use the **interquartile range** to describe the spread.

STOP and Reflect

Explain below which measures are most appropriate to describe the center and spread of a symmmetric distribution.

If there is an outlier, the distribution is not usually symmetric.

Example

3. The line plot shows the number of states visited by students in a class.

Number of States Visited

```
        X
   X  X
   X  X
X  X  X  X
X  X  X  X
X  X  X  X  X              X
+--+--+--+--+--+--+--+--+--+--+
10 11 12 13 14 15 16 17 18 19 20
```

a. Choose the appropriate measures to describe the center and spread of the distribution. Justify your response based on the shape of the distribution.

The data are not symmetric and there is an outlier, 19. The median and interquartile range are appropriate measures to use.

b. Write a few sentences describing the center and spread of the distribution using the appropriate measures.

The median is 12 states. The first quartile is 11. The third quartile is 13. The interquartile range is 13–11, or 2 states.

The data are centered around 12 states. The spread of the data around the center is about 2 states.

Got It? Do this problem to find out.

b. Describe the center and spread of the distribution. Justify your response based on the shape of the distribution. Then describe the center and spread.

Ages of Tennis Players (yr)

```
            X  X  X
      X  X  X  X  X
   X  X  X  X  X  X  X
X  X  X  X  X  X  X  X  X
+--+--+--+--+--+--+--+--+--+--+
24 25 26 27 28 29 30 31 32 33 34
```

b. _____

Show your work.

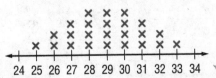
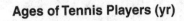

1. The histogram shows the wait times in minutes for entering a concert. Describe the shape of the distribution. (Example 1)

_____

_____

_____

_____

_____

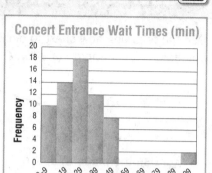

Concert Entrance Wait Times (min)

2. The box plot shows the weights in pounds of several dogs. Describe the shape of the distribution. (Example 2)

_____

_____

_____

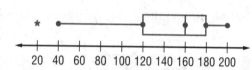

Weights of Dogs (lb)

3. The line plot shows the number of hours several students spent on the Internet during the week. (Example 3)

a. Choose the appropriate measures to describe the center and spread of the distribution. Justify your response based on the shape of the distribution. _____

_____

_____

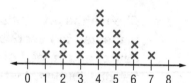

Number of Hours Spent on the Internet

b. Write a few sentences describing the center and spread of the distribution using the appropriate measures. Round to the nearest tenth if necessary.

_____

_____

_____

4. **Building on the Essential Question** Why does the choice of measure of center and spread vary based on the type of data display? _____

_____

_____

_____

Rate Yourself!

How well do you understand how to describe the shape of a distribution? Circle the image that applies.

Clear   Somewhat   Not So
              Clear   Clear

For more help, go online to access a Personal Tutor.

Tutor

Independent Practice

Go online for Step-by-Step Solutions

1 The histogram shows the average animal speeds in miles per hour of several animals. Describe the shape of the distribution. (Example 1)

The data is clustered from 1-79 mph. There is an outlier at 200-219.

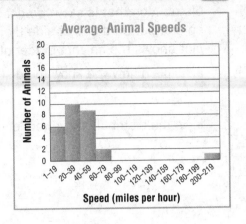

2. The box plot shows the science test scores for Mrs. Everly's students. Describe the shape of the distribution. (Example 2) The data

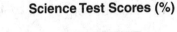

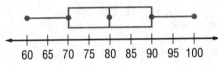

3 The line plot shows the number of text messages sent by different students in one day. (Example 3)

a. Choose the appropriate measures to describe the center and spread of the distribution. Justify your response based on the shape of the distribution.

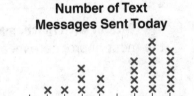

b. Write a few sentences describing the center and spread of the distribution using the appropriate measures.

4. **CCGPS** **Identify Structure** Fill in the graphic organizer to show when to use each measure regarding the shape of the distribution.

Measure	Symmetric or Not Symmetric
mean	
median	
interquartile range	
mean absolute deviation	

5. A distribution that is not symmetric is called *skewed*. A distribution that is *skewed left* shows data that is more spread out on the left side than on the right side. A distribution that is *skewed right* shows data that is more spread out on the right side than on the left side. The box plot shows the heights in feet of several trees.

Height of Trees (ft)

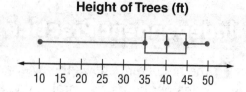

a. Explain how you know the distribution is not symmetric.

_____

b. Is the distribution skewed left or skewed right? Explain.

_____

_____

_____

c. Use appropriate measures to describe the center and spread of the distribution. Justify your choice of measure based on the shape of the distribution. _____

_____

_____

_____

 H.O.T. Problems Higher Order Thinking

6. CCGPS **Model with Mathematics** Draw a line plot for which the median is the most appropriate measure to describe the center of the distribution.

_____

7. CCGPS **Persevere with Problems** Explain why you cannot describe the specific location of the center and spread of the box plot shown using the most appropriate measures.

Calories in Servings of Fruits

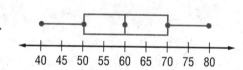

_____

_____

_____

Georgia Test Practice

8. The line plot shows the weekly attendance for a dance class. Which of the following statements is true?

Ⓐ The distribution is symmetric.

Ⓑ The distribution has an outlier.

Ⓒ The distribution has a peak.

Ⓓ There are no clusters.

Dance Class Attendance

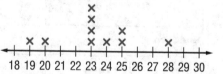

Extra Practice

9. The line plot shows the prices in dollars for several DVDs. Describe the shape of the distribution. _Sample answer:_ _The shape of the distribution is symmetric. The left side of the_ _data looks like the right side. There is a cluster from $13–$15._ _There are no gaps in the data. The peak of the distribution is_ _$14. There are no outliers._

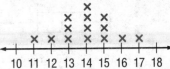

DVD Prices ($)

Homework Help ➤

10. The box plot shows donations in dollars to charity. Describe the shape of the distribution.

_____

_____

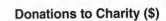

Donations to Charity ($)

11. The line plot shows the number of miles Elisa ran each week.

a. Choose the appropriate measures to describe the center and spread of the distribution. Justify your response based on the shape of the distribution. _____

_____

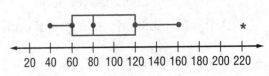

Miles Ran Each Week

b. Write a few sentences describing the center and spread of the distribution using the appropriate measures. Round to the nearest tenth if necessary. _____

12. **CCGPS** **Use Math Tools** The line plot shows the number of siblings for 18 students.

a. Explain how you know the distribution is not symmetric.

_____

_____

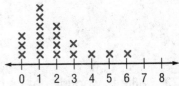

Number of Siblings

b. Is the distribution skewed left or skewed right? Explain.

_____

_____

c. Use appropriate measures to describe the center and spread of the distribution. Justify your choice of measure based on the shape of the distribution. _____

_____

13. Refer to the box plot below.

Roller Coaster Speeds (mph)

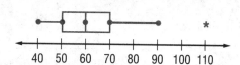

40 50 60 70 80 90 100 110   *

Which of the following statements is false?

Ⓐ The distribution is symmetric.

Ⓑ The distribution is not symmetric.

Ⓒ The distribution has an outlier.

Ⓓ The distribution has a gap of data.

14. Refer to the line plot below.

**Gas Mileage
(miles per gallon)**

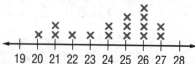

19 20 21 22 23 24 25 26 27 28

Which measure is the most appropriate to describe the variation (spread) of the distribution?

Ⓕ interquartile range

Ⓖ mean

Ⓗ mean absolute deviation

Ⓘ median

(CCGPS) Common Core Review

Graph the points on the coordinate plane. MCC5.G.2

15. F(2, 4)

16. K(4, 9)

17. G(1, 8)

18. L(5, 2)

19. H(2, 1)

20. M(9, 7)

21. I(8, 6)

22. N(5, 6)

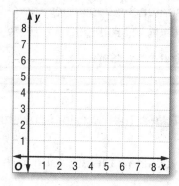

23. Callie is working on a small scrapbook. She completes 3 scrapbook pages each hour. How many pages will she complete in 12 hours?
MCC4.NBT.5

24. The table shows how many inches are in several feet. How many inches are in 4 feet? MCC6.RP.3a

Feet	Inches
1	12
2	24
3	36

CCGPS Content
Standards
MCC6.SP.4,
MCC6.SP.5,
MCC6.SP.5a,
MCC6.SP.5b,
MCC6.SP.5c,
MCC6.SP.5d

**Mathematical
Practices**
1, 3, 4

Inquiry HOW do you answer a statistical question?

Photos Aribelle surveyed students in the cafeteria lunch line. She asked the statistical question, *How many photos are currently stored in your cell phone?* She wants to organize the data and choose an appropriate way to display the results of her survey.

Investigation

You can collect, organize, display, and interpret data in order to answer a statistical question.

Step 1 Make a data collection plan. Aribelle chose to survey students in the cafeteria.

Step 2 Collect the data. The results of the survey are provided below.

55, 47, 58, 50, 66, 47, 54, 64, 47, 65,
43, 44, 51, 81, 54, 45, 57, 52, 58, 60

Step 3 Organize the data. Place the values in order from least to greatest.

_____

_____

Step 4 Describe the data. There were a total of ⬚ responses. The responses measure in the number of _____. The data was collected using a _____. One attribute of the data is the median, which is ⬚ photos. Another attribute is the interquartile range, which is ⬚ photos. There is an outlier at ⬚ photos.

Step 5 Create a display of the data. Explain why a box plot would be an appropriate display of Aribelle's data. _____

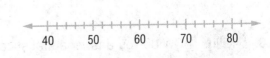

_____

_____

Work with a partner. Collect data in order to answer a statistical question.

1. Write a statistical question.

_____

2. Collect the data and record the results in a table.

3. Create a display of the data.

 Reflect

4. **CCGPS** **Model with Mathematics** Write a few sentences describing the results of your survey. Include the number of responses you recorded, how the responses were measured and/or gathered, and the overall pattern of the responses.

_____

_____

5. **CCGPS** **Reason Inductively** Write a few sentences describing the center and spread of the distribution.

_____

_____

6. **Inquiry** HOW do you answer a statistical question?

_____

_____

Interpret Line Graphs

What You'll Learn

Scan the lesson. Predict two things you will learn about line graphs.

- _____

- _____

 Essential Question

WHY is it important to carefully evaluate graphs?

Vocabulary

line graph

Common Core GPS

Content Standards
Extension of MCC6.SP.4

Mathematical Practices
1, 3, 4

 **Real-World Link**   Watch ▶

Golf The table shows the prize money for winners of the Masters Tournament.

Money Won by Masters Tournament Winners	
Year	Amount ($)
2005	1,170,000
2006	1,225,000
2007	1,305,000
2008	1,305,000
2009	1,350,000
2010	1,350,000

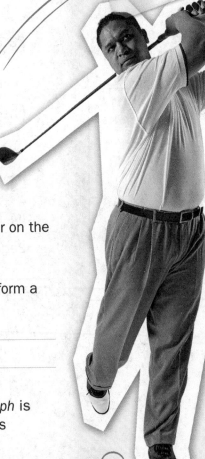

1. Fill in the dollar difference between each consecutive year on the lines above.

2. If the data were plotted, would the points (year, amount) form a straight line? Explain.

   _____

   _____

3. The Masters Tournament is held once a year. If a *line graph* is made of these data, will there be any realistic data values between tournament dates? Explain.

   _____

   _____

Make a Line Graph

A **line graph** is used to show how a set of data changes over a period of time. To make a line graph, decide on a scale and interval. Then graph pairs of data and draw a line to connect each point.

Example

1. Make a line graph of the data of Earth's Population. Describe the change in Earth's population from 1750 to 2000.

Earth's Population						
Year	1750	1800	1850	1900	1950	2000
Population (millions)	790	980	1,260	1,650	2,555	6,080

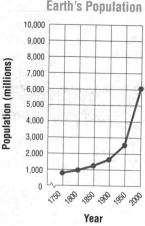

Earth's Population

> **Broken Line Graphs**
> Points are connected by a dotted line instead of a solid line when there are no realistic data values between the points.

Step 1 The data include numbers from 790 million to 6,080 million. So, a scale from 0 to 10,000 million and an interval of 1,000 million are reasonable.

Step 2 Let the horizontal axis represent the year. Let the vertical axis represent the population. Label the horizontal and vertical axes.

Step 3 Plot and connect the points for each year.

Step 4 Label the graph with a title.

Earth's population has increased drastically from 1750 to 2000.

Got It? Do this problem to find out.

a. Make a line graph of the data. Describe the change in the number of building permits filed from 2005 to 2010.

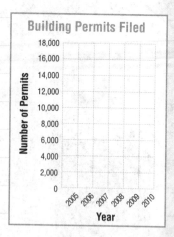

Building Permits Filed

Number of Building Permits Filed in a Major City						
Year	2005	2006	2007	2008	2009	2010
Building Permits Filed	16,000	15,500	13,900	11,000	8,200	5,900

a.

Interpret Line Graphs

By observing the upward or downward slant of the lines connecting the points, you can describe trends in the data and predict future events.

 Example

2. The line graph below shows the cost of tuition at a college during several years. Describe the trend. Then predict how much tuition will cost in 2020.

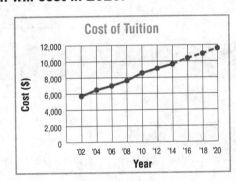

Notice that the increase from 2002 through 2012 is fairly steady. By extending the graph, you can predict that tuition in 2020 will cost a student about $11,500.

Got It? Do this problem to find out.

b. The line graph shows the growth of a plant over several weeks. Describe the trend. Then predict how tall the plant will be at 7 weeks.

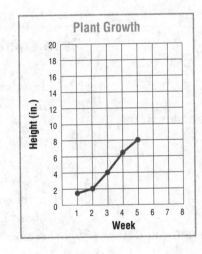

 Show your work.

b. _____

Example

3. **What does the graph tell you about the popularity of skateboarding?**

The graph shows that skateboard sales have been increasing each year. You can assume that the popularity of the sport is increasing.

Tutor

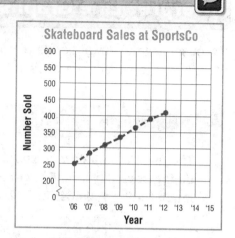

Guided Practice

Check ✓

1. Make a line graph of the data. (Example 1)

World's Tropical Rainforests								
Year	1940	1950	1960	1970	1980	1990	2000	2010
Remaining Tropical Rainforests (millions of acres)	2,875	2,740	2,600	2,375	2,200	1,800	1,450	825

2. Describe the change in the world's remaining rainforests from 1940 to 2010. (Example 1) _____

3. Describe the trend in the remaining tropical rainforests.

(Example 2) _____

4. Predict how many millions of acres there will be left in 2020. (Example 2) _____

5. What does the graph tell you about future changes in the remaining rainforests? (Example 3) _____

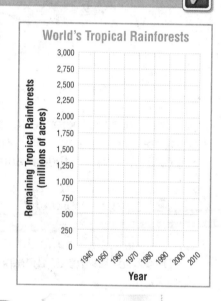

6. (e) **Building on the Essential Question** How can you use line graphs to predict data?

_____

Rate Yourself!

☐ I understand how to interpret line graphs.

▶▶ Great! You're ready to move on!

☐ I still have some questions about interpreting line graphs.

📖 No Problem! Go online to access a Personal Tutor.

Tutor

FOLDABLES Time to update your Foldable!

Independent Practice

Go online for Step-by-Step Solutions
eHelp

1 Make a line graph of the data. Then describe the change in the total amount Felisa saved from Week 1 to Week 5. (Example 1)

_____

_____

_____

_____

Felisa's Savings	
Week	**Total Amount ($)**
1	50
2	54
3	75
4	98
5	100

Felisa's Savings

2. Use the graph at the right. (Examples 2–3)

a. Describe the change in the winning times from 2006 to 2010.

_____

_____

b. Predict the winning time in 2015. _____

c. Predict when the winning time will be less than 500 minutes.

_____

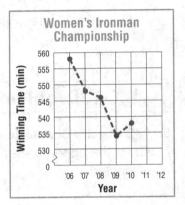

Women's Ironman Championship

Copy and Solve For Exercise 3, show your work on a separate piece of paper.

3. **CCGPS** **Model with Mathematics** Refer to the graphic novel frame below for Exercises a–b.

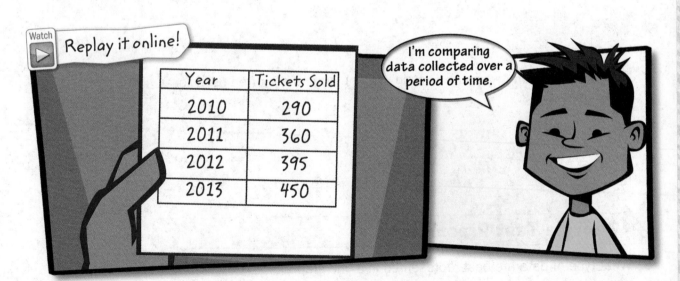

a. Use the information in the table and draw a line graph to show the changes in ticket sales over the past four years.

b. Predict what the ticket sales will be in 2015.

4. Use the graph that shows the distance traveled by two cars on the same freeway headed in the same direction.

Distance Traveled by Two Cars

a. Predict the distance traveled by Car A after 5 hours.

_____

b. Predict the distance traveled by Car B after 5 hours.

_____

c. How many miles do you think Car A will have traveled after 8 hours?

_____

d. Based on the graph, after how many hours will Car B have traveled about 360 miles? _____

e. Based on the graph, which car will reach a distance of 500 miles first? Explain your reasoning. _____

_____

_____

🔥 H.O.T. Problems Higher Order Thinking

5. **CCGPS** **Justify Conclusions** Can changes to the vertical scale or interval affect the appearance of a line graph? Justify your reasoning with examples.

_____

_____

_____

6. **CCGPS** **Persevere with Problems** Refer to the graph for Exercise 4. What can you conclude about the point at which the red and blue lines cross?

_____

_____

_____

7. **CCGPS** **Construct an Argument** Explain why line graphs are often used to make predictions.

_____

_____

_____

✏️ Georgia Test Practice

8. What type of data are best represented in a line graph?

Ⓐ data that show frequency

Ⓑ data that change over time

Ⓒ data that are grouped by category

Ⓓ data that compare totals

Extra Practice

9. **CCGPS** **Model with Mathematics** Make a line graph of the data. Describe the change in the online sales of movie tickets for Weeks 1 to 5.

Online Sales of Movie Tickets	
Week	Number of Tickets
1	1,200
2	1,450
3	1,150
4	1,575
5	1,750

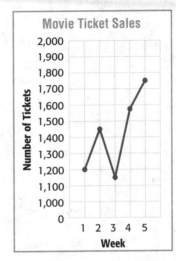

Movie Ticket Sales

Homework Help

The online sales of movie tickets increased from Week 1 to Week 2, decreased in Week 3 and then increased again for Weeks 4 and 5.

10. Use the graph at the right.

   a. Describe the change in depth from 10 minutes to 35 minutes.

   _____

   _____

   b. Predict the depth at 45 minutes. _____

   c. Predict when the depth will be more than 65 feet.

   _____

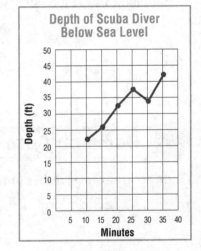

Depth of Scuba Diver Below Sea Level

11. Use the line graph at the right.

   a. Between which years did the winning time change the

   most? Explain. _____

   _____

   b. Make a prediction of the winning time in the 2020 Olympics.

   Explain your reasoning. _____

   _____

   _____

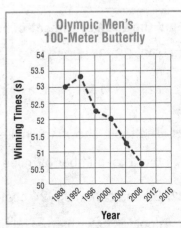

Olympic Men's 100-Meter Butterfly

Georgia Test Practice

12. Every Sunday, Kailey saves a portion of her weekly earnings. The table shows the total amount of money she has saved each week. What is the best prediction for the total amount she will have saved after Week 8?

Week	Total Amount Saved $)
1	15
2	34
3	42
4	60
5	78

- Ⓐ $100
- Ⓑ $130
- Ⓒ $150
- Ⓓ $170

13. For which year would the winning time in the Olympic Women's 3,000-Meter Speed Skating Relay have been the most difficult to predict based on previous results?

- Ⓕ 1994
- Ⓖ 1998
- Ⓗ 2002
- Ⓘ 2006

14. Short Response The graph shows the time Mia spent studying during one week. Describe the change in the number of hours Mia studied from Wednesday to Thursday.

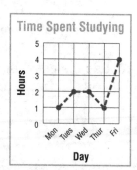

_____

_____

(CCGPS) # Common Core Review

Find the greatest number in the set. MCC4.NBT.2

15. {23, 34, 41, 25, 36}

_____

16. {65, 58, 64, 56, 62}

_____

17. {18, 16, 22, 19, 24}

_____

Find the total of the set of numbers. MCC4.NBT.4

18. {95, 88, 97, 89, 91}

_____

19. {56, 71, 68, 62, 74}

_____

20. {33, 36, 38, 29, 27}

_____

21. The table shows the miles the Smythe family traveled each day. What is the total number of miles they traveled? MCC4.NBT.4 _____

Day	Miles
Saturday	125
Sunday	84
Monday	112

22. Selena can make 24 cookies in 30 minutes. At this rate, how many cookies can she make in 90 minutes? MCC6.RP.3b _____

Select an Appropriate Display

What You'll Learn

Scan the lesson. Predict two things you will learn about selecting an appropriate display.

- _____
- _____

Essential Question

WHY is it important to carefully evaluate graphs?

 Common Core GPS

Content Standards
Extension of MCC6.SP.4

Mathematical Practices
1, 3, 4, 5, 6

 ## Real-World Link

Animals The displays show the maximum speed of six animals.

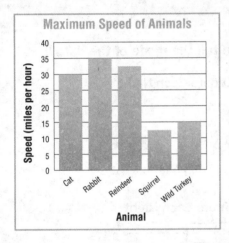

Animal Speeds	
Speeds	**Number of Animals**
1–5	
6–10	
11–15	
16–20	
21–25	
26–30	
31–35	

1. Use the bar graph to fill in the "Number of Animals" column in the table.

2. Which display allows you to find a rabbit's maximum speed?

   _____

3. In which display is it easier to find the number of animals with a maximum speed of 15 miles per hour or less? Explain.

   _____

   _____

| Key Concept | **Statistical Displays** |

Type of Display	Best used to
Bar Graph	show the number of items in specific categories
Box Plot	show measures of variation for a set of data, also useful for very large sets of data
Histogram	show frequency of data divided into equal intervals
Line Graph	show change over a period of time
Line Plot	show how many times each number occurs

Work Zone

Data can often be displayed in several different ways. The display you choose depends on your data and what you want to show.

Example

Tutor

1. **Which display allows you to tell the mode of the data?**

Lasagna Orders Each Night

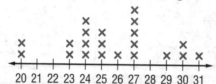

20 21 22 23 24 25 26 27 28 29 30 31

Lasagna Orders Each Night

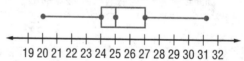

19 20 21 22 23 24 25 26 27 28 29 30 31 32

The line plot shows each night's data. The number of orders that occurs most frequently is 27. The box plot shows the spread of the data, but does not show individual data so it does not show the mode.

Show your work.

Got It? Do this problem to find out.

a. Which of the above displays allows you to easily find the median of the data?

a. _____

| Key Concept | **Statistical Displays** |

Type of Display	Best used to
Bar Graph	show the number of items in specific categories
Box Plot	show measures of variation for a set of data, also useful for very large sets of data
Histogram	show frequency of data divided into equal intervals
Line Graph	show change over a period of time
Line Plot	show how many times each number occurs

Work Zone

Data can often be displayed in several different ways. The display you choose depends on your data and what you want to show.

Example

1. **Which display allows you to tell the mode of the data?**

Lasagna Orders Each Night

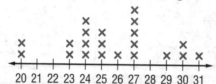

20 21 22 23 24 25 26 27 28 29 30 31

Lasagna Orders Each Night

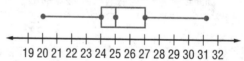

19 20 21 22 23 24 25 26 27 28 29 30 31 32

The line plot shows each night's data. The number of orders that occurs most frequently is 27. The box plot shows the spread of the data, but does not show individual data so it does not show the mode.

Show your work.

Got It? Do this problem to find out.

a. Which of the above displays allows you to easily find the median of the data?

a. _____

Examples

2. A survey compared different brands of hair shampoo. The table shows the number of first choice responses for each brand. Select an appropriate type of display to compare the number of responses. Justify your choice.

Favorite Shampoo Survey			
Brand	Responses	Brand	Responses
A	35	D	24
B	12	E	8
C	42	F	11

These data show the number of responses for each brand. A bar graph would be the best display to compare the responses.

3. Make the appropriate display of the data.

> **Step 1** Draw and label horizontal and vertical axes. Add a title.

> **Step 2** Draw a bar to represent the number of responses for each brand.

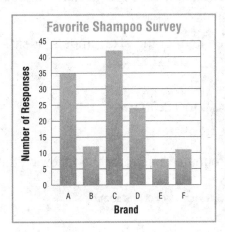

Got It? Do these problems to find out.

The table shows the quiz scores of Mr. Vincent's math class.

Math Quiz Scores											
70	70	75	80	100	85	85	65	75	85	95	90
90	100	85	90	90	95	80	85	90	85	90	75

b. Select an appropriate type of display to allow you to count the number of students with a score of 85. Explain your choice.

c. Make the appropriate display of the data.

b. _____

Check ✓

1. Which display makes it easier to determine the greatest number of calendars sold? Justify your reasoning. (Example 1)

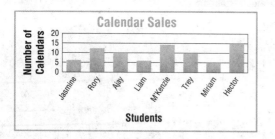

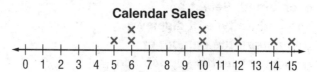

Select an appropriate type of display for data gathered about each situation. Justify your reasoning. (Example 2)

2. the favorite cafeteria lunch item of the sixth-grade students _____

3. the temperature from 6 A.M. to 12:00 P.M. _____

4. Select and make an appropriate display for the following data. (Example 3)

Number of Push-Ups Done by Each Student											
15	20	8	11	6	25	32	12	14	16	21	25
18	35	40	20	25	15	10	5	18	20	31	28

Show your work.

5. **Building on the Essential Question** Why is it important to choose the appropriate display for a set of data?

_____

_____

_____

Rate Yourself!

How confident are you about selecting an appropriate display? Shade the ring on the target.

I'm on target.

I need help.

For more help, go online to access a Personal Tutor.

Tutor

Independent Practice

Go online for Step-by-Step Solutions

1 Which display makes it easier to compare the maximum speeds of Top Thrill Dragster and Millennium Force? Justify your reasoning. (Example 1)

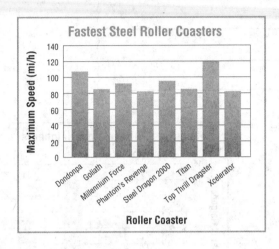

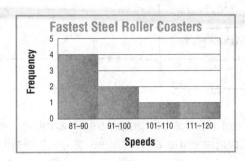

Select an appropriate type of display for data gathered about each situation. Justify your reasoning. (Example 2)

2. the test scores each student had on a language arts test

_____

3. the median age of people who voted in an election

_____

CCGPS **Use Math Tools** **Select and make an appropriate type of display for the situation.** (Example 3)

4.

South American Country	Water Area (km^2)	South American Country	Water Area (km^2)
Argentina	47,710	Guyana	18,120
Bolivia	15,280	Paraguay	9,450
Chile	12,290	Peru	5,220
Ecuador	6,720	Venezuela	30,000

5. **CCGPS** **Use Math Tools** Use the Internet or another source to find a set of data that is displayed in a bar graph, line graph, frequency table, or circle graph. Was the most appropriate type of display used? What other ways might these same data be displayed? _____

6. (CCGPS) **Be Precise** Fill in the graphic organizer below.

Display	What it shows
line plot	
histogram	
box-and-whisker plot	
bar graph	

7 Display the data in the bar graph using another type of display. Compare the advantages of each display.

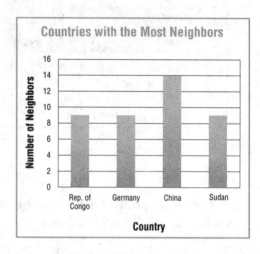

_____

_____

_____

_____

 H.O.T. Problems Higher Order Thinking

8. (CCGPS) **Construct an Argument** Determine whether the following statement is *true* or *false*. If true, explain your reasoning. If false, give a counterexample.

> *Any set of data can be displayed using a line graph.*

_____

9. (CCGPS) **Persevere with Problems** Which type of display allows you to easily

find the mode of the data? Explain your reasoning. _____

_____

Georgia Test Practice

10. Which of the following situations would involve data that are best displayed in a box plot?

Ⓐ the number of each type of drink a cafeteria sells

Ⓑ the response the most people gave to a survey on number of pets

Ⓒ the number of points Liam scored in each basketball game this season

Ⓓ the median age of a TV show's viewers

Extra Practice

11. Which display makes it easier to see the median distance? Justify your reasoning.

**Winning Distance of Men's Olympic
Javelin Throw Winners 1968–2008**

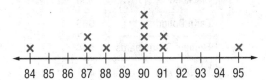

84 85 86 87 88 89 90 91 92 93 94 95

**Winning Distances of
Olympic Javelin Throw**

83 84 85 86 87 88 89 90 91 92 93 94 95

Homework Help

box plot; The median is easily seen on the box plot as the line in the box.

Select an appropriate type of display for data gathered about each situation. Justify your reasoning.

12. the amount of sales a company has over 6 months

_____

13. the prices of five different brands of tennis shoes at an athletic store

_____

14. the amount in a savings acount over a year

_____

15. the shape of the distribution of a team's football scores for one season

_____

CCGPS **Model with Mathematics** Select and make an appropriate type of display for the situation.

Show your work.

16.

Number of Counties in Various Southern States	
67	67
95	82
33	64
63	29
46	100
75	77
95	105

17. Which of the following situations would involve data that are best displayed in a line graph?

    Ⓐ the favorite subject of the students in Mrs. Ling's homeroom

    Ⓑ the weight a puppy gains in one year

    Ⓒ the number of hits Dylan got in each game this baseball season

    Ⓓ the number of miles each student travels to school

18. The table shows the prices of the skateboards Jacy might buy.

Skateboards	
Brand	**Price**
Blackbird	$55
Earth Bound	$68
Element Skateboards	$44
Venus Boards	$61
ZoomFast	$75

Which type of display would help Jacy best compare the prices of these skateboards?

    Ⓕ bar graph   Ⓗ line plot

    Ⓖ line graph   Ⓘ frequency table

19. **Short Response** The table shows the heights of 15 different Collie dogs. Which display would be most appropriate to show this data? Explain.

Height of Collies (in.)				
24	26	22	22	23
24	25	24	23	23
18	26	25	22	24

Common Core Review

Divide. MCC5.NBT.6

20. 36 ÷ 12 = _____

21. 108 ÷ 12 = _____

22. 138 ÷ 23 = _____

23. 204 ÷ 17 = _____

24. 192 ÷ 12 = _____

25. 390 ÷ 15 = _____

26. 324 ÷ 36 = _____

27. 540 ÷ 36 = _____

28. 792 ÷ 12 = _____

29. Measure the pencil below to the nearest centimeter. Then represent your measurement in meters. MCC5.MD.1 _____

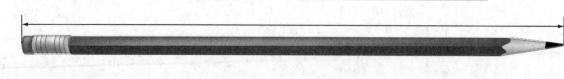

Inquiry HOW do you determine a measureable attribute?

 Content Standards
MCC6.SP.5,
MCC6.SP.5a,
MCC6.SP.5b,
MCC6.SP.5c

Mathematical Practices
1, 3, 4

School Each item in a backpack has different attributes such as color, size, and weight. Some of the attributes of the objects can be measured.

Investigation

You can choose the appropriate unit and tool to measure an object.

Step 1 Select an object in your classroom such as a desk, book, backpack, or trash can.

Step 2 List all of the measureable attributes of your object in the Step 3 table. Choose from among length, weight or mass, or capacity.

Step 3 Select an appropriate tool and measure each attribute. Record each measure using appropriate units in the table below.

Object	Attribute	Tool	Measurement

Step 4 Choose a different object with at least one attribute that requires the use of a different tool to measure. Then repeat steps 1–3.

Object	Attribute	Tool	Measurement

Step 5 Write and solve a real-world problem in which one of your measurements is needed to solve the problem.

_____

_____

Work with a partner. Choose an attribute common to several similar objects and use the appropriate unit and tool to measure.

1. Choose a set of objects and a measurable attribute.

   _____

2. Measure the attribute and record the results in a table.

3. Create a display of the data.

Reflect

4. **CCGPS** **Model with Mathematics** Write a few sentences describing your data. Include the number of observations, how the data was measured, and the overall pattern of the data. _____

   _____

   _____

5. **CCGPS** **Make a Conjecture** Explain how the way you measured the objects influenced the shape of the display. _____

   _____

   _____

6. **Inquiry** HOW do you determine a measureable attribute?

   _____

   _____

21ST CENTURY CAREER
in Envionmental Science

Environmental Engineer

Are you concerned about protecting the environment? If so, you should think about a career in environmental science. Environmental engineers apply engineering principles along with biology and chemistry to develop solutions for improving the air, water, and land. They are involved in pollution control, recycling, and waste disposal. Environmental engineers also determine methods for conserving resources and for reducing environmental damage caused by construction and industry.

College & Career READINESS

Explore college and careers at ccr.mcgraw-hill.com

Is This the Career for You?

Are you interested in a career as an environmental engineer? Take some of the following courses in high school.

◆ Algebra
◆ Biology
◆ Environmental Science
◆ Environmental History

Turn the page to find out how math relates to a career in Environmental Science.

Thinking Green!

Use the information in the table to solve each problem. Round to the nearest tenth if necessary.

1. Find the mean, median, and mode of the percent of recycled glass data. _____

_____

2. If Lee County is removed from the recycled aluminum cans data, which changes the most: the mean, median, or mode? Does this make sense? Explain your reasoning.

_____

_____

_____

3. Find the range, quartiles, and interquartile range of the percent of recycled newspapers data. _____

4. Find any outliers in the percent of recycled plastic bottles data. _____

5. Make a box plot of the percent of recycled glass data.

6. Refer to the box plot you made in Exercise 5. Compare the parts of the box and the lengths of the whiskers. What does this tell you about the data? _____

_____

_____

_____

_____

Percent of Materials That Are Recycled				
County	Aluminum Cans (%)	Glass (%)	Newspapers (%)	Plastic Bottles (%)
Broward	15	13	41	7
Dade	4	17	28	15
Duval	31	17	81	7
Hillsborough	14	21	38	23
Lee	48	16	66	53
Orange	12	29	33	16
Polk	6	26	22	8

Career Project

It's time to update your career portfolio! Describe an environmental issue that concerns you. Explain how you, as an environmental engineer, would work to resolve this issue. Then research how the issue is being addressed by envionmental scientists today.

_____

_____

_____

_____

Choose your favorite school activity or volunteer job. Could it lead to a possible career? If so, what is it?

_____

_____

_____

Vocabulary Check

Write the correct term for each clue in the crossword puzzle.

Across

4. the arrangement of a data set
6. a diagram that is constructed using five values
7. an empty space or interval in a set of data
9. a line plot using dots

Down

1. having one side of a distribution looking the same as the other side
2. a diagram that shows the frequency of data on a number line
3. a type of bar graph used to display numerical data that have been organized into equal intervals
5. data that are grouped closely together
8. the mode of the data

Key Concept Check

Use Your FOLDABLES

Use your Foldable to help review the chapter.

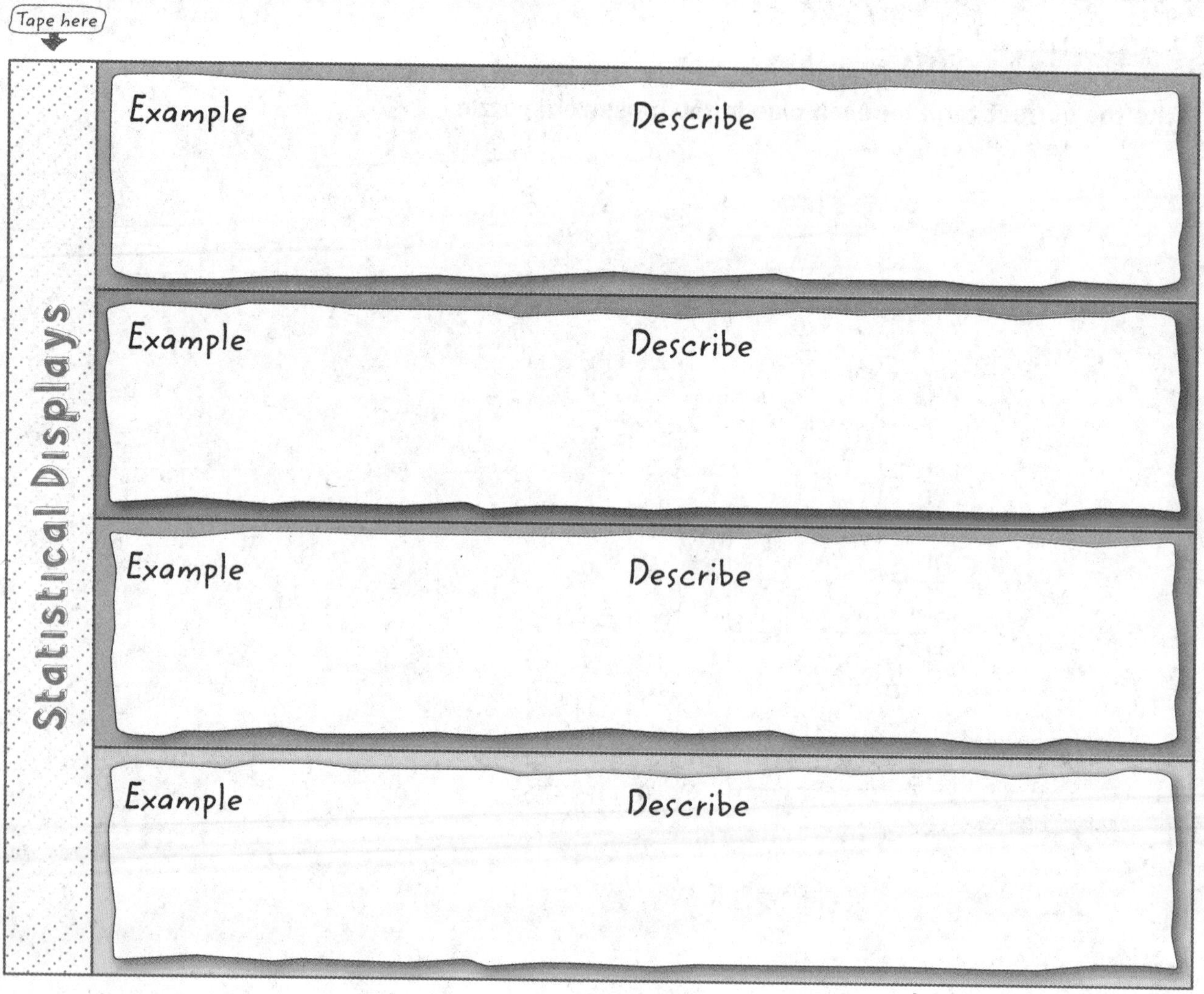

Tape here →

Statistical Displays

Example	Describe

Example	Describe

Example	Describe

Example	Describe

Got it?

Circle the correct term or number to complete each sentence.

1. It is best to use a (line plot, line graph) to show change over time.

2. A (cluster, gap) is the space on a graph that has no data values.

3. The median of a data set is easily seen in a (box plot, histogram).

4. A (line plot, box plot) will show the mode of the data set.

5. If a data set is symmetric, the spread should be described by the (interquartile range, mean absolute deviation).

Problem Solving

1. Jasmine asked her class how many pets they have. The line plot shows the results. Describe the distribution of the data.
(Lesson 1) __The mode is 1 pet.__

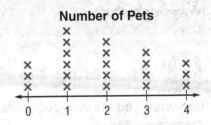

Number of Pets

2. Use the histogram. How many students complete 9 or less hours of homework a month? (Lesson 2)
__19 students__

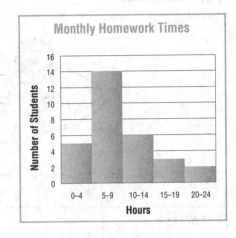

Monthly Homework Times

3. The box plot shows scores for a math test. Describe the distribution of the data. (Lesson 3) __The upper extreme is 98–99. The lower extreme = 67.5__

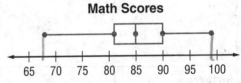

Math Scores

4. The line plot shows the cost of different video games at a store. Describe the shape of the distribution. (Lesson 4)
__Data clustered together at 30–50 dollars, gap from $15–$30__

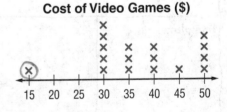

Cost of Video Games ($)

CCGPS Model with Mathematics Select the appropriate type of display for the data gathered in Exercises 5 and 6. (Lesson 6)

5. the number of students who have traveled to Arizona, Louisiana, Kansas, Florida, Michigan, and Wisconsin __Line Plot__

6. the change in the value of a house over a period of 30 years __Line Graph__

Reflect

 Answering the Essential Question

Use what you learned about staistical displays to complete the graphic organizer.

 Essential Question

WHY is it important to carefully evaluate graphs?

	When should I use it?
line graph	
histogram	
line plot	
box plot	

 Answer the Essential Question. WHY is it important to carefully evaluate graphs?

_____

_____

UNIT 7

Rational Explorations: Numbers and Their Opposites

Essential Question

HOW can mathematical ideas be represented?

Chapter 12

Integers and the Coordinate Plane

Integers, terminating decimals, and repeating decimals are rational numbers. In this chapter, you will compare and order rational numbers and graph points in four quadrants of the coordinate plane.

Chapter 12
Integers and the Coordinate Plane

 Essential Question

HOW are integers and absolute value used in real-world situations?

 CCGPS **Common Core GPS**

Content Standards
MCC6.NS.5, MCC6.NS.6, MCC6.NS.6a, MCC6.NS.6b, MCC6.NS.6c, MCC6.NS.7, MCC6.NS.7a, MCC6.NS.7b, MCC6.NS.7c, MCC6.NS.7d, MCC6.NS.8

Mathematical Practices
1, 2, 3, 4, 5, 7, 8

Math in the Real World

Rappelling Two friends rappel 35 feet down into a canyon. Their starting position is represented by 0 on the number line. Their ending position can be represented by −35.

Graph −35 on the number line below.

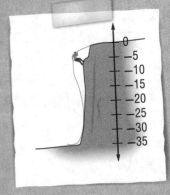

FOLDABLES
Study Organizer

1 Cut out the correct Foldable from the FL pages in the back of this book.

2 Place your Foldable on the Key Concept page toward the end of this chapter.

3 Use the Foldable throughout this chapter to help you learn about integers.

Vocabulary

absolute value	positive integer
bar notation	quadrants
integer	rational number
negative integer	repeating decimal
opposites	terminating decimal

Review Vocabulary

Using a graphic organizer can help you to remember important vocabulary terms. Fill in the graphic organizer below for the word *decimal*.

Decimal
Definition

Math Example	Real World Example

Are You Ready?

Try the Quick Check below.
Or, take the Online Readiness Quiz.

Example 1

Replace the ◯ with <, >, or = to make a true statement.

1.6 ◯ 1.3

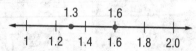

Since 1.6 is to the right of 1.3, 1.6 > 1.3.

Example 2

Replace the ◯ with <, >, or = to make a true statement.

$\frac{2}{5}$ ◯ $\frac{7}{10}$

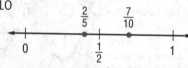

Since $\frac{2}{5}$ is less than $\frac{1}{2}$ and $\frac{7}{10}$ is greater than $\frac{1}{2}$, $\frac{2}{5} < \frac{7}{10}$.

Quick Check

Compare Decimals Replace each ◯ with <, >, or = to make a true statement.

Show your work.

1. 4.8 ◯ 4.80

2. 7.7 ◯ 7.5

3. 1.2 ◯ 2.1

Compare Fractions Replace each ◯ with <, >, or = to make a true statement.

4. $\frac{2}{11}$ ◯ $\frac{9}{10}$ =

5. $\frac{3}{5}$ ◯ $\frac{1}{4}$ =

6. $\frac{2}{3}$ ◯ $\frac{4}{6}$ =

7. Jahan bought $\frac{2}{3}$ pound of peanuts and $\frac{1}{4}$ pound of walnuts. Did Jahan buy more peanuts or more walnuts?

How Did You Do?

Which problems did you answer correctly in the Quick Check?
Shade those exercise numbers below.

① ② ③ ④ ⑤ ⑥ ⑦

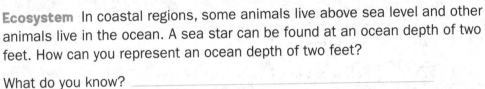

Inquiry HOW can positive and negative values be represented?

CCGPS **Content Standards**
MCC6.NS.5,
MCC6.NS.6,
MCC6.NS.6c

Mathematical Practices
1, 3, 4

Ecosystem In coastal regions, some animals live above sea level and other animals live in the ocean. A sea star can be found at an ocean depth of two feet. How can you represent an ocean depth of two feet?

What do you know? _____

_____

What do you need to find? _____

_____

Investigation

Sea level can be represented with the number 0.

To represent a location above sea level, use a positive number. A positive number can be written with or without a positive sign, such as 5 or +5.

To represent a location below sea level, use a negative number. A negative number is written with a negative sign, such as −5.

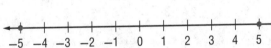

Write a number to represent an ocean depth of two feet.

Step 1 Determine if a positive sign or a negative sign should be used.

Since the location is below, or less than sea level,

use a _____ sign.

Step 2 Determine which number to use.

Use the number ☐ to represent two feet.

So, the number ☐ represents an ocean depth of two feet.

Collaborate

Work with a partner. Write the correct number to represent each location in relationship to sea level. The first one is done for you.

Show your work.

Animal	Elevation (ft)	Above or Below Sea Level	Number
Fiddler Crab	3	above sea level	+3
1. Eagle's Nest	75	above sea level	
2. Dolphin	10	below sea level	
3. Spider Crab	375	below sea level	
4. Blue Heron	4	above sea level	
5. Kelp Forest	656	below sea level	
6. White Egret	50	above sea level	

Reflect

7. **CCGPS Reason Inductively** What negative number is the same distance from 0 as the number +4? Explain. Graph both numbers on the number line below.

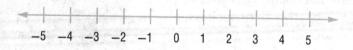

8. **CCGPS Model with Mathematics** Write about a real world situation that can be described using the number −6. Describe what the number 0 would represent.

9. **Inquiry** HOW can positive and negative values be represented?

Integers and Graphing

What You'll Learn

Scan the lesson. List two real-world scenarios in which you would use integers.

· _____

_____

· _____

_____

 Essential Question

HOW are integers and absolute value used in real-world situations?

 Vocabulary

integer
negative integer
positive integer

 Common Core GPS

Content Standards
MCC6.NS.5, MCC6.NS.6, MCC6.NS.6a, MCC6.NS.6c

Mathematical Practices
1, 3, 4, 5, 7

Real-World Link

Money The bar graph shows the amount of money remaining in the clothing budgets of four students at the end of one month. A value of −$2 means that someone overspent the budget and owes his or her parents 2 dollars.

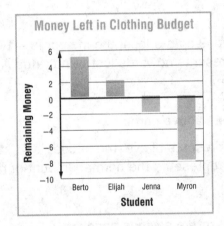

Money Left in Clothing Budget

1. What number represents owing 8 dollars? [ ]

2. What number represents having 5 dollars left? [ ]

3. Who has the most money left? Who owes the most? Explain.

_____

_____

_____

Use Integers to Represent Data

Positive whole numbers, their opposites, and zero are called **integers**. To represent data that are less than a 0, you can use **negative integers**. A negative integer is written with a − sign. Data that are greater than zero are represented by **positive integers**.

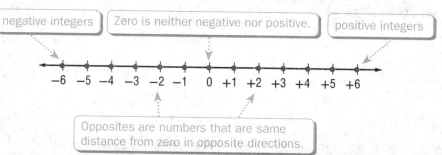

negative integers

Zero is neither negative nor positive.

positive integers

$$-6 \quad -5 \quad -4 \quad -3 \quad -2 \quad -1 \quad 0 \quad +1 \quad +2 \quad +3 \quad +4 \quad +5 \quad +6$$

Opposites are numbers that are same distance from zero in opposite directions.

Examples

Tutor

Write an integer for each situation. Explain the meaning of zero in each situation.

1. **a 10-yard loss**

Because it represents a loss, the integer is −10. In football, the integer 0 represents no yards lost or no yards gained.

2. **4 inches of rain above normal**

Because it represents above, the integer is 4. In this situation, the integer 0 represents the normal amount of rain.

3. **a $48 deposit into a savings account**

Because it represents an increase, the integer is ☐.

In this situation, the integer 0 represents _____

_____ .

Zero

The number zero can have different meanings based on real-world context. Sometimes zero represents an amount that does not change. Zero can also be used to represent real-world ideas, such as sea level.

Show your work.

Got It? Do these problems to find out.

Write an integer for each situation. Explain the meaning of zero in each situation.

a. a gain of $2 a share

b. 10 degrees below zero

a. _____2_____

b. _____−10_____

Graph Integers

Integers and sets of integers can be graphed on a horizontal or vertical number line. To graph a point on the number line, draw a point on the number line at its location. A set of integers is written using braces, such as {2, −9, 0}.

Examples

Tutor

4. **Graph −7 on a number line.**

> Draw a number line. Then draw a dot at the location that represents −7.

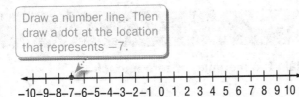

−10 −9 −8 −7 −6 −5 −4 −3 −2 −1 0 1 2 3 4 5 6 7 8 9 10

5. **Graph the set of integers {−4, 2, −1} on a number line.**

Draw a number line. Then draw a dot at the location of each integer.

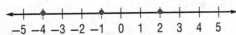

−5 −4 −3 −2 −1 0 1 2 3 4 5

6. **Graph the set of integers {0, 2, −3} on a number line.**

Draw a number line. Then draw a dot at the location of each integer.

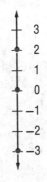

3
2
1
0
−1
−2
−3

Show your work.

10
8
6
4
2
0
−2
−4
−6
−8
−10

> **Got It?** Do these problems to find out.

Graph each set of integers on a number line.

c. {−3, 0, −2, 4}

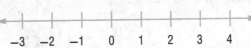

−3 −2 −1 0 1 2 3 4

d. {8, −6, −9, 5}

d. _____

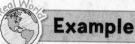

7. Alaina and her dad played golf on four different days. The data set {−1, +1, −3, +2} shows Alaina's scores in relation to par. Graph the scores. Explain the meaning of zero in this situation.

Draw a number line. Then draw a dot at the location of each golf score.

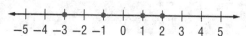

The integer 0 represents par.

Guided Practice

Write an integer for each situation. Explain the meaning of zero in each situation. (Examples 1–3)

1. 15-yard gain ____15____

2. loss of 2 hours ____−2____

Graph each integer or set of integers on a number line. (Examples 4–6)

3. −2

4. {−1, 1, 0}

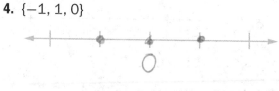

5. The data set {+5, 0, −15, +20} shows the number of points Delaney scored on each hand of a card game. Graph the scores. Explain the meaning of zero in this situation. (Example 7)

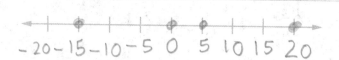

6.  **Building on the Essential Question** How can you use integers to represent data?

Rate Yourself!

How confident are you about integers and graphing? Check the box that applies.

For more help, go online to access a Personal Tutor.

Name _____ My Homework _____

Write an integer for each situation. Explain the meaning of zero in each situation. (Examples 1–3)

1. 3 miles below sea level _____ −3 _____

2. earning $45 _____ +45 _____

3 moving back 5 spaces on a game board _____
_____ −5 _____

Graph each integer or set of integers on a number line. (Examples 4–6)

4. −5

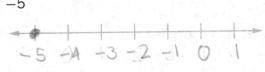

5 {2, −3, 0, 1}

6. The data set {+4, −1, −2, 0} shows a change in number of state representatives for four states after the last census. Graph the change in number of representatives. Explain the meaning of zero in this situation. (Example 7)

_____

7. **CCGPS** **Use Math Tools** The table shows the record low temperatures for several states. Graph the temperatures on a number line.

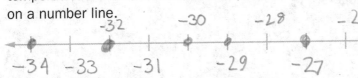

Record Low Temperature by State (°F)				
AL	**AK**	**CT**	**NJ**	**VA**
−27	−29	−32	−34	−30

8. **CCGPS** **Use Math Tools** The table shows the number of points earned for each action in a video game. While playing the video game, Kevin fell in water, jumped over a rock, touched a cactus and climbed a mountain. Graph the number of points he earned for each action on the number line.

Action	Points
fall in water	−10
walk over a bridge	+5
climb mountain	+10
jump over rock	+5
walk through quicksand	−15
touch cactus	−15

9. **Model with Mathematics** Complete the graphic organizer by writing words or symbols used to represent positive and negative integers.

Positive Integer	Negative Integer
•	•
•	•
•	•
•	•

H.O.T. Problems Higher Order Thinking

10. **CCGPS Persevere with Problems** A football team receives the ball on their own 10 yard line.

   a. They make a gain of 15 yards in the first play. What yard line is the ball on? _____

   b. What represents zero in this situation? Explain.

   _____

11. **CCGPS Justify Conclusions** The temperature outside is 15°F. If the temperature drops 20°, will the outside temperature be represented by a positive or negative integer? Explain your reasoning.

   _____
   _____
   _____

12. **CCGPS Identify Structure** Describe the characteristics of each set of numbers that make up the set of integers.

   _____
   _____
   _____

 Georgia Test Practice

13. The record low temperature for New Mexico is 50 degrees below zero Fahrenheit. The record low temperature for Hawaii is 12 degrees above zero Fahrenheit. What integer represents the record low temperature for New Mexico?

   Ⓐ 50
   Ⓑ 38
   Ⓒ −38
   Ⓓ −50

Extra Practice

Write an integer for each situation. Explain the meaning of zero in each situation.

14. 13° below zero   −13; The integer 0 represents zero degrees.

15. spending $25 _____

16. 13-yard gain _____

Graph each integer or set of integers on a number line.

17. −8

18. {0, −3, 1, −1}

19. {−1, 1, −2}

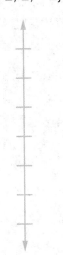

20. {3, −5, 4, −1}

21. {4, −2, 2}

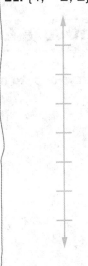

22. The data set {+3, −1, −2, +1} shows the moves a player made forward or backward in a board game. Graph the moves the player made. Explain the meaning of zero in this situation.

_____

23. **CCSS** **Model with Mathematics** The table shows the overnight low temperatures for 5 days in Minneapolis. Graph the temperatures on a number line.

Overnight Low Temperatures (°F)				
1	−1	3	−6	0

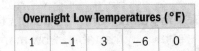

Georgia Test Practice

24. The lowest elevation in Vermont is 95 feet above sea level. The lowest elevation in Louisiana is 8 feet below sea level. What integer represents the lowest elevation in Vermont?

  (A) 8   (C) 95

  (B) −8   (D) −95

25. Short Response On Monday Kennedy spent $2 on lunch. On Tuesday she spent $1 on a snack. On Wednesday, her sister gave her $3. Graph the integers on the number line.

```
<-+--+--+--+--+--+--+--+--+--+--+->
```

26. On Friday, a school spirit shop gave away a free T-shirt with each purchase over $50. There were 47 purchases over $50. Which integer represents the change in the number of free T-shirts the spirit shop had in stock at the end of the day on Friday?

  (F) −50   (H) 47

  (G) −47   (I) 50

27. Short Response Jackson owes his sister Monica $15. Monica has a $10 bill in her pocket. Explain the meaning of zero in this situation.

_____

(CCGPS) **Common Core Review**

Fill in each ◯ with < or > to make the inequality true. MCC4.NBT.2

28. 26 ◯ 22

29. 11 ◯ 13

30. 2.5 ◯ 3

31. 44 ◯ 4.4

32. 15 ◯ 6.8

33. 1.8 ◯ 1.9

34. Ally bought $\frac{1}{12}$ pound of cashews and $\frac{5}{6}$ pound of granola. Plot the fractions on the number line. Which quantity is greater? Explain. MCC4.NF.3d

_____

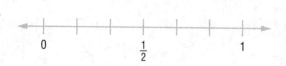

```
<---+----+----+----+----+----+----+----+--->
    0         1/2         1
```

35. The number of raffle tickets the student council sold over three days is shown in the table. How many total raffle tickets did they sell? MCC4.NBT.4

_____

Day	Tickets Sold
Wednesday	35
Thursday	23
Friday	46

Inquiry HOW can a number line help you find two integers that are the same distance from zero?

CCGPS Content Standards
MCC6.NS.5,
MCC6.NS.7,
MCC6.NS.7c,
MCC6.NS.7d
Mathematical Practices
1, 2, 3, 5

Hot Air Balloons Several hot air balloons were flying at the same height. The dashed line below represents their starting point. Which two balloons moved the same distance but in opposite directions?

Investigation

In the diagram below, +8 means Balloon A climbed 8 feet and −10 means Balloon B moved down 10 feet.

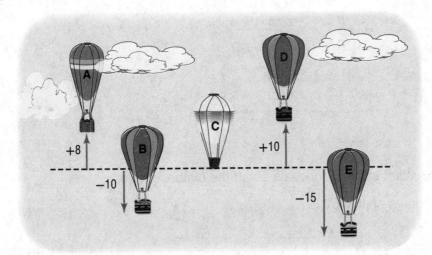

Use the diagram to compare the distance each balloon moved.

Step 1 Complete the chart to compare the distance each balloon moved from the dashed line.

Balloon	Integer	Direction	Distance Moved (ft)
C	0	none	0
D	+10		
E	−15		

Step 2 Determine which two balloons moved the same distance away from the dashed line.

So, Balloon ☐ and Balloon ☐ moved ☐ feet from the dashed line.

Collaborate

CCGPS **Use Math Tools** Use the number line to determine the distance
between each integer and zero.

Show your work.

$$\begin{array}{cccccccccccc} & | & | & | & | & | & | & | & | & | & | & | \\ -5 & -4 & -3 & -2 & -1 & 0 & 1 & 2 & 3 & 4 & 5 \end{array}$$

1. -2 _____

2. $+3$ _____

Work with a partner to complete the table. The first one is done for you.

	Integer	Distance Between Integer and Zero	Opposite Integer	Distance Between Opposite Integer and Zero
	3	3	−3	3
3.	4			
4.	7			
5.	−11			
6.	−13			
7.	19			
8.	−21			

9. CCGPS **Reason Inductively** What can you conclude about the distance from
zero for both an integer and its opposite? _____

_____

Reflect

10. CCGPS **Reason Abstractly** The movement of Balloon B in the Investigation
was represented by the number −10. What does zero represent in the
Investigation? _____

_____

11. (inquiry) HOW can a number line help you find two integers that are the
same distance from zero?

_____

_____

Absolute Value

Hill Street Studios/Getty Images

What You'll Learn

Scan the lesson. Predict two things you will learn about absolute value.

- _____
  _____

- _____

Essential Question

HOW are integers and absolute value used in real-world situations?

Vocabulary

absolute value
opposites

Common Core GPS

Content Standards
MCC6.NS.6, MCC6.NS.6a,
MCC6.NS.7, MCC6.NS.7c,
MCC6.NS.7d

Mathematical Practices
1, 2, 3, 4

Vocabulary Start-Up

The distance between a number and 0 on the number line is called its **absolute value**.

1. Each mark on the number line indicates one yard. Draw a tree three yards west of the house. Draw a mailbox three yards east of the house.

West   East

2. The distance between the house and the tree is _____ the distance between the house and the mailbox.

3. The tree and the mailbox are in _____ directions from the house.

4. How does the number line above help you to understand absolute value? _____

   _____

   _____

whew...

Real-World Link

5. **Errands** Jesse leaves home and walks 4 blocks west to the grocery store to buy milk then returns home. He then walks another 4 blocks east to the Post Office. Compare the distance and the direction of Jesse's house and the Post Office from the grocery store.

   _____

Find Opposites

Positive numbers, such as 2, are graphed to the right (or above) zero on a number line. Negative numbers, such as −2, are graphed to the left (or below) zero on a number line.

Opposites are numbers that are the same distance from zero in opposite directions. Since 0 is not negative nor positive, 0 is its own opposite. The opposite of the opposite of a number, is the number itself. For example, the opposite of the opposite of 3, −(−3), is 3.

| −2 is 2 units to the left of zero. | 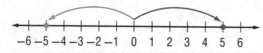 | 2 is 2 units to the right of zero. |

Examples

1. **Find the opposite of −5.**

> **Method 1** **Use a number line.**
>
> Draw a number line and graph −5.

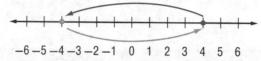

−5 is 5 units to the left of 0. The integer 5 is 5 units to the right of 0.

So, 5 is the opposite of −5.

> **Method 2** **Use symbols.**
>
> The integer −5 uses the negative symbol.
>
> The opposite of a negative symbol is a positive symbol.
>
> So, the opposite of −5 is +5, or 5.

2. **Find the opposite of the opposite of 4.**

-6 -5 -4 -3 -2 -1 0 1 2 3 4 5 6

The opposite of 4 is −4.
The opposite of −4 is 4.

So, 4 is the opposite of the opposite of 4.

Show your work.

Got It? Do these problems to find out.

a. _____

b. _____

a. What is the opposite of 3?

b. What is the opposite of the opposite of −2?

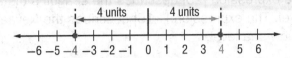

Absolute Value

Words   The absolute value of a number is the distance between the number and zero on a number line.

Model

```
      ←— 4 units —→|←— 4 units —→
  ←—+——+——+——+——+——+——+——+——+——+——+——+——→
    −6 −5 −4 −3 −2 −1  0  1  2  3  4  5  6
```

Symbols $|4| = 4$ The absolute value of 4 is 4.

$|-4| = 4$ The absolute value of −4 is 4.

The integers −4 and 4 are each 4 units from 0, even though they are on opposite sides of 0. $|-4|$ is read *absolute value of negative four*.

Examples

Tutor

Absolute Value

Since distance cannot be negative, the absolute value of a number is always positive or zero.

3. Evaluate $|-7|$.

```
   ←——— 7 units ———|
 ←—+——+——+——+——+——+——+——+——+——+——+——+——→
  −8 −7 −6 −5 −4 −3 −2 −1  0  1  2  3
```

The graph of −7 is 7 units from 0 on the number line.

So, $|-7| = 7$.

4. Evaluate $|5| + |-6|$.

$|5| + |-6| = 5 + |-6|$ The absolute value of 5 is 5.

$\qquad\qquad = 5 + 6$ The absolute value of −6 is 6.

$\qquad\qquad = 11$ Simplify.

5. Evaluate $|-7| - |3|$.

$|-7| - |3| = \boxed{} - \boxed{}$ Find the absolute value of −7 and 3.

$\qquad\qquad = \boxed{}$ Simplify.

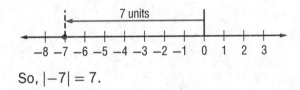

Show your work.

Got It?   Do these problems to find out.

c. $|14|$ **d.** $|-9| + |3|$ **e.** $|-8| - |-2|$

c. _____

d. _____

e. _____

 Example

6. A seagull is flying 25 feet above sea level. Nevaeh is diving 15 feet below sea level. What is the distance between Nevaeh and the seagull?

The expression |25| describes the seagull's distance above sea level. The expression |−15| describes the Nevaeh's distance below sea level.

To find the distance, add the absolute values.

$|25| + |-15| = 25 + |-15|$ The absolute value of 25 is 25.

$\qquad\qquad = 25 + 15$ The absolute value of −15 is 15.

$\qquad\qquad = 40$ Add.

So, the total distance is 40 feet.

Guided Practice

Check ✓

1. What is the opposite of 0? (Example 1)

Show your work.

2. What is the opposite of the opposite of 6? (Example 2)

Evaluate each expression. (Examples 3–5)

3. $|-5| = $ _____

4. $|20| - |-3| = $ _____

5. $|-16| + |-12| = $ _____

6. A game show contestant lost 15 points. He answered another question incorrectly and lost another 15 points. How many total points has he lost? (Example 6)

7. **Building on the Essential Question** How can absolute value help you to understand the size of a quantity? Give an example. _____

Rate Yourself!

How well do you understand opposites and absolute value? Circle the image that applies.

Clear   Somewhat Clear   Not So Clear

For more help, go online to access a Personal Tutor.

Tutor

Name _____ My Homework _____

Find the opposite of each integer. (Example 1)

1. 6 _____

2. −3 _____

3. 0 _____

Show your work.

Find the opposite of the opposite of each integer. (Example 2)

4. 12 _____

5. −9 _____

6. −17 _____

Evaluate each expression. (Examples 3–5)

7. $|-14| =$ _____

8. $|31| - |-1| =$ _____

9. $|-15| + |-6| =$ _____

10. Jayson spent $18 on a shirt. Then he spent $24 on a pair of pants. What is the total amount he spent? (Example 6) _____

11. Lilly saw a jelly fish at 6 feet below sea level. She saw a bright blue fish at 10 feet below sea level. What is the distance between the blue fish and the jelly fish? (Example 6) _____

12. **STEM** The table shows the melting points of various elements. Is the absolute value of the melting point of neon greater than or less than the absolute value of the melting point of hydrogen? _____

Element	Melting Point (°C)
Hydrogen	−259
Neon	−248
Oxygen	−218

13 **STEM** The surface of Jupiter is made of colorful clouds created by various chemicals in the atmosphere. The temperature at the top of the clouds is −230°F. The temperature below the clouds is 70°F. Which temperature has the lower absolute value? _____

CCGPS **Reason Abstractly** Evaluate each expression.

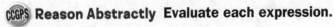

14. $-|3| =$ _____

15. $|5 + 9| =$ _____

16. $|17 - 8| =$ _____

17. **(CCGPS) Find the Error** Mei is evaluating an expression using absolute value. Find her mistake and correct it.

$|-14| = -14$

18. **(CCGPS) Which One Doesn't Belong?** Identify the phrase that *cannot* be described by the same absolute value as the other three. Explain your reasoning.

| a loss of 8 pounds | 8 miles above sea level | giving away $8 | 18° below normal |

(CCGPS) Persevere with Problems Determine whether each statement is *always*, *sometimes*, or *never* true. Explain.

19. The absolute value of a positive integer is a negative integer.

20. If a and b are integers and $a > b$, then $|a| > |b|$.

21. **(CCGPS) Reason Abstractly** Explain why the absolute value of a number is never negative.

22. **(CCGPS) Reason Abstractly** Explain why an account balance less than -40 dollars represents a debt greater than 40 dollars.

Georgia Test Practice

23. If $x = -2$ and $y = 2$, then which of the following statements is false?

Ⓐ $|x| > 1$ Ⓒ $|y| < 1$

Ⓑ $|x| = |y|$ Ⓓ $|x| = y$

Extra Practice

Find the opposite of each integer.

24. −2 _2_

25. 15 _____

26. 42 _____

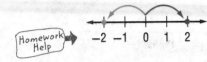
Homework Help →   −2 −1   0   1   2

Find the opposite of the opposite of each integer.

27. 9 _____

28. 0 _____

29. −8 _____

Evaluate each expression.

30. |18| = _____

31. |0| = _____

32. |25| _____

33. |2| + |−13| = _____

34. |−20| − |17| = _____

35. |−16| − |5| = _____

36. The balance of Bryce's account is $16. Jada's account is $5 overdrawn. What is the difference between their account balances?

_____

37. A football team lost 3 yards on their first play and 6 yards on their second play. How many total yards did they lose?

_____

38. The table shows the lowest elevations for several states. Is the absolute value of the lowest elevation of California greater than or less than the absolute value of the lowest elevation of Illinois?

State	Lowest Elevation (ft)
Oklahoma	289
Illinois	279
Kentucky	257
California	−282

CCGPS **Reason Abstractly** **Evaluate each expression.**

39. −|−10| = _____

40. |13 − 6| = _____

41. If $x = -1$ and $y = -2$, then which of the following statements is true?

- (A) $|x| > 1$
- (B) $|x| < |y|$
- (C) $|y| < 1$
- (D) $|y| < x$

42. Refer to the number line below. Which point represents the number with the greatest absolute value?

M   F   C   T

$-5 \ -4 \ -3 \ -2 \ -1 \ 0 \ 1 \ 2 \ 3 \ 4 \ 5$

- (F) point M
- (G) point F
- (H) point C
- (I) point T

43. A video game has different point values associated with different actions. The table shows some of the actions. Which action has associated points with the greatest absolute value?

Action	Points
collect gem	+5
fall in water	−10
build bridge	+12
climb tree	−15

- (A) collect gem
- (B) fall in water
- (C) build bridge
- (D) climb tree

44. Which expression has the greatest value?

- (F) $|-25|$
- (G) $|-16|$
- (H) $|18|$
- (I) $|22|$

45. Short Response The table shows the freezing point of different liquids. What liquid's freezing point has the greatest absolute value?

Liquid	Freezing Point (°F)
Water	32
Acetic Acid	62
Linseed Oil	−4
Acetone	−94

Common Core Review

Fill in each ◯ with >, <, or = to make a true statement. MCC4.NBT.2

46. 69.23 ◯ 69.25

47. 171.10 ◯ 171.09

48. 47.74 ◯ 47.740

49. Part of a sauce recipe is shown. If all the ingredients are mixed together, how much sauce will be made? MCC5.NF.1

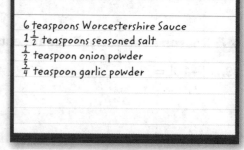

6 teaspoons Worcestershire Sauce
$1\frac{1}{2}$ teaspoons seasoned salt
$\frac{1}{2}$ teaspoon onion powder
$\frac{3}{4}$ teaspoon garlic powder

50. Caroline's soccer practice starts at quarter after 4 P.M. and ends at 5 P.M. How many minutes does her soccer practice last? MCC4.MD.2

Compare and Order Integers

What You'll Learn

Scan the lesson. List two real-world scenarios in which you would compare integers.

- _____

- _____

 Real-World Link

Essential Question

HOW are integers and absolute value used in real-world situations?

 Common Core GPS

Content Standards
MCC6.NS.7, MCC6.NS.7a, MCC6.NS.7b, MCC6.NS.7d

Mathematical Practices
1, 2, 3, 4, 5

Winter Fairbanks is located in interior Alaska. The average temperature for several months is shown.

1. The average temperature for December is −6.5°F and the average temperature for March is 11°F. Label December and March on the thermometer.

2. Which months have a greater average temperature

   than February? _____

3a. Which months have a lower average temperature

   than November? _____

3b. Complete the inequality to compare the temperatures of November and February.

   3 > ☐

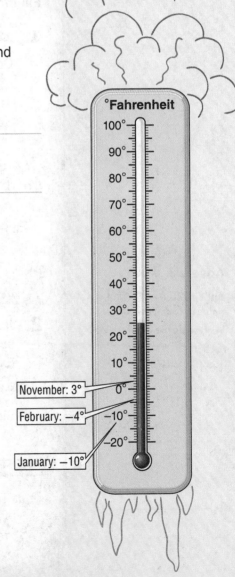

°Fahrenheit

November: 3°
February: −4°
January: −10°

Compare Integers

To compare integers, you can compare the signs as well as the magnitude, or size, of the numbers. Greater numbers are graphed farther to the right.

Compare the signs.

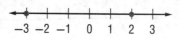

Positive numbers are greater than negative numbers. So, $2 > -3$.

Compare the position on the number line.

Since -2 is farther to the right, $-2 > -3$.

Example

Tutor

Fill in the ◯ with <, >, or = to make a true sentence.

1. 12 ◯ −4

Graph 12 and −4 on a number line. Then compare.

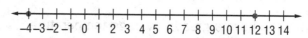

Since 12 is to the right of −4, $12 > -4$.

Got It? Do these problems to find out.

a. −3 ◯ −5   b. −5 ◯ 0   c. 6 ◯ −1

Real World

Example

Tutor

2. Justin has a score of −4 on the Trueville Trivia game. Desiree's score is −5. Write an inequality to compare the scores. Explain the meaning of the inequality.

$-4 > -5$ −4 is farther to the right on a number line than −5.

Since $-4 > -5$, Justin has a higher score than Desiree.

Got It? Do this problem to find out.

d. The temperature on Tuesday was 2°F. The temperature on Wednesday was −2°F. Write an inequality to compare the temperatures. Explain the meaning of the inequality.

Absolute Value
Although −5 is the least value in Example 2, it represents the greater point deficit.
$|-5| > |-4|$

Show your work.

d. _____

Order Integers

You can use a number line to order a set of integers. Integers can be ordered from least to greatest or from greatest to least.

Example

3. Order the set {−9, 6, −3, 0} from least to greatest.

> **Method 1** Use a number line.
> Graph the numbers on a number line.

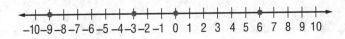

The order from left to right is −9, −3, 0, and 6.

> **Method 2** Compare signs and values.
> Compare negative numbers. Then compare positive numbers.
> The negative integers are −9 and −3. −9 < −3
> The integer 0 is neither positive nor negative.
> The positive integer is 6.

So, the order from least to greatest is −9, −3, 0, and 6.

Got It? Do these problems to find out.

Show your work.

e. Order the set {−4, 3, 11, −25} from greatest to least.

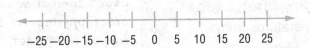

e. _____

f. Order the set {−18, 30, 12, −6, 3} from least to greatest.

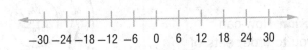

f. _____

Example

Tutor

4. **STEM** The table shows the lowest elevation for several continents. Order the elevations from least to greatest.

First, graph each integer. Then, write the integers as they appear on the number line from left to right.

Continent	Lowest Elevation (m)
Africa	−156
Asia	−418
Australia	−12
Europe	−28
North America	−86
South America	−105

```
−500−450−400−350−300−250−200−150 −100 −50   0
```

The elevations from least to greatest are −418, −156, −105, −86, −28, and −12.

Guided Practice

Check ✓

Fill in each ◯ with <, >, or = to make a true statement. (Example 1)

1. 17 ◯ 31

2. −6 ◯ −10

3. −83 ◯ −38

4. Andrew and his father are scuba diving at −38 feet and Tackle Box Canyon has an elevation of −83 feet. Write an inequality to compare the depths. Explain the meaning of the inequality. (Example 2)

_____

_____

5. **STEM** The daily low temperatures in Kate's hometown last week were 2°C, −9°C, −18°C, −6°C, 3°C, 0°C, and −7°C. Order the temperatures from greatest to least. (Examples 3 and 4)

_____

6. ⓔ **Building on the Essential Question** How can symbols and absolute value help you to order sets of integers?

_____

_____

Rate Yourself!

How confident are you about comparing and ordering integers? Shade the ring on the target.

I'm on target.

I need help.

For more help, go online to access a Personal Tutor.

Tutor

FOLDABLES Time to update your Foldable!

Independent Practice

eHelp
Go online for Step-by-Step Solutions

Fill in each ◯ with <, >, or = to make a true statement. (Example 1)

1. −2 ◯ −4

2. 1 ◯ −3

3. 5 ◯ 0

4. Amy is building a house. The basement floor is at −15 feet. The roof of the house is above the ground 25 feet. Write an inequality to compare the heights. Explain the meaning of the inequality. (Example 2)

_____

_____

5. The low temperature in Anchorage, Alaska, one day was −9°F. On the same day, the low temperature in Flagstaff, Arizona, was 26°F. Write an inequality to compare the temperatures. Explain the meaning of the inequality. (Example 2)

_____

_____

Order each set of integers from least to greatest. (Example 3)

6. {15, 17, 21, 6, 3}

7. {−55, 143, 18, −79, 44, 101}

_____

_____

8. The table indicates Xavier's cell phone use over the last four months. Positive values indicate the number of minutes he went over his allotted time, and negative values indicate the number of minutes he was under. Arrange the months from least to most minutes used. (Example 4)

_____

Month	Time (min)
February	−156
March	12
April	0
May	−45

9. CCGPS **Use Math Tools** Refer to the table and the following information. The apparent magnitude of an object measures how bright the object appears to the human eye. A negative magnitude identifies a brighter object than a positive magnitude.

a. Which object appears the brightest to the human eye?

_____

b. Order the objects from the brightest to the faintest.

_____

_____

c. Find the least apparent magnitude of this data set.

_____

Object	Approximate Apparent Magnitude
100-Watt Bulb	−19
Alpha Centauri	4
Andromeda Galaxy	0
Full Moon	−13
Sun	−27
Venus	−5

10. **CCGPS Justify Conclusions** Refer to the graphic novel frame below for exercises a–c.

a. If about 32,834.5 kilobytes of memory is still available, how many more pictures can they take? _____

b. Write an inequality to compare the number of pictures taken during school to the number of pictures taken after school. _____

c. Explain the meaning of the inequality. _____

H.O.T. Problems Higher Order Thinking

11. **CCGPS Model with Mathematics** Write a real-world situation to explain the inequality −$15 < $7. _____

12. **CCGPS Reason Abstractly** Explain why −11 is less than −7, but |−11| is greater than |−7|. _____

13. **CCGPS Persevere with Problems** Order the fractions $-\frac{1}{2}$, $\frac{5}{2}$, $-\frac{12}{4}$, $\frac{1}{6}$, and $\frac{7}{8}$ from least to greatest. _____

Georgia Test Practice

14. Order the set {−5, 3, 2, −7} from greatest to least.

  Ⓐ −7, −5, 3, 2   Ⓒ 2, 3, −5, −7

  Ⓑ −7, −5, 2, 3   Ⓓ 3, 2, −5, −7

Extra Practice

Fill in each ◯ **with <, >, or = to make a true statement.**

15. −2 (<) 4

 → Since −2 is to the left of 4, −2 < 4.

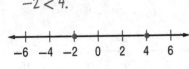

16. −6 ◯ 3

17. −3 ◯ 2

18. The elevation of Driskill Mountain, Louisiana, is 163 meters above sea level. Death Valley has an elevation of −86 meters. Write an inequality to compare the elevations. Explain the meaning of the inequality.

_____

_____

19. Yvonne owes her sister $25. Michael's checking account balance is −$20. Write an inequality to compare the amounts. Explain the meaning of the inequality.

_____

_____

Order each set of integers from least to greatest.

20. {14, 1, 6, 23, 7, 5}

_____

21. {−221, 63, 54, −89, −71, −10}

22. Gary, Sindhu, and Beth are all waiting for their trains to arrive. Gary's train leaves at 5 minutes before noon, Sindhu's leaves at 25 minutes after noon, and Beth's leaves 5 minutes before Sindhu's train. Order the three by who will leave first.

_____

23. **Use Math Tools** Use the bar graph and the information below. The bar graph gives the scores of four golfers (A, B, C, and D). The numbers indicate scores above and below par.

a. Order the scores on a number line.

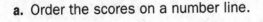

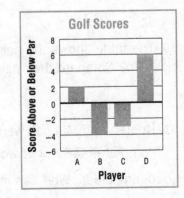

b. Which player had the worst score? Explain your answer.

_____

24. The table shows the temperatures for a four-day period.

Temperature (°F)	
Monday	−7
Tuesday	8
Wednesday	−2
Thursday	−1

Which list shows the temperatures from least to greatest?

Ⓐ 8, −2, −1, −7

Ⓑ 8, −1, −2, −7

Ⓒ −7, −2, −1, 8

Ⓓ −7, −1, −2, 8

25. Verónica (V) was 12 minutes early to class, Deshawn (D) was right on time, and Kendis (K) was 3 minutes late. Which time line represents the students' arrival to class?

Ⓕ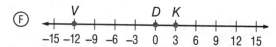

Ⓖ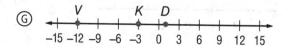

Ⓗ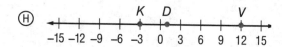

Ⓘ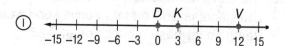

26. **Short Response** The table shows the scores for a game of miniature golf. The integer 0 represents par. Arrange the players from least shots taken to most shots taken.

Player	Score
Cristian	−6
Bailey	2
Liam	−3
Marisol	5

_____

Write each fraction as a decimal. MCC5.NF.5b

27. $\frac{3}{4} =$ _____

28. $\frac{1}{5} =$ _____

29. $\frac{3}{20} =$ _____

30. The table shows the heights of Sonya's siblings. Who is taller, Frieda or Julio? Compare their heights using the symbol >. MCC4.NBT.2

Member	Height (ft)
Frieda	$5\frac{1}{4}$
Julio	$5\frac{5}{6}$

_____

31. Kristen and Mitchell were given the same math assignment. Kristen completes 0.8 of her work in class. Mitchell completes 0.75 of his work during class. Who has more homework remaining after class? MCC5.NBT.3

_____

Content Standards
MCC6.NS.5
Mathematical Practices
1, 3

Case #1 Hit the Slopes!

Marissa and her family are on a ski trip at Mount Washington in New Hampshire. They returned from the slopes at 6 P.M. By 9 P.M., the temperature had fallen 18° to the day's low temperature of −8°F.

What was the temperature at 6 P.M.?

Understand *What are the facts?*
- By 9 P.M., the temperature had fallen 18°.
- The day's low temperature was −8°F.

Plan *What is your strategy to solve this problem?*
Work backward from the low temperature at 9 P.M. Use a thermometer diagram to find the temperature at 6 P.M.

Solve *How can you apply the strategy?*

Start at ☐ °F. Shade the thermometer ☐ degrees

to find the temperature at 6 P.M.

So, the temperature at 6 P.M. was _____ .

°Fahrenheit
50°
40°
30°
20°
10°
0°
−10°

Check *Does the answer make sense?*

−8°F is 8 degrees away from 0°F. 18 − 8 = 10

So, add to ☐ to 0°F. Since 0 + ☐ = ☐ , the answer is reasonable.

Analyze the Strategy [Tutor]

Justify Conclusions The high temperature was 36°F. How far away from −8°F is 36°F? Explain. _____

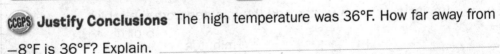

Case #2 Get Ready, Get Set, Go

The table shows the amount of time it takes Henry to do different activities before going to soccer practice.

If he needs to be at practice at 8:15 A.M., what time should he wake up in the morning to get to the soccer field?

Activity	Time (minutes)
Travel to field from home	15
Eating breakfast	35
Changing into uniform	10
Checking E-mail messages	20

 Understand

Read the problem. What are you being asked to find?

I need to find _____.

Underline key words and values. What information do you need to know?

The table shows the time it takes Henry to do each activity. It takes him ☐ minutes to get to the field, ☐ minutes to eat, ☐ minutes to change for practice, and ☐ minutes to check his email.

 Plan

Choose a problem-solving strategy.

I will use the _____ strategy.

 Solve

Use your problem-solving strategy to solve the problem.

8:15 A.M. − 20 min = _____ A.M.   7:45 A.M. − 35 min = _____ A.M.

7:55 A.M. − 10 min = _____ A.M.   7:10 A.M. − 15 min = _____ A.M.

So, Henry should wake up at _____.

 Check

Use information from the problem to check your answer.

Begin at _____ A.M. and add the minutes from the table.

☐ + ☐ + ☐ + ☐ = ☐ minutes

_____ A.M. plus ☐ minutes is 8:15 A.M.

HOW can you use a number line to model and compare positive and negative rational numbers?

Content Standards
MCC6.NS.6,
MCC6.NS.6c,
MCC6.NS.7

Mathematical Practices
1, 3, 4

Beach Marcus and Silvio are at the beach. Marcus builds a sandcastle 0.6 meter high. Silvio digs a hole in the sand 0.8 meter deep.

Investigation 1

Just as you can graph integers on a number line, you can graph positive and negative fractions and decimals. Recall that positive numbers are to the right of zero on the number line and negative numbers are to the left of zero.

Step 1 Complete the number line from −1 to 1, with increments of 0.2.

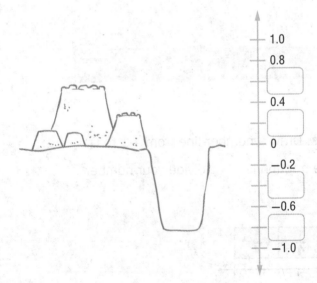

Step 2 The sandcastle is above sea level. Its height is *greater than zero* on the number line, so draw a dot at ☐ to represent the sandcastle.

Step 3 The hole is below sea level. Its depth is *less than zero* on the number line. So draw a dot at ☐ to represent the hole.

Collaborate

CCGPS **Model with Mathematics** Work with a partner. Graph each number on a number line.

1. −2.4

Show your work.

2. 0.1

3. −4.5

4. −6.8

Investigation 2

Tools

Graph $-\frac{3}{4}$ on a number line.

Step 1 Model $-\frac{3}{4}$ using fraction tiles. Draw a number line from −1 to 0.

Since the denominator of the fraction is ☐ , divide your number

line into ☐ equal parts.

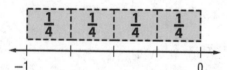

Step 2 Each mark on the number line represents $\dfrac{\boxed{}}{\boxed{}}$. Label the number

line with $-\frac{3}{4}$, $-\frac{2}{4}$, and $-\frac{1}{4}$.

Step 3 Draw a dot to graph $-\frac{3}{4}$ on the number line above.

CCGPS **Model with Mathematics** Work with a partner. Graph each number on a number line.

5. $-\dfrac{4}{5}$

Show your work.

6. -5.75

7. $\dfrac{7}{10}$

8. $-\dfrac{3}{8}$

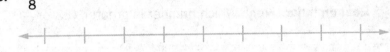

9. 8.75

10. $-\dfrac{3}{10}$

11. $-\dfrac{5}{12}$

Work with a partner to complete the table. The first one is done for you.

Number	Positive or Negative	Greater Than or Less Than Zero	Left or Right of 0 on the Number Line
-3.5	negative	$<$	left
12. $+\dfrac{4}{5}$			
13. $-\dfrac{1}{3}$			
14. $+0.3$			

15. **CCGPS Reason Inductively** Which number is greater, 0.3 or -0.7? Explain.

_____

_____

16. **CCGPS Reason Inductively** Jacyln thinks that $-\dfrac{1}{2}$ is greater than $\dfrac{1}{4}$ because it is farther from zero on the number line. Is her thinking correct? Explain.

_____

_____

_____

_____

 Reflect

17. **CCGPS Model with Mathematics** Write a real-world problem that involves a positive and a negative value. Then graph the values used in the problem on a number line. Compare the values.

_____

_____

_____

_____

18. **Inquiry** HOW can you use a number line to model and compare positive and negative rational numbers?

_____

_____

Terminating and Repeating Decimals

What You'll Learn

Scan the lesson. Predict two things you will learn about terminating and repeating decimals.

- _____
  _____

- _____
  _____

Vocabulary Start-Up

Any number that can be written as a fraction is called a **rational number**. Every rational number can be written as either a **terminating decimal** or a **repeating decimal**.

Draw lines from each word to its matching statement.

| terminating decimal |

| the decimal form of a rational number; 0.33333... |

| repeating decimal |

| the decimal form of a rational number which has a repeating digit of zero; 06.25 |

Real-World Link

Party Favors Jude is buying fruit snacks for party favors. He asks the cashier for a half pound of fruit snacks.

1. Express one half as a fraction.

   _____

2. Write the decimal that represents half a pound.

   _____

3. Suppose Jude wanted to buy one third of a pound. What decimal would the scale show?

   _____

Key Concept ⟩ Rational Numbers

Words   Rational numbers can be written as fractions.

Algebra $\frac{a}{b}$, where a and b are integers and $b \neq 0$.

Model

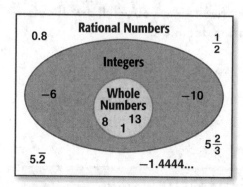

Work Zone

Fractions, terminating and repeating decimals, percents, and integers are all rational numbers. Every rational number can be expressed as a decimal by dividing the numerator by the denominator.

Rational Number	Repeating Decimal	Terminating Decimal
$\frac{3}{10}$	0.300...	0.3
$\frac{4}{5}$	0.800...	0.8
$\frac{5}{6}$	0.833...	does not terminate

To indicate the number pattern that repeats indefinitely, use bar notation. **Bar notation** is a bar placed over the digits that repeat.

$$0.545454... = 0.\overline{54} \qquad\qquad 0.583333... = 0.58\overline{3}$$

Example

Tutor

1. Write $\frac{5}{12}$ as a decimal.

$$
\begin{array}{r}
0.4166 \\
12\overline{)5.000} \\
-48 \\
\hline
20 \\
-12 \\
\hline
80 \\
-72 \\
\hline
80 \\
-72 \\
\hline
8
\end{array}
$$

Divide 5 by 12.

The remainder will never be zero.

So, $\frac{5}{12} = 0.4166...$ or $0.41\overline{6}$.

Got It? Do these problems to find out.

Write each fraction as a decimal. Use bar notation if necessary.

a. $\frac{1}{6}$ b. $\frac{8}{9}$ c. $\frac{2}{11}$

a. _____

b. _____

c. _____

Write a Negative Fraction as a Decimal

When writing negative fractions as decimals, the process is the same. Divide as with positive fractions. Write the negative sign in front of the decimal.

Examples

 Tutor

2. Write $-\frac{2}{9}$ as a decimal.

$$
\begin{array}{r}
0.222 \\
9\overline{)2.000} \\
-18 \\
\hline
20 \\
-18 \\
\hline
20 \\
-18 \\
\hline
2
\end{array}
$$

Divide 2 by 9.

The remainder will never be zero.

So, $-\frac{2}{9} = -0.222\ldots$ or $-0.\overline{2}$.

> **Repeating Decimals**
> When dividing, it is sometimes helpful to divide until the repeated pattern is shown at least three times.

3. Write $-2\frac{2}{3}$ as a decimal.

$-2\frac{2}{3}$ can be rewritten as $-\frac{8}{3}$.

The mixed number $-2\frac{2}{3}$ can be written as $-2.\overline{6}$.

$$
\begin{array}{r}
2.6\ldots \\
3\overline{)8.0} \\
-6 \\
\hline
20 \\
-18 \\
\hline
2
\end{array}
$$

d. _____

e. _____

Got It? Do these problems to find out.

Write each fraction as a decimal. Use bar notation if necessary.

d. $-\frac{1}{4}$ e. $-\frac{5}{6}$ f. $-2\frac{1}{6}$

f. _____

Tutor

Example

4. Frankie made 34 out of 44 free throws this season. To the nearest thousandth, what is his free-throw average?

Using a calculator, divide 34 by 44.

34 ÷ 44 **ENTER** 0.77272727

To the nearest thousandth, his free-throw average is 0.773.

Got It? Do this problem to find out.

g. Of nine students surveyed, four said they prefer exercising in the morning rather than in the evening. Express this fraction as a decimal. Use bar notation if necessary.

Show your work.

g. _____

Guided Practice

Check ✓

Write each fraction as a decimal. Use bar notation if necessary. (Examples 1–3)

1. $\dfrac{7}{9}$ = _____

2. $-\dfrac{1}{33}$ = _____

3. $-2\dfrac{5}{6}$ = _____

4. $\dfrac{10}{15}$ = _____

5. $-\dfrac{4}{5}$ = _____

6. $1\dfrac{5}{9}$ = _____

7. Dana bought $\dfrac{2}{3}$ yard of fabric to make a new purse. Write the amount of fabric she used as a decimal. (Example 4)

_____

8. ⓔ **Building on the Essential Question** How are repeating decimals used in real-world situations?

_____

_____

_____

Rate Yourself!

Are you ready to move on? Shade the section that applies.

- I have a few questions.
- I'm ready to move on.
- I have a lot of questions.

For more help, go online to access a Personal Tutor.

Tutor

Independent Practice

 Go online for Step-by-Step Solutions

Write each fraction as a decimal. Use bar notation if necessary.
(Examples 1–3)

1. $\frac{7}{15} =$ _____

2. $\frac{8}{18} =$ _____

3. $-\frac{8}{12} =$ _____

Show your work.

4. $-\frac{6}{7} =$ _____

5. $3\frac{15}{44} =$ _____

6. $-2\frac{5}{22} =$ _____

7. Sarafina had 34 out of 99 hits when she was at bat during the softball season. What was her batting average? (Example 4)

_____

8. Shiv and his friends ate $3\frac{1}{6}$ pizzas. Write this amount as a decimal. (Example 4)

_____

Write each decimal as a fraction or mixed number in simplest form.

9. $-0.9 =$ _____

10. $-0.85 =$ _____

11. $-3.8 =$ _____

Evaluate each expression.

12. $|-2.3| =$ _____

13. $\left|\frac{4}{13}\right| =$ _____

14. $\left|-8\frac{7}{11}\right| =$ _____

15. **STEM** There are over 2,700 species of snakes in the world. Over 600 species are venomous. Write the fraction of species that are *not* venomous as a decimal. _____

16. **CCGPS** **Justify Conclusions** The ratio of the circumference of a circle to its diameter is represented by the number π. The number π is a decimal that does not repeat. The fraction $\frac{22}{7}$ is sometimes used as an estimate of π. Is $\frac{22}{7}$ a repeating decimal? Explain.

_____

17. **CCGPS Reason Abstractly** Refer to the graphic novel frame below for Exercises a–b.

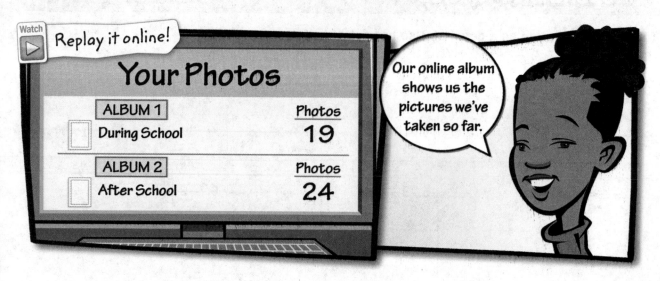

a. How many total photos were taken? _____

b. What fraction of the photos were taken after school? Write this fraction as a decimal. Round to the nearest thousandth. _____

H.O.T. Problems Higher Order Thinking

18. **CCGPS Identify Structure** Write a fraction and an equivalent terminating decimal between 0.2 and 0.6. _____

19. **CCGPS Persevere with Problems** Predict whether or not the decimal equivalent to $\frac{17}{36}$ is terminating. Explain your reasoning. Check your prediction with a calculator. _____

_____

20. **CCGPS Which One Doesn't Belong?** Identify the decimal equivalent that does *not* have the same characteristic as the other three. Explain.

| $\frac{1}{12}$ | $\frac{2}{12}$ | $\frac{3}{12}$ | $\frac{4}{12}$ |

Georgia Test Practice

21. Which decimal represents the shaded portion of the figure below?

    Ⓐ 0.4   Ⓒ 0.5

    Ⓑ $0.\overline{4}$ Ⓓ $0.\overline{5}$

Extra Practice

Write each fraction as a decimal. Use bar notation if necessary.

22. $\frac{32}{75} =$ 0.42$\overline{6}$

$$
\begin{array}{r}
0.42\overline{6} \\
75\overline{)32.000} \\
-300 \\
\hline
200 \\
-150 \\
\hline
500 \\
-450 \\
\hline
50
\end{array}
$$

Homework Help →

23. $\frac{3}{11} =$ _____

24. $-\frac{5}{8} =$ _____

25. $-\frac{7}{10} =$ _____

26. $2\frac{5}{7} =$ _____

27. $-1\frac{80}{99} =$ _____

28. Cris answered 61 out of 66 questions correctly on a test. What is his test average to the nearest thousandth? _____

Write each decimal as a fraction or mixed number in simplest form.

29. $-0.15 =$ _____

30. $-7.75 =$ _____

31. $-12.54 =$ _____

32. CCSS **Identify Repeated Reasoning** The table shows the decimal equivalent to fractions with a denominator of 7.

a. What do you notice about the pattern of the six repeated numbers?

_____

Fraction	Decimal	Fraction	Decimal
$\frac{1}{7}$	$0.\overline{142857}$	$\frac{4}{7}$	$0.\overline{571428}$
$\frac{2}{7}$	$0.\overline{285714}$	$\frac{5}{7}$	$0.\overline{714285}$
$\frac{3}{7}$	$0.\overline{428571}$	$\frac{6}{7}$	$0.\overline{857142}$

b. Using the decimals, add the first half of each pattern to the numbers in the last half. For example, $\frac{1}{7} = 0.\overline{142857}$, so add $142 + 857$. What pattern do you notice? _____

c. Using a calculator, try the same experiment with $\frac{5}{13}$. Is the result the same? Justify your reasoning. _____

33. Which decimal represents the shaded portion of the figure below?

Ⓐ 0.16   Ⓒ 0.17

Ⓑ 0.1$\overline{6}$ Ⓓ 1.6

34. Which of the following is *not* equivalent to 0.$\overline{3}$?

Ⓕ $\frac{1}{3}$

Ⓖ $\frac{3}{9}$

Ⓗ $\frac{3}{10}$

Ⓘ $\frac{11}{33}$

35. **Short Response** Write −1.25 as a fraction.

_____

ⒸⒸⒼⓅⓈ **Common Core Review**

Fill in each ◯ **with < or > to make a true statement.** MCC4.NBT.2

36. 4,556 ◯ 4,565

37. 8,698 ◯ 8,689

38. 47,872 ◯ 47,871

39. 26,525 ◯ 26,522

40. 1,123,004 ◯ 1,123,040

41. 5,776,050 ◯ 5,775,005

42. The table shows the number of miles Katie walked for two weeks. Compare the distances using the < symbol. MCC5.NBT.3b

_____

Week	Number of Miles
1	5.78
2	5.691

43. The table shows the amount of different colored paints in a bin in art class. Compare the amount of blue and orange paint using the > symbol.
MCC5.NBT.3

_____

Color	Number of Ounces
Blue	47.362
Green	47.637
Orange	47.394
Yellow	47.583

Compare and Order Rational Numbers

What You'll Learn

Scan the lesson. List two headings you would use to make an outline of the lesson.

• _____

_____

• _____

_____

 Essential Question

HOW are integers and absolute value used in real-world situations?

CCGPS **Common Core GPS**

Content Standards
MCC6.NS.6, MCC6.NS.6c, MCC6.NS.7, MCC6.NS.7a, MCC6.NS.7b

Mathematical Practices
1, 2, 3, 4, 5, 7

Real-World Link

Insects The lengths of several common types of insects are shown in the table.

Insect	Length (in.)
Green June Beetle	$\frac{3}{4}$
Cricket	$\frac{1}{1}$
Fire ant	$\frac{1}{3}$
Firefly	$\frac{3}{4}$
Housefly	$\frac{1}{4}$
Japanese beetle	$\frac{1}{2}$
Mosquito	$\frac{5}{8}$

1. Which of the insects is the longest?

_____

2. Shade each fraction strip to represent the lengths of a fire ant and a housefly. Which is longer, the fire ant or housefly?

_____

3. How many of the insects are longer than 0.5 inch?

_____

4. Order the lengths of a housefly, a Green June beetle, and a fire ant from the shortest to longest.

Compare Decimals and Fractions

Positive and negative rational numbers can be represented on a number line. You can use a number line to help you compare and order rational numbers.

Examples

Tutor

Fill in each ◯ with <, >, or = to make a true statement.

1. −1.2 ◯ 0.8

Graph the decimals on a number line.

$$-1.4\ -1.2\ -1\ -0.8\ -0.6\ -0.4\ -0.2\ \ 0\ \ 0.2\ 0.4\ 0.6\ 0.8\ \ 1\ \ 1.2\ 1.4$$

Since −1.2 is to the left of 0.8, −1.2 < 0.8.

2. −1.40 ◯ −1.25

Graph the decimals on a number line.

Since −1.40 is below −1.25, −1.40 < −1.25.

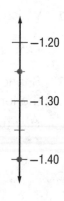

−1.20

−1.30

−1.40

3. $-\dfrac{3}{8}$ ◯ $-\dfrac{5}{16}$

Rename the fractions using the least common denominator.

$$-\frac{3}{8} = -\frac{3 \times 2}{8 \times 2} = -\frac{6}{16} \qquad\qquad -\frac{5}{16} = -\frac{5 \times 1}{16 \times 1} = -\frac{5}{16}$$

Since $-6 < -5$, $-\dfrac{6}{16} < -\dfrac{5}{16}$ and $-\dfrac{3}{8} < -\dfrac{5}{16}$.

Check

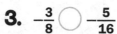

$$-\frac{6}{16} \quad -\frac{5}{16} \quad -\frac{4}{16} \quad -\frac{3}{16} \quad -\frac{2}{16} \quad -\frac{1}{16} \quad 0$$

✓

Got It? Do these problems to find out.

a. 3.1 ◯ −3.7

b. −4.5 ◯ −4.49

c. $\dfrac{9}{16}$ ◯ $\dfrac{12}{16}$

d. $-\dfrac{7}{10}$ ◯ $-\dfrac{4}{5}$

Compare and Order Rational Numbers

To compare and order rational numbers, first write them in the same form.

Examples

Fill in each ◯ with <, >, or = to make a true statement.

4. -0.51 ◯ $-\dfrac{8}{15}$

Rename $-\dfrac{8}{15}$ as a decimal. Then graph both decimals on a number line.

$$-0.5\overline{3} \quad -0.51$$

−0.6 −0.55 −5 −0.5 −0.45 −0.4

$-\dfrac{8}{15} = -0.5\overline{3}$

Since -0.51 is to the right of $-0.5\overline{3}$ on the number line, $-0.51 > -\dfrac{8}{15}$.

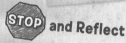

STOP and Reflect

How could you represent that −8.3 feet is deeper than −5.7 feet? Explain.

---

5. Order the set $\left\{-2.46, -2\dfrac{22}{25}, -2\dfrac{1}{10}\right\}$ from least to greatest.

Write $-2\dfrac{22}{25}$ and $-2\dfrac{1}{10}$ as decimals to the hundredths place.

$$-2\dfrac{22}{25} = -2.88 \qquad -2\dfrac{1}{10} = -2.1$$

−2.88   −2.46   −2.1

−3.00 −2.75 −2.50 −2.25 −2.00

Graph the decimals on the number line.

From least to greatest, the order is $-2\dfrac{22}{25}$, -2.46, and $-2\dfrac{1}{10}$.

Got It? Do these problems to find out.

Show your work.

Fill in each ◯ with <, >, or = to make a true statement.

e. $-3\dfrac{5}{8}$ ◯ -3.625 **f.** $\dfrac{3}{7}$ ◯ 0.413

g. Order the set $\left\{-7\dfrac{13}{20}, -7.78, -7\dfrac{17}{100}\right\}$ from greatest to least.

g. _____

Example

6. Mr. Plum's science class is growing plants under different conditions. The table shows the difference from the average for some students' plants. Order the differences from least to greatest.

Student	Difference (in.)
Ricky	$3\frac{1}{4}$
Debbie	-2.2
Suni	1.7
Leonora	$-1\frac{7}{10}$

Express each number as a decimal.

Ricky's plant: $3\frac{1}{4} = 3.25$ Debbie's plant: -2.2

Suni's plant: 1.7 Leonora's plant: $-1\frac{7}{10} = -1.7$

From least to greatest, the differences are -2.2, $-1\frac{7}{10}$, 1.7, and $3\frac{1}{4}$.

Guided Practice

Check ✓

Fill in each ◯ with <, >, or = to make a true statement. (Examples 1–4)

1. 9.7 ◯ -10.3

2. $\frac{5}{8}$ ◯ $-\frac{3}{8}$

3. -6.7 ◯ $-6\frac{7}{10}$

4. $-\frac{5}{6}$ ◯ -0.94

Show your work.

Order the following sets of numbers from least to greatest. (Example 5)

5. $\left\{-3\frac{1}{3},\ 3.3,\ -3\frac{3}{4},\ 3.5\right\}$ _____

6. $\left\{2.\overline{1},\ -2.1,\ 2\frac{1}{11},\ -2\right\}$ _____

7. **Financial Literacy** Steve recorded these amounts in his checkbook: $-\$6.50$, $\$7.00$, $-\$6.75$, and $\$7.25$. Order these amounts from least to greatest. (Example 6)

_____

8. **Building on the Essential Question** How can a number line help in ordering rational numbers?

_____

_____

Rate Yourself!

Are you ready to move on? Shade the section that applies.

YES   ?   NO

For more help, go online to access a Personal Tutor.

Tutor

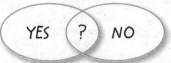 *Time to update your Foldable!*

Independent Practice

Go online for Step-by-Step Solutions

eHelp

Fill in each ⬭ **with <, >, or = to make a true statement.** (Examples 1–4)

1. $\frac{5}{4}$ ⬭ $-\frac{1}{4}$

Show your work.

2. $-6\frac{1}{3}$ ⬭ -6.375

3 $-\frac{3}{5}$ ⬭ -0.6

4. $-9\frac{2}{7}$ ⬭ -9.3

Order each set of numbers from least to greatest. (Example 5)

5 $\left\{2.8, -2\frac{3}{4}, 3\frac{1}{8}, -2.\overline{2}\right\}$ _____

6. $\left\{\frac{2}{3}, -0.6, 0.65, \frac{4}{5}\right\}$ _____

7. **Financial Literacy** The change in four stocks during a day are: $-4\frac{1}{2}$, 5.6, $-2\frac{3}{8}$, and 1.35.

   Order the changes from least to greatest. (Example 6)

   _____

8. **CCGPS Multiple Representations** Consider the inequality $-3.5 < -1.5$.
   a. **Words** Write a real-world problem that could be represented by the inequality.

   _____

   _____

   b. **Number Line** Graph -3.5 and -1.5 on the number line.

   c. **Symbols** Use the symbol > to compare -3.5 and -1.5.

   _____

9. For a STEM competition, Julienne constructed a model rocket. The rocket can reach an average height of 545 feet. Find the differences between the average height and the actual heights reached. Then write them as positive and negative rational numbers. Order the differences from least to greatest.

   _____

Trials	Actual Height (ft)
1	534.2
2	556.4
3	554.0
4	535.3

10. ![CCGPS] **Identify Structure** Fill in the diagram with appropriate numbers.

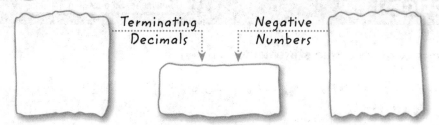

Terminating
Decimals

Negative
Numbers

🔥 **H.O.T. Problems** Higher Order Thinking

11. ![CCGPS] **Reason Inductively** Determine whether the following statement is *always*, *sometimes*, or *never* true. Give examples to justify your answer. If x and y are both greater than zero and $x > y$, then $-x < -y$.

_____

_____

12. ![CCGPS] **Justify Conclusions** Determine whether the fractions $-\frac{4}{5}$, $-\frac{4}{6}$, $-\frac{4}{7}$, and $-\frac{4}{8}$ are arranged in order from least to greatest. Explain.

_____

_____

_____

13. ![CCGPS] **Reason Abstractly** Explain why -0.33 is greater than $-0.\overline{33}$.

_____

_____

14. ![CCGPS] **Persevere with Problems** Compare the set $\left\{-0.\overline{7}, -0.\overline{67}, -\frac{7}{9}, -\frac{2}{3}\right\}$. Explain your answer.

_____

_____

✏️ **Georgia Test Practice**

15. Which of the following numbers is less than $-\frac{2}{3}$?

Ⓐ 0.6

Ⓒ $0.\overline{6}$

Ⓑ $\frac{1}{3}$

Ⓓ $-\frac{5}{6}$

Extra Practice

Fill in each ◯ with <, >, or = to make a true statement.

16. -18.6 ⬤< -18.06

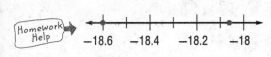

17. -4.08 ◯ -4.7

18. $-\dfrac{3}{7}$ ◯ $-\dfrac{2}{5}$

19. -3.375 ◯ $-3\dfrac{4}{10}$

20. $-5\dfrac{1}{5}$ ◯ -5.2

21. $-8\dfrac{2}{5}$ ◯ -8.3

Order the following sets of numbers from least to greatest.

22. $\left\{ \dfrac{1}{8}, -0.02\overline{5}, 0.2, -\dfrac{1}{7} \right\}$ _____

23. $\left\{ 1.25, 1\dfrac{3}{4}, 1.2\overline{5}, 1\dfrac{1}{5} \right\}$ _____

24. CCGPS **Reason Inductively** The average amount of time Brent spent in-line skating for one week was 34 minutes. During the next week, the difference between the average time and actual time spent skating was 4.2 minutes, $-5\dfrac{1}{3}$ minutes, $-2\dfrac{1}{2}$ minutes, and 3.75 minutes.

Order these differences from least to greatest. _____

Fill in each ◯ with <, >, or = to make a true statement.

25. $-4\dfrac{4}{5}$ ◯ $-4.\overline{7}$

26. $-3.2\overline{5}$ ◯ $-3.\overline{2}$

27. $-5.\overline{31}$ ◯ $-5.\overline{313}$

28. The table shows the profit or loss of the after-school snack stand.

   a. Write each profit as a positive number and each loss as a negative

      number. _____

   b. Order the numbers from least to greatest.

   _____

Day	Profit or Loss	($)
1	Profit	7.50
2	Loss	3.50
3	Loss	6.00
4	Profit	4.50

Lesson 5 Compare and Order Rational Numbers **885**

29. Which point shows the approximate location of $-\frac{1}{3}$?

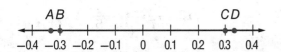

Ⓐ point A   Ⓒ point C

Ⓑ point B   Ⓓ point D

30. Which number has the least value?

Ⓕ $-2\frac{3}{10}$ Ⓗ -3.62

Ⓖ -2.47 Ⓘ $-3\frac{17}{20}$

31. Refer to the number line. Which inequality is true?

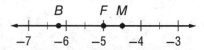

Ⓐ point B > point M

Ⓑ point F < point B

Ⓒ point M < point F

Ⓓ point F < point M

32. Which of the following numbers is the greatest?

Ⓕ -0.73 Ⓗ -0.21

Ⓖ 0.32 Ⓘ 0.19

33. Short Response Student Council's goal was to raise $50 each week for 4 weeks to have enough money for the school dance. The table shows the difference between the goal and the actual amount raised. Order these amounts from least to greatest.

Week	1	2	3	4
Difference ($)	5.50	−6.25	7.80	−2.45

Graph the points on the coordinate plane. MCC5.G.1

34. H(1, 6)

35. M(7, 0)

36. I(5, 8)

37. N(4, 9)

38. J(6, 3)

39. O(7, 5)

40. L(3, 1)

41. P(2, 2)

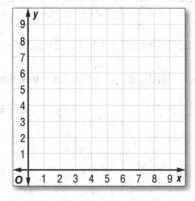

42. Graph the point on the number line that represents $\frac{3}{10}$ and label it A. MCC4.NF.6

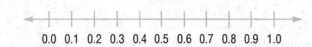

The Coordinate Plane

What You'll Learn

Scan the lesson. List two real-word scenarios where you would use the coordinate plane.

- $Q1 = X + Y +$
- $Q2 = X - Y +$
- $Q3 = X - Y -$
- $Q4 = X + Y -$

 Real-World Link

Maps The map shows the layout of a small town. The locations of buildings are described in respect to the town hall. Each unit on the grid represents one block.

1. Describe the location of the barber shop in relation to the town hall. _____

   _____

2. What building is located 7 blocks east and 5 blocks north of the town hall? _____

3. Violeta is at the library. Describe how many blocks and in what direction she should travel to get to the supermarket. _____

   _____

4. Town Hall and the bank are both located on the same vertical number line. The number 0 represents the location of Town Hall on the number line. What number represents the location of the bank? ☐

 Essential Question

HOW are integers and absolute value used in real-world situations?

Vocab **Vocabulary**

quadrants

CCGPS **Common Core GPS**

Content Standards
MCC6.NS.6, MCC6.NS.6b, MCC6.NS.6c

Mathematical Practices
1, 3, 4, 5, 7

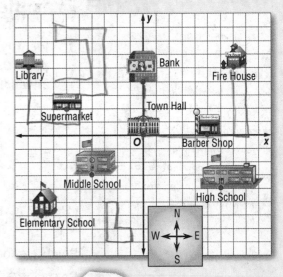

Reflect over
Y-Axis:
Keep the
same Y-
coordinate,
X is opp.

X-Axis:
Keep X: Same
Y is Opp

Ordered Pairs

A point located on the
x-axis will have a
y-coordinate of 0. A point
located on the y-axis will
have an x-coordinate of 0.
Points located on an axis are
not in any quadrant.

Reflect over
X-Axis:

$(-3, -2)$

$(-77, -123)$

$(1, 1)$

Identify Points and Ordered Pairs

A coordinate plane is formed when the x-axis and y-axis intersect at their zero points. The axes separate the coordinate plane into four regions called **quadrants**.

You can use the location on the plane or use the x-coordinates and y-coordinates to identify the quadrant in which a point is located.

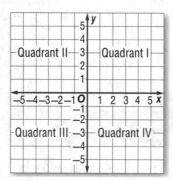

Quadrant	x-coordinate	y-coordinate	Example
I	positive	positive	(2, 5)
II	negative	positive	(−2, 5)
III	negative	negative	(−2, −5)
IV	positive	negative	(2, −5)

Examples

Tutor

1. Identify the ordered pair that names point C. Then identify the quadrant in which it is located.

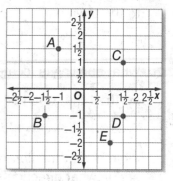

Step 1 Start at the origin. Move right on the x-axis. The x-coordinate of point C is $1\frac{1}{2}$.

Step 2 Move up the y-axis. The y-coordinate is 1.

Point C is located at $\left(1\frac{1}{2}, 1\right)$. Both coordinates are positive.

So, point C is in Quadrant I.

- -

2. Identify the point located at $\left(-1\frac{1}{2}, -1\right)$. Then identify the quadrant in which it is located.

Step 1 Start at the origin. Move left on the x-axis. The x-coordinate is $-1\frac{1}{2}$.

Step 2 Move down the y-axis. The y-coordinate is −1.

Point B is located at $\left(-1\frac{1}{2}, -1\right)$. Both coordinates are negative.

So, point B is in Quadrant III.

> **Got It?** Do these problems to find out.

   a. Identify the ordered pair that names point A. Then identify the quadrant in which it is located.

   b. Identify the point located at (1, −2). Then identify the quadrant in which it is located.

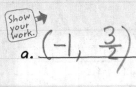

a. $\left(-1, \dfrac{3}{2}\right)$

b. E, Q4

Reflections on the Coordinate Plane

You can use what you know about number lines and opposites to compare locations on the coordinate plane. Consider the number line and coordinate plane below.
The number line shows that −4 and 4 are opposites.

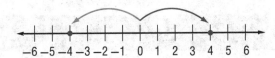

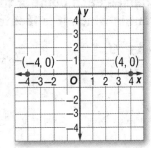

The coordinate plane shows that the points (−4, 0) and (4, 0) are the same distance from the *y*-axis in opposite directions. So, they are *reflected* across the *y*-axis. Notice that the *y*-coordinates did not change and that the *x*-coordinates are opposites.

Example

 Tutor

3. **Name the ordered pair that is a reflection of (−3, 2) across the *x*-axis.**

To reflect across the *x*-axis, keep the same *x*-coordinate, −3, and take the opposite of the *y*-coordinate. The opposite of +2 is −2.

So, (−3, 2) reflected across the *x*-axis is located at (−3, −2).

c. (1, 4)

d. (−2, −5)

> **Got It?** Do these problems to find out.

Name the ordered pair that is a reflection of each point across the *x*-axis.

   c. (1, −4)   **d.** (−2, 5)   **e.** (−3, −1)

e. (−3, 1)

Example

4. Kendall is building a square fence. She places fence posts at the locations indicated on the grid. What is the location of the post that reflects (−4, 4) across the y-axis?

To reflect across the y-axis, keep the same y-coordinate, 4.

The opposite of the x-coordinate, −4, is 4.

So, (−4, 4) reflected across the y-axis is (4, 4).

Got It? Do this problem to find out.

Show your work.

f. _____

f. Kendall also placed a fence post at (−4, −4). What is the location of the post that reflects (−4, −4) across the y-axis?

Guided Practice

Identify the ordered pair that names each point or the name of each point. Then identify the quadrant in which it is located. (Examples 1 and 2)

1. T

Q3

2. $\left(-1\frac{1}{2}, 0\right)$

None

3. $\left(-2, 2\frac{1}{2}\right)$

Q2

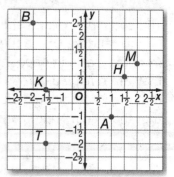

4. Refer to the diagram of a school. (Examples 3 and 4)

   a. What is located at the reflection of (−3, −4) across the y-axis. What are the coordinates of this location?

   (3, -4)

   b. What is located at the reflection of the science labs across the x-axis? What are the coordinates of this location?

   (-3, -2), (-3, 2)

5.  **Building on the Essential Question** How are number lines and the coordinate plane related?

   You use the opposite.

Rate Yourself!

Are you ready to move on? Shade the section that applies.

YES   ?   NO

For more help, go online to access a Personal Tutor.

Independent Practice

Go online for Step-by-Step Solutions

Identify the ordered pair that names each point. Then identify the quadrant in which it is located. (Example 1)

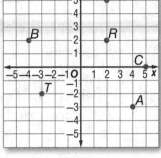

1. R

$Q-1$

Show your work.

2. G

_____

3. B

_____

4. T

_____

 5. C

_____

6. A

_____

Identify the name of each point. Then identify the quadrant in which it is located. (Example 2)

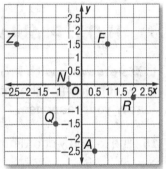

 7. (−2.5, 1.5)

_____

8. (1, 1.5)

_____

9. (0.5, −2.5)

_____

10. (2, −0.5)

_____

11. (−0.5, 0)

_____

12. (−1, −1.5)

_____

13. CCGPS **Use Math Tools** Refer to the map of Wonderland Park. (Examples 3 and 4)

a. What is located closest to the origin?

_____

b. Liza is standing at (2, 4). What is located at the reflection of (2, 4) across the *x*-axis? What are the coordinates of this location?

_____

c. What is located at the reflection of (3, 1) across the *y*-axis? What are the coordinates of this

location? _____

d. The Pipeline Plunge is reflected across the *x*-axis. What are the coordinates of its new

location? _____

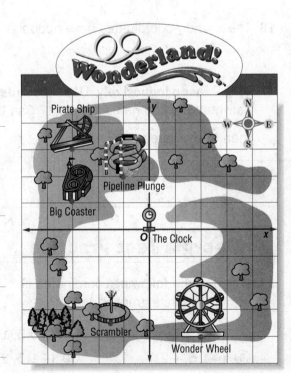

14. CCGPS **Identify Structure** Fill in the graphic organizer below. Consider the point (−3, 2).

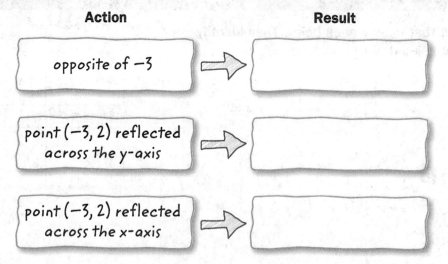

Action | Result

opposite of −3 ⇒

point (−3, 2) reflected across the y-axis ⇒

point (−3, 2) reflected across the x-axis ⇒

H.O.T. Problems Higher Order Thinking

CCGPS **Persevere with Problems** Without graphing, identify the quadrant(s) for which each of the following statements is true for any point (*x*, *y*). Justify your response.

15. The *x*- and *y*-coordinates have the same sign.

_____

_____

16. The *x*- and *y*-coordinates have opposite signs. _____

_____

17. CCGPS **Reason Inductively** Does the order of the numbers in an ordered pair matter when naming a point? Can that point be represented by more

than one ordered pair? _____

_____

_____

Georgia Test Practice

18. Which of the following coordinates lie within the circle graphed below?

Ⓐ (−1, 1.5)   Ⓒ (−0.5, 1)

Ⓑ (−1.5, −2)   Ⓓ (−1.5, 2)

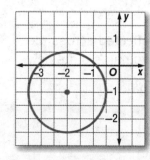

892 **Chapter 12** Integers and the Coordinate Plane

Extra Practice

Identify the ordered pair that names each point. Then identify the quadrant in which it is located.

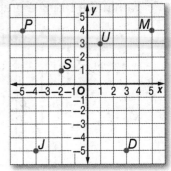

19. *U*

(1, 3); I

Both numbers are
positive so it is in
the first quadrant.

20. *D*

_____

_____

21. *S*

_____

_____

22. *P*

_____

23. *J*

_____

24. *M*

_____

Identify the name of each point. Then identify the quadrant in which it is located.

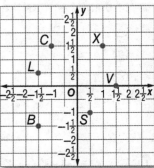

25. $\left(-1\frac{1}{2}, \frac{1}{2}\right)$

_____

26. $\left(1, 1\frac{1}{2}\right)$

_____

27. $\left(\frac{1}{2}, -1\right)$

_____

28. $\left(1\frac{1}{2}, 0\right)$

_____

29. $\left(-1\frac{1}{2}, -1\frac{1}{2}\right)$

_____

30. $\left(-1, 1\frac{1}{2}\right)$

_____

31. CCGPS **Model with Mathematics** Luke is making a model of a park. He has the basketball court drawn on his model.

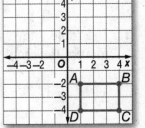

a. The swing set is located at the reflection of point *B* across the *x*-axis. What ordered pair describes the location of the swing set?

_____

b. The slide is located at the reflection of point *C* across the *x*-axis. What ordered pair describes the location of the slide?

_____

c. A water fountain is located at the reflection of point *D* across the *y*-axis. What ordered pair describes the location of the water fountain?

_____

32. Which of the following coordinates lie within the triangle graphed below?

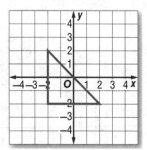

Ⓐ (1, 0) Ⓒ (−1, 2)

Ⓑ (−2, −3) Ⓓ (−1, −1)

33. Identify the point for the ordered pair (−3, 5).

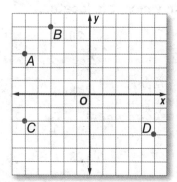

Ⓕ Point A Ⓗ Point C

Ⓖ Point B Ⓘ Point D

34. Which ordered pair represents the reflection of point J across the y-axis?

Ⓐ (−4, −2)

Ⓑ (4, 4)

Ⓒ (4, 2)

Ⓓ (2, 2)

Common Core Review

Represent the set of numbers as decimals on the number line. MCC4.NF.6

35. $\left\{3\frac{1}{10}, 2\frac{7}{10}, 2\frac{9}{10}\right\}$

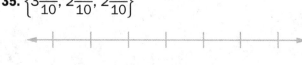

36. $\left\{5\frac{3}{10}, 5\frac{1}{10}, 5\right\}$

37. The table shows how many magazines three co-workers sold in one month. How many magazines did they sell in total? MCC4.NBT.4

Name	Number of Magazines
Julie	12
Dion	0
Calvin	7

38. Draw a line of symmetry on the figure shown. MCC4.G.3

Graph on the Coordinate Plane

What You'll Learn

Scan the lesson. Predict two things you will learn about graphing on the coordinate plane.

- _____
  _____

- _____
  _____

 Essential Question

HOW are integers and absolute value used in real-world situations?

 Common Core GPS

Content Standards
MCC6.NS.6, MCC6.NS.6b, MCC6.NS.6c, MCC6.NS.8

Mathematical Practices
1, 2, 3, 4, 7

 Real-World Link

Scavenger Hunt Maria hid the clues to a scavenger hunt for her hiking club. Use the map to show where she hid the clues. Identify the location of each clue.

1. The first clue is hidden near a tree. What ordered pair describes its location?

   $(4, 2)$

2. Maria hid the next clue at a location reflected across the y-axis. Where is it hidden?

   $(-4, 2)$

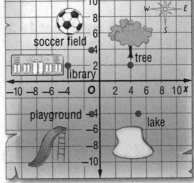

3. She walks 3 blocks east and 2 blocks north to place the next clue. Where is it hidden?

   $(-1, 4)$

4. The next clue is at a location reflected across the x-axis. Where is it hidden?

   _____

5. Maria hid the next clue under a rock by the lake. How many blocks east did she walk to the lake?

   _____

6. The final clue tells the hikers to walk 5 blocks north and three blocks east to find the prize. What ordered pair describes the location of the prize?

   _____

Graph Ordered Pairs

To graph an ordered pair, draw a dot at the point that corresponds to the coordinates.

Examples

Tutor

1. Graph point *M* at (−3, 5).

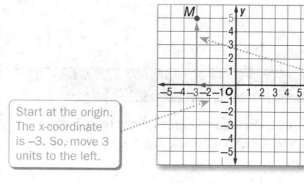

Start at the origin. The x-coordinate is −3. So, move 3 units to the left.

Next, since the y-coordinate is 5, move 5 units up. Draw a dot.

2. Graph point *N* at $\left(-2\frac{1}{2}, -3\frac{1}{2}\right)$.

The x-coordinate $-2\frac{1}{2}$ is between −2 and −3.

Start at the origin and move $2\frac{1}{2}$ units left.

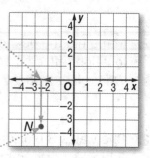

The y-coordinate $-3\frac{1}{2}$ is between −3 and −4.

Next, move $3\frac{1}{2}$ units down. Draw a dot.

Got It? Do these problems to find out.

Graph and label each point on the coordinate plane below.

   a. P(−2, 4)

   b. Q(0, −4)

   c. $R\left(-\frac{1}{2}, -2\frac{1}{2}\right)$

   d. S(4.5, 1)

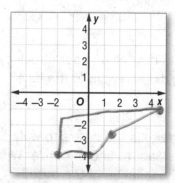

Graph Reflections on the Coordinate Plane

You can graph points that are reflected across the *x*- and *y*-axes. Remember that points reflected across the *x*-axis will have the same *x*-coordinates and their *y*-coordinates will be opposites. Points reflected across the *y*-axis will have the same *y*-coordinates and their *x*-coordinates will be opposites.

Examples

3. **Graph A(2, −4). Then graph its reflection across the x-axis.**

Graph point *A*.

To reflect across the *x*-axis, keep the same *x*-coordinate, 2, and take the opposite of the *y*-coordinate.

The opposite of −4 is 4.

So, point *A* reflected across the *x*-axis is located at point A′(2, 4). Graph point A′.

4. **Graph B(−1.5, 3). Then graph its reflection across the y-axis.**

Graph point *B*.

To reflect across the *y*-axis, keep the same *y*-coordinate and take the opposite of the *x*-coordinate.

The opposite of −1.5 is 1.5.

So, point *B* reflected across the *y*-axis is point B′(1.5, 3).

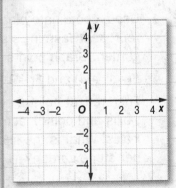

Got It? Do these problems to find out.

e. Graph C(1, 5). Then graph its reflection across the *x*-axis.

f. Graph $D\left(2, 3\frac{1}{2}\right)$. Then graph its reflection across the *y*-axis.

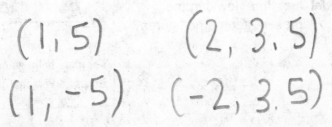

$$(1, 5) \qquad (2, 3.5)$$
$$(1, -5) \qquad (-2, 3.5)$$

Tutor

5. Mr. Martin is using a coordinate plane to design a logo. He graphs points at (2, 4) and (2, −2). He reflects (2, −2) across the y-axis. Then he reflects the new point across the x-axis. What figure is Mr. Martin using for his logo?

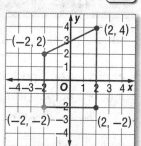

Graph (2, 4) and (2, −2). (2, −2) reflected across the y-axis is (−2, −2).
Graph (−2, −2). (−2, −2) reflected across the x-axis is (−2, 2).
Graph (−2, 2).

So, the figure is a trapezoid.

 Got It? Do this problem to find out.

9. _____

g. Ms. Shaull is drawing a map of the school. Her room is at (−3, 4) and the gym is at (3, 4). The library is a reflection of (3, 4) across the x-axis. This point is reflected across the y-axis to graph the office. What figure is graphed on the map?

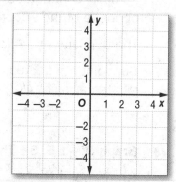

Guided Practice

Check

1. Use a coordinate plane to represent Jasmine's stone garden. Graph points E(−1, −4) and F$\left(-3\frac{1}{2}, 4\right)$.
Then reflect point E across the y-axis and point F across the x-axis. What is the shape of her stone garden? (Examples 1–5)

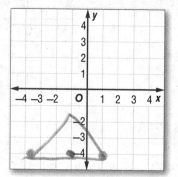

Show your work.

Rate Yourself!

How confident are you about graphing on the coordinate plane? Check the box that applies.

2. **Building on the Essential Question** How can the coordinate plane be used to represent geometric figures?

For more help, go online to access a Personal Tutor.

Tutor

Independent Practice

Go online for Step-by-Step Solutions
eHelp

Graph and label each point on the coordinate plane to the right.
(Examples 1 and 2)

1. $T(0, 0)$

2. $D(2, 1)$

3. $K(-3.25, 3)$

4. $N\left(0, -1\frac{1}{2}\right)$

5. $F(-4.5, 0)$

6. $A\left(-3\frac{1}{2}, -3\right)$

7. $L(2.5, -3.5)$

8. $S\left(4, 2\frac{1}{2}\right)$

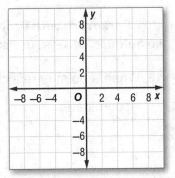

9. Graph $U(3.5, -3)$ on the coordinate plane to the right.
   Then graph its reflection across the x-axis. (Example 3)

10. Graph $B(-7, 6)$ on the coordinate plane on the right.
    Then graph its reflection across the x-axis. (Example 3)

11. Graph $R(-2, 5)$ on the coordinate plane to the right.
    Then graph its reflection across the y-axis. (Example 4)

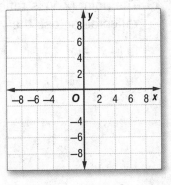

12. Amelia is drawing a map of the park. She graphs the entrance at
    $(2, -3)$. She reflects $(2, -3)$ across the y-axis. Then Amelia reflects
    the new point across the x-axis. What figure is graphed on the map?
    (Example 5)

    _____

13. A point is reflected across the y-axis. The new point is located at
    $(-4.25, -1.75)$. Write the ordered pair that represents the

    original point. _____

14. **CCGPS** **Model with Mathematics** A point is reflected across the x-axis. The
    new point is $(-7.5, 6)$. What is the distance between the two points?

    _____

15 On a coordinate plane, draw triangle *ABC* with vertices *A*(−1, −1), *B*(3, −1), and *C*(−1, 2). Find the area of the triangle in square units.

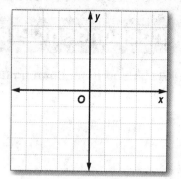

_____

16. The points (4, 3) and (−4, 0) are graphed on a coordinate plane. The point (4, 3) is reflected across the *x*- and *y*-axes. If all four points are connected, what figure is graphed?

_____

 H.O.T. Problems Higher Order Thinking

17. CCGPS **Identify Structure** Three vertices of a quadrilateral are (−1 −1), (1, 2), and (5, −1). What are the coordinates of two vertices that will form

two different parallelograms? _____

CCGPS **Persevere with Problems** Determine whether each statement is *sometimes*, *always*, or *never* true. Give an example or a counterexample.

18. When a point is reflected across the *y*-axis, the new point has a negative

x-coordinate. _____

_____

_____

19. The point (*x*, *y*) is reflected across the *x*-axis. Then the new point is reflected across the *y*-axis. The location of the point after both reflections

is (−*x*, −*y*). _____

_____

_____

Georgia Test Practice

20. What are the coordinates of *Y*′ after *Y*(−3.5, 5) is reflected across the *x*-axis?

Ⓐ (3.5, −5)　　　Ⓒ (5, −3.5)

Ⓑ (−3.5, −5)　　Ⓓ (3.5, 5)

Extra Practice

Graph and label each point on the coordinate plane to the right.

21. $B(-3, 4)$ *The x-coordinate is −3. The y-coordinate is 4.*

22. $D(-1.5, 2.5)$

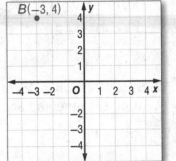

23. $A\left(4\frac{3}{4}, -1\frac{1}{4}\right)$

24. $J\left(2\frac{1}{2}, -2\frac{1}{2}\right)$

25. $C(1, 4.5)$

26. $F(-4, -3.5)$

27. $G\left(3\frac{1}{2}, 3\right)$

28. $H\left(-3, -1\frac{1}{2}\right)$

29. Graph $N(1, -3)$ on the coordinate plane to the right.
Then graph its reflection across the *y*-axis.

30. Graph $H(7, 8)$ on the coordinate plane on the right.
Then graph its reflection across the *x*-axis.

31. Graph $F(-6, 5.5)$ on the coordinate plane to the right.
Then graph its reflection across the *x*-axis.

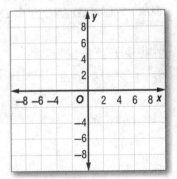

32. Marcus is drawing a plan for his vegetable garden. He graphs one
corner at $(-7.5, 2)$ and one corner at $(7.5, 2)$. He reflects $(-7.5, 2)$
across the *x*-axis. Then Marcus reflects the new point across the
y-axis. What shape is the vegetable garden?

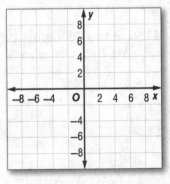

_____

33. A point is reflected across the *x*-axis. The new point is located at
$(4.75, -2.25)$. Write the ordered pair that represents the original point.

_____

34. 🅒🅒🅖🅟🅢 **Model with Mathematics** A point is reflected across the
x-axis. The new point is $(5, -3.5)$. What is the distance between
the two points?

_____

Lesson 7 Graph on the Coordinate Plane   **901**

Georgia Test Practice

35. What are the coordinates of B(−0.5, 2) after it is reflected across the y-axis?

Ⓐ (0.5, −2) Ⓒ (2, −0.5)

Ⓑ (−0.5, −2) Ⓓ (0.5, 2)

36. What figure is made when the points (−1, 2), (2, 2), (2, −1), and (−1, −1) are connected?

Ⓕ triangle Ⓗ trapezoid

Ⓖ rectangle Ⓘ square

37. **Short Response** What are the coordinates of point H after it is reflected across the x-axis, and then reflected across the y-axis? _____

_____

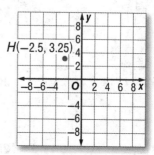

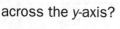 **Common Core Review**

Multiply. MCC4.NBT.5

38. $1 \times 1 \times 1 =$ _____

39. $3 \times 3 \times 3 =$ _____

40. $6 \times 6 \times 6 =$ _____

41. Use the geometric pattern below to find the number of squares in the next figure. MCC4.OA.5

_____

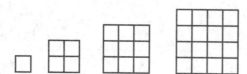

42. Alexa saved a total of $210. Each week she saved the same amount of money. She has been saving for 7 weeks. How much money did Alexa save each week? MCC5.NBT.6

_____

WHAT is the relationship between coordinates and distance?

CCGPS Content Standards
MCC6.NS.8
Mathematical Practices
1, 3, 4

Maps Taylor's house and school are each shown on the map. What is the distance between the two points?

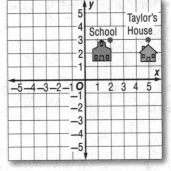

What do you know? _____

_____

_____

What do you need to find? _____

_____

_____

Investigation 1

Find the distance between Taylor's house and the school.

Step 1 Find the coordinates of Taylor's house.

_____

Step 2 Find the coordinates of the school.

_____

Step 3 Draw a line between the points. The line is horizontal, so the *y*-coordinates are the same.

Step 4 To find the distance, count the number of units between the *x*-coordinates.

Location	*x*-coordinate
house	
school	

So, there are ☐ units between Taylor's house and the school.

Investigation 2

Find the distance between point *A* and point *B* on the coordinate plane.

Step 1   Determine the coordinates for point *A*.

_____

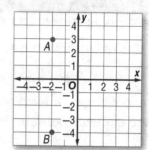

Step 2   Determine the coordinates for point *B*.

_____

Step 3   Draw a line between the points. The line is
vertical, so the *x*-coordinates are the same.

Step 4   Count the number of units between each
y-coordinate and the *x*-axis.

Point	y-coordinate	Distance from x-axis
A		
B		

Step 5   To find the distance between the two points,
add the distance from the *x*-axis to each point.

$$\boxed{} + \boxed{} = \boxed{}$$

So, the distance between point *A* and point *B* is $\boxed{}$ units.

 **Collaborate**

**CCGPS Model with Mathematics Work with a partner. Draw a line between
each pair of points. Find the distance between each pair of points.**

1. _____

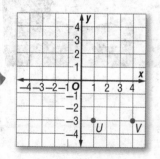

2. _____

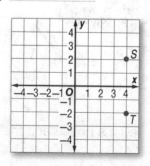

Collaborate

CCGPS Model with Mathematics Work with a partner. Plot each pair of points on the coordinate plane. Find the distance between each pair of points.

3. C(−3, −6), D(−3, −1) —5 units

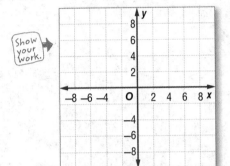

Show your work.

4. E(−6, −2), F(1, −2) 7 Units

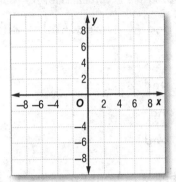

5. G(1, −4), H(4, −4) 3 units

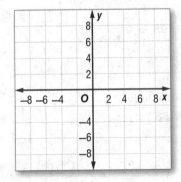

6. K(3, −4), L(3, 2) 6 units

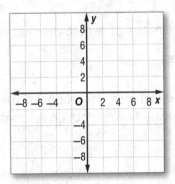

7. M(5, 1), N(−1, 1) —6 Units

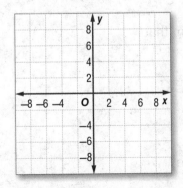

8. O$\left(5\frac{1}{2}, 6\right)$, P$\left(5\frac{1}{2}, 2\right)$ —4 Units

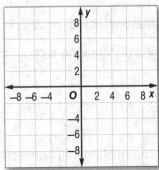

With a partner to complete the table below. Use your answers from Exercises 3–6. The first one is done for you.

Exercise	Coordinates Used	Horizontal or Vertical Line?	Same or Different Quadrant?	Line Length
2	2 and −2	horizontal	different	4 units
9. 3	and			
10. 4	and			
11. 5	and			
12. 6	and			

13. Compare your answers from Exercises 11 and 12. What is the relationship between the coordinates used and the length of each line?

_____

_____

_____

14. Name the coordinates of two points that have the same x-coordinates and are 8 units apart. _____

15. (CCGPS) **Reason Inductively** Use absolute value to write a rule for determining the distance between two points on a coordinate plane that have the same x-coordinate. _____

_____

_____

 Reflect

16. (CCGPS) **Model with Mathematics** Write and solve a real-world problem that involves determining distance on a coordinate plane. _____

_____

_____

17. (Inquiry) WHAT is the relationship between coordinates and distance?

_____

_____

Polygons on the Coordinate Plane

What You'll Learn

Scan the rest of the lesson. List two headings you would use to make an outline of the lesson.

- _____

- _____

 Essential Question

HOW does measurement help you solve problems in everyday life?

CCGPS **Common Core GPS**

Content Standards
MCC6.G.1, MCC6.G.3, MCC6.NS.8

Mathematical Practices
1, 2, 3, 4, 5, 7

 ## Real-World Link

Maps Graph points on a coordinate plane to draw a map of an outdoor stadium. Complete the table to identify each shape.

Location	Vertices	Shape
Stage	(2, 6), (2, 9), (6, 9), (6, 6), (5, 5), (3, 5)	
Bleachers	(7, 5), (7, 9), (9, 9), (9, 5)	
Concession Stand	(5, 2), (5, 4), (7, 4), (7, 2)	

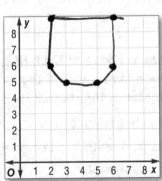

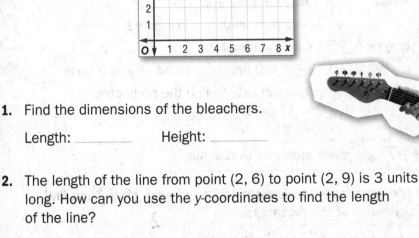

1. Find the dimensions of the bleachers.

   Length: _____   Height: _____

2. The length of the line from point (2, 6) to point (2, 9) is 3 units long. How can you use the y-coordinates to find the length of the line?

   _____

Find Perimeter

You can use the coordinates of a figure to find its dimensions by finding the distance between two points. To find the distance between two points with the same *x*-coordinates, subtract their *y*-coordinates. To find the distance between two points with the same *y*-coordinates, subtract their *x*-coordinates.

Examples

1. A rectangle has vertices A(2, 8), B(7, 8), C(7, 5), and D(2, 5). Use the coordinates to find the length of each side. Then find the perimeter of the rectangle.

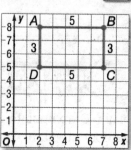

Width: Find the length of the horizontal lines.

$\overline{AB}$ is 5 units long. $\overline{CD}$ is 5 units long.

Length: Find the length of the vertical lines.

$\overline{BC}$ is 3 units long. $\overline{DA}$ is 3 units long.

Add the lengths of each side to find the perimeter.

$5 + 5 + 3 + 3 = 16$ units

So, rectangle ABCD has a perimeter of 16 units.

Perimeter and Area

Remember that perimeter is the distance around a closed figure. Area is the number of square units needed to cover the surface enclosed by a geometric figure.

2. Rectangle ABCD has vertices A(2, 1), B(2, 5), C(4, 5), and D(4, 1). Use the coordinates to find the length of each side. Then find the perimeter of the rectangle.

Width: Subtract *y*-coordinates.

AB: $5 - 1 = 4$ units   CD: $5 - 1 = 4$ units

Length: Subtract *x*-coordinates.

AD: $4 - 2 = 2$ units   BC: $4 - 2 = 2$ units

Add the lengths of each side to find the perimeter.

$4 + 2 + 4 + 2 = 12$ units

Show your work.

Got It? Do these problems to find out.

a. $\underline{\quad 8 \quad u^2}$

b. $\underline{\qquad\qquad}$

Use the coordinates to find the length of each side. Then find the perimeter of the rectangle.

a. E(3, 6), F(3, 8), G(7, 8), H(7, 6)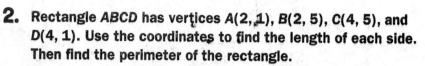

b. I(1, 4), J(1, 9), K(8, 9), L(8, 4)

Example

3. Each grid square on the zoo map has a length of 200 feet. Find the total distance, in feet, around the zoo.

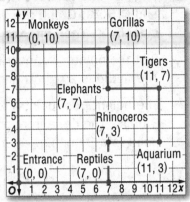

When *x*-coordinates are the same, subtract the *y*-coordinates. When *y*-coordinates are the same, subtract the *x*-coordinates.

$10 + 7 + 3 + 4 + 4 + 4 + 3 + 7 = 42$ units

Multiply by 200 feet to find the total distance.

$42 \times 200 = 8{,}400$ feet. The total distance is 8,400 feet.

Got It? Do this problem to find out.

c. The coordinates of the vertices of a garden are (0, 1), (0, 4), (8, 4), and (8, 1). If each unit represents 12 inches, find the perimeter in inches of the garden.

Show your work.

c. _____

Find Area

You can find the area of a figure that has been drawn grid paper or graphed on the coordinate plane.

Example

4. Find the area of the figure in square units.

The figure can be separated into a rectangle and a trapezoid.

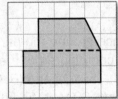

Area of rectangle

$A = \ell \times w$

$A = 5 \times 2$ or 10

Area of trapezoid

$A = \frac{1}{2}h(b_1 + b_2)$

$A = \frac{1}{2}(2)(3 + 4)$ or 7

So, the area of the figure is 10 + 7 or 17 square units.

Got It? Do this problem to find out.

d. Find the area, in square units, of the figure at the right.

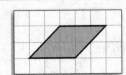

d. _____

$$a^2 + b^2 = c^2$$

$$3^2 + 3^2$$

$$18 \neq 9$$

Show your work.

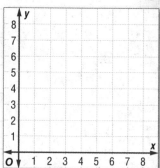
e. _____

5. A figure has vertices $A(2, 5)$, $B(2, 8)$, and $C(5, 8)$. Graph the figure and classify it. Then find the area.

Plot the points. Connect the vertices. The figure is a right triangle.

The height from point A to point B is 3 units. The base from point B to point C is 3 units.

$A = \frac{1}{2}bh$ Area formula of a triangle

$A = \frac{1}{2}(3)(3)$ Replace b with 3 and h with 3.

$A = 4.5$ Multiply.

Triangle ABC has an area of 4.5 square units.

Got It? Do this problem to find out.

Graph the figure and classify it. Then find the area.

e. $A(3, 3)$, $B(3, 6)$, $C(5, 6)$, $D(8, 3)$

Guided Practice

Check

Use the coordinates to find the length of each side of the rectangle. Then find the perimeter. (Examples 1 and 2)

1. $L(3, 3)$, $M(3, 5)$, $N(7, 5)$, $P(7, 3)$

2. $P(3, 0)$, $Q(6, 0)$, $R(6, 7)$, $S(3, 7)$

Show your work.

3. Mrs. Piel is building a fence around the perimeter of her yard for her dog. The coordinates of the vertices of the yard are $(0, 0)$, $(0, 10)$, $(5, 10)$, and $(5, 0)$. If each grid square has a length of 100 feet, find the amount of wire, in feet, needed for the fence. What is the shape of her yard? (Example 3) _____

4. **Building on the Essential Question** How can coordinates help you to find the area of figures on the coordinate plane? _____

_____

Rate Yourself!

How well do you understand polygons on the coordinate plane? Circle the image that applies.

Clear   Somewhat   Not So
            Clear   Clear

For more help, go online to access a Personal Tutor.

Tutor

Independent Practice

Go online for Step-by-Step Solutions

Use the coordinates to find the length of each side of the rectangle. Then find the perimeter. (Examples 1 and 2)

1 $D(1, 2)$, $E(1, 7)$, $F(4, 7)$, $G(4, 2)$

 Show your work. _____

2. $Q(0, 0)$, $R(4, 0)$, $S(4, 4)$, $T(0, 4)$

_____

3. Natasha is building a rectangular picture frame for her favorite photo. The coordinates of the vertices of the frame are (0, 0), (0, 8), (12, 8), and (12, 0). Each grid square has a length of 3 centimeters. Find the amount of wood, in centimeters, needed for the perimeter. (Example 3)

_____

_____

Find the area of each figure in square units. (Example 4)

4. _____

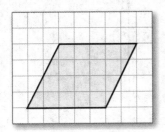

5. _____

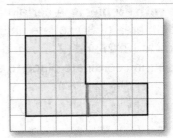

Graph each figure and classify it. Then find the area. (Example 5)

6. $R(3, -2)$, $S(7, -2)$, $T(8, -6)$, $V(1, -6)$

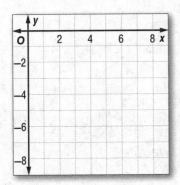

7 $A(-3, -4)$, $B(-3, 5)$, $C(2, 5)$, $D(2, -4)$

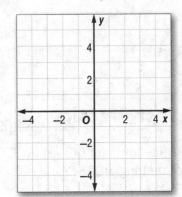

8. **CCGPS** **Use Math Tools** A rectangle has a perimeter of 20 units. The coordinates of three of the vertices are (0, 0), (6, 0), and (6, 4) as shown on the graph.

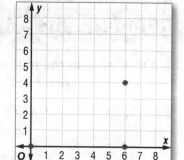

a. What is the coordinate of the missing vertex?

_____

b. Plot points (6, 6) and (2, 4). Connect these points to create a composite figure.

c. What is the area of the composite figure? _____

H.O.T. Problems Higher Order Thinking

9. **CCGPS** **Use Math Tools** Draw a rectangle on a coordinate plane that has a perimeter of 16 units. Label all of the vertices with the coordinates. Then find the area of the rectangle. _____

_____

10. **CCGPS** **Persevere with Problems** A certain rectangle has a perimeter of 22 units and an area of 30 square units. Two of the vertices have coordinates at (2, 2) and (2, 7). Find the two missing coordinates. Use the coordinate plane to support your answer.

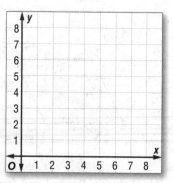

_____

_____

11. **CCGPS** **Identify Structure** Explain the steps you would use to find the perimeter of a rectangle using the coordinates of the vertices.

_____

_____

_____

_____

_____

Georgia Test Practice

12. Rectangle QRST has vertices Q(3, 2), R(3, 8), S(7, 8), and T(7, 2). What is the perimeter of rectangle QRST?

Ⓐ 14 units

Ⓑ 15 units

Ⓒ 18 units

Ⓓ 20 units

Name _____ My Homework _____

Extra Practice

Use the coordinates to find the length of each side of the rectangle. Then find the perimeter.

13. A(5, 2), B(5, 4), C(2, 4), D(2, 2)

AB = 2 units, BC = 3 units, CD = 2 units, DA = 3 units; 10 units

14. M(1, 1), N(1, 9), P(7, 9), Q(7, 1)

15. **CCGPS Reason Abstractly** Andre is creating a border around his rectangular patio with paver bricks. The coordinates of the vertices of the patio are (1, 5), (6, 5), (6, 1), and (1, 1). Each grid square has a length of 3 feet.

Find the amount of brick, in feet, needed for the perimeter. _____

Find the area of each figure in square units.

16. _____

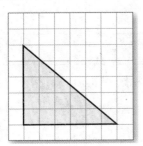

17. _____

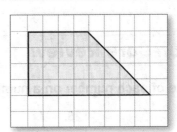

Graph each figure and classify it. Then find the area.

18. G(−4, 1), H(4, 1), I(3, −3), J(−1, −3)

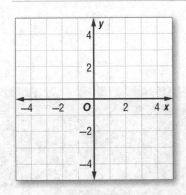

19. X(−7, 2), Y(−7, 6), Z(−4, 2)

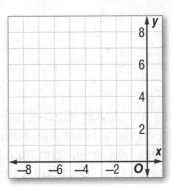

Copy and Solve Graph each figure and classify it. Then find the area.

20. K(−2, 2), L(3, 2), M(2, −2), N(−3, −2)

21. Q(−2, 4), R(0, −2), S(−4, −2)

Copyright © The McGraw-Hill Companies, Inc.

Lesson 8 Polygons on the Coordinate Plane **913**

22. Which is *not* a characteristic of the figure with vertices at coordinates $A(8, 5)$, $B(7, 2)$, $C(4, 2)$, and $D(2, 5)$?

Ⓐ one set of parallel sides

Ⓑ four vertices

Ⓒ two sets of parallel sides

Ⓓ two acute angles

23. Short Response A triangle on a coordinate plane has vertices with coordinates of (2, 2), (8, 2), and (8, 9). Each grid square has a length of one foot. Find the area of the triangle in square feet.

24. Short Response Each grid square represents one square centimeter.

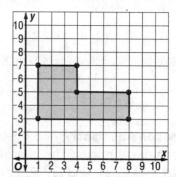

Use the coordinates of the vertices to find the area of the figure.

Graph the opposite of each number on a number line. MCC6.NS.6a

25. 0

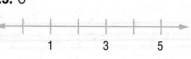

26. −7

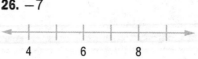

27. 5

28. Graph 2 and 9. Then use the number line to find the distance between

9 and 2. MCC6.NS.8, MCC6.NS.5 _____

29. John and his dad are playing catch on the football field. John is standing on the 10-yard line. His dad is standing on the 25-yard line. How far is John from his dad? If his dad moves to the 20-yard line, what is the distance between them now? MCC4.OA.3

21ST CENTURY CAREER
in Art

Scientific Illustrator

If you are artistic and have a strong interest in science, you should think about a career as a scientific illustrator. Scientific illustrators combine their artistic abilities with their scientific backgrounds to draw scientifically accurate images. Karen Carr, a wildlife and natural history artist, has artwork in scientific publications, museums, and zoos. To draw animals that are extinct, she examines fossils, talks to scientists, and uses measurements and proportions from scientific literature.

Explore college and careers at ccr.mcgraw-hill.com

Is This the Career for You?

Are you interested in a career as a scientific illustrator? Take some of the following courses in high school.

◆ Algebra
◆ Biology
◆ Geometry
◆ Life/Figure Drawing
◆ Physics

Find out how math relates to a career in Art.

You be the Scientfic Illustrator!

Use the information in the table to solve each problem. Write in simplest form.

1. Write the length and height of an Argentinosaurus as decimals. Use bar notation if necessary.

   _____

2. How much taller was a Velociraptor than a Microraptor? Write your answer as a

   decimal. _____

3. Which is greater, the height of the Argentinosaurus or the length of the

   Camptosaurus? _____

4. How much longer was a Camptosaurus than a Velociraptor? Plot your answer on the number line.

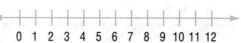

5. Compare the heights of all four dinosaurs. Order them from least to greatest.

   _____

6. An artist is creating a mural in which a Microraptor is $1\frac{1}{2}$ times the actual size. What is the length of the dinosaur in the

   mural? _____

Dinosaur Measurements		
Dinosaur	Length (ft)	Height (ft)
Argentinosaurus	$114\frac{5}{6}$	$24\frac{1}{10}$
Camptosaurus	$16\frac{2}{5}$	$11\frac{4}{5}$
Microraptor	$2\frac{5}{8}$	$\frac{24}{25}$
Velociraptor	$5\frac{9}{10}$	$3\frac{7}{25}$

Career Project

It's time to update your career portfolio! Investigate the education and training requirements for a career as a scientific illustrator.

_____

_____

_____

_____

_____

What are some short-term goals you need to achieve to become a scientific illustrator?

- _____

- _____

- _____

- _____

Vocabulary Check

Complete the puzzle by unscrambling the letters below to reveal words from the vocabulary list at the beginning of the chapter.

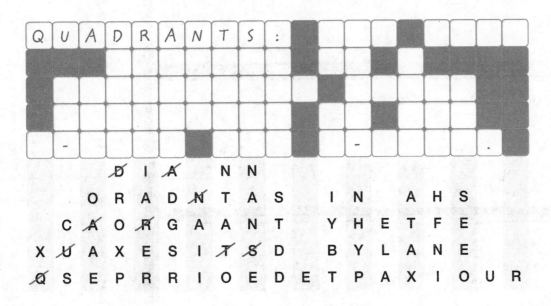

Q U A D R A N T S :

    D I A   N N

  O R A D N T A S   I N   A H S

  C A O R G A A N T   Y H E T F E

  X U A X E S I T S D   B Y L A N E

  Q S E P R R I O E D E T P A X I O U R

Complete each sentence using the vocabulary list at the beginning of the chapter.

1. A _____ is a number that can be written as a fraction.

2. A number that is less than zero is a _____.

3. A number that is greater than zero is a _____.

4. The _____ of a number is the distance between the number and zero on a number line.

5. The division of a _____ ends.

6. A decimal whose digits repeat in groups of one or more is a _____.

Use Your FOLDABLES

Use your Foldable to help review the chapter.

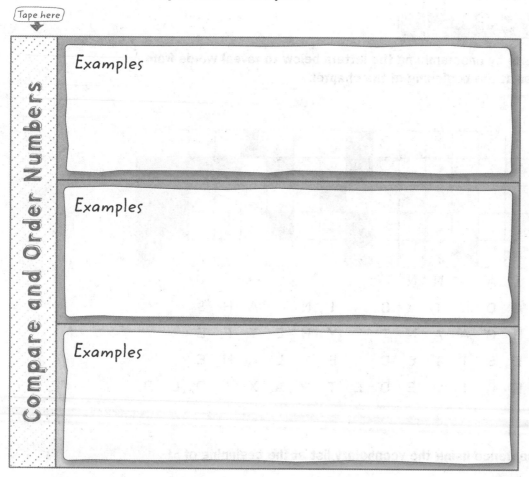

Tape here

Compare and Order Numbers

Examples

Examples

Examples

Got it?

Circle the correct term or number to complete each sentence.

1. The opposite of −4 is (−4, 4).

2. The distance of a number from 0 is its (opposite, absolute value).

3. The value listed first in an ordered pair is the (x-coordinate, y-coordinate).

4. The absolute value of 17 is (−17, 17).

5. $(1.\overline{25}$, 6.543) is a terminating decimal.

Problem Solving

1. Kirk bought songs for his MP3 player. He needed 6 more songs to have a total of 100. Write an integer to represent how many more songs Kirk needs. (Lesson 1)

2. In a football game, the quarterback was tackled behind the line of scrimmage and lost 7 yards. Represent the loss of 7 yards as an integer. (Lesson 1)

3. Kelsey's bank transactions are shown in the table. A positive number represents a deposit and a negative number represents a withdrawal. What is the absolute value of the transaction in Week 3? (Lesson 2)

Week	Transaction
1	50
2	−15
3	−20
4	30

4. The high temperatures in a city during a 5 day period were −6°, 8°, −2°, 6°, and 11°. Place the temperatures in order from least to greatest. (Lesson 3)

5. **CCGPS Use Math Tools** Refer to the diagram. Which building is located at (−2, −4)? (Lesson 6)

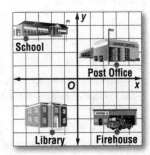

School · Post Office · Library · Firehouse

6. **CCGPS Be Precise** Farah made 28 out of 84 shots on a goal in a recent hockey season. Write her shots made out of shots attempted as a decimal. (Lesson 4)

7. The heights of the lifeguard chairs are $66\frac{1}{3}$ inches and $72\frac{5}{8}$ inches. One section of the lake has a depth of $\frac{203}{4}$ inches, and another section has a depth of $\frac{109}{2}$ inches. Represent each height and depth using a positive or negative number. Then order the numbers from least to greatest. (Lesson 5)

Answering the Essential Question

Use what you learned about integers and the coordinate plane to complete the graphic organizer.

 Essential Question

HOW are integers and absolute value used in real-world situations?

Vocabulary	Definition
integer	
absolute value	

Describe a real-world situation that can be represented by the absolute value of 27.

Describe a real-world situation that can be represented by the absolute value of −16?

 Answer the Essential Question. HOW are integers and absolute value used in real-world situations?

COLLABORATIVE PROJECT

People Everywhere Federal, state, and local governments use population data that are gathered from the U.S. Census to help them plan what services communities need. In this project you will:

- **Collaborate** with your classmates to collect data and to compare populations within our state, county, or city.

- **Share** the results of your research in a creative way.

- @ **Reflect** on how you use mathematics to describe change and model real-world situations.

By the end of this project, you will have a better understanding of the population of people that live around you!

 Collaborate

Go Online Work with your group to research and complete each activity. You will use your results in the Share section on the following page.

1. Use the U.S. Census Web site to find the total population for your state. Then compare the following:
   - the ratio of males to females
   - the ratio of people in your age group to those in any other age group

2. Research the population density of your state. Compare the results with all of the surrounding states. Plot your results on a number line. How does your state compare to others?

3. Research the growth rate of the population of your state over the past ten U.S. Census reports. Display your results in a table and a line graph. Describe any patterns in the line graph.

4. Explain in a journal entry or blog how you could use population data to predict the population of your state in 2020.

5. One way federal funds are distributed to states and counties is based on their population. Research the population of your county, as well as the surrounding counties. If $1,000,000 is to be divided among the counties, about what fraction of the money do you think your county would receive? Why?

Share

With your group, decide on a way to present what you have learned from each of the activities about the population of your state according to the U.S. Census. Some suggestions are listed below, but you can also think of other creative ways to present your information. Remember to show how you used math to complete each of the activities in this project!

- Create a presentation using the data you collected. Your presentation should include a spreadsheet, graph, and one other visual display.
- Write a persuasive letter to a local government official. In the letter, explain what you have learned in this project. Then lobby to have a new service provided for your community. This could be a new park, school, hospital, or whatever you think your community needs.

Check out the note on the right to connect this project with other subjects.

connect with Science

Environmental Literacy Select two states, other than your own, and research the types of landforms found in these states. Some questions to consider are:

- What different types of landforms are found in these states?

- How do the landforms found in these states compare with those found in your state?

Reflect

6. **Ⓠ Answer the Essential Question** How can you use mathematics to describe change and model real-world situations?

   a. How did you use what you learned about ratios and rates to describe change and model the real-world situations in this project?

   _____

   _____

   _____

   b. How did you use what you learned about fractions, decimals, and percents to describe change and model the real-world situations in this project?

   _____

   _____

   _____

COLLABORATIVE PROJECT

Get Out the Map! If you could go anywhere in the world, where would you go? This is your chance to explore someplace new. In this project you will:

- **Collaborate** with your classmates as you investigate a new place you would like to travel.
- **Share** the results of your research in a creative way.
- ℯ **Reflect** on how mathematical ideas can be represented.

By the end of this project, you will have a better understanding of how to use a map to plan the perfect adventure!

Collaborate

⏻ Go Online Work with your group to research and complete each activity. **You will use your results in the Share section on the following page.**

1. Think of someplace new that you would like to travel. Investigate the population of the area you choose as well as any interesting geographical features. Make a list of area attractions that you'd like to visit, such as museums, amusement parks, historical sites, national parks, and so on.

2. Research information about the climate for the area of your location in the time of year you are planning to travel. Important information could include the monthly rainfall, the average daily high and low temperatures, humidity levels, and wind speeds. Create a visual display to share your results.

3. Find lodging in the location you chose. Then, using maps and descriptions available on the Internet, plot three or four area attractions on a coordinate plane. Label each point.

4. Create a budget for each day of the trip showing the cost of the travel, lodging, daily activities, and food. Calculate the cost for your entire family, not just yourself.

5. Use an online map or GPS device to determine the actual distances you will need to travel to get from where you are staying to any attraction you plan to visit. Then find the total distance you will travel during the entire trip.

Share

With your group, decide on a way to present what you have learned from each of the activities about the planning the perfect adventure. Some suggestions are listed below, but you can also think of other creative ways to present your information. Remember to show how you used math to complete each of the activities in this project!

- Create a travel brochure for your current location. Your objective is to increase the tourists for your town. The brochure should include each of the following: a detailed map, recommended restaurants, area attractions, and fun facts.
- Write a journal entry from the perspective of an early explorer who, 1,000 years ago, traveled to the location you chose. Then describe how technology makes planning, budgeting, and navigating at the same location much easier today.

Check out the note on the right to connect this project with other subjects.

 connect with Science

Use the Internet to research what technology was used by early explorers to navigate through unknown territories. Some questions to consider are:

- What tools were used to help explorers travel in the right direction?

- What constellations were used by the explorers and how were they used?

Reflect

6. **Answer the Essential Question** How can mathematical ideas be represented?

   a. How did you use what you learned about computing with multi-digit numbers, and multiplying and dividing fractions to represent mathematical ideas in this project?

   _____

   _____

   _____

   b. How did you use what you learned about integers and the coordinate plane to represent mathematical ideas in this project?

   _____

   _____

   _____

COLLABORATIVE PROJECT

Watch ▶

It's Out of This World How fast do objects in our solar system travel through space? Let's explore the orbital speed of different planets and satellites! In this project you will:

- **Collaborate** with your classmates as you investigate the orbital speed of three planets.

- **Share** the results of your research in a creative way.

- **ⓔ Reflect** on how you communicate mathematical ideas effectively.

Collaborate

Ⓤ Go Online Work with your group to research and complete each activity. You will use your results in the Share section on the following page.

1. Choose three planets in our solar system. Use the Internet to research each planet and find its average orbital speed in miles per second or kilometers per second. Organize the information in a table.

2. Find and record the orbital distance traveled in 1, 2, and 3 seconds for each planet you chose in Exercise 1. Then describe how the orbital distance of each planet changes with time.

3. For your three planets, list the ordered pairs representing (time, distance). Graph each set of ordered pairs on a coordinate plane and connect each set of points with a line. Compare the graphs. Then write equations to represent each relationship.

4. Research artificial satellites, such as the Hubble Space Telescope, that are orbiting Earth. Use the Internet to research three different satellites and determine the purpose of those satellites. Write a summary of your findings.

5. For each satellite you found in Exercise 4, find and record its average orbital speed in miles per second or kilometers per second. Organize the information in a table. Compare the orbital speeds.

With your group, decide on a way to present what you have learned from each of the activities. Some suggestions are listed below, but you can also think of other creative ways to present your information. Remember to show how you used math to complete each of the activities of this project!

 **connect** with **Social Studies**

Global Awareness Research the history of space exploration and write a summary of your findings. Some questions to consider are:

- What have scientists in the U.S. and other countries discovered recently about the solar system?
- Which countries have contributed the most to space exploration?

- Create a presentation using the data you collected. Your presentation should include a spreadsheet, graph, and one other visual display.
- Write an article that would be published in a magazine from the perspective of a scientist. Include any important information that you found while researching the orbital speed of each planet.

Check out the note on the right to connect this project with other subjects.

 Reflect

6. **Ⓔ Answer the Essential Question** How can you communicate mathematical ideas effectively?

a. How did you use what you learned about expressions and equations to communicate mathematical ideas effectively in this project?

_____

_____

_____

b. How did you use what you learned about functions and inequalities to communicate mathematical ideas effectively in this project?

_____

_____

_____

COLLABORATIVE PROJECT

Watch ▶

A New Zoo A zoo is a great place to explore wild animals and learn about their habitats. In this project you will:

- **Collaborate** with your classmates as you explore some animals at the zoo and design your own zoo.

- **Share** the results of your research in a creative way.

- **℮ Reflect** on how you use different measurements to solve real-life problems.

By the end of this Project, you may be interested in working at the zoo or even working as a designer to help create new living areas for the animals.

Collaborate

⏻ Go Online Work with your group to research and complete each activity. You will use your results in the Share section on the following page.

1. Choose 10 zoo animals. Research various characteristics of each animal, such as average weight, lifespan, incubation period, and the temperature of its natural habitat. Write a brief summary for each animal that you choose.

2. Create a bar graph that shows the average weight, the average lifespan, and the average incubation period for the 10 animals you chose.

3. Organize the characteristics found in Exercise 1 for each animal in a table or spreadsheet. Then describe how you could use these characteristics to help you design the animals' living spaces.

4. Research the amount of living space needed for each animal. Use this information to design and draw your own zoo. Be sure to include the dimensions and area. Which animals have the largest living areas? Explain why.

5. Find the area of each animal's enclosure that you designed in Exercise 4. Also, find the volume and surface area of any buildings at the zoo you designed.

Share

With your group, decide on a way to present what you have learned about designing a zoo. Some suggestions are listed below, but you can also think of other creative ways to present your information. Remember to show how you used mathematics to complete this project!

- Design a web page that can be used to describe the zoo. Some questions to consider are:
  - Which zoo attractions should be promoted to get more tourists to visit your zoo?
  - Include a map of your zoo.
- Design a living area for a giant panda exhibit. Be sure to include drawings and explanations of why you designed the exhibit the way you did.

Check out the note on the right to connect this project with other subjects.

connect with **Science**

Environmental Literacy
Research the living conditions for animals in zoos today compared to the living conditions of the past. How has it changed over time? Things to consider:
- size of living space
- average lifespan difference
- behavior changes

Reflect

6. @ **Answer the Essential Question** How can you use different measurements to solve real-life problems?

    a. How did you use what you learned about area to solve real-life problems?

    _____

    _____

    _____

    b. How did you use what you learned about volume and surface area to solve real-life problems?

    _____

    _____

    _____

COLLABORATIVE PROJECT

Watch ▶ **Let's Exercise** Regular physical activity not only keeps you fit, but helps you think clearly and improve your mood. In this project you will:

- **Collaborate** with your classmates as you research physical fitness.

- **Share** the results of your research in a creative way.

- @ **Reflect** on why learning mathematics is important.

By the end of this project, you just might be your family's personal trainer!

 Collaborate

⏻ **Go Online** Work with your group to research and complete each activity. You will use your results in the Share section on the following page.

1. Survey at least ten students about the number of times they participate in sports or other physical activities each week. Find the mean. Then make a dot plot of the data.

2. Research 15 physical activities and the number of Calories burned per hour for each activity. Record the information and draw a box plot to represent the data.

3. Create a jogging schedule to train for a 5K run. Include the number of weeks needed to train and the increments of miles you would need to run. Calculate the number of Calories burned per run. Draw a line graph to represent the data.

4. Look up a fast food restaurant's menu that includes the number of Calories for each item. Record the number of Calories a person would consume if they ate at that restaurant for each meal in one day. Construct an appropriate graph to display your results.

5. Look at what the USDA considers a healthy diet. Based on what you learn, plan one day's worth of meals. Use a statistical display to compare this day's diet with the day's diet in Exercise 4.

Share

With your group, decide on a way to share what you have learned about physical fitness. Some suggestions are listed below, but you can also think other creative ways to present your information. Remember to show how you used mathematics to complete each of the activities of this project!

· Write an article for the food or health section of an online magazine.
· Act as a pediatrician and create a digital presentation that promotes physical fitness.

Check out the note on the right to connect this project with other subjects.

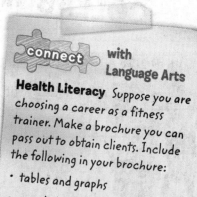

connect with **Language Arts**

Health Literacy Suppose you are choosing a career as a fitness trainer. Make a brochure you can pass out to obtain clients. Include the following in your brochure:

· tables and graphs
· sample testimonials from satisfied customers.

Reflect

6. @ **Answer the Essential Question** Why is learning mathematics important?

  a. How did you use what you learned about statistical measures to help you to understand why learning mathematics is important?

  _____

  _____

  _____

  b. How did you use what you learned about statistical displays to help you to understand why learning mathematics is important?

  _____

  _____

  _____

Glossary/Glosario

Go online for the eGlossary.

Vocab

The eGlossary contains words and definitions in the following 13 languages:

Arabic	Cantonese	Hmong	Spanish	Urdu
Bengali	English	Korean	Tagalog	Vietnamese
Brazilian Portuguese	Haitian Creole	Russian		

English

Español

Aa

absolute value The distance between a number and zero on a number line.

acute angle An angle with a measure greater than 0° and less than 90°.

acute triangle A triangle having three acute angles.

Addition Property of Equality If you add the same number to each side of an equation, the two sides remain equal.

algebra A mathematical language of symbols, including variables.

algebraic expression A combination of variables, numbers, and at least one operation.

analyze To use observations to describe and compare data.

angle Two rays with a common endpoint form an angle. The rays and vertex are used to name the angle.

∠ABC, ∠CBA, or ∠B

valor absoluto Distancia entre un número y cero en la recta numérica.

ángulo agudo Ángulo que mide más de 0° y menos de 90°.

triángulo acutángulo Triángulo con tres ángulos agudos.

propiedad de adición de la igualdad Si sumas el mismo número a ambos lados de una ecuación, los dos lados permanecen iguales.

álgebra Lenguaje matemático que usa símbolos, incluyendo variables.

expresión algebraica Combinación de variables, números y, por lo menos, una operación.

analizar Usar observaciones para describir y comparar datos.

ángulo Dos rayos con un extremo común forman un ángulo. Los rayos y el vértice se usan para nombrar el ángulo.

∠ABC, ∠CBA o ∠B

arithmetic sequence   A sequence in which the difference between any two consecutive terms is the same.

sucesión aritmética   Sucesión en la cual la diferencia entre dos términos consecutivos es constante.

Associative Property   The way in which numbers are grouped does not change the sum or product.

propiedad asociativa   La forma en que se agrupan tres números al sumarlos o multiplicarlos no altera su suma o producto.

average   The sum of two or more quantities divided by the number of quantities; the mean.

promedio   La suma de dos o más cantidades dividida entre el número de cantidades; la media.

bar notation   A bar placed over digits that repeat to indicate a number pattern that repeats indefinitely.

notación de barra   Barra que se coloca sobre los dígitos que se repiten para indicar el número de patrones que se repiten indefinidamente.

base   Any side of a parallelogram.

base   Cualquier lado de un paralelogramo.

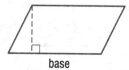

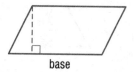

base   One of the two parallel congruent faces of a prism.

base   Una de las dos caras paralelas congruentes de un prisma.

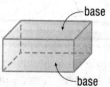

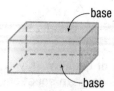

base   In a power, the number used as a factor. In 10^3, the base is 10. That is, $10^3 = 10 \times 10 \times 10$.

base   En una potencia, el número usado como factor. En 10^3, la base es 10. Es decir, $10^3 = 10 \times 10 \times 10$.

box plot   A diagram that is constructed using five values.

diagrama de caja   Diagrama que se construye usando cinco valores.

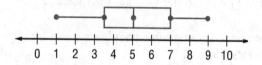

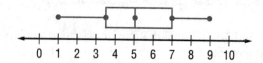

center   The given point from which all points on a circle are the same distance.

centro   Un punto dado del cual equidistan todos los puntos de un círculo o de una esfera.

circle   The set of all points in a plane that are the same distance from a given point called the center.

círculo   Conjunto de todos los puntos en un plano que equidistan de un punto dado llamado centro.

circle graph   A graph that shows data as parts of a whole. In a circle graph, the percents add up to 100.

gráfica circular   Gráfica que muestra los datos como partes de un todo. En una gráfica circular los porcentajes suman 100.

Area of Oceans

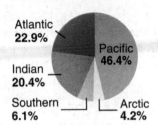

Área de superficie de los océanos

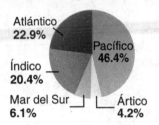

circumference   The distance around a circle.

circunferencia   La distancia alrededor de un círculo.

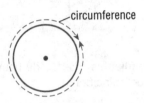

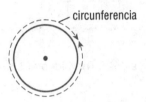

cluster   Data that are grouped closely together.

agrupamiento   Conjunto de datos que se agrupan.

coefficient   The numerical factor of a term that contains a variable.

coeficiente   El factor numérico de un término que contiene una variable.

Commutative Property   The order in which numbers are added or multiplied does not change the sum or product.

propiedad commutativa   La forma en que se suman o multiplican dos números no altera su suma o producto.

compatible numbers   Numbers that are easy to use to perform computations mentally.

números compatibles   Números que son fáciles de usar para realizar computations mentales.

complementary angles   Two angles are complementary if the sum of their measures is 90°.

ángulos complementarios   Dos ángulos son complementarios si la suma de sus medidas es 90°.

∠1 and ∠2 are complementary angles.

∠1 y ∠2 son complementarios.

composite figure   A figure made of triangles, quadrilaterals, semicircles, and other two-dimensional figures.

figura compuesta   Figura formada por triángulos, cuadriláteros, semicírculos y otras figuras bidimensionales.

congruent   Having the same measure.

cóngruente   Ques tienen la misma medida.

congruent figures Figures that have the same size and same shape; corresponding sides and angles have equal measures.

constant A term without a variable.

coordinate plane A plane in which a horizontal number line and a vertical number line intersect at their zero points.

corresponding sides The sides of similar figures that "match."

cubic units Used to measure volume. Tells the number of cubes of a given size it will take to fill a three-dimensional figure.

3 cubic units

figuras congruentes Figuras que tienen el mismo tamaño y la misma forma; los lados y los ángulos correspondientes con igual medida.

constante Un término sin una variable.

plano de coordenadas Plano en que una recta numérica horizontal y una recta numérica vertical se intersecan en sus puntos cero.

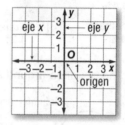

lados correspondientes Lados de figuras semejantes que coinciden.

unidades cúbicas Se usan para medir el volumen. Indican el número de cubos de cierto tamaño que se necesitan para llenar una figura tridimensional.

3 unidades cúbicas

Dd

data Information, often numerical, which is gathered for statistical purposes.

decagon A polygon having ten sides.

defining the variable Choosing a variable and deciding what the variable represents.

dependent variable The variable in a relation with a value that depends on the value of the independent variable.

diameter The distance across a circle through its center.

diameter

datos Información, con frecuencia numérica, que se recoge con fines estadísticos.

decágono Un polígono con diez lados.

definir la variable Elegir una variable y decidir lo que representa.

variable dependiente La variable en una relación cuyo valor depende del valor de la variable independiente.

diámetro La distancia a través de un círculo pasando por el centro.

diámetro

dimensional analysis The process of including units of measurement when you compute.

análisis dimensional Proceso que incluye las unidades de medida al hacer cálculos.

distribution The arrangement of data values.

distribución El arreglo de valores de datos.

Distributive Property To multiply a sum by a number, multiply each addend by the number outside the parentheses.

propiedad distributiva Para multiplicar una suma por un número, multiplica cada sumando por el número fuera de los paréntesis.

Division Property of Equality If you divide each side of an equation by the same nonzero number, the two sides remain equal.

propiedad de igualdad de la división Si divides ambos lados de una ecuación entre el mismo número no nulo, los lados permanecen iguales.

dot plot A diagram that shows the frequency of data on a number line. Also known as a line plot.

diagrama de puntos Diagrama que muestra la frecuencia de los datos sobre una recta numérica.

equals sign A symbol of equality, =.

signo de igualdad Símbolo que indica igualdad, =.

equation A mathematical sentence showing two expressions are equal. An equation contains an equals sign, =.

ecuación Enunciado matemático que muestra que dos expresiones son iguales. Una ecuación contiene el signo de igualdad, =.

equilateral triangle A triangle having three congruent sides.

triángulo equilátero Triángulo con tres lados congruentes.

equivalent expressions Expressions that have the same value.

expresiones equivalentes Expresiones que poseen el mismo valor, sin importer los valores de la(s) variable(s).

equivalent ratios Ratios that express the same relationship between two quantities.

razones equivalentes Razones que expresan la misma relación entre dos cantidades.

evaluate To find the value of an algebraic expression by replacing variables with numbers.

evaluar Calcular el valor de una expresión sustituyendo las variables por número.

exponent In a power, the number that tells how many times the base is used as a factor. In 5^3, the exponent is 3. That is, $5^3 = 5 \times 5 \times 5$.

exponente En una potencia, el número que indica las veces que la base se usa como factor. En 5^3, el exponente es 3. Es decir, $5^3 = 5 \times 5 \times 5$.

face A flat surface.

cara Una superficie plana.

factor the expression The process of writing numeric or algebraic expressions as a product of their factors.

factorizar la expresión El proceso de escribir expresiones numéricas o algebraicas como el producto de sus factores.

first quartile For a data set with median M, the first quartile is the median of the data values less than M.

primer cuartil Para un conjunto de datos con la mediana M, el primer cuartil es la mediana de los valores menores que M.

formula   An equation that shows the relationship among certain quantities.

fórmula   Ecuación que muestra la relación entre ciertas cantidades.

fraction   A number that represents part of a whole or part of a set.
$$\frac{1}{2}, \frac{1}{3}, \frac{1}{4}, \frac{3}{4}$$

fracción   Número que representa parte de un todo o parte de un conjunto.
$$\frac{1}{2}, \frac{1}{3}, \frac{1}{4}, \frac{3}{4}$$

frequency distribution   How many pieces of data are in each interval.

distribución de frecuencias   Cantidad de datos asociada con cada intervalo.

frequency table   A table that shows the number of pieces of data that fall within the given intervals.

tabla de frecuencias   Tabla que muestra el número de datos en cada intervalo.

function   A relationship that assigns exactly one output value to one input value.

función   Relación que asigna exactamente un valor de salida a un valor de entrada.

function rule   An expression that describes the relationship between each input and output.

regla de funciones   Expresión que describe la relación entre cada valor de entrada y de salida.

function table   A table organizing the input, rule, and output of a function.

tabla de funciones   Tabla que organiza las entradas, la regla y las salidas de una función.

Gg

gap   An empty space or interval in a set of data.

laguna   Espacio o intervalo vacío en un conjunto de datos.

geometric sequence   A sequence in which each term is found by multiplying the previous term by the same number.

sucesión geométrica   Sucesión en la cual cada término después del primero se determina multiplicando el término anterior por el mismo número.

graph   To place a dot at a point named by an ordered pair.

gráfica   Colocar una marca puntual en el punto que corresponde a un par ordenado.

Greatest Common Factor (GCF)   The greatest of the common factors of two or more numbers.

The greatest common factor of 12, 18, and 30 is 6.

máximo común divisor (MCD)   El mayor de los factores comunes de dos o más números.

El máximo común divisor de 12, 18 y 30 es 6.

Hh

height   The shortest distance from the base of a parallelogram to its opposite side.

altura   La distancia más corta desde la base de un paralelogramo hasta su lado opuesto.

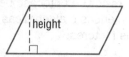

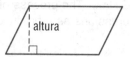

heptagon   A polygon having seven sides.

heptágono   Polígono con siete lados.

hexagon   A polygon having six sides.

hexágono   Polígono con seis lados.

histogram   A type of bar graph used to display numerical data that have been organized into equal intervals.

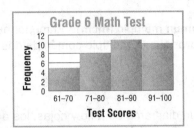

histograma   Tipo de gráfica de barras que se usa para exhibir datos que se han organizado en intervalos iguales.

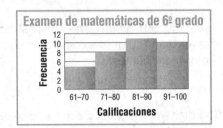

Identity Properties   Properties that state that the sum of any number and 0 equals the number and that the product of any number and 1 equals the number.

propiedades de identidad   Propiedades que establecen que la suma de cualquier número y 0 es igual al número y que el producto de cualquier número y 1 es igual al número.

independent variable   The variable in a function with a value that is subject to choice.

variable independiente   Variable en una función cuyo valor está sujeto a elección.

inequality   A mathematical sentence indicating that two quantities are not equal.

desigualdad   Enunciado matemático que indica que dos cantidades no son iguales.

integer   Any number from the set {... −4, −3, −2, −1, 0, 1, 2, 3, 4 ...} where ... means *continues without end.*

entero   Cualquier número del conjunto {... −4, −3, −2, −1, 0, 1, 2, 3, 4 ...} donde ... significa que *continúa sin fin.*

interquartile range   A measure of variation in a set of numerical data, the interquartile range is the distance between the first and third quartiles of the data set.

rango intercuartil   El rango intercuartil, una medida de la variación en un conjunto de datos numéricos, es la distancia entre el primer y el tercer cuartil del conjunto de datos.

intersecting lines   *Lines* that meet or cross at a common *point.*

rectas secantes   *Rectas* que se intersectan o se cruzan en un *punto* común.

interval   The difference between successive values on a scale.

intervalo   La diferencia entre valores sucesivos de una escala.

inverse operations   Operations which *undo* each other. For example, addition and subtraction are inverse operations.

operaciones inversas   Operaciones que *se anulan* mutuamente. La adición y la sustracción son operaciones inversas.

isosceles triangle   A triangle having at least two congruent sides.

triángulo isósceles   Triángulo que tiene por lo menos dos lados congruentes.

lateral face   Any face that is not a base.

least common denominator (LCD)   The least common multiple of the denominators of two or more fractions.

least common multiple (LCM)   The smallest whole number greater than 0 that is a common multiple of each of two or more numbers.

The LCM of 2 and 3 is 6.

leaves   The digits of the least place value of data in a stem-and-leaf plot.

like terms   Terms that contain the same variable(s) to the same power.

line   A set of *points* that form a straight path that goes on forever in opposite directions.

linear function   A function that forms a line when graphed.

line graph   A graph used to show how a set of data changes over a period of time.

line of symmetry   A line that divides a figure into two halves that are reflections of each other.

line of symmetry

line plot   A diagram that shows the frequency of data on a number line. Also known as a dot plot.

line segment   A part of a *line* that connects two points.

line symmetry   Figures that match exactly when folded in half have line symmetry.

cara lateral   Cualquier superficie plana que no sea la base.

mínimo común denominador (mcd)   El menor múltiplo común de los denominadores de dos o más fracciones.

mínimo común múltiplo (mcm)   El menor número entero, mayor que 0, múltiplo común de dos o más números.

El mcm de 2 y 3 es 6.

hoja   En un diagrama de tallo y hojas, los dígitos del menor valor de posición.

términos semejantes   Términos que contienen la misma variable o variables elevadas a la misma potencia.

recta   Conjunto de *puntos* que forman una trayectoria recta sin fin en direcciones oputestas.

función lineal   Función cuya gráfica es una recta.

gráfica lineal   Gráfica que se use para mostrar cómo cambian los valores durange un período de tiempo.

eje de simetría   Recta que divide una figura en dos mitades especulares.

eje de simetría

esquema lineal   Diagrama que muestra la frecuencia de los datos sobre una recta numérica.

segmento de recta   Parte de una *recta* que conecta dos puntos.

simetría lineal   Exhiben simetría lineal las figuras que coinciden exactamente al doblarse una sobre otra.

Mm

mean   The sum of the numbers in a set of data divided by the number of pieces of data.

media   La suma de los números en un conjunto de datos dividida entre el número total de datos.

mean absolute deviation A measure of variation in a set of numerical data, computed by adding the distances between each data value and the mean, then dividing by the number of data values.

desviación media absoluta Una medida de variación en un conjunto de datos numéricos que se calcula sumando las distancias entre el valor de cada dato y la media, y luego dividiendo entre el número de valores.

measures of center Numbers that are used to describe the center of a set of data. These measures include the mean, median, and mode.

medidas del centro Numéros que se usan para describir el centro de un conjunto de datos. Estas medidas incluyen la media, la mediana y la moda.

measures of variation A measure used to describe the distribution of data.

medidas de variación Medida usada para describir la distribución de los datos.

median A measure of center in a set of numerical data. The median of a list of values is the value appearing at the center of a sorted version of the list—or the mean of the two central values, if the list contains an even number of values.

mediana Una medida del centro en un conjunto de datos numéricos. La mediana de una lista de valores es el valor que aparece en el centro de una versión ordenada de la lista, o la media de los dos valores centrales si la lista contiene un número par de valores.

mode The number(s) or item(s) that appear most often in a set of data.

moda Número(s) de un conjunto de datos que aparece(n) más frecuentemente.

Multiplication Property of Equality If you multiply each side of an equation by the same nonzero number, the two sides remain equal.

propiedad de multiplicación de la igualdad Si multiplicas ambos lados de una ecuación por el mismo número no nulo, lo lados permanecen iguales.

---

negative integer A number that is less than zero. It is written with a − sign.

entero negativo Número que es menor que cero y se escribe con el signo −.

net A two-dimensional figure that can be used to build a three-dimensional figure.

red Figura bidimensional que sirve para hacer una figura tridimensional.

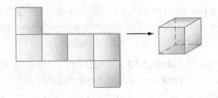

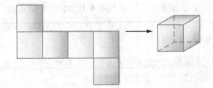

nonagon A polygon having nine sides.

enágono Polígono que tiene nueve lados.

numerical expression A combination of numbers and operations.

expresión numérica Una combinación de números y operaciones.

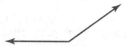

obtuse angle   Any angle that measures greater than 90° but less than 180°.

ángulo obtuso   Cualquier ángulo que mide más de 90° pero menos de 180°.

obtuse triangle   A triangle having one obtuse angle.

triángulo obtusángulo   Triángulo que tiene un ángulo obtuso.

octagon   A polygon having eight sides.

octágono   Polígono que tiene ocho lados.

opposites   Two integers are opposites if they are represented on the number line by points that are the same distance from zero, but on opposite sides of zero. The sum of two opposites is zero.

opuestos   Dos enteros son opuestos si, en la recta numérica, están representados por puntos que equidistan de cero, pero en direcciones opuestas. La suma de dos opuestos es cero.

ordered pair   A pair of numbers used to locate a point on the coordinate plane. The ordered pair is written in the form (*x*-coordinate, *y*-coordinate).

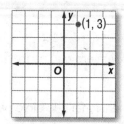

par ordenado   Par de números que se utiliza para ubicar un punto en un plano de coordenadas. Se escribe de la forma (coordenada *x*, coordenada *y*).

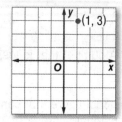

order of operations   The rules that tell which operation to perform first when more than one operation is used.

1. Simplify the expressions inside grouping symbols, like parentheses.
2. Find the value of all powers.
3. Multiply and divide in order from left to right.
4. Add and subtract in order from left to right.

orden de las operaciones   Reglas que establecen cuál operación debes realizar primero, cuando hay más de una operación involucrada.

1. Primero ejecuta todas las operaciones dentro de los símbolos de agrupamiento.
2. Evalúa todas las potencias.
3. Multiplica y divide en orden de izquierda a derecha.
4. Suma y resta en orden de izquierda a derecha.

origin   The point of intersection of the *x*-axis and *y*-axis on a coordinate plane.

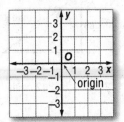

origen   Punto de intersección de los ejes axiales en un plano de coordenadas.

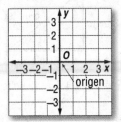

outlier   A value that is much higher or much lower than the other values in a set of data.

valor atípico   Dato que se encuentra muy separado de los otros valores en un conjunto de datos.

Pp

parallel lines   Lines in a plane that never intersect.

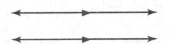

rectas paralelas   Rectas en un plano que nunca se intersecan.

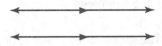

parallelogram   A quadrilateral with opposite sides parallel and opposite sides congruent.

paralelogramo   Cuadrilátero cuyos lados opuestos son paralelos y congruentes.

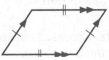

peak   The most frequently occurring value in a line plot.

pico   El valor que ocurre con más frecuencia en un diagrama de puntos.

pentagon   A polygon having five sides.

pentágono   Polígono que tiene cinco lados.

percent   A ratio that compares a number to 100.

por ciento   Razón en que se compara un número a 100.

percent proportion   One ratio or fraction that compares part of a quantity to the whole quantity. The other ratio is the equivalent percent written as a fraction with a denominator of 100.

$$\frac{\text{part}}{\text{whole}} = \frac{\text{percent}}{100}$$

proporción porcentual   Razón o fracción que compara parte de una cantidad a toda la cantidad. La otra razón es el porcentaje equivalente escrito como fracción con 100 de denominador.

$$\frac{\text{parte}}{\text{todo}} = \frac{\text{porcentaje}}{100}$$

perfect square   Numbers with square roots that are whole numbers. 25 is a perfect square because the square root of 25 is 5.

cuadrados perfectos   Números cuya raíz cuadrada es un número entero. 25 es un cuadrado perfecto porque la raíz cuadrada de 25 es 5.

perimeter   The distance around a figure.

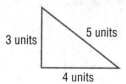

$$P = 3 + 4 + 5 = 12 \text{ units}$$

pi   The ratio of the circumference of a circle to its diameter. The Greek letter π represents this number. The value of pi is always 3.1415926....

plane   A flat surface that goes on forever in all directions.

point   An exact location in space that is represented by a dot.

polygon   A simple closed figure formed by three or more straight line segments.

population   The entire group of items or individuals from which the samples under consideration are taken.

positive integer   A number that is greater than zero. It can be written with or without a + sign.

powers   Numbers expressed using exponents. The power 3^2 is read *three to the second power,* or *three squared.*

prism   A three-dimensional figure with at least three rectangular lateral faces and top and bottom faces parallel.

properties   Statements that are true for any number.

proportion   An equation stating that two ratios or rates are equivalent.

pyramid   A three-dimensional figure with at least three triangular sides that meet at a common vertex and only one base that is a polygon.

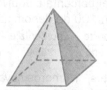

perímetro   La distancia alrededor de una figura.

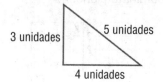

$$P = 3 + 4 + 5 = 12 \text{ unidades}$$

pi   Razón de la circunferencia de un círculo al diámetro del mismo. La letra griega π representa este número. El valor de pi es siempre 3.1415926....

plano   Superficie plana que se extiende infinitamente en todas direcciones.

punto   Ubicación exacta en el espacio que se representa con un marca puntual.

polígono   Figura cerrada simple formada por tres o más segmentos de recta.

población   El grupo total de individuos o de artículos del cual se toman las muestras bajo estudio.

entero positivo   Número que es mayor que cero y se puede escribir con o sin el signo +.

potencias   Números que se expresan usando exponentes. La potencia 3^2 se lee *tres a la segunda potencia* o *tres al cuadrado.*

prisma   Figura tridimensional que tiene por lo menos tres caras laterales rectangulares y caras paralelas superior e inferior.

propiedades   Enunciados que son verdaderos para cualquier número.

proporción   Ecuación que indica que dos razones o tasas son equivalentes.

pirámide   Una figura de tres dimensiones con que es en un un polígono y tres o mas caras triangulares que se encuentran en un vértice común.

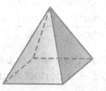

Qq

quadrants The four regions in a coordinate plane separated by the *x*-axis and *y*-axis.

cuadrantes Las cuatro regiones de un plano de coordenadas separadas por el eje *x* y el eje *y*.

quadrilateral A closed figure having four sides and four angles.

cuadrilátero Figura cerrada que tiene cuatro lados y cuatro ángulos.

quartiles Values that divide a data set into four equal parts.

cuartiles Valores que dividen un conjunto de datos en cuatro partes iguales.

Rr

radical sign The symbol used to indicate a nonnegative square root, $\sqrt{}$.

signo radical Símbolo que se usa para indicar una raíz cuadrada no negativa, $\sqrt{}$.

radius The distance from the center to any point on the circle.

radio Distancia desde el centro de un círculo hasta cualquier punto del mismo.

range The difference between the greatest number and the least number in a set of data.

rango La diferencia entre el número mayor y el número menor en un conjunto de datos.

rate A ratio comparing two quantities with different kinds of units.

tasa Razón que compara dos cantidades que tienen diferentes tipos de unidades.

rate of change A rate that describes how one quantity changes in relation to another. A rate of change is usually expressed as a unit rate.

tasa de cambio Tasa que describe cómo cambia una cantidad con respecto a otra. Por lo general, se expresa como tasa unitaria.

ratio A comparison of two quantities by division. The ratio of 2 to 3 can be stated as 2 out of 3, 2 to 3, 2 : 3, or $\frac{2}{3}$.

razón Comparación de dos cantidades mediante división. La razón de 2 a 3 puede escribirse como 2 de cada 3, 2 a 3, 2 : 3 ó $\frac{2}{3}$.

rational number A number that can be written as a fraction.

número racional Número que se puede expresar como fracción.

ratio table A table with columns filled with pairs of numbers that have the same ratio.

tabla de razones Tabla cuyas columnas contienen pares de números que tienen una misma razón.

ray A line that has one endpoint and goes on forever in only one direction.

rayo Recta con un extremo y la cual se extiende infinitamente en una sola dirección.

reciprocals Any two numbers that have a product of 1. Since $\frac{5}{6} \times \frac{6}{5} = 1$, $\frac{5}{6}$ and $\frac{6}{5}$ are reciprocals.

recíproco Cualquier par de números cuyo producto es 1. Como $\frac{5}{6} \times \frac{6}{5} = 1$, $\frac{5}{6}$ y $\frac{6}{5}$ son recíprocos.

rectangle A parallelogram having four right angles.

rectángulo Paralelogramo con cuatro ángulos rectos.

rectangular prism A prism that has rectangular bases.

prisma rectangular Una prisma que tiene bases rectangulares.

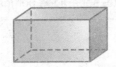

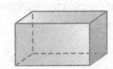

reflection   The mirror image produced by flipping a figure over a line.

reflexión   Transformación en la cual una figura se voltea sobre una recta. También se conoce como simetría de espejo.

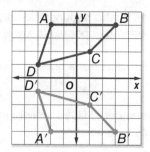

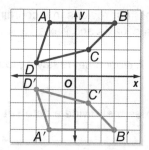

relation   A set of ordered pairs such as (1, 3), (2, 4), and (3, 5). A relation can also be shown in a table or a graph.

relación   Conjunto de pares ordenados como (1, 3), (2, 4) y (3, 5). Una relación también se puede mostrar en una tabla o una gráfica.

repeating decimal   The decimal form of a rational number.

decimal periódico   La forma decimal de un número racional.

rhombus   A parallelogram having four congruent sides.

rombo   Paralelogramo que tiene cuatro lados.

right angle   An angle that measures exactly 90°.

ángulo recto   Ángulo que mide exactamente 90°.

right triangle   A triangle having one right angle.

triángulo rectángulo   Triángulo que tiene un ángulo recto.

Ss

sample   A randomly selected group chosen for the purpose of collecting data.

muestra   Grupo escogido al azar o aleatoriamente que se usa con el propósito de recoger datos.

scale   The set of all possible values of a given measurement, including the least and greatest numbers in the set, separated by the intervals used.

escala   Conjunto de todos los valores posibles de una medida dada, incluyendo el número menor y el mayor del conjunto, separados por los intervalos usados.

scale The scale gives the ratio that compares the measurements of a drawing or model to the measurements of the real object.

escala Razón que compara las medidas de un dibujo o modelo a las medidas del objeto real.

scale drawing A drawing that is used to represent objects that are too large or too small to be drawn at actual size.

dibujo a escala Dibujo que se usa para representar objetos que son demasiado grandes o demasiado pequeños como para dibujarlos de tamaño natural.

scalene triangle A triangle having no congruent sides.

triángulo escaleno Triángulo sin lados congruentes.

scaling To multiply or divide two related quantities by the same number.

homotecia Multiplicar o dividir dos cantidades relacionadas entre un mismo número.

sequence A list of numbers in a specific order, such as 0, 1, 2, 3, or 2, 4, 6, 8.

sucesión Lista de números en un orden específico como, por ejemplo, 0, 1, 2, 3 ó 2, 4, 6, 8.

similar figures Figures that have the same shape but not necessarily the same size.

figuras semejantes Figuras que tienen la misma forma, pero no necesariamente el mismo tamaño.

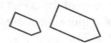

slant height The height of each lateral face.

altura oblicua Altura de cada cara lateral.

solution The value of a variable that makes an equation true. The solution of $12 = x + 7$ is 5.

solución Valor de la variable de una ecuación que hace verdadera la ecuación. La solución de $12 = x + 7$ es 5.

solve To replace a variable with a value that results in a true sentence.

resolver Reemplazar una variable con un valor que resulte en un enunciado verdadero.

square A rectangle having four right angles and four congruent sides.

cuadrado Rectángulo con cuatro ángulos rectos y cuatro lados congruentes.

square root The factors multiplied to form perfect squares.

raíz cuadrada Factores multiplicados para formar cuadrados perfectos.

statistical question A question that anticipates and accounts for a variety of answers.

cuestión estadística Una pregunta que se anticipa y da cuenta de una variedad de respuestas.

statistics Collecting, organizing, and interpreting data.

estadística Recopilar, ordenar e interpretar datos.

stem-and-leaf plot A system where data are organized from least to greatest. The digits of the least place value usually form the leaves, and the next place-value digits form the stems.

diagrama de tallo y hojas Sistema donde los datos se organizan de menor a mayor. Por lo general, los dígitos de los valores de posición menores forman las hojas y los valores de posición más altos forman los tallos.

Stem	Leaf
1	2 4 5
2	
3	1 2 3 3 9
4	0 4 6 7

4 | 7 = 47

Tallo	Hojas
1	2 4 5
2	
3	1 2 3 3 9
4	0 4 6 7

4 | 7 = 47

stems   The digits of the greatest place value of data in a stem-and-leaf plot.

tallo   Los dígitos del mayor valor de posición de los datos en un diagrama de tallo y hojas.

straight angle   An angle that measures exactly 180°.

ángulo llano   Ángulo que mide exactamente 180°.

Subtraction Property of Equality   If you subtract the same number from each side of an equation, the two sides remain equal.

propiedad de sustracción de la igualdad   Si sustraes el mismo número de ambos lados de una ecuación, los dos lados permanecen iguales.

supplementary angles   Two angles are supplementary if the sum of their measures is 180°.

ángulos suplementarios   Dos ángulos son suplementarios si la suma de sus medidas es 180°.

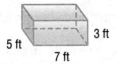

∠1 and ∠2 are supplementary angles.

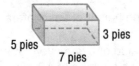

∠1 y ∠2 son suplementarios.

surface area   The sum of the areas of all the surfaces (faces) of a three-dimensional figure.
S.A. = 2ℓh + 2ℓw + 2hw

área de superficie   La suma de las áreas de todas las superficies (caras) de una figura tridimensional.
S.A. = 2ℓh + 2ℓw + 2hw

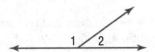

$S.A. = 2(7 \times 3) + 2(7 \times 5) + 2(3 \times 5)$
$= 142$ square feet

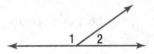

$S.A. = 2(7 \times 3) + 2(7 \times 5) + 2(3 \times 5)$
$= 142$ pies cuadrados

survey   A question or set of questions designed to collect data about a specific group of people, or population.

encuesta   Pregunta o conjunto de preguntas diseñadas para recoger datos sobre un grupo específico de personas o población.

symmetric distribution   Data that are evenly distributed.

distribución simétrica   Datos que están distribuidos.

term   Each number in a sequence.

término   Cada uno de los números de una sucesión.

term   Each part of an algebraic expression separated by a plus or minus sign.

término   Cada parte de un expresión algebraica separada por un signo más o un signo menos.

terminating decimal   A decimal is called terminating if its repeating digit is 0.

decimal finito   Un decimal se llama finito si el dígito que se repite es 0.

third quartile   For a data set with median M, the third quartile is the median of the data values greater than M.

tercer cuartil   Para un conjunto de datos con la mediana M, el tercer cuartil es la mediana de los valores mayores que M.

three-dimensional figure   A figure with length, width, and height.

figura tridimensional   Una figura que tiene largo, ancho y alto.

trapezoid   A quadrilateral with one pair of parallel sides.

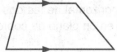

trapecio   Cuadrilátero con un único par de lados paralelos.

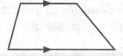

triangle   A figure with three sides and three angles.

triangular prism   A prism that has triangular bases.

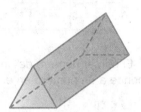

triángulo   Figura con tres lados y tres ángulos.

prisma triangular   Prisma con bases triangulares.

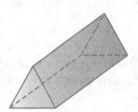

Uu

unit price   The cost per unit.

unit rate   A rate that is simplified so that it has a denominator of 1.

unit ratio   A unit rate where the denominator is one unit.

precio unitario   El costo por cada unidad.

tasa unitaria   Tasa simplificada para que tenga un denominador igual a 1.

razón unitaria   Tasa unitaria en que el denominador es la unidad.

Vv

variable   A symbol, usually a letter, used to represent a number.

vertex   The point where three or more faces intersect.

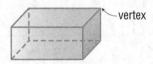

variable   Un símbolo, por lo general, una letra, que se usa para representar un número.

vértice   El punto en que se intersecan dos o más caras del prisma.

volume   The amount of space inside a three-dimensional figure. Volume is measured in cubic units.

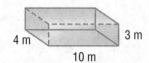

$V = 10 \times 4 \times 3 = 120$ cubic meters

volumen   Cantidad de espacio dentro de una figura tridimensional. El volumen se mide en unidades cúbicas.

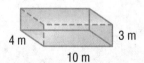

$V = 10 \times 4 \times 3 = 120$ metros cúbicos

x-axis   The horizontal line of the two perpendicular number lines in a coordinate plane.

eje x   La recta horizontal de las dos rectas numéricas perpendiculares en un plano de coordenadas.

x-coordinate   The first number of an ordered pair. The x-coordinate corresponds to a number on the x-axis.

coordenada x   El primer número de un par ordenado, el cual corresponde a un número en el eje x.

Yy

y-axis   The vertical line of the two perpendicular number lines in a coordinate plane.

eje y   La recta vertical de las dos rectas numéricas perpendiculares en un plano de coordenadas.

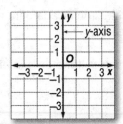

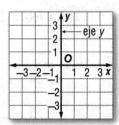

y-coordinate   The second number of an ordered pair. The y-coordinate corresponds to a number on the y-axis.

coordenada y   El segundo número de un par ordenado, el cual corresponde a un número en el eje y.

Selected Answers

Chapter 1 Compute with Multi-Digit Numbers

Chapter 1   Are You Ready?

1. 300   **3.** 1,078   **5.** 49   **7.** 4 million albums

Lesson 1-1   Independent Practice

1. 16.7   **3** 103.01   **5.** 80.02   **7** 1.73 s
9. $24.85   **11.** Luis did not annex a zero before
subtracting. $8.9 - 3.72 = 5.18$ **13.** Sample answer:
When you add the whole numbers the sum is 20. The sum
of the decimals will be added on, which will make the sum
greater than 20.   **15.** 6; A zero is annexed to subtract from
8.5. So, you will subtract $10 - 4$ to find the value in the
hundredths place.

Lesson 1-1   Extra Practice

17. 7.9   **19.** 39.99   **21.** 14.82   **23.** $207.85   **25.** 34.15
degrees Celsius   **27.** B   **29.** 166.85 miles   **31.** 34
33. Thursday

Lesson 1-2   Independent Practice

1. 30; $10 \times 3 = 30$ **3** 160; $20 \times 8 = 160$
5. 240; $30 \times 8 = 240$ **7.** about 80 million tons
9 More; her wage and hours worked were rounded up,
so the actual total is less than the estimate.   **11a.** Raj
needs to save $132 more.   **11b.** No; $6 \times 20 = $120
13. about $12   **15.** B

Lesson 1-2   Extra Practice

17. $30 \times 80 = 2,400$ **19.** about 90   **21.** yes   **23.** no; 32
25. Calories: 400; Vitamin C: 400 mg; carbohydrates:
100 g; calcium: 80 mg   **27.** yes; $4 \times $3.69 \approx 4 \times $4 =$
$16   **29.** B   **31.** 345   **33.** $4.37

Lesson 1-3   Independent Practice

1. 8.4   **3.** 2.6   **5.** 0.06   **7** $215.27   **9** 134.6°F;
Sample answer: $1,346 \times 10 = 13,460$. Since 13.46 has
2 decimal places, $13.46 \times 10 = 134.60$.
11. Sample answer: 32 mm; $20 \times 1.95 = 39$; $4 \times 1.75 =$
7; $39 - 7 = 32$ **13.** Sample answer: First evaluate
1.17×100 to be 117. Then, multiply 117 by 5.4 to get
the answer of 631.8. Or first evaluate 5.4×100 to be
540. Then multiply 540 by 1.17 to get the answer of
631.8. Or first evaluate 5.4×10 to be 54 and 1.17×10
to be 11.7. Then multiply 54 by 11.7 to get the answer of
631.8.   **15.** No; zero represents the number of hundredths
and should be counted.

Lesson 1-3   Extra Practice

17. 8.5   **19.** 19.2   **21.** 0.084   **23.** 2.24 g   **25.** 93.5 in^2
27. 7.44 miles   **29.** 4,515 square inches   **31.** 6   **33.** 13
35. 5; 3; 35

Lesson 1-4   Independent Practice

1. 0.28   **3** 1.092   **5.** 167.0067
7 84.474 ft; $46.93 \times 1.8 \approx 45 \times 2 = 90$; $84.474 \approx 90$
9 $5.76; Each price is about $1. He bought about
6 pounds of fruit. $6 \times 1 = 6 \approx 5.76 **11.** 1.03515
13.

×	2	0.2	0.02	0.002
3	6	0.6	0.06	0.006
0.3	0.6	0.06	0.006	0.0006
0.03	0.06	0.006	0.0006	0.00006
0.003	0.006	0.0006	0.00006	0.000006

Sample answer: The factor 0.002 has three decimal
places and the factor 0.003 has three decimal places.
So, the product will have six decimal places.
15. 32.013341...; Sample answer: 3.9853×8.032856
rounds to $4 \times 8 = 32$, so the answer must be about 32.
17. greater than 0.4; It is being multiplied by a decimal
greater than 1.   **19.** D

Lesson 1-4   Extra Practice

21. 2.48   **23.** 16.128   **25.** 0.02255   **29a.** Junnie
29b. 0.62 mile farther   **31.** G   **33.** 7.275 mi   **35.** 12
37. 7 boxes

Problem-Solving Investigation   Look for a Pattern

Case 3. $47.70   **Case 5.** 30.5, 39, 48.5; Add 3.5; then
add 4.5; then add 5.5, and so on.

Lesson 1-5   Independent Practice

1. 29   **3.** 15   **5** 130 R30   **7.** 170   **9** 60 mi
11. 175 names   **13.** 144 cups   **15.** Sample answer: Mary
saved $2,400 in 12 months. What was the average
amount she saved each month?; $200   **17.** No; Sample
answer: if the remainder equals the divisor, then the
quotient should be increased by 1.   **19.** B

Lesson 1-5   Extra Practice

21. 57 R3   **23.** 10 R21   **25.** 166 R24   **27.** 224 R1
29. 845 cups   **31.** B   **33.** H   **35.** 60   **37.** 700
39. 10 vans

Lesson 1-6   Independent Practice

1. $33 \div 3 = 11$ **3.** $36 \div 12 = 3$ **5** Sample answer:
about 3   **7** about 6 gal; $53 \div 8.5 \approx 54 \div 9 = 6$ **9.** 1;
2; 4; 8   **11.** Sample answer: $160.23 \div 6.54$ **13.** B

Lesson 1-6 Extra Practice

15. $46 \div 23 = 2$ **17.** about 7 inches; $45.9 \div 7 \approx 49 \div 7 = 7$ **19** $\$474.72 \div 12 \approx \$480 \div 12 = \$40$
21a. 5; $100 \times 5 = 500$ **21b.** 10 **23.** about 12 children
25. $490 \div 70 = 7$ **27.** 0.147 **29.** 7.3456; 0.73456; 0.073456; Sample answer: Divide by ten to move the decimal point one place value to the left.

Lesson 1-7 Independent Practice

1. 13.1 **3** 23.7 **5.** 1.2 **7.** $770.56 **9** 22.8 ft; Area of a rectangle is length times width, so divide the area by the length to find the width. $752.4 \div 33 = 22.8$ **11.** Brand B; The cost of each bottled water for Brand B is about $0.44. For Brand A the cost is about $0.58 and for Brand C the cost is about $0.46. So Brand B has the best cost per bottle. **13.** Amanda placed the decimal point in the wrong place of the quotient. $11.2 \div 14 = 0.8$ **15.** Since $40 \div 20 = 2$, the answer is about 2.

Lesson 1-7 Extra Practice

17. 18.4 **19.** 1.6 **21.** 1.9 **23.** $3.75 **25.** Dominoes; The cost of each domino set is about $0.66. The cost of each peg game is about $0.83, and the cost of each mini football is about $0.75. So, the domino set has the best cost per toy. **27.** $62.46 **29.** 83 **31.** 31.1 **33.** 8.8 kg

Lesson 1-8 Independent Practice

1. 3.6 **3** 250 **5.** 450 **7.** 20 steps **9a.** 24 h
9b. 21.12 h **11 a.** 2.2 times **b.** 3.8 times **13.** $49 \div 7$; the quotient is 7 and all of the other problems have a quotient of 0.7.

Lesson 1-8 Extra Practice

15. 0.2 **17.** 0.0492 **19.** 420 **21.** 6 pieces **23.** about 4.4 times **25.** D **27.** I **29.** < **31.** > **33.** $\frac{7}{12}$ of her free time

Chapter Review Vocabulary Check

Across
1. compatible numbers **5.** decimal
Down
3. multidigit **5.** dividend

Chapter Review Key Concept Check

Across
1. 483 **3.** 178 **5.** 21 **9.** 4930 **13.** 203
Down
1. 40 **3.** 108 **5.** 239 **7.** 72 **9.** 463 **11.** 880

Chapter Review Problem Solving

1. 60 mph × 3 h = 180 mi **3.** 73.08 ft² **5.** 186,000
7. about 4.5 feet; 5.75 × 0.8 is about 6 × 0.8 or 4.8, which is closest to 4.5

Chapter 2 Multiply and Divide Fractions

Chapter 2 Are You Ready?

1. 12 **3.** 6 **5.** $4\frac{11}{21}$ **7.** $6\frac{7}{8}$ in.

Lesson 2-1 Independent Practice

1. $\frac{1}{4} \times 20 = 5$

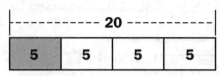

3. $1 \times 0 = 0$ **5** $12 \times \frac{1}{4} = 3$ pizzas **7a.** about 20 lb
7b. about $75 **9** Sample answer: $10 \times 3 = 30$ in²
11. Sample answer: $\frac{5}{9}$; $8\frac{1}{2}$ is about $\frac{5}{9} \times 9 = 5$. **13.** C

Lesson 2-1 Extra Practice

15. 14 **17.** $\frac{2}{9} \times 90 = 20$ **19.** $\frac{1}{2} \times 4 = 2$ **21.** $8 \times 1 = 8$ cm² **23.** 23 movies **25.** B **27.** C **29.** $\frac{1}{2}$ **31.** 0
33.

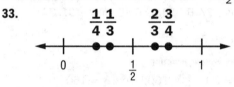

35. 120 square feet

Lesson 2-2 Independent Practice

1. 15 **3.** 2 **5.** $\frac{22}{5}$ or $4\frac{2}{5}$ **7** $2\frac{2}{5}$ in. **9** neither; $\frac{4}{5} \times 30 = 24$ and $\frac{2}{3} \times 36 = 24$. So, $24 = 24$.
11. seventh **13.** He multiplied by $\frac{8}{8}$ instead of multiplying by $\frac{8}{1}$. $\frac{3}{4} \times \frac{8}{1} = \frac{24}{4}$ or 6. **15.** C

Lesson 2-2 Extra Practice

17. 6 **19.** $\frac{7}{5}$ or $1\frac{2}{5}$ **21.** $\frac{25}{2}$ or $12\frac{1}{2}$ **23.** 146 days **25.** B
27. 6 yd **29.** 286 **31.** 153 **33.** 3 inches

Lesson 2-3 Independent Practice

1. $\frac{2}{15}$ **3** $2\frac{2}{3}$ **5.** $\frac{1}{6}$ **7** $\frac{3}{8}$ **9** $\frac{3}{10}$
11a. Sample answer: Olivia withdrew $\frac{3}{4}$ of her savings. She used $\frac{1}{5}$ of what was left to buy a book. If she had $100 in savings, how much did she spend on the book?

11b.

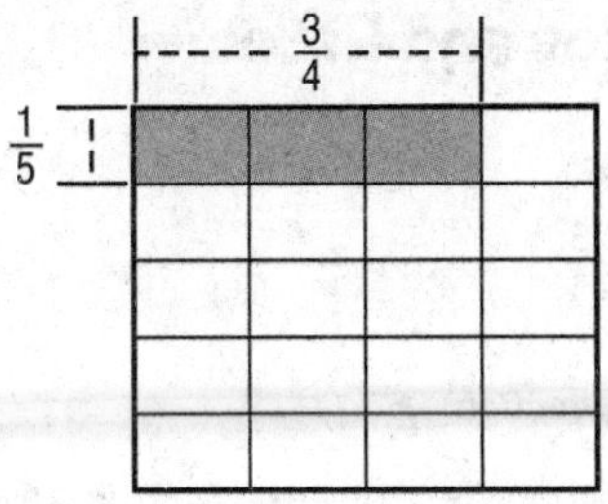

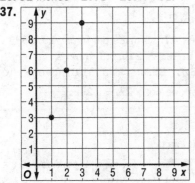

11c. Sample answer: Multiply $\frac{1}{5} \times \frac{1}{4}$. Multiply the product, $\frac{1}{20}$ by \$100. She spent \$5 on a book.   **13.** Sample answer: $a = \frac{3}{8}$ and $b = \frac{5}{7}$; $a = \frac{5}{8}$ and $b = \frac{3}{7}$; $a = \frac{5}{14}$ and $b = \frac{3}{4}$ **15.** C

Lesson 2-3   Extra Practice

17. $\frac{6}{35}$ **19.** $4\frac{1}{8}$ **21.** $\frac{1}{3}$ **23.** Nyemi: 138; Luke: 69; Natalie: 23   **25.** $\frac{1}{2}$ c; $\frac{3}{4} \times \frac{2}{3} = \frac{3 \times 2}{4 \times 3} = \frac{1}{2}$ **27.** H
29. 648   **31.** 1,320   **33.** A; The product must be less than 5 because the factors are 5 and a fraction less than 1.

Lesson 2-4   Independent Practice

1. $1\frac{1}{6}$ **3.** $2\frac{27}{32}$ **5.** 9   **7** $9\frac{1}{4}$ mi   **9** $3\frac{3}{8}$ c
11a. about $69\frac{27}{40}$ million mi   **11b.** about $139\frac{7}{20}$ million mi
11c. about $487\frac{29}{40}$ million mi   **11d.** about $882\frac{11}{20}$ million mi
13. $1\frac{1}{24}$ **15.** B; the product must be greater than $\frac{2}{3}$ and less than $2\frac{1}{2}$.

Lesson 2-4   Extra Practice

17. $2\frac{1}{8}$ **19.** $\frac{17}{20}$ **21.** $12\frac{3}{4}$ **23.** $1,259\frac{1}{4}$ in^2
25. 31 inches   **27.** D   **29.** H   **31.** 4   **33.** 8   **35.** 3
37.

(graph with points plotted at approximately (1, 3), (2, 6), (3, 9); y-axis labeled 1–9, x-axis labeled 1–9)

Lesson 2-5   Independent Practice

1. 6   **3** 52   **5.** $2\frac{1}{2}$ **7** 1,500 lb   **9.** $4\frac{4}{5}$ oz
11a. The x-value represents the number of quarts and the y-value represents the equivalent number of gallons.
11b. Sample answer: The point on the line whose y-value is equal to 2.5 is (10, 2.5), so 10 qt = 2.5 gal.   **13.** 16 in. is equivalent to 1 ft 4 in.; $1\frac{1}{2}$ ft is equivalent to 1 ft 6 in.; So, 16 in. < $1\frac{1}{2}$ ft.   **15.** Sample answer: 5 pt; 80 fl oz

Lesson 2-5   Extra Practice

17. $4\frac{1}{2}$ **19.** 24   **21.** $6\frac{1}{2}$ **23.** 3,520 ft   **25.** No; 15 in. + $4\frac{1}{2}$ in. + $6\frac{3}{4}$ in. = $26\frac{1}{4}$ in.; $2\frac{1}{2}$ ft = 30 in.; So, $26\frac{1}{4}$ in. < 30 in.   **27.** $\frac{1}{2}$ **29.** D   **31.** D   **33.** 39
35. 7.5   **37.** $41\frac{2}{3}$ feet

Problem-Solving Investigation   Draw a Diagram

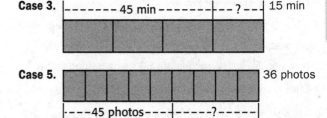

Case 3. 45 min | ? | 15 min

Case 5. 36 photos | 45 photos | ?

Lesson 2-6   Independent Practice

1. $\frac{5}{3}$ **3.** 1   **5.** $6\frac{2}{3}$ **7.** 10   **9** $4\frac{1}{2}$ **11** 110 horses
13. 6 activities; $4 \div \frac{2}{3} = 4 \times \frac{3}{2} = \frac{12}{2} = 6$ **15.** Daniella did not multiply by the reciprocal of 4, which is $\frac{1}{4}$. $\frac{8}{9} \div 4 = \frac{8}{9} \times \frac{1}{4} = \frac{8}{36}$ or $\frac{2}{9}$ **17.** D

Lesson 2-6   Extra Practice

19. $\frac{9}{7}$ **21.** $3\frac{1}{3}$ **23.** $3\frac{3}{5}$ **25.** $7\frac{1}{5}$ **27.** 8 dinners   **29.** A
31. 16 bags; He can only fill another $\frac{2}{3}$ of a bag, so he can't make 17 bags.   **33.** 12   **35.** 15   **37.** 16
39. 84 people

Lesson 2-7   Independent Practice

1. $\frac{1}{4}$ **3** $\frac{1}{12}$ **5.** $\frac{1}{24}$ **7.** Sample answer: David has $\frac{5}{6}$ foot of tape. He uses $\frac{1}{12}$ foot of tape to hang each photo on the bulletin board. How many photos can he hang on the bulletin board? 10 photos

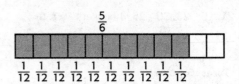

$\frac{5}{6}$

$\frac{1}{12}$ $\frac{1}{12}$ $\frac{1}{12}$ $\frac{1}{12}$ $\frac{1}{12}$ $\frac{1}{12}$ $\frac{1}{12}$ $\frac{1}{12}$ $\frac{1}{12}$ $\frac{1}{12}$

9 $\frac{3}{4} \div \frac{3}{8} = 2$; 2 T-shirts
11.

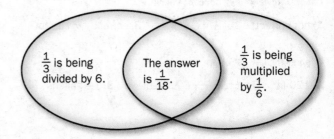

$\frac{1}{3}$ is being divided by 6.   The answer is $\frac{1}{18}$. $\frac{1}{3}$ is being multiplied by $\frac{1}{6}$.

13. greater than 1; the dividend is greater than the divisor; less than 1; the dividend is less than the divisor   **15.** D

Lesson 2-7   Extra Practice

17. $\frac{1}{20}$ **19.** $\frac{1}{7}$ **21.** $\frac{5}{12}$ **23.** $\frac{1}{10} \div 4 = \frac{1}{40}$; $\frac{1}{40}$ kilometer
25. $\frac{7}{8} \div \frac{1}{24} = 21$; 21 cycles   **27.** D   **29.** I   **31.** 4   **33.** 4
35. 4   **37.** 2 feet

Lesson 2-8   Independent Practice

1. $\frac{5}{12}$ **3** $\frac{2}{3}$ **5** 28 slices   **7.** fraction; improper; reciprocal; fractions   **9.** less than; Sample answer: The expression $5\frac{1}{6} \div 3\frac{5}{8}$ represents $5\frac{1}{6}$ being divided into a greater number of parts than the expression $5\frac{1}{6} \div 2\frac{2}{5}$. If $5\frac{1}{6}$ is divided into a greater number of parts, each part will be smaller. So, $5\frac{1}{6} \div 3\frac{5}{8} < 5\frac{1}{6} \div 2\frac{2}{5}$.

Lesson 2-8   Extra Practice

11. $2\frac{3}{4}$ **13.** $2\frac{2}{3}$ **15.** 2   **17.** 2   **19.** $2\frac{1}{10}$ **21.** $6\frac{3}{8} \div \frac{3}{8}$; 17 bags   **23.** D   **25.** 20 books; Twenty books weigh 25 pounds and twenty-one books weigh $26\frac{1}{4}$ pounds, so the bag can hold 20 books.   **27.** $\frac{6}{7}$ **29.** $\frac{1}{8}$ **31.** $\frac{1}{2}$
33. 6 groups

Lesson 2-9   Independent Practice

1. 2   **3.** 7   **5.** 30   **7** 60   **9** 9 pansies   **11.** 30 days
13. Sample answer: A gardener has 27 daisies and 36 marigolds. An equal number of each of flower is planted in each row. What is the greatest number of marigolds in each row? 9 marigolds   **15.** Yes; Sample answer: when 1 is the only common factor of two numbers, then the GCF is one. The GCF of 5 and 7 is one because they are both prime numbers.

Lesson 2-9   Extra Practice

17. 5   **19.** 6   **21.** 15   **23.** 30   **25.** 4 baskets   **27.** C
29. 24 inches   **31.** $\frac{3}{5}$ **33.** $\frac{8}{10}$

Chapter Review   Vocabulary Check

1. mixed number   **3.** reciprocal   **5.** denominator
7. unit ratio   **9.** Compatible numbers

Chapter Review   Key Concept Check

1. not correct; $13 \times \frac{1}{3} = \frac{13}{5}$ or $4\frac{1}{3}$ **3.** correct   **5.** correct

Chapter Review   Problem Solving

1. 120 in^2 **3.** $\frac{7}{16}$ **5.** $\frac{1}{20}$ **7.** 8,800 yd   **9.** $1\frac{2}{5}$ gallons

Chapter 3 Ratios and Rates

Chapter 3   Are You Ready?

1. 29   **3.** 6   **5.** $\frac{1}{4}$ **7.** $\frac{13}{25}$

Lesson 3-1   Independent Practice

1. $\frac{2}{1}$; For every 2 flutes, there is 1 drum.   **3.** $\frac{2}{5}$; For every 2 boys, there are 5 girls in the class.   **5.** 12, 21   **7a.** $\frac{5}{16}$, 5 to 16, or 5:16; The Rangers have made 5 Stanley Cup Finals appearances for every 16 appearances made by the Canadiens.   **7b.** $\frac{23}{17}$, 23 to 17, 23:17; The Maple Leafs have made 23 Stanley Cup appearances to every 17 Bruins' appearances.   **9.** 1,440; The ratios are 1:2, 1:3, 1:4, and 1:5.

Lesson 3-1   Extra Practice

11. $\frac{1}{4}$; for every 1 triangle there are 4 rectangles.   **13.** $\frac{1}{3}$; For every 1 puppy, there are 3 kittens available for adoption.   **15.** $\frac{2}{7}$, 2 to 7, or 2:7; Two out of every 7 food items donated were cans of fruit.   **17.** $\frac{1}{3}$; 1:3; or 1 to 3; Sample answer: If 6 students own a cell phone, 24 − 6 or 18 do not. The ratio is $\frac{6}{18}$ or $\frac{1}{3}$.   **19.** G   **21.** B   **23.** 4
25. 195 miles   **27.** 15 girls

Lesson 3-2   Independent Practice

1. $\frac{12 \text{ oz}}{1 \text{ steak}}$ **3.** $\frac{5.1 \text{ gal}}{1 \text{ container}}$ **5.** Divide the time by the number of laps. Evans drove the fastest at 2.3 minutes per lap.   **7.** $4 per mile   **9a.** 268 miles   **9b.** about 2 h
11. A unit rate has a denominator of 1.
$\frac{\$108}{6 \text{ weeks}} = \frac{\$18}{1 \text{ week}}$ **13.** B

Lesson 3-2   Extra Practice

15. 4 tulips per minute   **17.** 15 miles per hour   **19.** $63 per ticket   **21a.** 10.4 m per s   **21b.** 9.3 m per s
21c. 10.3 m per s   **23.** C   **25.** first kind: $1.67 for one box; second kind: $1.50 for one box   **27.** $\frac{1}{5}$ **29.** $\frac{6}{25}$
31. 53 miles per hour

Lesson 3-3   Independent Practice

1

Number of Pies	5	10	20	8 pounds
Pounds of Apples	2	4	8	

3

American Dollars	270	27	9	$9
Mexican Pesos	3,000	300	100	

5a.

People Served	24
Liters of Soda	4
Pints of Sherbet	2
Cups of Ice	6

5b. 2 L soda, 1 pt sherbet, 3 c ice; 6 L soda, 3 pt sherbet, 9 c ice **5c.** 3 L soda, 1.5 pt sherbet, 4.5 c ice; Since 18 is half of 36, half the recipe that serves 36 people will serve 18 people. 6 L ÷ 2 = 3 L, 3 pt ÷ 2 = 1.5 pt, and 9 c ÷ 2 = 4.5 c. **7.** Larger Quantity: ×; larger batches, Smaller Quantity: ÷; unit rate

9.

Girls	10	5	15
Boys	8	4	12

No; if 5 girls and 5 boys are added, there would be 15 girls and 13 boys in the class. Using the ratio table, you can see that there should be 12 boys for 15 girls.

Lesson 3-3   Extra Practice

11.

Number of Adults	1	2	3	4	4 adults
Number of Students	7	14	21	28	

13.

Ounces of Nectar	16	2	12	60 birds
Number of Birds Fed	80	10	60	

15. 160 mi **17.** B **19.** 8; Sample answer: There are 60 minutes in an hour. 15 × 4 = 60, so 2 × 4 = 8.
21. 7; 3

Lesson 3-4   Independent Practice

1

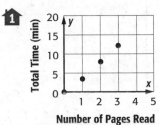

3.

Ken's Home Supply		
Fencing (ft), *x*	Cost ($), *y*	(*x, y*)
1	5	(1, 5)
2	10	(2, 10)
3	15	(3, 15)
4	20	(4, 20)

Wayne's Warehouse		
Fencing (ft), *x*	Cost ($), *y*	(*x, y*)
1	6	(1, 6)
2	12	(2, 12)
3	18	(3, 18)
4	24	(4, 24)

5 Sample answer: As the number of feet of fencing increases, the cost at Wayne's Warehouse increases at a faster rate than the cost at Ken's Home Supply. The cost at Wayne's Warehouse is shown on the graph as a steeper

line.   **7.** Sample answer: Lauren earns $7 an hour tutoring. Make a table showing the relationship between the number of hours she tutors and the amount of money she earns.

9.

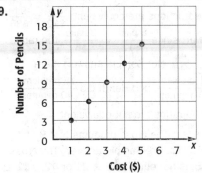

Sample answer: The points at (1, 3), (2, 6), (3, 9), and (5, 15) represent a ratio equivalent to 1:3. The ratio 4:12 is equivalent to 1:3. So, the cost of 12 pencils is $4.

Lesson 3-4   Extra Practice

11.

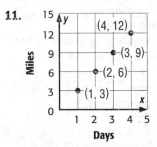

13.

Tiger Exhibit		
Animals, *x*	Employees, *y*	(*x, y*)
1	2	(1, 2)
2	4	(2, 4)
3	6	(3, 6)
4	8	(4, 8)

Elephant Exhibit		
Animals, *x*	Employees, *y*	(*x, y*)
1	4	(1, 4)
2	8	(2, 8)
3	12	(3, 12)
4	16	(4, 16)

15. Sample answer: The number of employees for the elephant exhibit increases at a faster rate than the number of employees for the tiger exhibit. The line representing the elephant exhibit is a steeper line.   **17.** $90   **19.** $\frac{1}{5}$

21. 6 students

Problem-Solving Investigation   The Four-Step Plan

Case 3. 6,482 steps   **Case 5.** $890

Lesson 3-5 Independent Practice

1 No; Since the unit rates, $\frac{\$0.50}{1 \text{ bagel}}$ and $\frac{\$0.38}{1 \text{ bagel}}$, are not the same, the rates are not equivalent. **3** Yes; Since $\frac{3 \text{ h} \times 3}{\$12 \times 3} = \frac{9 \text{ h}}{\$36}$, the fractions are equivalent; $\frac{3 \text{ h}}{\$12} = \frac{9 \text{ h}}{\$36}$. **5.** No; Sample answer: since $\frac{8 \text{ pairs}}{\$12} \neq \frac{3 \text{ pairs}}{\$6}$, the ratios are not equivalent. **7** No; Sample answer: Kiera did $\frac{6 \text{ problems}}{30 \text{ minutes}}$ or $\frac{1 \text{ problem}}{5 \text{ minutes}}$, and Heath did $\frac{18 \text{ problems}}{40 \text{ minutes}}$ or $\frac{9 \text{ problems}}{20 \text{ minutes}}$. So, the ratios are not equivalent. **9a.** Yes; Sample answer: The cross products 5×9 and 3×15 are both 45. **9b.** No; Sample answer: The cross product 7×5 or 35, is not equal to 2×21 or 42. **11.** B

Lesson 3-5 Extra Practice

13. Yes; Since the unit rates are the same, $\frac{32 \text{ words}}{1 \text{ minute}}$, the rates are equivalent; $\frac{96 \text{ words}}{3 \text{ minutes}} = \frac{160 \text{ words}}{5 \text{ minutes}}$. **15.** No; Since $\frac{16 \text{ students}}{28 \text{ students}} \neq \frac{240 \text{ students}}{560 \text{ students}}$, the ratios are not equivalent. **17.** yes; The length to width ratio for the model and sofa form equivalent fractions. **19.** Yes; sample answer: $\frac{\$35}{5 \text{ weeks}} = \frac{\$7}{1 \text{ week}}$ and $\frac{\$56}{56 \text{ days}} = \frac{\$56}{8 \text{ weeks}}$ or $\frac{\$7}{1 \text{ week}}$. **21.** H **23.** 150 **25.** 126 **27.** \$4

Lesson 3-6 Independent Practice

1. 90 cookies **3** 840 gal **5** 60 students **9.** Elisa did not set up the equivalent ratios in the correct order. She should have set it up as $\frac{1}{12} = \frac{\blacksquare}{276}$. There are 23 teachers at the preschool. **11.** 15 people

Lesson 3-6 Extra Practice

13. 54 teenagers **15.** 3 baseballs **17.** 28 DVDs **19.** C **21.** 27 **23.** $\frac{1}{7}$ **25.** $\frac{1}{6}$ **27.** 32 cars

Chapter Review Vocabulary Check

Across
3. ordered pair **9.** graph **11.** y coordinate
Down
1. y axis **5.** scaling **7.** ratio table

Chapter Review Key Concept Check

1. d **3.** a **5.** b

Chapter Review Problem Solving

1. $\frac{1}{3}$, 1 to 3, or 1:3; one out of 3 DVDs Amos owns is an action DVD.
3.

Number of Trucks	3	24	48
Number of Vehicles	8	64	128

48 trucks

5. yes; $\frac{4}{90} = \frac{2}{45}$ and $\frac{2}{45} = \frac{2}{45}$ **7.** 72 students

Chapter 4 Fractions, Decimals, and Percents

Chapter 4 Are You Ready?

1. 4 **3.** 18 **5.** 60 **7.** 3 rotations

Lesson 4-1 Independent Practice

1. $\frac{1}{2}$ **3.** $\frac{33}{100}$ **5** 0.385 **7.** 0.16 **9** Mercury: 87.96; Venus: 224.7; Mars: 686.98 **11a.** meat: $\frac{7}{20}$; vegetables: $\frac{3}{20}$; sauce: $\frac{1}{20}$; bread: $\frac{1}{20}$ **11b.** $\frac{1}{5}$ lb **11c.** $\frac{3}{5}$ lb **13** Sample answer: $\frac{1}{5}$ in. and $\frac{7}{20}$ in. **15.** Always; a decimal that ends in the thousandths place can have a denominator of 1,000. Since 1,000 is divisible by 2 and 5, the denominator of every such terminating decimal is divisible by 2 and 5. **17.** C

Lesson 4-1 Extra Practice

19. $\frac{13}{20}$ **21.** $9\frac{7}{20}$ **23.** 0.622 **25.** 14.6 **27.** 23.375 **29.** 0.6 **31.** D **33.** $\frac{4}{5}$ **35.** 1; 5 **37.** 18; 25
39.

Multiplication Problem	Product
36 × 100	3,600
36 × 10	360
36 × 1	36
36 × 0.1	3.6
36 × 0.01	0.36

Lesson 4-2 Independent Practice

1 $\frac{1}{50}$ **3.** $\frac{17}{20}$ **5.** 20% **7.** 35% **9.** $\frac{7}{25}$ **11** $\frac{9}{50}$ **13.** Do not prefer: 80%, prefer: 20%; the sum of the percents is 100. **15.** Sample answer: $\frac{11}{20} = \frac{55}{100}$ or 55%, $\frac{3}{5} = \frac{60}{100}$ or 60%, $\frac{7}{10} = \frac{70}{100}$ or 70% **17.** $\frac{8}{45}$; The other numbers are equivalent to $\frac{9}{20}$. **19.** D

Lesson 4-2 Extra Practice

21. $\frac{47}{100}$ **23.** $\frac{22}{25}$ **25.** 84% **27.** 72% **29.** 95% **31a.** 44% **31b.** 16% **31c.** 60% **31d.** 40% **33.** H **35.** 68.5 **37.** 325.5 **39.** \$2.76

Lesson 4-3 Independent Practice

1 0.35 **3.** 0.31 **5.** 22% **7.** 10% **9.** 0.04 **11** 12% **13.** C: \$59.50, A: \$70, B: \$87.50 **15.** 0.88, 0.90, 0.92 **17.** Sample answer: Since $\frac{3}{4}$ is equal to 0.75, write $43\frac{3}{4}\%$ as 43.75%. Then change 43.75% to the decimal 0.4375. **19.** D

Lesson 4-3 Extra Practice

21. 0.03 **23.** 0.11 **25.** 62% **27.** 87% **29.** 0.65
31. 82% **33.** D **35.** 0.25 **37.** = **39.** >
41. Aliah's brother

Lesson 4-4 Independent Practice

1. 3.5; $3\frac{1}{2}$ 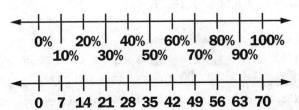 **3** 0.0015; $\frac{3}{2,000}$ **5.** 250% **7.** 420%
9. 850% **11.** 0.9% **13** 140% **15.** 0.003; $\frac{3}{1,000}$;
3 out of every 1,000 people are Japanese. **17a.** 0.0005
17b. sulfur **19.** 30 mph **21.** B

Lesson 4-4 Extra Practice

23. 4; 4 **25.** 0.0004; $\frac{1}{2,500}$ **27.** 3,500% **29.** 0.77%
31. 9.8% **33.** 0.0012 **35.** 125% **37.** 133% **39.** D
41. <
43.

```
←——+——+——+——+——+——+——+——+——+——+——→
   0  0.1 0.2 0.3 0.4 0.5 0.6 0.7 0.8 0.9  1
```

Problem-Solving Investigation Solve a Simpler Problem

Case 3. 2 books **Case 5.** 21 bracelets

Lesson 4-5 Independent Practice

1. < **3** < **5.** $\frac{1}{4}, \frac{1}{2}, \frac{2}{3}, \frac{5}{6}$ **7.** Alex; 0.35 < 0.40
9a. 0.20, 0.25, 0.20 **9b.** Two are the same; 0.25 is the
greatest score. **11** 8%, 17%, 0.2, $\frac{11}{20}$ **13.** $\frac{3}{9}, \frac{3}{8}$, and $\frac{3}{7}$;
Because the numerators are the same, the larger the
denominator, the smaller the fraction. **15.** A

Lesson 4-5 Extra Practice

17. = **19.** > **21.** $\frac{1}{2}, \frac{9}{16}, \frac{5}{8}, \frac{3}{4}$ **23.** 3%, $\frac{2}{50}$, 0.08
25. $\frac{1}{2}$, 0.55, $\frac{5}{7}$ **27.** B **29.** $\frac{1}{8}, \frac{3}{16}, \frac{11}{32}, \frac{3}{4}$ **31.** 4.29 **33.** $\frac{37}{50}$

Lesson 4-6 Independent Practice

1 $\frac{1}{2}$ of $120 is $60. **3** $\frac{2}{5}$ of 15 is 6. **5.** 24 + 24 +
24 = 72 **7.** $\frac{3}{4}$ of 20 yr is 15 yr. **9a.** No; 40% is $\frac{2}{5}$. $\frac{2}{5}$ of
15 is 6. He needs 7 baskets to win a prize. **9b.** about 50%
11 Sample answer 71 − 37 = 34 missed shots and $\frac{34}{71}$
is about $\frac{35}{70}$ or $\frac{1}{2}$. Since $\frac{1}{2}$ = 50%, he missed about 50% of
his shots. **13.** about 75% **15.** More; Rachel rounded
$32 down to $30, so the actual amount she will save will
be more than $12. **17.** Sample answer: First, round 42%
to 40%, and $122 to $125. Next, rewrite 40% as $\frac{2}{5}$. Then
find $\frac{1}{5}$ of $125. Finally, multiply this result by 2 to find $\frac{2}{5}$ of
$125.

Lesson 4-6 Extra Practice

19. $\frac{1}{2}$ of 60 is 30. **21.** $\frac{1}{4}$ of 120 is 30. **23.** 19 + 19 +
19 = 57 **25.** 61 + 61 + 61 + 61 = 244 **27.** $\frac{3}{4}$ of 8 h is
6 h. **29.** about 423; 47 × 9 = 423 **31.** about 75% **33.** B
35. G **37.** 0.07 **39.** 0.15 **41.** 0.06 **43.** 22.5 ft²

Lesson 4-7 Independent Practice

1. 46 **3.** 92 **5** 9 **7.** 336 **9** $8.40 **11.** No; 70%
of 30 is 21, not 24. 80% of 30 is 24. **13.** Sample
answers given for examples. Percent: equal to; 100%; less
than; 25%; greater than; 125%. Fraction: equal to; $\frac{3}{3}$; less
than; $\frac{1}{3}$; greater than; $\frac{4}{3}$ **15.** Yes; 16% of 40 is 6.4 and
40% of 16 is 6.4 **17.** C

Lesson 4-7 Extra Practice

19. 16.5 **21.** 161 **23.** 159.84 **25.** 0.45 **27.** 18 ounces
of bleach **29.** 398.24 **31.** 212.85 **33.** C **35.** Sample
answer: about 135 cars; Round 28% to 30%; 30% of 450
is 135. **37.** 90 **39.** 7.5 **41.** 4.8
43.

Trip	Part of Club
Carnegie Museum of Art	0.32
Fallingwater	0.20
Westemoreland Museum of American Art	0.48

Lesson 4-8 Independent Practice

1. 70

3 $\frac{22}{\blacksquare} = \frac{44}{100}$; 50 **5** $50 **7.** 15 cups **9.** 20 cups
11. Sample answer: $\frac{\blacksquare}{25} = \frac{84}{100}$; 21 **13.** 18 karats; 24 is
the whole and 75 is the percent, so $\frac{18}{24} = \frac{75}{100}$. **15.** B

Lesson 4-8 Extra Practice

17. 400

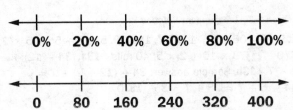

19. $\frac{270}{\blacksquare} = \frac{90}{100}$; 300   **21.** 24   **23.** 300 students
25. 240 ounces   **27.** H   **29.** 300 cans   **31.** 49   **33.** 123
35. 16   **37.** 4.5 miles

Chapter Review   Vocabulary Check

1. percent   **3.** percent proportion   **5.** least common
denominator

Chapter Review   Key Concept Check

1. not correct;

$$\frac{4}{5} \rightarrow 5\overline{)4.0}$$
$$\begin{array}{r}0.8\\ -40 \\ \hline 0\end{array}$$

3. not correct;

$$120\% = \frac{120}{100}$$
$$= \frac{6}{5}$$
$$= 1\frac{1}{5}$$

Chapter Review   Problem Solving

1. savings: $\frac{2}{5}$; charity: $\frac{3}{20}$; shopping: $\frac{9}{20}$ **3.** $\frac{4}{5}$ **5.** Miguel
7. 15 in.; Sample answer: $\frac{1}{4}$ of 60 is 15.

Chapter 5 Expressions

Chapter 5   Are You Ready?

1. 343   **3.** 6,561   **5.** $1\frac{5}{9}$ **7.** $\frac{1}{20}$

Lesson 5-1   Independent Practice

1. 6^2 **3.** 5^6 **5.** 27^4 **7.** $6 \times 6 \times 6 \times 6$; 1,296
9. $\frac{1}{8} \times \frac{1}{8} = \frac{1}{64}$ **11.** 1.0625   **13.** 1,100.727
15a. The next values are found by dividing the previous
power by 2.   **15b.** The next values are found by dividing the
previous power by 4.   **15c.** The next values are found by
dividing the previous power by 10.   **17.** D

Lesson 5-1   Extra Practice

19. 10^3 **21.** 9^2 **23.** 13^5 **25.** 0.06×0.06; 0.0036
27. 8,100 square feet   **29.** 42.875 miles   **31.** 145
33. 48   **35.** 6   **37.** $43

Lesson 5-2   Independent Practice

1. 9   **3.** 106   **5.** 117   **7.** 112   **9.** $5 \times 7 + 5^2 + 5 \times 2$;
$70   **11.** $3 \times 10 + 2 \times 5$; 40 rolls   **13a.** $(34 - 12) \div$
$2 + 7$ **13b.** Sample answer: $34 - (12 \div 2) + 7 =$
$34 - 6 + 7 = 28 + 7 = 35$ **15.** D

Lesson 5-2   Extra Practice

17. 13   **19.** 3   **21.** 99   **23.** 38   **25.** $2\frac{1}{2} \times 8 \times 5$; 100 oz

27. G   **29.** 9   **31.** 14   **33.** $37

Lesson 5-3   Independent Practice

1. 12   **3.** 18   **5.** 1   **7.** 20   **9.** $\frac{1}{8}$ m³   **11.** $415.80
13. 29   **15.** 7 ft²   **17.** Sample answer: Both numerical
expressions and algebraic expressions use operations, for
example $6 + 7$ and $8 \div n$. An algebraic expression, such
as $6 + a$, includes numbers and variables, where a
numerical expression, such as, $6 + 3$ only includes
numbers.

Lesson 5-3   Extra Practice

19. 24   **21.** 14   **23.** 3   **25.** 22   **27.** $117   **29.** $81\frac{1}{2}$
31. 180   **33.** B   **35.** I   **37.** >   **39.** $2 + 4 = 6$ **41.** 12 miles

Lesson 5-4   Independent Practice

1. w = the width; $w - 6$ **3.** t = Tracey's age; $t - 6$
5. s = the number in the Senate; $4s + 35$;
435 members   **7.** $2.54x$; 30.48 cm   **9.** m = Marcella's
age; $\frac{1}{3}m + 2$; Justin is 23 years old and Aimee is 42 years
old.   **11.** c = total customer order; $2 + 0.2c$ **13.** C

Lesson 5-4   Extra Practice

15. s = number of Ruben's shoes; $s + 10$
17. m = the number of ringtones Mary has; $2m + 3$
19. c = cost of one drink; $4c + 12.75$; $24.75
21. p = number of purses in Aisha's collection; $\frac{1}{2}p + 3$;
Cierra has 9 purses.   **23.** H   **25.** 7.8   **27.** 14.5
29. $3 \times 4 = 12$ and $4 \times 3 = 12$; 12 tiles

Problem-Solving Investigation   Act It Out

Case 3. Team 3   **Case 5.** 13 toothpicks

Lesson 5-5   Independent Practice

1. yes; Associative Property   **3.** no; The first expression
is equal to 17 and the second is equal to 1.   **5.** No; the
first expression is equal to 32, not 0.   **7.** $75,000 \cdot 5$
and $5 \cdot 75,000$ **9.** $42r$ **11.** 3   **13.** Sample answer:
$12 + (8 + 5)$ and $(12 + 8) + 5$ **15.** Sample answer:
$24 \div 12 = 2$ and $12 \div 24 = 0.5$

Lesson 5-5   Extra Practice

17. yes; Identity Property   **19.** No; the first expression is
equal to 4 and the second is equal to $\frac{1}{4}$ or 0.25.
21. No; the first expression is equal to 13, not 1.
23. The expressions $\frac{1}{2}(37)(20)$ and $\frac{1}{2}(20)(37)$ are
equivalent. Either one can be used to find how much
money she will donate. Half of 20 is 10 and $10 \cdot 37$ is
370. She will donate $370.   **25.** $b + 4$ **27.** $120y$
29. $36w$ **31.** I   **33.** $(2 \times 7) \times 6$ and $2 \times (7 \times 6)$
35. $30 + 7$ **37.** four $10 bills and three $1 bills

Lesson 5-6 Independent Practice

1. $9(40) + 9(4) = 396$ 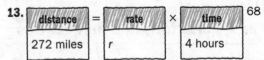 **3** $7(3) + 7(0.8) = 26.6$
5. $66 + 6x$ **7** $6(43) - 6(35) = 6(43 - 35)$; 48 mi
9. $6(9 + 4)$ **11.** $11(x + 5)$ **13.** $7(11x + 3)$ **15.** 0.37;
Sample answer: $0.1(3.7) = 0.1(3) + 0.1(0.7) = 0.3 + 0.07 = 0.37$ **17.** Sample answer: The friend did not
multiply 5 and 2. The expression $5(x + 2) = 5x + 10$.

Lesson 5-6 Extra Practice

19. 152 **21.** 11.7 **23.** $3x + 21$ **25.** $9(2.50 + 4) = 9(2.50) + 9(4)$; \$58.50 **27.** $3(9 + 4)$ **29.** $4(4 + 5)$
31. $6(5 + 2x)$ **33.** B **35.** $4(x + 5)$ **37.** 0 **39.** \$65;
Since $20 + 15 + 10 + 20 = 15 + 20 + 10 + 20$, they
each saved the same amount.

Lesson 5-7 Independent Practice

1. $11x$ **3** $45x$ **5.** $21x + 35y$ **7** $6(4x + 3y)$
9. $4(x + 6) + 4x$; $8x + \$24$ **11** $6(3t + 2c) = 18t + 12c$ **13.** 9 **15a.** $3(x + 0.75) + 2x$; $\$5x + \$2.25$
15b. $6(x + 3.75) + 2x$; $\$8x + \$22.50$ **15c.** $2(x + 1.50) + 3x$; $\$5x + \$3$ **17.** The expressions are equivalent because
they name the same number regardless of which number
stands for y. **19.** $6x + (-21)$ or $6x - 21$

Lesson 5-7 Extra Practice

21. $9x$ **23.** $21x$ **25.** $28x + 20y$ **27.** $5(2x + 3y)$
29. $4(x + 3 + 2)$; $\$4x + \$20$ **31.** $4(5t + 3j) = 20t + 12j$
33. terms: $2x, 3y, x, 7$; like terms: $2x, x$; coefficients: 1, 2, 3;
constant: 7 **35.** I **37.** 1;8 **39.** 5;9 **41.** 28

Chapter Review Vocabulary Check

Across
1. algebraic **7.** powers **9.** base **13.** coefficient
Down
3. perfect square **5.** like terms **11.** variable

Chapter Review Key Concept Check

1. $12x + 12$ **3.** $3x - 6$ **5.** $2(x + 3)$

Chapter Review Problem Solving

1. $3 \times 5 + 7$; 22 motorcycles **3.** $m =$ amount of memory
that is music; $m + 0.5$ **5.** $14 + (16 + 11)$ and
$(14 + 16) + 11$ **7.** $3(x + 2) + 2x$; $\$5x + \$6$

Chapter 6 Equations

Chapter 6 Are You Ready?

1. 1.11 **3.** 2.69 **5.** $\frac{1}{3}$ **7.** $\frac{13}{40}$ mi

Lesson 6-1 Independent Practice

1 25 **3.** 5 **5.** 13 **7.** 3 **9.** 11 **11.** 5 games
13 35 students **15.** Sample answer: $m + 8 = 13$
17. True; $m + 8$ is not equal to any specific value, so there
are no restrictions placed upon the value of m. **19.** D

Lesson 6-1 Extra Practice

21. 31 **23.** 9 **25.** 8 **27.** 5 **29.** 2 **31.** 6 members
33. C **35.** F **37.** 63 **39.** 115 **41.** 93 **43.** \$7.69

Lesson 6-2 Independent Practice

1 3 **3.** 2 **5** $m + 22 = 118$; 96 in. **7.** $\frac{2}{5}$ **9** $\frac{1}{4}$
11. 0, 1, 2 **13.** D

Lesson 6-2 Extra Practice

15. 3 **17.** 5 **19.** 5 **21.** $9 + x = 63$; 54 inches **23.** $\frac{1}{10}$
25. $\frac{1}{2}$ **27.** G **29.** 14 **31.** 15 **33.** 52 **35.** $\frac{1}{3}$ more of a
pizza

Lesson 6-3 Independent Practice

1. 9 **3** 4 **5.** 3.4 **7.** $a - 6 = 15$; 21 years old **9.** 21
11. 1 **13** $x - 56 = 4$; \$60 **15.** Elisa did not perform the
inverse operation. Add 6 to each side to undo subtracting 6.
17. Sample answer: I would use what I know about fact
families to rewrite the equation $b + 7 = 16$. The solution
is 9.

Lesson 6-3 Extra Practice

19. $f = 6$ **21.** 4 **23.** 14.7 **25.** $15 = v - 12$; 27 votes
27. 19 **29.** $\frac{1}{2}$ **31.** $x - 12 = 3$; \$15 **33.** H **35.** 504
37. 135 **39.** 144 **41.** 16 cars

Problem-Solving Investigation Guess, Check, and Revise

Case 3. five problems worth 2 points each and two
problems worth 4 points each **Case 5.** $3 \times 4 + 6 \div 1 = 18$

Lesson 6-4 Independent Practice

1 6 **3.** 6 **5.** 2 **7.** $4e = 58$; \$14.50 **9.** $\frac{1}{2}$
11a. $26p = 2,002$; 77 points **b.** $16p = 1,736$;
108.5 points

13.

distance	=	rate	×	time	68
272 miles		r		4 hours	

15. $4b = 7$; The solution for the other equations is 4. **17.** B

Lesson 6-4 Extra Practice

19. 5 **21.** 4 **23.** 2 **25.** 7 **27.** $1,764 = 28r$; 63 mph
29. 5 **31.** 3 **33.** 4 **35.** A **37.** 32 grams **39.** 16
41. 31 **43.** 63 **45.** $\frac{1}{8}$ pie

Lesson 6-5 Independent Practice

1 20 **3** 15.04 **5** $\frac{x}{4} = 3$; 12 dozen

7.

+	−
Subtraction Property of Equality	Addition Property of Equality
×	÷
Division Property of Equality	Multiplication Property of Equality

9. True; Sample answer: Dividing by 3 is the same as multiplying by $\frac{1}{3}$. **11.** A

Lesson 6-5 Extra Practice

13. 84   **15.** 169   **17.** 56   **19.** 3   **21.** $\frac{x}{3} = 2$; 6 eggs
23. $\frac{r}{4} = 16$; 64 in.   **25.** B   **27.** $\frac{x}{3} = 6$; 18 mi   **29.** >
31. <   **33.** <   **35.** 28

Chapter Review Vocabulary Check

Across
1. division property   **5.** solution   **7.** addition property
Down
3. inverse operations

Chapter Review Key Concept Check

1. $x = 16$ **3.** $x = 24$ **5.** $x = 68$

Chapter Review Problem Solving

1. 9 h   **3.** $4 + x = 10$; 6 ft   **5.** $25t = 5$; $0.20   **7.** $\frac{b}{4} = 10$;
40 min

Chapter 7 Functions and Inequalities

Chapter 7 Are You Ready?

1. >   **3.** <   **5.** 46   **7.** 3

Lesson 7-1 Independent Practice

1.

Input (x)	3x + 5	Output
0	3(0) + 5	5
3	3(3) + 5	14
9	3(9) + 5	32

3.

Input (x)	x + 2	Output
0	0 + 2	2
1	1 + 2	3
6	6 + 2	8

5.

Number of Guests (x)	30 ÷ x	Cupcakes per Guest (y)
6	30 ÷ 6	5
10	30 ÷ 10	3
15	30 ÷ 15	2

7. 56 miles

9.

Years (x)	223 million × $10 × x
1	$2,230,000,000
2	$4,460,000,000
3	$6,690,000,000

11. B

Lesson 7-1 Extra Practice

13.

Input (x)	4x + 2	Output
1	4(1) + 2	6
3	4(3) + 2	14
6	4(6) + 2	26

15.

Input (x)	2x − 6	Output
3	2(3) − 6	0
6	2(6) − 6	6
9	2(9) − 6	12

17.

Hours (x)	55x	Miles (y)
3	55(3)	165
4	55(4)	220
5	55(5)	275

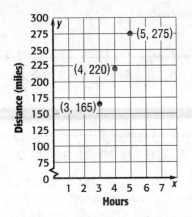

19. F **21.** 14 **23.** 32 **25.** 48 **27.** $4.80

Lesson 7-2 Independent Practice

1 add 9 to the position number; $n + 9$; 21 **3.** Sample answer: This is a geometric sequence. Each term is found by multiplying the previous term by 3; 486, 1,458, 4,374

5. add 12; 52, 64 **7.** add $\frac{1}{2}$; $4\frac{1}{4}$, $4\frac{3}{4}$ **9.** 29.6

11. arithmetic sequence; 4.75, 5.75 **13** arithmetic sequence; Each term is found by adding 2 to the previous term.; $10 + 2 = 12$; 12 boxes **15.** The value of each term is the square of its position; n^2; 10,000.

Lesson 7-2 Extra Practice

17. subtract 4 from the position number; $n - 4$; 8

19. Each term is found by multiplying the previous term by 3; 324, 972, 2,916 **21.** add 3; 13, 16

23. add $1\frac{1}{2}$; $7\frac{1}{2}$, 9 **25.** 19.3 **27.** H **29.** 186

31. 128 **33.** 162 **35.** $13.50

Lesson 7-3 Independent Practice

1. $y = 6x$

3

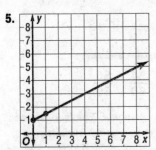

5.

7

Input (x)	1	2	3	4
Output (y)	5	10	15	20

$y = 5x$

9. Sample answer: Ray is saving $7 per week to buy a new DVD player. The variable y represents the total amount he has saved. The variable x represents the number of weeks.

11. B

Lesson 7-3 Extra Practice

13. $y = 10x$

15.

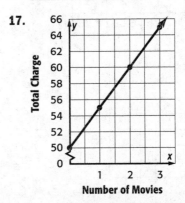

17.

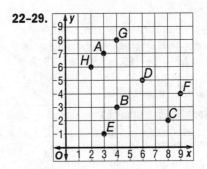

19. C **21.**

Number of Days	Total Cost
4	$28
8	$56
12	$84

22–29.

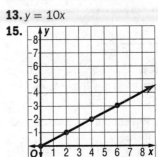

31. $1.95

Lesson 7-4 Independent Practice

1 a. $v = 400d$

b.

Number of Days, d	1	2	3
Pounds Eaten, v	400	800	1200

c.

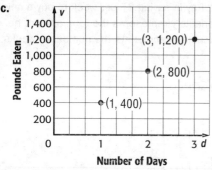

The graph is a line because with each day the amount of vegetation increases by 400.

3 a. $t = 3 + 1.75c$; where t represents the total earned and c represents the number of chores

b.

Number of Chores, c	1	2	3
Total Earned ($), t	4.75	6.50	8.25

c.

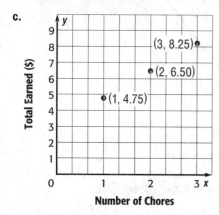

d. $11.75   **5.** No; the graphs of the lines will never meet other than at zero hours.   **7.** C

Lesson 7-4   Extra Practice

9. Music Man: $t = 45n$; Road Tunes: $t = 35n$; where t represents the total cost and n represents the number of hours   **11.** C   **13.** $p = 2m + 5s$ **15.** >   **17.** <   **19.** <

Problem-Solving Investigation   Make a Table

Case 3. 35 cubes   **Case 5.** 25 toothpicks

Lesson 7-5   Independent Practice

1 5   **3.** yes   **5.** flying, stand up, or suspended

7 Jan. and Feb.; $0.75   **9.** Sample answer: 0, 1, and 2   **11.** $a > c$; if $a > b$, then it is to the right of b on the number line. If $b > c$, then it is to the right of c on the number line. Therefore, a is to the right of c on the number line.   **13.** D

Lesson 7-5   Extra Practice

15. 0   **17.** no   **19.** Carmen, Eliot, and Ryan   **21.** A   **23.** 5 + 3   **25.** 5 × 8   **27.** 6; 4

Lesson 7-6   Independent Practice

1. $p \leq 35$ **3** $p < 437$

5.

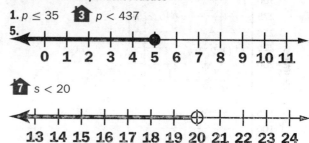

7 $s < 20$

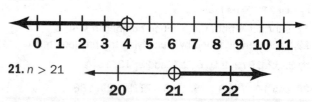

9. She used the incorrect symbol. "at least" means the values will be larger than 10, but include 10; $c \geq 10$
11. When an inequality uses the greater than or less than symbols, it does not include the number given. So, $x > 5$ and $x < 7$ do not include 5 or 7 respectively. When the greater than or equal to and less than or equal to symbols are used, the given numbers are included. So, $x \geq 5$ and $x \leq 7$ include 5 and 7, respectively.

Lesson 7-6   Extra Practice

13. $s \leq 50$ **15.** $h > 200$

17.

19. $t < 4$

21. $n > 21$

23. H   **25.** 11   **27.** 13   **29.** 12

Lesson 7-7   Independent Practice

1. $y \leq 1$

3 $x > 8$

5 $0.1x \leq 5.00$; $x \leq 50$

7 $p > \frac{53}{60}$

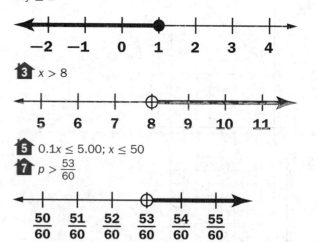

9. Sample answer: An airplane can hold 53 passengers and there are currently 32 passengers on board. How many more passengers can board the airplane?   **11.** Yes; Sample answer: $x > 5$ is not the same relationship as $5 > x$. However, $x > 5$ is the same relationship as $5 < x$.

Lesson 7-7 Extra Practice

13. $a < 5$

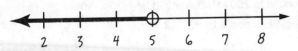

15. $d \geq 9$

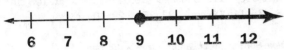

17. $g < 12$

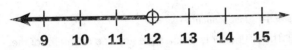

19. $25b \geq 5,000$; $b \geq 200$

21. $n \geq \dfrac{3}{14}$

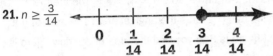

23. A **25.** A **27.** 144 **29.** 192 **31.** 66 **33.** 15 ft²

Chapter Review Vocabulary Check

Across
3. function rule **5.** geometric sequence **9.** sequence
Down
1. arithmetic sequence **7.** inequality

Chapter Review Key Concept Check

1. 24 **3.** geometric **5.** function

Chapter Review Problem Solving

1.

Games (n)	4(n)	Cost (t)
1	4(1)	4
2	4(2)	8
3	4(3)	12

3. $t = 10p$

5.

Number of Dogs Washed (d)	Total Earned (t)
1	28
2	31
3	34

$25 + 3d = t$

7. $4g \leq 12$; $g \leq 3$

Chapter 8 Area

Chapter 8 Are You Ready?

1. 32 cm² **3.** 18 cm² **5.** 14 **7.** 12

Lesson 8-1 Independent Practice

1. 9 units² **3** 72 cm² **5.** $166\frac{1}{2}$ ft²

7 No; in order for the area of the first floor to be 20,000 ft² and the base 250 feet, the height must be 20,000 ÷ 250 or 80 feet.

9a. Sample answers are given.

Base (cm)	Height (cm)	Area (cm²)
1	4	4
2	4	8
3	4	12
4	4	16
5	4	20

9b.

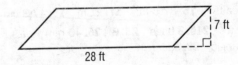

9c. It appears to form a line. **11.** Sample answer: Both parallelograms and rectangles have bases and heights. So, the formula $A = bh$ can be used for both figures. The height of a rectangle is the length of one of its sides while the height of a parallelogram is the length of the altitude.

Lesson 8-1 Extra Practice

13. 20 units² **15.** 180 in² **17.** 325 yd² **19.** 25 mm
21. Sample answer: 196 ft²

7 ft

28 ft

23. 84 cm² **25.** G
27.

29.

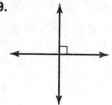

31. isosceles triangle; Sample answer: It is a closed three-sided figure with two congruent sides.

Lesson 8-2 Independent Practice

1. 24 units^2 **3.** 747 ft^2 **5.** 19 cm

7. a. $\frac{5n}{2}$ **b.**

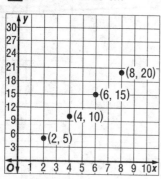

c. The points appear to form a line.

9. The formula is $\frac{1}{2}bh$, not bh.

$$100 = \frac{b \cdot 20}{2}$$
$$b = 10 \text{ m}$$

11.

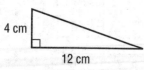

Sample answer: Area of first triangle is 24 cm^2; Area of second triangle is 48 cm^2; 1:2 or $\frac{1}{2}$.

Lesson 8-2 Extra Practice

13. $7\frac{1}{2}$ units^2 **15.** 87.5 m^2 **17.** 21 m **19.** 47.3 cm
21a. 27 ft^2 **21b.** 3 bags **23.** B **25.** 40 mm
27. rectangle **29.** square

Lesson 8-3 Independent Practice

1. 168 yd^2 **3.** 112 m^2 **5.** 16 mm **7. a.** 7,000 ft^2
b. 4 bags
9. Sample answer:

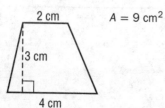

$A = 9$ cm^2

11. Sample answer: The lengths of the bases can be rounded to 20 m and 30 m, respectively. The area can be rounded to 250 m^2. Divide 250 by $\frac{1}{2}(20 + 30)$ or 25. The height h is about 10 m. **13.** D

Lesson 8-3 Extra Practice

15. 161.5 ft^2 **17.** 10 inches **19.** 1,557 mi^2 **21.** 108 cm^2
23. B **25.** 11,000 cm^2 **27.** 256 **29.** 30 cm

Problem-Solving Investigation Draw a Diagram

Case 3. 15 balloons **Case 5a.** 120 ft^2 **Case 5b.** 2 qt

Lesson 8-4 Independent Practice

1. The perimeter is 4 times greater. The perimeter of the original figure is 36 cm and the perimeter of the new figure is 144 cm; 144 cm ÷ 36 cm = 4. **3.** The area is multiplied by $\frac{1}{3} \cdot \frac{1}{3}$ or $\frac{1}{9}$ the original area. The area of the original figure is 315 yd^2 and the area of the new figure is 35 yd^2; 35 yd^2 ÷ 315 yd^2 = $\frac{1}{9}$. **5.** Use the area and the length to find the width of the queen-size bed. The width of the bed is 4,800 ÷ 80, or 60 inches. So, the width of the dollhouse bed is 60 · $\frac{1}{12}$, or 5 inches. The length of the dollhouse bed is 80 · $\frac{1}{12}$ or $6\frac{2}{3}$ inches.
7. Sample answer:

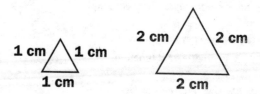

9. A

Lesson 8-4 Extra Practice

11. The perimeter is 6 times greater. The perimeter of the original figure is 30 ft and the perimeter of the new figure is 180 ft; 180 ft ÷ 30 ft = 6. **13.** The perimeter is $\frac{1}{4}$ the original perimeter. The perimeter of the original figure is 80 m and the perimeter of the new figure is 20 m; $\frac{1}{4} \cdot 80$ m = 20 m. The area is $\frac{1}{4} \cdot \frac{1}{4}$ or $\frac{1}{16}$ the original area. The area of the original figure is 240 m^2 and the area of the new figure is 15 m^2; 15 m^2 ÷ 240 m^2 = $\frac{1}{16}$.
15. C **17.** I
19. Opposite sides are congruent and parallel. **21.** square

Lesson 8-5 Independent Practice

🏠**1** 58.6 in^2 **3.** 189 ft^2 🏠**5 a.** 467.4 ft^2 **b.** 467.4 ÷ 350 ≈ 1.34; Since only whole gallons of paint can be purchased, you will need 2 gallons of paint. At $20 each, the cost will be 2 × $20 or $40. **7.** Sample answer: Add the areas of a rectangle and a triangle. Area of rectangle: 3 × 4 = 12; Area of triangle: $\frac{1}{2}$ × 3 × 3 = 4.5; 12 + 4.5 = 16.5. So, an approximate area is 16.5 × 2,400 or 39,600 mi^2. **9.** B

Lesson 8-5 Extra Practice

11. 66.2 m^2 **13.** 10,932 ft^2 **15.** A **17.** 3,150 ft^2
19. 1,065 **21.** 105 cm^3

Chapter Review Vocabulary Check

1. polygon **3.** parallelogram **5.** rhombus
7. composite figure

Chapter Review Key Concept Check

1. $A = \frac{1}{2}h(b_1 + b_2)$ **3.** $A = \frac{1}{2}(9.8)(7 + 12)$ **5.** $A = 93.1$

Chapter Review Problem Solving

1. 6 ft **3.** 66.5 ft^2 **5.** 100 ft^2 **7.** The perimeter is 0.5 or $\frac{1}{2}$ the original perimeter. The perimeter of the original figure is 36 cm and the perimeter of the new figure is 18 cm; 18 cm ÷ 36 cm = 0.5.

Chapter 9 Volume and Surface Area

Chapter 9 Are You Ready?

1. 214.5 **3.** 172.8 **5.** 44 **7.** 101

Lesson 9-1 Independent Practice

1. 132 m^3 🏠**3** 171 in^3 **5.** 17 m **7.** 3 mm
🏠**9 a.** $50\frac{5}{8}$ in^3 **b.** $16\frac{7}{8}$ in^3 **c.** 75% **11.** No; the volume of the figure is 3^3 or 27 cubic units. If the dimensions doubled, the volume would be 6^3 or 216 cubic units, eight times greater. **13.** C

Lesson 9-1 Extra Practice

15. 1,430 ft^3 **17.** 2,702.5 in^3 **19.** 360 mi^3 **21.** C
23. 20 in. **25.** obtuse triangle
27.

Lesson 9-2 Independent Practice

1. 336 m^3 🏠**3** 104.0 cm^3 🏠**5** 108 in^3 **7.** 8 in.
9. 10 yd **11.** To find the base area, Amanda should have multiplied by $\frac{1}{2}$. The base area of the prism is 6 cm^2, not 12 cm^2. So, the volume of the prism is 42 cm^3.

13. The rectangular prism will hold more mints than the triangular prism. The rectangular prism has a volume of 144 in^3 while the triangular prism has a volume of 72 in^3.

Lesson 9-2 Extra Practice

15. 346.5 ft^3 **17.** 380 in^3 **19.** 10,395 in^3 **21.** 15 m
23. 48 ft^3 **25.** C **27.** Cabinet A: 3,888 in^3; Cabinet B: 4,760 in^3; Tia should purchase cabinet B. **29.** 18 units^2
31. 12 times

Problem-Solving Investigation Make a Model

Case 3. yes; Sample answer: 8 + 10 + 12 + 14 + 16 + 18 + 20 = 98; Since 98 < 100, there are enough chairs. **Case 5.** 16 boxes

Lesson 9-3 Independent Practice

1. 2,352 yd^2 🏠**3** 3,668.94 m^2 **5.** 1,162 cm^2
🏠**7** Package A: 492 in^2; Package B: 404 in^2; Package A has a greater surface area. No, the volume of Package B is greater. **9.** 48 in^2; 144 in^2 **11.** B

Lesson 9-3 Extra Practice

13. 324 m^2 **15.** 384.62 cm^2 **17a.** 316.5 in^2
17b. 534 in^2 **17c.** 207.75 in^2 **19.** H **21.** 224
23. 1,701 **25.** right angle

Lesson 9-4 Independent Practice

1. 1,152 yd^2 🏠**3** 13.6 m^2 🏠**5** about 21.4 yd^2
7. 279.2 in^2 **9.** 7.5 in. **11.** Sample answer: Prism A with bases that are right triangles that measure 3 by 4 by 5 and with a height of 1. Prism B with bases that are right triangles that measure 1 by 1 by 1.4 and with a height of 10. Prism A has a greater volume while Prism B has a greater surface area.

Lesson 9-4 Extra Practice

13. 537 ft^2 **15.** 70.8 in^2 **17.** 282.7 cm^2 **19.** 428.1 cm^2
21. D **23.** H **25.** acute **27.** square

Lesson 9-5 Independent Practice

1. 24 m^2 🏠**3** 126.35 cm^2 **5.** 143.1 mm^2 🏠**7** 52 cm^2
9. 132 in^2 **11.** 110 ft^2; Sample answer: A pyramid has only one square base. To find the surface area, add 25 + (4 · 21.25). **13.** C

Lesson 9-5 Extra Practice

15. 223.5 ft^2 **17.** 383.25 cm^2 **19.** 923 in^2 **21.** 14 in.
23. 671.6 in^2 **25.** 24 **27.** 60 **29.** 5 cm

Chapter Review Vocabulary Check

1. three-dimensional figure **3.** volume **5.** rectangular prism **7.** vertex **9.** lateral face

Chapter Review Key Concept Check

Across
1. 480.4 **5.** 8

Down
1. 40   **3.** 520

Chapter Review   Problem Solving

1. 1,845,720 yd³   **3.** 76 ft²   **5.** 84.8 ft²

Chapter 10 Statistical Measures

Chapter 10   Are You Ready?

1. 68.75   **3.** $21.60   **5.** 24.20   **7.** 115.2 miles

Lesson 10-1   Independent Practice

1 88%   **3** $25   **5.** 88   **7.** Sample answer: pages read: 27, 38, 26, 39, 40   **9.** C

Lesson 10-1   Extra Practice

11. 56 in.   **13.** 26 tickets   **15.** C   **17.** G   **19.** >   **21.** >   **23.** >

Lesson 10-2   Independent Practice

1 89; none; There is no mode to compare.
3. The values are close. The median and mode are equal, 44 mph, and the mean, 45.58 mph, is slightly more. The data follows the measures of center in the way that they are close to the measure of center.   **5** Mode; The mode of the temperatures in Louisville is 70° and the mode for Lexington's temperatures is 76°. Since 76° − 70° = 6°, the mode was used to make this claim.   **7.** $21
9. Sample answer: The median or mode best represents the data. The mean, 8, is greater than all but one of the data values.

Lesson 10-2   Extra Practice

11. median: 23; mode: 44; The mode is 21 years more than the median.   **13.** median: 12.5; mode: none; There is no mode to compare.   **15.** Sample answers are given.

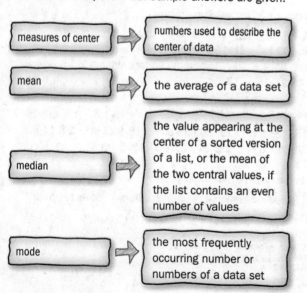

measures of center	numbers used to describe the center of data
mean	the average of a data set
median	the value appearing at the center of a sorted version of a list, or the mean of the two central values, if the list contains an even number of values
mode	the most frequently occurring number or numbers of a data set

17. $7.45   **19.** 35   **21.** 84   **23.** 22   **25.** 5.2 miles

Problem-Solving Investigation   Use Logical Reasoning

Case 3. 42 customers   **Case 5.** 6 students; 10 students

Lesson 10-3   Independent Practice

1 a. 1,028   b. 923.5; 513; 1,038   c. 525   d. none
3 median: 357.5, Q_1: 298, Q_3: 422, IQR: 124
5. range: 63, median: 7.5, Q_3: 30.5, Q_1: 0.5, IQR: 30; Sample answer: The number of moons for each planet varies greatly. The IQR and range are both large.
7. Sample answer: The median is correct, but Hiroshi included it when finding the third and first quartiles. The first quartile is 96, the third quartile is 148, and the interquartile range is 52.   **9.** Sample answer: The third quartile is the median of the upper half of the data and the first quartile is the median of the lower half of the data.   **11.** B

Lesson 10-3   Extra Practice

13a. NFC   **13b.** NFC—median: 86, Q_3: 113, Q_1: 68, IQR: 45; AFC—median: 80, Q_3: 94, Q_1: 76, IQR: 18
13c. Sample answer: The AFC had a median of 80 penalties and the NFC had a median of 86 penalties. The AFC had an IQR of 18 penalties while the NFC had an IQR of 45 penalties. The ranges were 47 penalties for the AFC and 78 penalties for the NFC.   **15.** D   **17.** 14 months; 10 months; 8.5 months; 13.5 months; 5 months   **19.** 23.5   **21.** 17.5   **23.** 12.4   **25.** 7 hours

Lesson 10-4   Independent Practice

1 17.88 moons; Sample answer: The average distance each data value is from the mean is 17.88 moons.
3. United States: 9.77 km; Europe: 2.87 km; Sample answer: The mean absolute deviation in bridge lengths in the U.S. is greater than the mean absolute deviation of the bridge lengths in Europe. The lengths of the bridges in Europe are closer to the mean.   **5** eight   **7.** yes; Sample answer: Twice the mean absolute deviation is 2 × 1.50 million, or 3.00 million. Since 5.86 million > 3.00 million, the population of 8.4 million is greater than 3.00 million away from the mean.   **9.** Sample answer: It helps me to remember to take the absolute value of the difference between each data value and the mean.
11. with the data value of 55: 5.33 miles per hour; without the data value of 55: 2 miles per hour   **13.** Sample answer: The mean absolute deviation is the average distance that each data value is from the mean. Since distance cannot be negative, the absolute values of the differences are used.

Lesson 10-4   Extra Practice

15. $26.76; The average distance each data value is from the mean is $26.76.   **17.** Sixth grade: $10.67; Seventh grade: $16.67; Sample answer: The mean absolute deviation of the money raised by sixth grade homerooms is less than the mean absolute deviation of the money raised by seventh grade classrooms. The amounts of the money raised by the sixth grade homerooms are closer to the mean. **19.** B **21.** 45.33 Calories **23.** 23.75 **25.** 6.3 **27.** 5.8 **29.** 15.75 **31.** 235 cones

Lesson 10-5 Independent Practice

1 The mean best represents the data. There are no extreme values. mean: 56.4 minutes **3 a.** 1,148
b. With the outlier, the mean is 216.83 ft, the median is 33.5 ft, there is no mode, and the range is 1,138 ft. Without the outlier, the mean is 30.6 ft, the median is 24 ft, there is no mode, and the range is 52 ft. **c.** With the outlier, the best measure is the median depth; without the outlier, the best measure is the mean. **5.** Pilar did not include the outlier. The mean is 20. The median, which is 15.5, best describes the data because the outlier affects the mean more than it affects the median. **7.** Sample answer: 125, 32, and 19

Lesson 10-5 Extra Practice

9. Since the set of data has no extreme values or numbers that are identical, the mean or median, 6 songs, would best represent the data. **11a.** 62° **11b.** With the outlier, the mean is 32.71°, the median is 29°, the mode is 29° and the range is 37°. Without the outlier, the mean is 27.83°, the median is 28.5°, the mode is 29°, and the range is 4°.
11c. Sample answer: With the outlier, the best measure is the mode; without the outlier, the best measure is the mode; the outlier does not affect the mode, but affects the mean and median. **13.** The median best describes the data with and without the outlier of 98 because it changes the least. With the outlier, the median is 36. Without the outlier, the median is 35, so it only decreased by 1. **15.** Sample answer: the mean and median times best represent the data. The mean is 12.56 s and the median is 12.55 s. There are no extreme values. **17.** 260 **19.** 154

Chapter Review Vocabulary Check

1. mode **3.** range **5.** interquartile range

Chapter Review Key Concept Check

Across
1. 505 **3.** 249 **5.** 138 **9.** 96 **11.** 8312
Down
1. 53 **3.** 281 **7.** 691 **11.** 83

Chapter Review Problem Solving

1. 72 mph **3.** 82°; 82° **5.** $1.17; Sample answer: The average distance each price is from the median is $1.17. **7.** Sample answer: The median or mode; the mode is not affected by the outlier and the median only varies by 1 percentage point with and without the outlier.

Chapter 11 Statistical Displays

Chapter 11 Are You Ready?

1. 16 **3.** 27 **5.** 57 **7.** 84.5

Lesson 11-1 Independent Practice

1

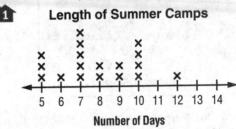

Length of Summer Camps

Number of Days

median: 7.5; mode: 7; range: 7; no outlier; There are a total of 18 summer camps represented. The median means that one half of the summer camps are longer than 7.5 days and one half are less. More camps are 7 days than any other number of days. **3** Sample answer: There are 15 play lists represented. mean: 40; median: 40; modes: 40 and 42; So, the majority of the data is close to the measures of center. Q_1: 38; Q_3: 42; IQR: 4, which means half the playlists have between 38 and 42 songs; there is an outlier at 25. **5.** 11 **7.** The outlier of the data set is 29°F, not 20°F. **9.** 24 cm **11.** C

Lesson 11-1 Extra Practice

13.

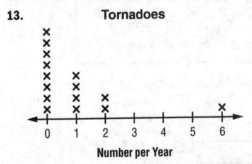

Tornadoes

Number per Year

median: 0; mode: 0; range: 6; outlier: 6 There were 15 tornadoes represented. The median means that half the number of tornadoes was greater than zero and half the number of tornadoes was zero.
15. Sample answer: The median, range, and outliers do not exist because the data are not numerical. The mode is pepperoni, because more students prefer pepperoni than any other topping. The plot shows responses for 10 people. There are five different toppings. Two topping preferences were chosen by only one person. **17.** G
19. > **21.** < **23.** > **25.** 6 students

Lesson 11-2 Independent Practice

1. Sample answer: 24 cyclists participated. No one finished with a time lower than 60 minutes. **3** 60–64

5.

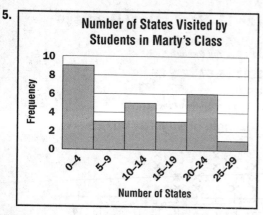

Number of States Visited by Students in Marty's Class

7 6th grade   **9.** Sample answer: ages of students at summer camp: 3, 4, 5, 7, 7, 8, 8, 10, 10, 11, 13, 14, 15, 15
11. D

Lesson 11-2   Extra Practice

13. 24–27   **15.** 17

17.

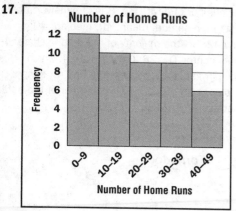

Number of Home Runs

19. A   **21.** H   **23.** 53   **25.** 65.4   **27.** 210.5

Lesson 11-3   Independent Practice

1

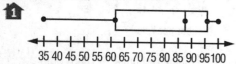

3 a.   Length of Coastline (mi)

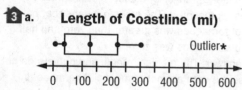

3b. 127 mi   **c.** Sample answer: The length of the box plot shows that the number of miles of coastline for the top 25% of states varies greatly. The number of miles of coastline for the bottom 25% of states is concentrated.

5a.   Ticket Sales

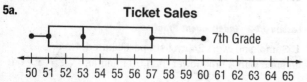

5b. Grade 6; Sample answer: The median, upper extreme, and first and third quartiles are higher for the grade 6 data.
7. Sample answer: {28, 30, 52, 68, 90, 92}

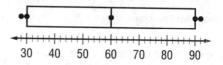

Lesson 11-3   Extra Practice

9.

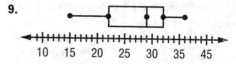

11a. 96   **11b.** Sample answer: The scores were closer together between 82 and 86.   **11c.** 75%   **11d.** 82   **13.** A
15.

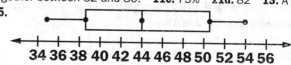

17. 125   **19.** 280   **21.** 200

Problem-Solving Investigation   Use a Graph

Case 3. 5 lawns
Case 5. 91

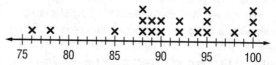

Lesson 11-4   Independent Practice

1 Sample answer: The shape of the distribution is not symmetric. There is a cluster from 1–79. The distribution has a gap from 80–199. The peak of the distribution is on the left side of the data in the interval 20–39. There is an outlier in the interval 200–219.   **3 a.** median and interquartile range; Sample answer: The distribution is not symmetric.   **b.** Sample answer: The data are centered around 23.5 text messages. The spread of the data around the center is about 3 text messages.   **5a.** Sample answer: The lengths of the whiskers are not the same.
5b. skewed left; Sample answer: The data are more spread out on the left side due to the long left whisker.   **5c.** Sample answer: Use the median and interquartile range to describe the center and spread since the distribution is not symmetric. The data are centered around 40 feet. The spread of the data around the center is 10 feet.   **7.** Sample answer: The distribution is symmetric. The appropriate measures to describe the center and spread are the mean and mean absolute deviation. A box plot shows the measures to describe the center and spread are the mean and mean absolute deviation. A box plot shows the location of the median and interquartile range but it does not show the location of the mean or the mean absolute deviation.

Lesson 11-4   Extra Practice

9. Sample answer: The shape of the distribution is symmetric. The left side of the data looks like the right side. There is a cluster from $13–$15. There are no gaps in the data. The peak of the distribution is $14. There are no outliers.   **11a.** mean and mean absolute deviation; Sample answer: The distribution is symmetric and there are no outliers.   **11b.** Sample answer: The data are centered around 31 miles. The spread of the data around the center is about 1.3 miles.   **13.** A

15–22.

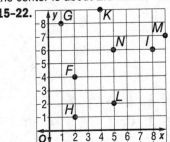

23. 36 pages

Lesson 11-5   Independent Practice

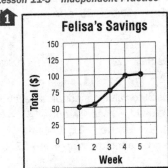

Sample answer: Felisa's total savings increased slowly for Weeks 1 and 2, then increased more dramatically for Weeks 3 and 4 with a slower increase for Week 5.

3a.

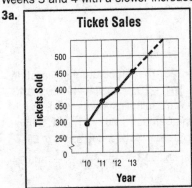

3b. 500 tickets   **5.** Sample answer: If the vertical scale is much higher than the highest value, it makes the graph flatter. Changing the interval does not affect the graph.
7. Sample answer: Line graphs are often used to make a prediction because they show changes over time and they allow the viewer to see data trends and make predictions.

Lesson 11-5   Extra Practice

9.

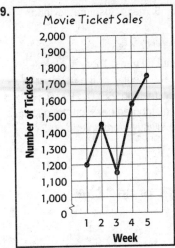

The online sales of movie tickets increased from Week 1 to Week 2, decreased in Week 3 and then increased again for Weeks 4 and 5.   **11a.** 1992 and 1996; The winning time decreased by about 1 second.   **11b.** Sample answer: 48.50 seconds; Based on the trend from 1992 to 2008, the winning time decreased.   **13.** I   **15.** 41   **17.** 24   **19.** 331
21. 321 miles

Lesson 11-6   Independent Practice

1 bar graph; The bar graph shows the maximum speeds, not just the interval in which the data occurs.   **3.** box plot; A box plot easily displays the median.

7   **Number of Neighbors**

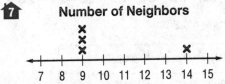

Sample answer: The line plot allows you to easily see how many countries have a given number of neighbors. The bar graph, however, allows you to see the number of neighbors for each given country.   **9.** Sample answer: line plot; You can easily locate the values with the most Xs to find the mode.

Lesson 11-6   Extra Practice

11. box plot; The median is easily seen on the box plot as the line in the box.   **13.** bar graph; A bar graph allows for the prices to be compared.   **15.** Sample answer: box plot; A box plot easily shows the spread of data.   **17.** B
19. Sample answer: line plot; It shows each piece of the data individually.   **21.** 9   **23.** 12   **25.** 26   **27.** 15
29. 15 cm; 0.15 m

Chapter Review   *Vocabulary Check*

Across
7. gap   **9.** dot plot
Down
1. symmetric   **3.** histogram   **5.** cluster

Chapter Review   Key Concept Check

1. line graph   **3.** box plot   **5.** mean absolute deviation

Chapter Review   Problem Solving

1. Sample answer: There are no gaps. There is a peak at 1 and a cluster from 0–4. The median of the data set is 2 pets.   **3.** Sample answer: median: 85; Q_1: 81; Q_3: 90; IQR: 9; The data is evenly distributed between the quartiles. The left side of the data is slightly more spread out.
5. bar graph

Chapter 12 Integers and the Coordinate Plane

Chapter 12   Are You Ready?

1. =   **3.** <   **5.** >   **7.** peanuts

Lesson 12-1   Independent Practice

1. −3; The integer 0 represents at sea level.
3 −5; The integer 0 represents neither moving backward nor moving forward.

5
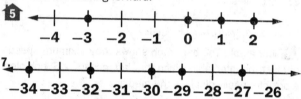

7.
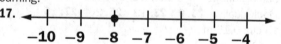

9. Sample answers are given.

Positive Integer	Negative Integer
• gain	• lose
• above	• below
• earn	• spend
• +	• −

11. Negative; Sample answer: A drop of 15° would result in a temperature of 0°F. Since the drop of 20° is greater than 15°, the temperature is below zero and will be represented by a negative integer.   **13.** D

Lesson 12-1   Extra Practice

15. −25; The integer 0 represents neither spending nor earning.
17.
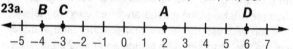

19.   **21.**
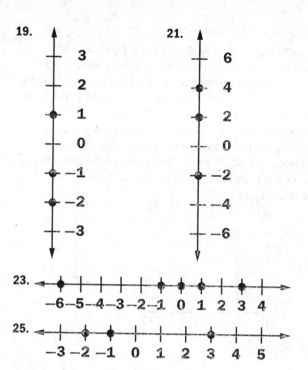

23.

```
←―●―┼―┼―┼―┼―●―┼―●―●―┼―●―┼→
  −6 −5 −4 −3 −2 −1  0  1  2  3  4
```

25.

```
←―┼―●―┼―●―┼―┼―●―┼―●―┼→
  −3 −2 −1  0  1  2  3  4  5
```

27. The integer 0 represents neither owing money nor having money.   **29.** <   **31.** >   **33.** <   **35.** 104 raffle tickets

Lesson 12-2   Independent Practice

1. −6   **3.** 0   **5.** −9   **7.** 14   **9** 21   **11.** 4 feet
13 70°F   **15.** 14   **17.** Absolute value cannot be a negative number. So, the absolute value of −14 is 14, not −14.
19. Never; distance cannot be negative.   **21.** Absolute value is distance and distance cannot be negative.   **23.** C

Lesson 12-2   Extra Practice

25. −15   **27.** 9   **29.** −8   **31.** 0   **33.** 15   **35.** 11
37. 9 yards   **39.** −10   **41.** B   **43.** D   **45.** Acetone   **47.** >
49. $8\frac{3}{4}$ tsp

Lesson 12-3   Independent Practice

1. >   **3.** >   **5** −9 < 26; The temperature in Flagstaff, Arizona, was warmer.   **7** −79, −55, 18, 44, 101, 143
9a. Sun   **9b.** Sun, 100-Watt Bulb, Full Moon, Venus, Andromeda Galaxy, Alpha Centauri   **9c.** −27   **11.** Sample answer: Elise owes her brother $15. Jacob has $7. Elise has less money than Jacob.   **13.** $-\frac{12}{4}, -\frac{1}{2}, \frac{1}{6}, \frac{7}{8}$, and $\frac{5}{2}$

Lesson 12-3   Extra Practice

15. <   **17.** <   **19.** −20 > −25; Michael owes less money than Yvonne.   **21.** −221, −89, −71, −10, 54, 63
23a.

```
    B  C              A           D
←―┼―●―●―┼―┼―┼―┼―●―┼―┼―┼―●―┼→
 −5 −4 −3 −2 −1  0  1  2  3  4  5  6  7
```

23b. D; Since −4 < −3 < 2 < 6, player D had the most strokes over par.   **25.** F   **27.** 0.75   **29.** 0.15   **31.** Mitchell

Problem-Solving Investigation Work Backward

Case 3. 1,220 meters   **Case 5.** 3

Lesson 12-4   Independent Practice

1 $0.4\overline{6}$ **3.** $-0.\overline{6}$ **5.** $3.34\overline{09}$ **7.** $0.\overline{34}$ **9.** $-\dfrac{9}{10}$

11. $-3\dfrac{4}{5}$ **13.** $\dfrac{4}{13}$ **15** $0.\overline{7}$ **17a.** 43   **17b.** $\dfrac{24}{43}$; 0.558

19. $\dfrac{17}{36}$ is not a terminating decimal since decimals are based on powers of 10 and 36 is not a factor of any power of 10.   **21.** B

Lesson 12-4   Extra Practice

23. $0.\overline{27}$ **25.** -0.7 **27.** $-1.\overline{80}$ **29.** $-\dfrac{3}{20}$ **31.** $-12\dfrac{27}{50}$

33. B   **35.** $-\dfrac{5}{4}$ **37.** >   **39.** >   **41.** >

43. $47.394 > 47.362$

Lesson 12-5   Independent Practice

1. >   **3** =   **5** $-2\dfrac{3}{4}, -2.\overline{2}, 2.8, 3\dfrac{1}{8}$ **7.** $-4\dfrac{1}{2}, -2\dfrac{3}{8},$
$1.35, 5.6$ **9** $-10.8, -9.7, 9.0, 11.4$ **11.** always; The greater a number is, the farther away from zero. Therefore, its opposite will also be farther from zero.   **13.** The first decimal is a terminating decimal, so its thousandths place is zero. The second decimal has a repeating digit of 3 so its thousandths place is 3. $-0.330 > -0.\overline{333}$ **15.** D

Lesson 12-5   Extra Practice

17. >   **19.** >   **21.** <   **23.** $1\dfrac{1}{5}, 1.25, 1.2\overline{5}, 1\dfrac{3}{4}$ **25.** <
27. >   **29.** A   **31.** D   **33.** $-6.25, -2.45, 5.50, 7.80$

35–41.
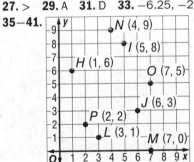

Lesson 12-6   Independent Practice

1. (2, 2); I   **3.** (−4, 2); II   **5** (5, 0); none   **7** Z; II
9. A; IV   **11.** N; none   **13a.** The Clock   **13b.** the Wonder Wheel; (2, −4)   **13c.** the Big Coaster; (−3, 1)
13d. (−1, −2)   **15.** Quadrants I and III; Sample answer: In Quadrant I, both coordinates are positive and in Quadrant III, both coordinates are negative.   **17.** Sample answer: The first coordinate tells the location in relation to the *y*-axis. The second coordinate tells the location in relation to the *x*-axis. Any point is defined by only one ordered pair.

Lesson 12-6   Extra Practice

19. (1, 3); I   **21.** (−2, 1); II   **23.** (−4, −5); III   **25.** L; II
27. S; IV   **29.** B; III   **31a.** (4, 2)   **31b.** (4, 4)   **31c.** (−1, −4)
33. G

35.
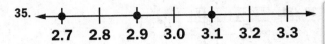
2.7 2.8 2.9 3.0 3.1 3.2 3.3

37. 19 magazines

Lesson 12-7   Independent Practice

1–8.
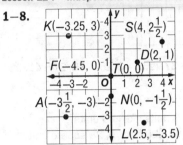

9 –11.
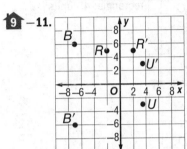

13. (4.25, −1.75)

15
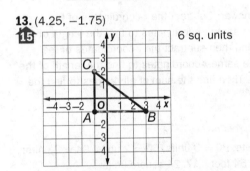
6 sq. units

17. Sample answer: (7, 2), (−5, 2)   **19.** always; The *y*-coordinate will be the opposite of the original following the reflection across the *x*-axis. The *x*-coordinate will be the opposite of the original following the reflection across the *y*-axis.

Lesson 12-7   Extra Practice

21–28.
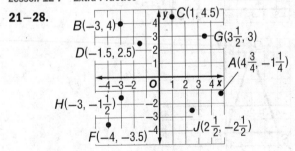

29–31.

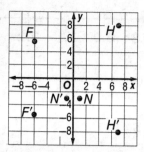

33. (4.75, 2.25)   **35.** D   **37.** (2.5, −3.25)   **39.** 27   **41.** 25

Lesson 12-8   Independent Practice

1 $DE = 5$ units, $EF = 3$ units, $FG = 5$ units, $GD = 3$ units; 16 units   **3.** 120 cm   **5.** 28 square units

7

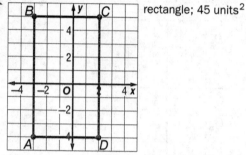

rectangle; 45 units^2

11. Sample answer: Subtract the *x*-coordinates of the points with the same *y*-coordinates to find the length of 2 of the sides and then subtract the *y*-coordinates of the points with the same *x*-coordinates to find the length of the other 2 sides. Then find the sum of all 4 sides to find the perimeter.

Lesson 12-8   Extra Practice

13. $AB = 2$ units, $BC = 3$ units, $CD = 2$ units, $DA = 3$ units; 10 units   **15.** 54 feet   **17.** 24 square units

19.

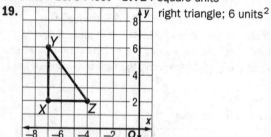

right triangle; 6 units^2

21.

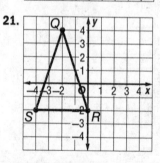

isosceles triangle; $A = 12$ units^2 **23.** 21 ft2

25.

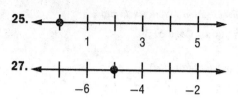

27.

29. 15 yd; 10 yd

Chapter Review   Vocabulary Check

1. rational number   **3.** positive integer
5. terminating decimal

Chapter Review   Key Concept Check

1. 4   **3.** x-coordinate   **5.** 6.543

Chapter Review   Problem Solving

1. 6   **3.** 20   **5.** library
7. $-\dfrac{109}{2}$ in., $-\dfrac{203}{4}$ in., $66\dfrac{1}{3}$ in., $72\dfrac{5}{8}$ in.

Index

Index

Name ____

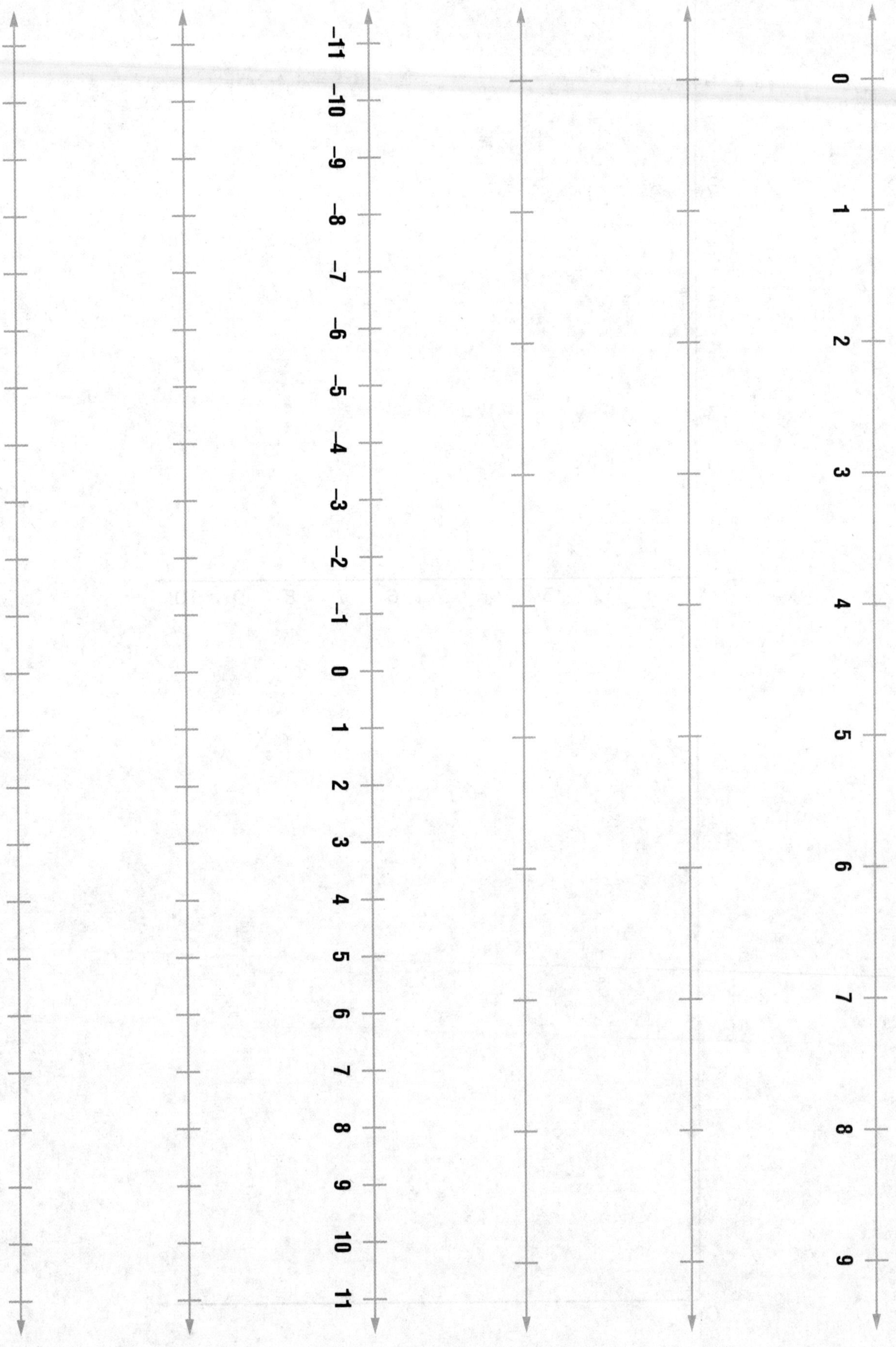
0 1 2 3 4 5 6 7 8 9
–11 –10 –9 –8 –7 –6 –5 –4 –3 –2 –1 0 1 2 3 4 5 6 7 8 9 10 11

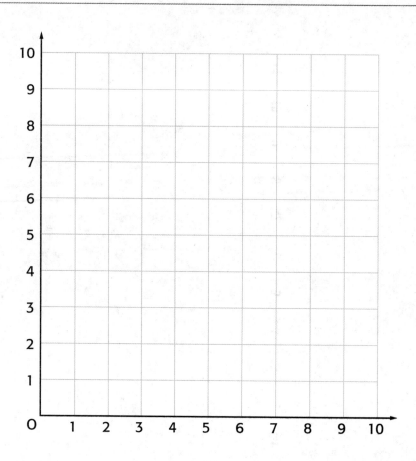

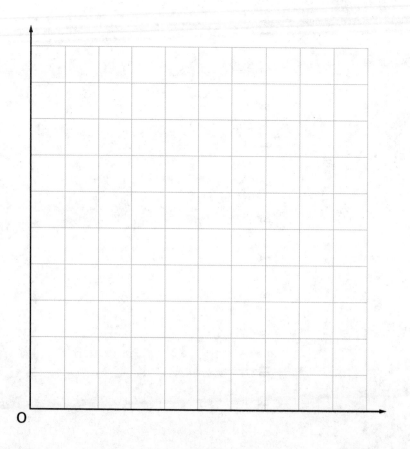

WM2   First Quadrant Grids

Name _____

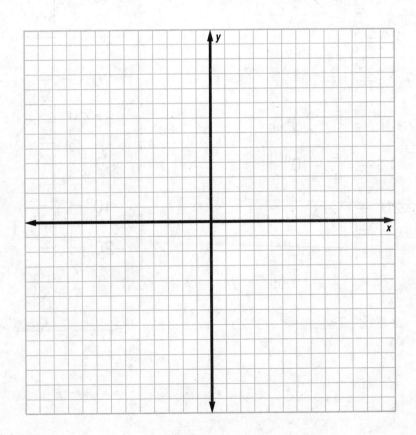

Coordinate Planes   WM3

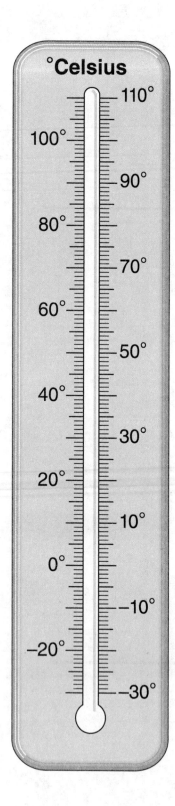

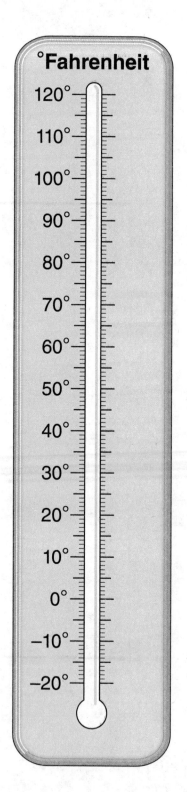

=

Equation Mat **WM5**

Work Mats

WM6   **Centimeter Grid**

Name _____

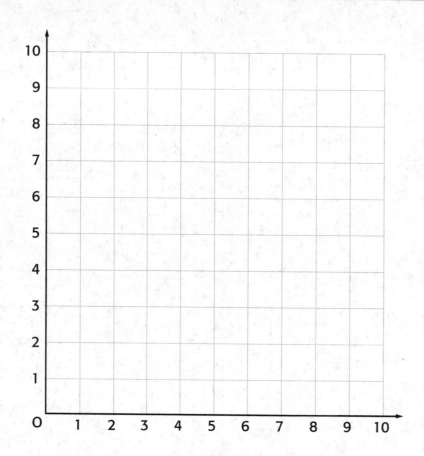

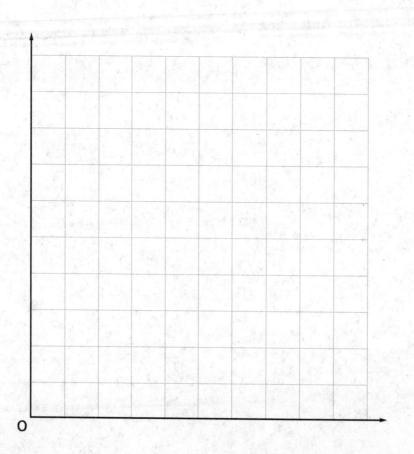

WM8 **First Quadrant Grids**

What Are Foldables and How Do I Create Them?

Foldables are three-dimensional graphic organizers that help you create study guides for each chapter in your book.

Step 1 Go to the back of your book to find the Foldable for the chapter you are currently studying. Follow the cutting and assembly instructions at the top of the page.

Step 2 Go to the Key Concept Check at the end of the chapter you are currently studying. Match up the tabs and attach your Foldable to this page. Dotted tabs show where to place your Foldable. Striped tabs indicate where to tape the Foldable.

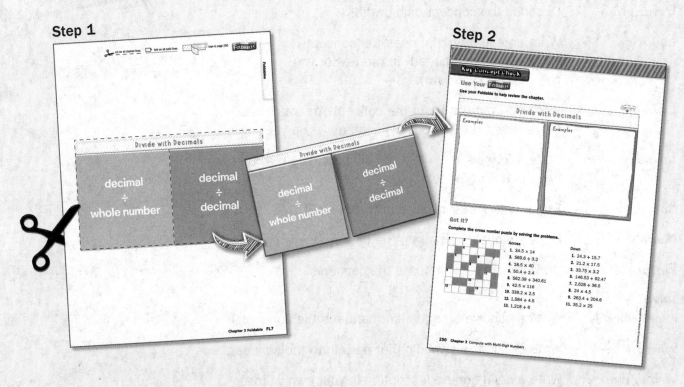

How Will I Know When to Use My Foldable?

When it's time to work on your Foldable, you will see a Foldables logo at the bottom of the **Rate Yourself!** box on the Guided Practice pages. This lets you know that it is time to update it with concepts from that lesson. Once you've completed your Foldable, use it to study for the chapter test.

How Do I Complete My Foldable?

No two Foldables in your book will look alike. However, some will ask you to fill in similar information. Below are some of the instructions you'll see as you complete your Foldable. **HAVE FUN** learning math using Foldables!

Instructions and what they mean

Best Used to...	Complete the sentence explaining when the concept should be used.
Definition	Write a definition in your own words.
Description	Describe the concept using words.
Equation	Write an equation that uses the concept. You may use one already in the text or you can make up your own.
Example	Write an example about the concept. You may use one already in the text or you can make up your own.
Formulas	Write a formula that uses the concept. You may use one already in the text.
How do I ...?	Explain the steps involved in the concept.
Models	Draw a model to illustrate the concept.
Picture	Draw a picture to illustrate the concept.
Solve Algebraically	Write and solve an equation that uses the concept.
Symbols	Write or use the symbols that pertain to the concept.
Write About It	Write a definition or description in your own words.
Words	Write the words that pertain to the concept.

Key Concept Check
Use Your FOLDABLES
Use your Foldable to help review the chapter.
Divide with Decimals
Examples
Examples
Tape here

Meet Foldables Author Dinah Zike

Dinah Zike is known for designing hands-on manipulatives that are used nationally and internationally by teachers and parents. Dinah is an explosion of energy and ideas. Her excitement and joy for learning inspires everyone she touches.

I ♡ Foldables!

Divide with Decimals

decimal
÷
whole number

decimal
÷
decimal

✂ cut on all dashed lines   ⊏⊐ fold on all solid lines   tape to page 80   **FOLDABLES**

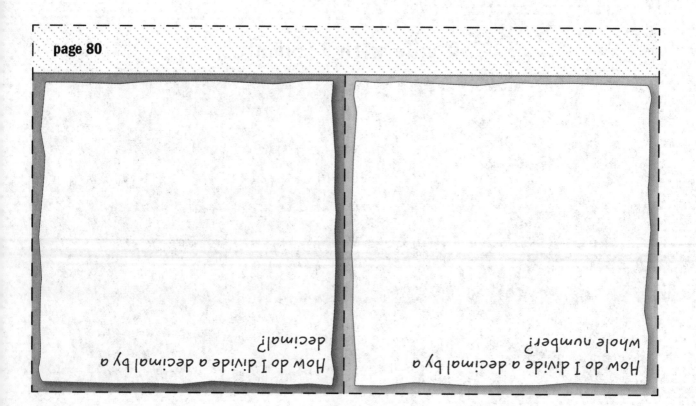

page 80

How do I divide a decimal by a decimal?

How do I divide a decimal by a whole number?

Multiply and Divide Fractions

multiply

divide

Example

Example

fraction x whole number

whole number ÷ fraction

Example

Example

fraction x fraction

fraction ÷ fraction

✂ cut on all dashed lines   ⬜ fold on all solid lines   tape to page 174   **FOLDABLES**

page 174

Tab 3

How do I divide a whole number
by a fraction?

How do I multiply a fraction
by a whole number?

page 174

Tab 2

How do I divide a fraction
by a fraction?

How do I multiply a fraction
by a fraction?

page 174

Tab 1

How do I divide a mixed number
by a fraction?

How do I multiply a fraction
by a mixed number?

FL6   **Chapter 2 Foldable**

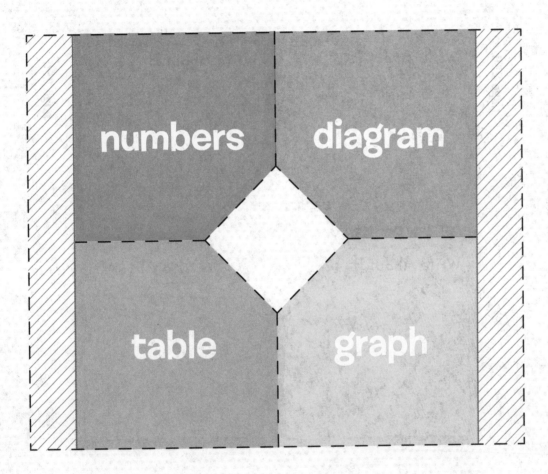

✂ cut on all dashed lines   ⬜ fold on all solid lines   ▨ tape to page 250   **FOLDABLES**

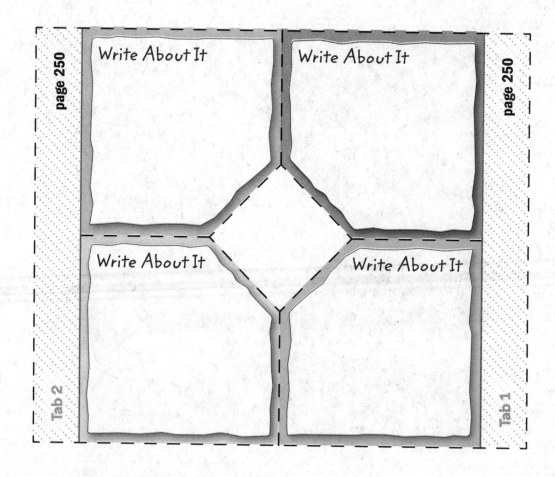

page 250

page 250

Tab 2

Tab 1

Write About It

Write About It

Write About It

Write About It

FL8 **Chapter 3 Foldable**

Fractions, Decimals, and Percents

percents and fractions

percents and decimals

percent of a number

✂ cut on all dashed lines   ▭ fold on all solid lines   tape to page 334   FOLDABLES

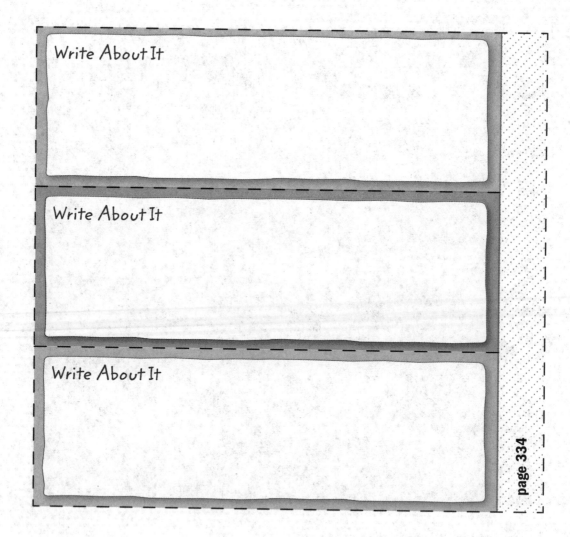

Write About It

Write About It

Write About It

page 334

Foldables

Properties of Addition

Commutative	Associative	Identity
+	+	+
×	×	×
Commutative	Associative	Identity

Properties of Multiplication

✂ cut on all dashed lines   ⬜ fold on all solid lines   tape to page 420   **FOLDABLES**®

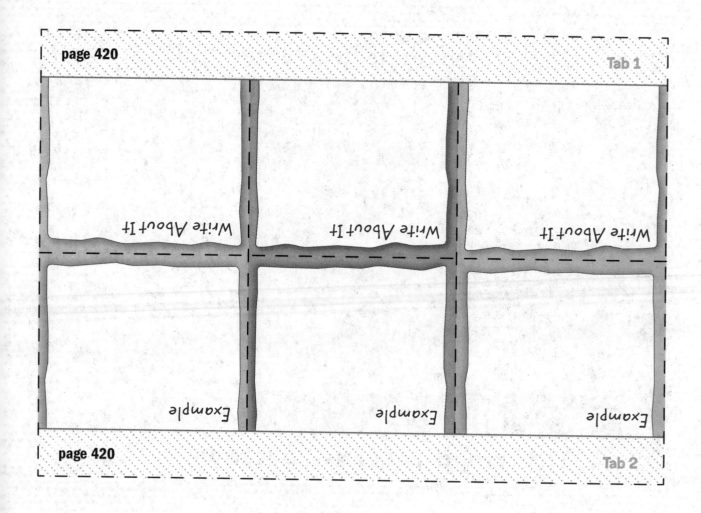

page 420   Tab 1

Write About It   Write About It   Write About It

Example   Example   Example

page 420   Tab 2

Foldables

equations

Models   Symbols

addition (+)

Models   Symbols

subtraction (−)

Models   Symbols

multiplication (×)

✂ cut on all dashed lines   ▭ fold on all solid lines   tape to page 488   **FOLDABLES**

page 488   Tab 4

Write About It

page 488   Tab 3

Write About It

page 488   Tab 2

Write About It

page 488   Tab 1

Write About It

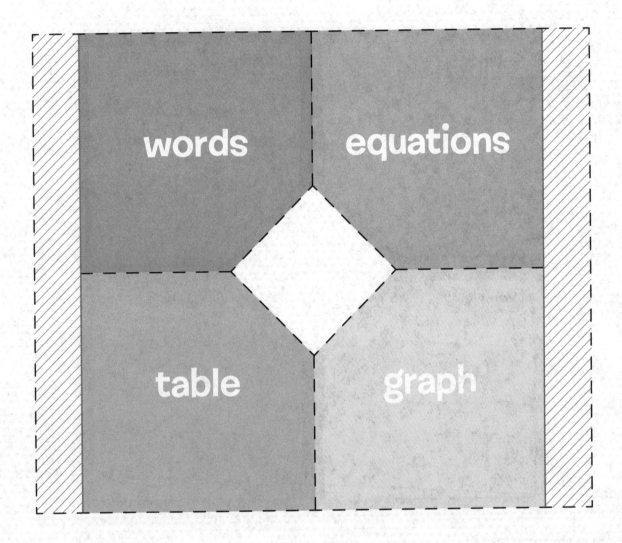

✂ cut on all dashed lines   ⬓ fold on all solid lines   tape to page 562   **FOLDABLES**

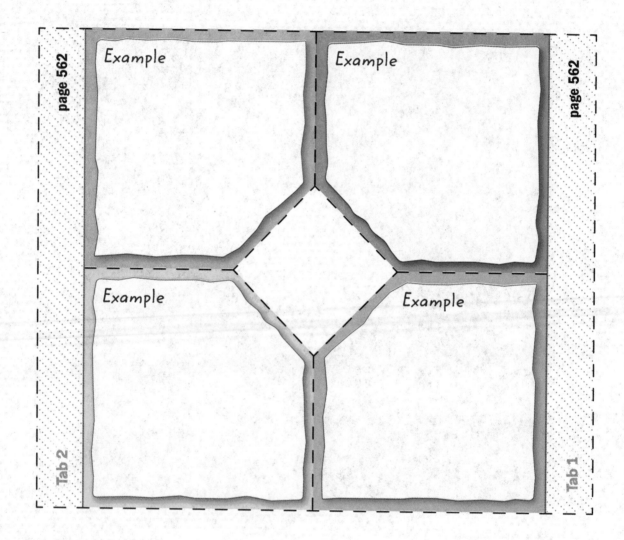

page 562   Tab 2

page 562   Tab 1

Example

Example

Example

Example

cut on all dashed lines | fold on all solid lines | tape to page 634

FOLDABLES

Area

parallelograms	triangles	trapezoids

✂ cut on all dashed lines   ⬜ fold on all solid lines   tape to page 634

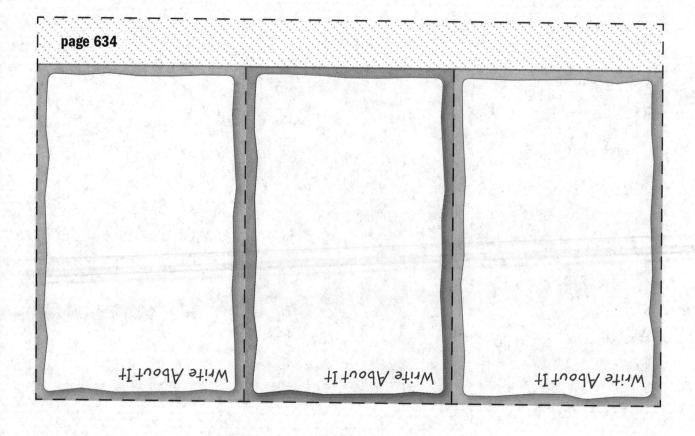

page 634

Write About It

Write About It

Write About It

volume

surface area

cut on all dashed lines   fold on all solid lines   tape to page 700

FOLDABLES®

---

page 700   Tab 1

Model   *Formulas*

Real-World Examples

page 700   Tab 2

FL20   **Chapter 9 Foldable**

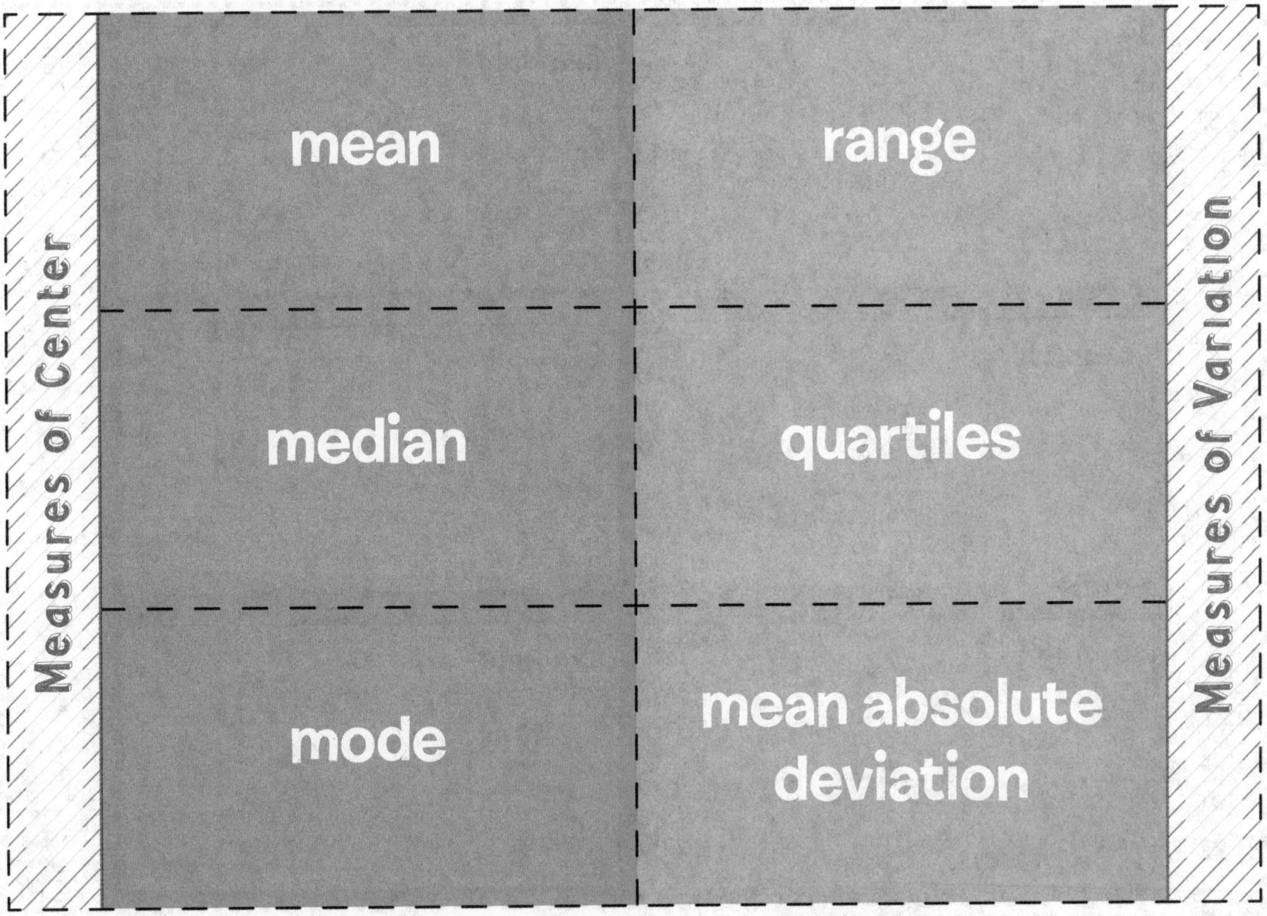

Measures of Center

mean	range
median	quartiles
mode	mean absolute deviation

Measures of Variation

✂ cut on all dashed lines   📁 fold on all solid lines   📑 tape to page 760   **FOLDABLES**

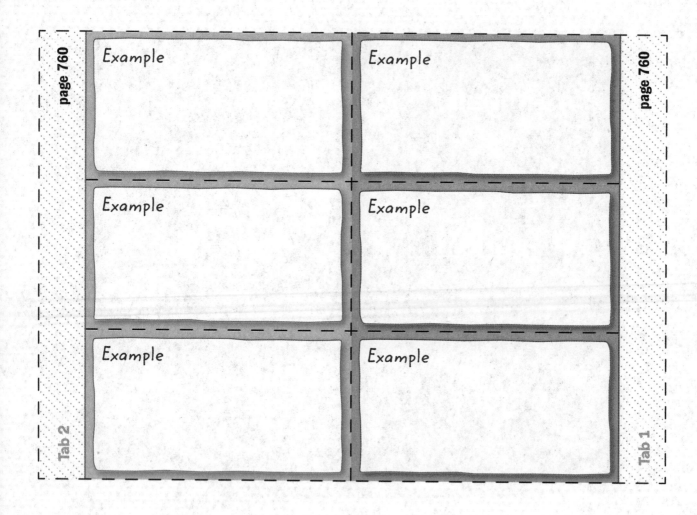

page 760

Example

Example

Example

Example

Example

Example

Tab 2

Tab 1

page 760

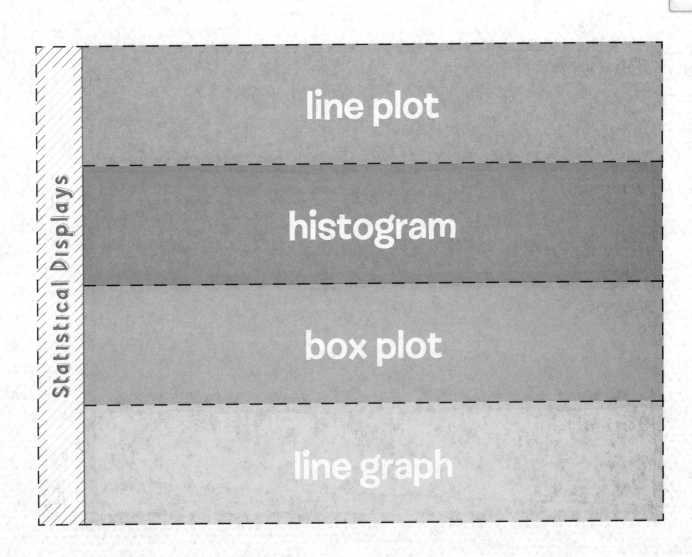

Statistical Displays

line plot

histogram

box plot

line graph

cut on all dashed lines   fold on all solid lines   tape to page 826   FOLDABLES

Best used to...

Best used to...

Best used to...

Best used to...

page 826

FL24   **Chapter 11 Foldable**

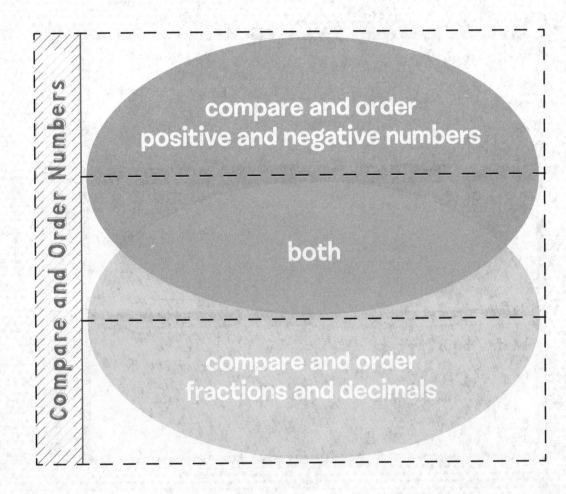

Compare and Order Numbers

compare and order
positive and negative numbers

both

compare and order
fractions and decimals

Write About It

Write About It

Write About It

page 918